The Forgotten Air Force
The Royal Air Force in the War
Against Japan 1941–1945

The last resting place of an unknown airman: Kranji War Cemetery, Singapore
(*author's photograph*)

The Forgotten Air Force

The Royal Air Force in the War Against Japan 1941–1945

Henry Probert

BRASSEY'S
London · Washington

Copyright © 1995 Henry Probert

First English Edition 1995
Reprinted 1996

UK editorial offices:
Brassey's, 33 John Street, London WC1N 2AT
UK orders: Marston Book Services, PO Box 269, Abingdon, OX14 4SD

North American Orders: Brassey's Inc., PO Box 960,
Herndon, VA 22070, USA

Henry Probert has asserted his moral right to be identified as
the author of this work.

Library of Congress Cataloging in Publication Data
available

British Library Cataloguing in Publication Data
A catalogue record for this book is available from the British Library

ISBN 1 85753 065 9 Hardcover

Photoset in North Wales by
Derek Doyle & Associates, Mold, Clwyd.
Printed in Great Britain by
BPC Wheatons, Exeter.

I do not think such devotion has ever been surpassed in any air force, and I doubt if it has been equalled.

(Field Marshal Sir William Slim:
Defeat into Victory)

Contents

Foreword

Air Chief Marshal Sir Lewis Hodges KCB CBE DSO DFC

Many books have been written about the war in South-East Asia and the Burma campaign in particular, but they have tended to concentrate mainly on the course of the land battle; there has been no comprehensive study of air operations in that distant theatre as a whole. This volume fills that gap. Air Commodore Probert has undertaken an in-depth study of all aspects of the air war: beginning with the disasters associated with the fall of Singapore he goes on to describe how the Royal Air Force recovered and, co-operating closely with the United States Army Air Force, contributed to the defeat of Japan. Its many roles are covered, ranging from air defence and the close air support of the 14th Army to air transport in aid of the land forces – supplying the Army with all its needs from the air; to the long-range interdiction operations carried out by the bomber squadrons and the photographic reconnaissance work; and the role of the maritime squadrons in the protection of shipping in the Indian Ocean.

In my own experience the major differences between operations in Europe and the Far East theatre were the very great distances involved, the nature of the terrain – the very rugged, mountainous, jungle-covered country making navigation extremely difficult – and the appalling weather conditions in the monsoon period from May to October. I was flying long-range Liberators on Special Duties work – parachuting agents and stores to Resistance groups in the Japanese-occupied territories. In the case of Malaya this involved sorties of 20 hours or more from our bases in East Bengal – or, more usually, Ceylon. Similarly operations to Indo-China involved very long flights over the most inhospitable terrain to reach the Hanoi area.

In covering this wide canvas of the air war in the Far East the author has succeeded in producing a very readable and informative account of an extremely complex subject – the totality of air operations in South-East Asia from the disastrous days of 1941 and 1942 when the Japanese swept all before them, to the turning of the tide as the longer range and more modern aircraft became available and the

Anglo-American forces were able to gain the initiative leading to eventual victory.

1995 marks the 50th Anniversary of the end of the war against Japan, which makes this work a particularly timely addition to the literature of the Far East conflict. I believe it will be of great value to students of the history of this critical but widely ignored aspect of the Second World War.

Preface

It was as a 15-year-old schoolboy that I heard the chilling news of the sinking of HMS *Prince of Wales* and HMS *Repulse* off the coast of Malaya. We at home were used to disasters, yet somehow all believed that Britain's position in the Far East, centred upon so-called Fortress Singapore, could never be successfully challenged. We were in for a rude awakening. For the next two years little good news for the British was to come from the Far East and we put events there to the back of our minds. Even in 1944 and 1945, after our attention had been drawn briefly to the battles of Imphal and Kohima, all eyes remained focused on the climax of the European war; only occasionally did news of 14th Army's advance through Burma make the headlines. If there was an awareness of the great war being waged by the Allies against Japan it was largely in terms of the amphibious campaigns conducted in the Pacific theatre chiefly by the Americans.

Then when the Far East war at last ended it was generally perceived as an American victory – and let no one doubt that to them belongs the lion's share of the credit. Recovering from the shock of Pearl Harbor and a series of shattering reverses in the south-west Pacific they gradually regained the sea and air supremacy needed to capture one island base after another in readiness for the attack on Japan itself, and prior to administering the *coup de grâce* in August 1945 they were mounting a massive air assault. This is the picture that has so widely persisted, one of a war in which the British played but a marginal role amid a dearth of publicity epitomised in the description of General Slim's forces as 'The Forgotten Army'.

My personal interest in the story began when my RAF career took me to Singapore in 1963. Changi, where I was to spend two and a half years, was a fine, well appointed air base which also housed the Headquarters of the Far East Air Force, yet surprisingly all too few of the thousands of men and women serving there seemed to know much about its antecedents. Hardly had I arrived than I was asked as one of my subsidiary duties to compile a short history. The task was to prove an eye-opener. First I had to recount the building of the base between the wars as part of the fixed defences of the island, and to explain something of the rationale. I had then to attempt to describe the wartime years when Changi and the nearby prison were used to house in increasingly inhuman conditions many many thousands of prisoners-of-war, most of them captured when Singapore fell. My researches fascinated and appalled me, and I quickly came to understand the deep loathing felt towards their captors by most of those who survived. Then, when I visited the vast war cemetery at Kranji, overlooking the Johore Strait, I was reminded of the cost to the British Commonwealth in human terms of the war in South-East Asia. My little book attracted much interest not just at Changi but also among former prisoners-of-war at home and in Australia, and ever since I have felt a deep commitment to the history of their war.

Then in 1978 I became Head of the Air Historical Branch and found much of my work to be connected with the Royal Air Force's role in the Second World War. It brought me into touch with many of those who took part and with many of the war historians, and I became caught up in numerous questions relating to the RAF's achievements and the controversies surrounding them. Yet it was nearly always the European war that featured, with the Battle of Britain, the strategic bomber offensive and the final campaign in north-west Europe dominating the picture. I found this totally understandable yet felt sad that so little attention was paid to those who had fought all or part of their war on the other side of the world. True, there were many books which dealt with specific parts of the Far Eastern story, there were squadron histories, there were more general accounts which touched on aspects of the RAF's activities. Not, however, since Hilary Saunders wrote about the Japanese war in the three volume history of the RAF in the Second World War had anyone attempted to put the whole story together under one cover. Even when my friend John Terraine wrote his fine book about the RAF in the Second World War, *The Right of the Line*, he felt obliged to confine its scope to the war against Germany and Italy. I therefore resolved, with John's encouragement, to attempt to fill the gap myself.

In so doing I have ignored the conventional Staff College teaching that one should never have a divided aim. In fact I have set myself three. First, I have tried to contribute to the understanding of the RAF's war in South-East Asia by placing it in the context of the strategic priorities of the war as a whole. Second, I have attempted to bring out the main lessons of my Service's role in the conflict against Japan for the application of air power; never before nor since has the RAF taken part in a jungle war on anything approaching this scale, and it forms a unique part of its history. Finally, and most important, I have sought to pay tribute to all who served in that war and whose efforts and achievements have been too readily forgotten amid the plethora of other fiftieth anniversary celebrations. Nothing has changed. They felt equally forgotten at the time as, in partnership with their Army and Navy comrades, they came back from defeat and eventually triumphed over the allegedly invincible Japanese. In so doing they demonstrated levels of skill, flexibility and sheer determination which have few parallels in the history of air warfare. It is a story of which not only the Royal Air Force but our whole nation should feel justly proud.

For reasons of time and space I have had to confine my account essentially to the work of the Royal Air Force and units of other air forces which served under RAF command. Thus the major contributions of the Australian and New Zealand airmen to the war in the south-west Pacific are outside my scope. So too are the vast campaigns fought by the Americans in the Pacific. Moreover, while some discussion of the work of the USAAF in South-East Asia is essential to the RAF's story, I am unable to go into it in any detail.

Obviously in a war whose central feature was close co-operation between the land and air forces I have needed to provide brief explanation of the Army's operations but readers who wish full accounts will need to turn to the various histories of the land war, some of which are mentioned in the Bibliography. The same applies to the naval operations which the RAF supported.

There is vast source material available for a history of this kind and I have had no choice but to cut many corners. Fortunately my successor as Head of the Air Historical Branch, Group Captain Ian Madelin, has kindly given me full access to the Branch archives, and the official narratives and monographs covering the Far East war have been invaluable. Without them I should have faced an impossible task in the time available. The many other essential sources provided by the Branch have included commanders' despatches, intelligence summaries and unit histories. The Cabinet Office histories have also been of great help, as have commercially published works ranging from campaign histories, biographies and memoirs to short accounts of individual squadrons. My main sources are listed in the Bibliography.

Of much assistance too have been the many people 'who were there' and responded to my requests for help. Inevitably I received far more material than I could possibly use, but thanks to their generosity I have been able to draw on personal recollections so as to provide local colour and convey at least some feel for what their war was actually like. Some have also lent me photographs, and I am most grateful to them all for their interest and encouragement. My thanks go too to a number of people who have given their time to meet me and to offer criticisms of my drafts. All are named in my Acknowledgements.

Finally, and most important, I am indebted to my wife Audrey. Under the expert guidance of my son-in-law, Andrew Sturla, she mastered our computer and converted my scrawl into polished text, a task requiring skills of which I was quite incapable. Without all her

efforts, coupled with great patience and forbearance, this book would
have been impossible.

Acknowledgements

I wish to acknowledge the generous assistance I have received from a great many individuals. First and foremost are Ian Madelin and his staff in the Air Historical Branch – in particular Sebastian Cox, who has read and commented on the entire manuscript, and Peter Singleton, who has provided invaluable assistance with photographs. Norman Franks also has helped greatly with the photographs, and my friend and neighbour Kenneth Burton with the research. My publishers too have been extremely supportive, especially Brigadier Bryan Watkins with his constructive advice on both the content and the presentation, and the RAF Historical Society, led by its Chairman Air Marshal Sir Frederick Sowrey, has given me much encouragement. Thanks go also to the staffs at the Ministry of Defence Library, the Imperial War Museum, the RAF Museum, Christ Church Library and the Liddell Hart Centre.

I am most grateful too to several who have commented on sections of the account on the basis of their own experience. In particular Marshal of the Royal Air Force Sir Denis Spotswood, who served on Mountbatten's planning staff, has read all the later chapters and Air Chief Marshal Sir Lewis Hodges, who commanded 357 Squadron, has seen the whole manuscript and very kindly contributed the Foreword.

My thanks go too to the many people – some, alas, no longer with us – who sent me recollections of their time in the Far East, sometimes accompanied by photographs, and to others who encouraged me and who pointed me towards sources of which I might not otherwise have been aware. It gives me great pleasure to list their names: Squadron Leader R J Allanson, Professor Louis Allen, Mr M J Applegarth, Squadron Leader JFP Archbold, Group Captain R H Arscott, Mr P J M Ballard, Group Captain P H Baldwin, Dr A Banks, Mr R Barkus, Mr P G Bates, Air Commodore L J Birchall RCAF, Mr H Bird, Mr J S Bishop, Mr J G Booth, Air Commodore E Burchmore, Mr J Burgess, Mr W R Burkitt, Mrs B Burton, Mr A G Cameron, Mr F Card, Dr T C Carter, Mr L W Chapman, Mr R Chappell, Mr M E J Clack, Mr F W Cooper, Mr C A Couch, Air Chief Marshal Sir Kenneth Cross, Mr C E Crawford, Mr C W Crocker, Group Captain D Croucher, Mr J Cutler, Mr W Croot, Mr H A Cullingworth, Group Captain D David, Mr R

Davies, Mr W Day, Mr B Dennis, Air Vice-Marshal D Dick, Flight Lieutenant J H J Dix RCAF, Mr J E G Dixon, Mr J Dunbar, Mr D C Elliott, Mr E Ellwood-Wade, Wing Commander L Ercolani, Mr W J M Ewing, Mr S Fielding, Squadron Leader R Fletcher, Mr A J Fowden, Mr A Fox, Mr S Goldberg, Mr H A Griffiths, Group Captain D W Groocock, Mr L Gwinnell, Mr J Hall, Mr R Hammersley, Mr C Hardman, Mr D F Harris, Mr H T Hathaway, Mr E Hayes, Flight Lieutenant D K Healey, Mr E R Henman, Mr T L Henthorne, Mr F Higgins, Professor R Higham, Mr W F Holder, Mr D L Holloway, Mr G D Hooper, Mr N C Horton, Flight Lieutenant L L Hunt, Mr P L Hunt, Mr C G Hutchings, Mr R Jackson, Mr D J Johnson, Mr J Johnson, Mr W H Jones, Mr A Kelsall, Major General C Kinvig, Mr S Lawrence, Mr F W Lewis, Mr H Liffen, Mr J S Linn, Mr J Linnell, Mr S Linsley, Mr D H G Lyon, Mr A C MacDougall, Mr W MacKenzie, Mr H W McOwan, Mr N Macrae, Mr R Mager, Mr L Maidment, Group Captain A S Mann, Wing Commander D D Martin, Mr J F Midgley, Mr J Milner, Squadron Leader R Mitchell, Mr E A Munday, Mr D R Neate, Mr P N Negretti, Mr R Nesbit, Mr P Nevill, Mr C Newton, Mr T O'Brien, Mr S Overend, Group Captain J S Owen, Mr E Palmer, Mr L Parry, Dr A N H Peach, Mr A Pearcy, Mr C P C Peart, Air Vice-Marshal Sir Richard Peirse, Mr P Pigott, Mr L E Ransom, Mr A J W Reid, Mr J Reid, Flight Lieutenant P Reynolds, Sir Robert Rhodes-James, Mr R S Ridgway, Mr C F Shores, Squadron Leader R J Skinner, Mrs E Smith, Squadron Leader G Smith, Mr C Smyth, Squadron Leader J A Stephen, Mr T Stocks, Mr A A M Stripp, Mr L Stubbs, Flight Lieutenant J R Taylor, Mr M Tomlinson, Mr H Toy, Squadron Leader C R Turner, Mr D Turner, Mr D J Waite, Mr G L Waltham, Mr W R Washington, Professor K P Werrell, Mr D Wilcox, Lieutenant Colonel M Wilcox, Mr L Wilde, Mr D Williams, Mr B J W Winterbottom, Mr M V Winton, Mr F Wooldridge, Mr H H Wynn, and Mr S Yates.

Maps

1 Towards the Rising Sun

On 17 October 1927 four Supermarine Southampton flying boats took off from Cattewater, near Plymouth, under the command of Group Captain H M Cave-Brown-Cave. Flying in formation at their cruising speed of 83 mph they set course across France for the Mediterranean. Four months later, on 28 February 1928, having worked their way by stages via Egypt, the Persian Gulf, India, Burma and Malaya, they reached Singapore, alighting in the Straits of Johore near Seletar. So successful had the flight been that they continued on to Australia where they circumnavigated the continent before returning to Singapore on 28 December – in total a 28,000 mile trip. A few days later, on 8 January 1929, the Far East Flight, as it had hitherto been known, was re-designated No 205 Squadron and placed under the command of Squadron Leader G E Livock. The first permanent Royal Air Force unit had now arrived in Singapore and been warmly welcomed. Thirteen years later the RAF would depart under very different circumstances.

To start our story, however, we must go back to 1921, when on 16 June the British Cabinet decided to establish a naval base in Singapore.[1] The reason, briefly stated, was the threat which an emergent Japan might one day pose to Great Britain's many interests in the Far East – the dominions of Australasia, the colonial possessions of South-East Asia, her trading outlets and routes, her sources of raw materials. Although Japan had been an ally during the First World War, there was increasing clash of interest between her and the United States and once the UK had terminated the Anglo-Japanese Alliance in favour of links with the USA it became clear that Japan's desire to control her own supplies of raw materials could sooner or later lead to conflict. The answer, as argued by the Royal Navy and supported in almost all quarters, lay in the application of the time-honoured principles of sea-power: there must be a permanent Far Eastern Fleet and a base to maintain it. Given, however, the shortage of money for defence in the aftermath of war, together with the philosophy of the 'ten-year rule' – the policy assumption that there would be no major war for ten years – and the Washington Naval Treaty, the government decided it could not spare enough ships for a

1

permanent fleet; all that could be done was to build a base able to receive a battle fleet in an emergency. Hong Kong and Sydney having been quickly rejected, the choice fell on Singapore.

Clearly many questions now needed resolution, but the main one that concerns us here was what role, if any, should be allotted to the aeroplane in the defence of the base. That there would be a role of some sort was clear almost immediately, when Wing Commander F E T Hewlett was sent to represent the Air Ministry on the Admiralty committee that first considered the siting of the naval base; in December 1921 he chose Seletar for the associated airfield and seaplane base.[2] But it was not until 1925 that the real debate began. The decision to site the naval base on the Johore Strait having been taken in February 1923,[3] was it to be defended essentially by fixed gun batteries, or by aircraft, or by a mix of the two? At this stage there was no thought of its being threatened by land from the north; according to the Chief of the Imperial General Staff the Malayan jungles were impassable.[4] So any threat could come only from the sea, and for the Admiralty and the Army the permanent siting of 15″ guns would suffice. The airmen, however, had other ideas. Trenchard, who as Chief of Air Staff had been fighting ever since the end of the First World War to establish what he saw as the proper roles of British air power and with them the permanent status of the RAF, considered that the Navy was wrong to discount the increasing range, mobility and strike power of the torpedo bomber. He had therefore been urging that at least some of the guns should be replaced by the RAF in the interests of both security and economy.[5] Then at the end of 1924 – after the short-lived first Labour government had attempted to cancel the whole project – the new Conservative administration appointed a sub-committee of the Committee of Imperial Defence under Lord Curzon to re-examine the Singapore plan, including the possible use of aircraft.[6] In July 1925 Trenchard appeared before the sub-committee. His approach was bold. Stating his conviction that the defence of Singapore was 'a vital stage in the development of the air', he argued strongly against the traditional approach, seeing no need to decide now to spend large sums installing 15″ guns which could be out of date when actually required:

> In a few years' time the whole air situation in the East may have been transformed; any change that occurs will strengthen and not diminish the potentialities of air power for the defence of Singapore and the Far East.[7]

When the sub-committee reported in October it was unable to resolve the differences.[8] Whereas the Navy and Army remained committed to guns, the RAF saw torpedo bombers, supported by fighter and reconnaissance aircraft, as adequate and cheaper, and also mobile –

the squadrons could be stationed elsewhere in peacetime and moved in only if war were imminent. Not unreasonably the other Services pointed out that they might not in fact be available at the critical moment; only if based there permanently would they serve to deter. As Sir John Slessor later quoted their view: 'How are we to know that when the enemy attack upon Singapore materialises your squadrons will not be committed somewhere else?'[9] The inevitable unsatisfactory compromise was reached in August 1926, after Trenchard had reluctantly agreed to the initial installation of three 15'' guns, leaving further consideration of the merits of heavy guns and aircraft to be postponed. 'It was the worst blunder of my career; I was too trusting' said Trenchard in later years to his biographer, Andrew Boyle. Nevertheless he had at least obtained agreement to the organisation of a chain of airfields leading to Calcutta and the Far East, and to the development of the torpedo bomber.[10]

As we reflect on this early debate in the light of what happened later it is all too easy to be critical, but it was certainly much too optimistic to assume that sufficient aircraft of the right types and quality could ever be moved into such a distant theatre at short notice and then operate effectively. Nor, as Louis Allen observes, 'was there any proof available at that time that the torpedo bomber would be effective against modern battleships possessing air cover of their own'.[11] On the other hand, as the Second World War would eventually demonstrate, Trenchard had correctly perceived the long-term significance of the torpedo bomber in maritime war.

More than five years were to elapse before the main arguments would be resumed. These were Churchill's 'locust years', the period when the threat of major war seemed remote, when economic troubles made resources for defence particularly hard to come by, and when much international effort was devoted to the cause of disarmament. Progress on the Singapore project was therefore slow – indeed work was suspended for a time – and the RAF was able to do little beyond developing the facilities at Seletar, basing 205 Squadron there in 1929 for maritime reconnaissance duties, and sending out 36 Squadron, equipped with Horsley torpedo bombers, in December 1930.[12] 100 Squadron, equipped with Vildebeests, followed three years later.

In September 1931, however, started a series of incidents which culminated in the Japanese seizure of Manchuria, and were followed in 1932 by an attempt to stir up trouble in Shanghai. The Chiefs of Staff, well aware of the total inadequacy of Britain's Far Eastern position, urged the Cabinet to abandon the 'ten-year rule' and authorise the strengthening of Britain's defences.[13] Meanwhile a CID sub-committee had been formed under Mr Baldwin in December 1931 to consider coast defence and port security throughout the Empire, with special reference to the role of air forces, and central to its work was the situation of Singapore. Inevitably the arguments of 1925 were reiterated, with Sir John Salmond, Trenchard's successor as CAS, able to point to improved aircraft performance and weapon techniques. He therefore claimed that air forces were essential not only to meet the threat of air attack but also to provide a better insurance against ship bombardment than fixed defences could offer, owing to their greater range.[14] The Navy and Army strongly disagreed, and the sub-committee confirmed that the fixed guns should comprise the main deterrent to naval attack. At the same time, however, they stated that the defence of the base required the co-operation of all three Services, with the RAF providing air defence, reconnaissance, and an offensive capability against ships.

Its role thus defined, the RAF was now authorised to construct a second airfield, for which a site at Sembawang was selected, and on 1 December 1933 it formed its own headquarters, located at Seletar. A Chiefs of Staff analysis undertaken soon afterwards confirmed that the main air threat was likely to come from carriers; attack from land-based aircraft was discounted. To meet this threat, the existing flying boat squadron and two torpedo bomber squadrons should be supplemented by another flying boat squadron, a fighter bomber squadron and a spotter flight, and work should continue on the air route to the Far East so that reinforcements could be sent in wartime.[15]

If this be thought a meagre force, let it be remembered that its task was limited to the defence of the naval base against seaborne attack; there was still no serious consideration of a threat from any other direction. Moreover in 1934 the RAF was still relatively small; only in that year was the first of the expansion schemes announced, and there were many other pressing calls on its limited strength – most notably to prepare to meet the new threat from Hitler's Germany. John Terraine reminds us of a session of the Ministerial Committee on Disarmament in May-July (the title itself is revealing) at which a report of the Defence Requirements Committee was considered: even though DRC still saw Japan as the immediate threat, Chamberlain, the Chancellor of the Exchequer, made the significant statement that 'we cannot provide simultaneously for hostilities with Japan and Germany, and the latter is the problem to which we must now address ourselves'. He did not think Japan would attack the British Empire unless Britain was preoccupied with hostilities in Europe, so a deterrent against Germany would also be a deterrent against Japan. Consequently he was opposed to proposals to increase RAF strength overseas; public opinion would not think much of arguments to increase the air forces at such places as Penang.[16] Such a view, expressed by a man who was to be at the heart of the nation's affairs for the next six years, gives a good indication of the great difficulty that any of the military leaders were bound to face in pleading for higher priority to be given to the needs of the Far East. Moreover there was much truth in what he said: the United Kingdom would never be strong enough to cope with both Germany and Japan on her own – an underlying fact which needs to be constantly remembered as our story unfolds.

At about the same time another major factor was coming into play. Hitherto it had always been assumed that, in emergency, a major part of the British Fleet would be sent to Singapore; this after all was the whole point of constructing the naval base with all its extensive facilities. But in December 1934 Japan denounced the Washington Naval Treaty, which since 1922 had limited the tonnage of capital ships possessed by the Great Powers. Then in June 1935, in the hope that it would lead to a further international treaty, Britain signed a bilateral agreement with Germany, giving Hitler the right to build up to 35 per cent of the surface tonnage of the Royal Navy. Although intended as a step towards arms control, the appearance of the new German navy which the agreement heralded changed the whole balance of naval power. It meant in effect that most of the British Fleet would always have to be kept in home waters.[17] So from now on the Admiralty faced a permanent dilemma, though it would be several years before it came to be accepted that the Far East would not merely have to wait for its fleet to arrive but might well have to be content with little more than a token force. For the future, we could argue, the whole concept of the naval base was flawed – though we should recognise that its presence and its ability to receive the fleet were primarily intended as a deterrent. It was in reality a gigantic piece of bluff, one which the Japanese would successfully call in 1941.

In the meantime it was becoming increasingly clear that the defence of the base against seaborne attack would have to rely in at least the earlier stages of an emergency largely on aircraft. Up to 1935, as we have seen, the RAF presence was confined to Singapore Island but by the end of that year the staff were beginning to realise that aerial reconnaissance over the South China Sea would be very restricted unless airfields were available further north. It was but a short step from this to appreciate the value of forward bases for offensive operations. So by 1936 plans were afoot for three airfields near Kota Bharu, on the north-east coast of Malaya, for two more at Kuantan and Kahang, and also – as a separate measure for the defence of Penang (notwithstanding Chamberlain's strictures) – one at Butterworth. Others soon followed, most notably Alor Star, not far from the Siamese frontier (Map 1).

The siting of these airfields has been the subject of considerable controversy. General Percival, writing after the war, considered it one of the greatest failures to face realities of the pre-war period: in his

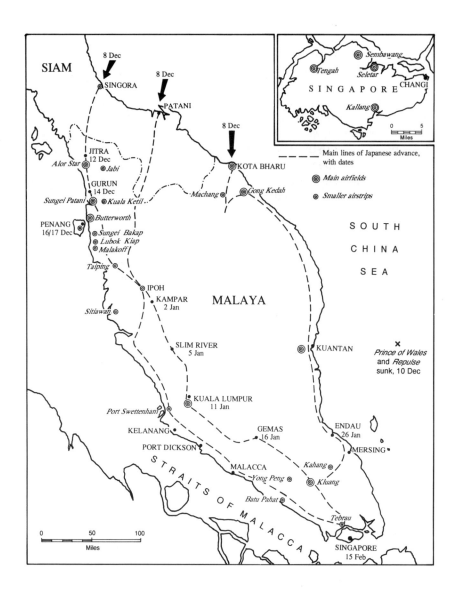

Map 1   Malaya 1941/42

view it accounted for much of the weakness of the Army's dispositions.[18] His point was that unless there were going to be enough aircraft to deal the enemy a shattering blow, they should have been built further inland where they would have been easier to defend and more difficult to capture; as actually located – particularly those near Kota Bharu – their defence against ground attack presented the Army with severe problems, and proved in the event virtually impossible. As the chief Army planner in Singapore in 1936/37 he had himself argued the case at the time, but site selection was then a purely RAF responsibility and there was in fact no joint consultation. To us looking back this seems incredible, but under the circumstances of the day it may not be so surprising: it still needed the experience of the Second World War to demonstrate the crucial importance of the ground defence of airfields.

For the airmen what mattered was that the airfields should be as far forward as possible so as to ensure the early detection of enemy convoys and to enable them to be attacked more than once before reaching the eastern coast of Malaya.[19] Brooke-Popham, the later C-in-C (see p.21), made the same point, adding that there must be sufficient airfields to enable a large proportion of the squadrons to be concentrated in any given area.[20] The eventual assumption was that there would be 336 aircraft, and the long time needed to build airfields in the local conditions meant that the work had to be put in hand before anyone could be certain that all would materialise. In the event they did not and the Army was left with severe defensive problems, but, Brooke-Popham contended, this could not have been foreseen. He certainly accepted that the tactical siting of some of the airfields could have been better – some were sited 'solely with reference to their suitability for flying operations' without any thought to ground defence – but given the assumption that air power was to be primarily responsible for the defence of Malaya he was convinced that the overall airfield pattern was sound, given that there would be enough aircraft. It is all very well for critics to say they should have been elsewhere and not, as Louis Allen, for example, says, 'at the end of very awkward lines of communication which made their defence and reinforcement by land almost an impossibility'.[21]

It is worth reminding ourselves that the whole centre of the Malayan peninsula was filled by a rugged, heavily forested, mountain mass which not only offered physical obstruction but also bred adverse meteorological conditions. There were practically no roads or railways in the mountain area nor were the rivers adequate as communication routes, and much of the rest of the land area was covered with a medley of broken hills which offered poor locations for airfields. There was therefore no choice but to place many of them near the coasts where they were difficult to defend without control of the seas.[22] To be realistic, therefore, all the airfields would have had to be placed on the western side of the Malayan mountain chain, which would have been unsound for the purpose of air operations. Certainly there should have been joint consultation on the tactical siting, but the fundamental planning was not necessarily at fault – provided it could be followed up by the necessary aircraft.

The need for airfields in Malaya brings us to the wider discussions that engaged the Army planners and their RAF opposite numbers in Singapore during the late 1930s. It was General Dobbie, GOC Malaya, who in 1937 gave the impetus to new thinking about the shape of a possible Japanese attack. Having carried out exercises at Mersing to test the feasibility of seaborne landings, he concluded that they would be possible on the east coast between October and March, and the appreciation which Colonel Percival (the later GOC) then produced for him proved particularly astute in the light of later events. Argued from the Japanese point of view it postulated the establishment of advanced air bases in Siam, and landings at Singora and Patani in Siam and at Kota Bharu in Malaya. At the same time Dobbie reassessed the assumption that the Malayan jungles were impassable for infantry, and in July 1938 warned that the greatest danger to Singapore now lay in a land attack from the north, following a landing in Johore. His recommendation that the southern shore of the island should be given coast defences and defence works be built in south Johore was accepted and in 1939 he received £60,000 for the purpose.[23] Given the many pressures nearer home this was an achievement, but the sum was hardly enough to be significant.

So the later 1930s were marked by a more realistic attitude in at least some quarters, and also – as Percival wrote in July 1937 – by the building up of a system of close co-operation between the Services. This was done by regular monthly staff conferences, by conferences of commanders to discuss specific matters, and by visits to each other's offices whenever necessary.[24] That Percival thought he needed to say this may surprise us, but clearly it was a step in the right direction, and it may be significant that in October 1936 the first AOC in the Far East, Air Commodore Sidney Smith, was succeeded by Air Commodore Arthur Tedder – one of the RAF's great co-operators as he subsequently proved in the Second World War. On 1 April 1937 he moved his Headquarters from Seletar to the Union Building in Singapore, where he would be close to his colleagues.[25]

Unfortunately, Percival's praise did not extend to the civilian government: 'there is not that combined examination of problems which is so necessary when a fortress like Singapore is under construction'.[26] Throughout these years, it has to be said, the local administration and much of the local population exhibited a degree of complacency that made the task of the military men far more difficult than it should have been – and it was in all conscience difficult enough.

The anxieties about Japanese intentions were not confined to the British. By 1937 the Dominions of Australia and New Zealand were becoming worried, and the government rashly promised them that in the event of a Japanese attack a fleet large enough to contain the enemy battle fleet would be despatched immediately.[27] It was to be a different story two years later. The Dutch, too, had fears about their far-flung and ill-defended empire in the East Indies; indeed as early as 1936 they had proposed informal defence conversations. The CID was, however, reluctant to commit itself to an Anglo-Dutch defence scheme, though confidential discussions were held between the Dutch authorities and the Air Ministry on technical matters.[28] There were worries also in France, whose possessions in Indo-China were becoming increasingly exposed, and in the course of Anglo-French discussions in May 1939 about the overall threat posed by the three Axis powers it was recognised that they ought to plan for two extreme contingencies: the temporary abandonment of naval control in either the Far East or the eastern Mediterranean. Following up these conversations a month later in Singapore, both parties expressed grave concern over the inadequacy of naval and air forces in the Far East, for it was becoming clear that since naval commitments in Europe precluded reinforcement in peacetime, larger air forces must be provided on a permanent basis.[29]

So by 1939 the rapidly deteriorating situation in Europe was imposing its compelling logic on the Far East. Up to 1937 it had been assumed that the promised naval force would reach Singapore in 42 days; the 'period before relief' was then extended to 70 days (assuming the Mediterranean route was closed);[30] and in June 1939 the Chiefs of Staff declared that it was now impossible to say definitely how soon after Japanese intervention a fleet could be despatched, or its size. The planning staff was therefore ordered to re-examine the whole Far Eastern position, and in the meantime the period before relief was extended to 90 days. A study appearing soon afterwards indicated that – given the need to defend against all three Axis powers – it would be possible to spare only two battleships for the Far East. The Japanese had nine.[31]

Could air power, therefore, fill the gap? In theory yes, but as Slessor – Air Ministry Director of Plans in the late 1930s – reminds us, Britain was completely unable 'to direct further air forces for the protection of Singapore in view of the position in Europe'. Even so he was far from unaware of the threat: 'Japan became increasingly insolent and aggressive in China as the year (1938) wore on, which could not fail to alarm us'.[32] The intelligence reports being circulated around the Air Ministry and the RAF[33] also conveyed their warnings: the Japanese were developing a system of air raid precautions (September 1938);

Map 2   South-East Asia

they were taking drastic measures to improve the quality of their aircraft industry (November); they were funding a major expansion of the Naval Air Force (April 1939). There were regular reports on the contribution of the Japanese air forces to the war in China – losses between July 1937 and March 1939 allegedly amounted to 1,050 aircraft, some slight indication of the scale of operations and the experience being acquired. Perhaps most significant was the statement in June 1939 that four airfields were being built on the recently captured Chinese island of Hainan, not far from French Indo-China (Map 2). But all these things were happening a long way from Singapore, and those concerned on the spot could do little more than take note and make the best of the slender resources being given them.

In August 1938 Air Vice-Marshal John Babington had taken over from Tedder – not perhaps an ideal appointment, for he had spent the previous ten years as Air Representative to the League of Nations, AOC at Halton, and AOC 24 (Training) Group. He stayed until 1941, doing the best he could for his Command at a time when it was always at the bottom of the priority list, but not always hitting it off with his Army opposite number, as we shall see.

The biggest task he and his staff faced was already under way by the time he arrived, namely the building of the new airfields. Construction was usually slow, chiefly because of the shortage of mechanical plant, the poor condition of most of it, and the insufficiency of qualified operators. Nor did it help that the civil authorities rarely understood the gravity of the situation and failed to accord land acquisition and airfield work proper priority. A further factor was the need to combat malaria in the very difficult climatic conditions of Malaya; much effort had to be devoted to controlling undergrowth, to drainage and to oiling nearby water while building the airfields, and then to maintenance of the precautions once work was complete. Not surprisingly therefore, construction took much longer than in most other parts of the world; Seletar took five years for example, and Sembawang and Tengah each three years, partly due to the large volumes of material to be excavated. While considerable additional work remained to be done, most of the airfields that would be used in 1941 were at least open by September 1939; on Singapore Island, in addition to the three mentioned above, the civil airport at Kallang could now take an RAF squadron, and on the mainland there were nine available. Apart from Penang and Alor Star, which had 950 and 1000 yard tarmac runways respectively, all were grass. Given all the difficulties this was a fine achievement on the part of the Air Ministry Works Directorate's local organisation.[34]

Another major task was to provide the maintenance facilities for what it was always assumed would be several hundred aircraft. Seletar had been constructed not only as the home for four squadrons but also as the main support unit, and such was its growth that in January 1938 the relevant parts of the station became the Aircraft Depot, Far East, which now undertook aircraft repairs for both the RAF and the Fleet Air Arm. Then with the repair commitment continuing to increase – particularly for engines – it became clear that Seletar could not cope on its own, and in August 1939 Babington proposed that further engine repair work should be undertaken at Kuala Lumpur, where technical trade schools already existed and skilled labour would be more easily available. This was approved on 12 September; no longer would the RAF presence on the mainland be limited to operational squadrons and all the support concentrated in Singapore.[35]

By the outbreak of war in Europe, therefore, much of the RAF infrastructure was coming into place, but what of the aircraft? Way back in 1934, as we have seen, there were four squadrons, two of torpedo bombers and two of flying boats, and there were still no more in 1938 – although during a reinforcement exercise early that year several squadrons of Blenheims had flown in from India and Iraq. By the summer of 1939, however, there were two such squadrons based in Singapore, and the Chiefs of Staff, convinced of the possibility of war breaking out within two or three months, decided to strengthen its defences by sending out another two, which arrived on 8 and 22 September.[36] So on the outbreak of war with Germany, Britain's air defences in the Far East rested on the shoulders of 24 Blenheims, the reasonably modern medium bombers of the day (and about to be supplemented by 24 more), 10 flying boats – four of them modern Sunderlands, the rest aged Singapores – and 24 torpedo bombers, the equally aged Vildebeests. In addition there was a handful of Fleet Air Arm aircraft – Swordfish and Walrus. But not a single fighter – despite what the CID had said in 1931.

For an explanation of this parlous state of affairs we can perhaps look to the narrow concept of the RAF's role at that time, namely to locate and attack shipping, especially carriers, to the east of Singapore, and to oppose the establishment of air bases within range of the island.[37] And if we wonder why fighters were not needed as escorts, it needed the experience of Bomber Command over the North Sea in the winter of 1939/40 to show that they did. But for the main bases and Singapore City itself to be totally without air defence – even at a time when it was in reality unlikely that the Japanese would strike – does seem, to say the least, surprising. Nor was there any civil defence or ARP system, but to few did it seem to matter; the indigenous population was indifferent and apathetic.[38] So we come back to the fundamental truth about the Far East in 1939:

The defence of Hong Kong and Malaya and the great Naval Base at Singapore had to be assured not by the land, sea and air forces considered to be necessary, but by such forces as could be spared.[39]

They were precious few.

2   The Years of Neglect

The Early Policy Debate

It was Sir Robert Brooke-Popham who wrote about 'the feeling of being neglected' that affected him and his colleagues in Singapore in 1941;[1] the term 'neglect' is probably as good as any to describe the British government's approach to its military commitments in the Far East throughout the period between September 1939 and December 1941. We have already considered the dilemma posed by Singapore during the 1930s; this could only become more acute once Britain was at war with Germany, though not until the fall of France would the possibility of Japanese intervention begin to be taken seriously. As Churchill wrote of September 1939: 'there is no sign at this moment of any hostile action or intent upon the part of Japan'. Nothing which threatened in the Far East, he went on, must divert us from our prime objectives in Europe, and the furthest point we could defend if Japan came in would be the fortress of Singapore.[2] The term 'fortress' was, of course, totally inappropriate as the events of 1941/42 would show, but in the intervening years the concept seems to have dominated the thinking of many in London who should have known better.

Those on the spot, of course, did know better, and Air Vice-Marshal Babington and his new Army opposite number, General Bond (who had taken over from General Dobbie on 1 August 1939), had to concentrate their minds on how best to discharge their responsibilities under the new circumstances. Sadly, however, as Brooke-Popham would later observe on his arrival in Singapore, relations between the two Services were not happy; they were marked by jealousy, lack of co-operation, and a tendency for one Service to work out a plan and then see how the other could come in.[3] Louis Allen, who writes of the 'intense hostility' that developed between Babington and Bond, tells us that when Bond arrived in Singapore he refused to accept the constitutional position held by Mr Vlieland as Secretary of Defence and began pressing for a return to the earlier committee system whereby the Army ruled the roost.[4] Clearly there was not the close working relationship between the Army and RAF that there should have been, and this was well illustrated when the Governor, Sir Shenton Thomas,

14

attempted to work out a coordinated policy in the early part of 1940.

Bond, convinced that the Army's main role must be the close defence of Singapore and its approaches and anxious for more manpower, had been pressing for the introduction of compulsory military service, a measure bound to be unpopular and difficult to implement. The Governor, on the other hand, was mindful of the economic importance of Malaya for the British war effort; she produced 38 per cent of the world's rubber and 58 per cent of its tin, and £93 million of her £131 million worth of exports went to foreign countries, mainly the USA, where they earned dollars. Given that a Japanese attack did not seem all that likely – she was already deeply committed in China – he judged that absolute priority should be given to the claims of industry.[5] He was certainly not, however, opposed to the strengthening of Malaya's defences and saw the building up of the air forces – which would not entail conscription – as the best means of doing so. As he saw it, if the Japanese were to attack they would first need to acquire an advanced base within striking distance of Singapore, and such action could be opposed only by air forces.[6]

This advocacy of an appreciable increase in RAF strength as the primary means of defence – and hopefully deterrence – was influenced by Vlieland and firmly endorsed by Babington. Recognising that the defence could not rely on the despatch of the Main Fleet, which was heavily committed against Germany, and that the military garrison could do little outside Singapore, south Johore and Penang, the AOC was certain that Singapore's fate would be sealed if the enemy were to gain a foothold in Malaya; only air power could prevent this.[7] Moreover if such a strategy were accepted it would free the Army from their localised role near Singapore and enable them to support the defensive structure that the air forces would require.[8]

The despatch which the Governor sent to London embodying these views was considered by the Overseas Defence Committee on 20 March 1940 (ie., shortly before the extension of the war by the German attack on Norway and Denmark).[9] Its conclusions were as follows:

a. Although the security of Singapore is vital to the safety of the British Empire, it is not proposed to refer the matter to the Chiefs of Staff, as it is out of the question to make any change in present policy.

b. Owing to the need to expand the RAF to achieve superiority over the Germans, only a minimum can be spared for such places where danger is not imminent. Preparations are in hand for an increase in the Middle East and India, which would form a strategic reserve for the Far East.

c. Whilst it is realised that RAF strength in Singapore is only half the wartime establishment, it is impracticable to consider any increase in the near future of the responsibilities borne by the RAF in Singapore.[10]

This was an unequivocal statement, hardly surprising in its message but utterly unhelpful to its recipients, especially when accompanied by an injunction to rely on their own resources by raising the standard of the local volunteers and introducing conscription. In effect the government had resolved to leave a small, widely dispersed air force without a single air defence fighter, thereby ensuring its destruction should Malaya or Singapore come under Japanese attack. That the ODC should have decided the matter was unworthy of reference to the Chiefs of Staff seems astonishing.

Babington lost no time in reminding the Air Ministry of his opinion that ground forces could not hold Malaya or Singapore, and requested details of the strategic reserve in India to which the ODC had referred, so that he could at least be ready to receive reinforcements,[11] but these and other protests fell on deaf ears. When the ODC next met, on 16 May, it indicated that there was no way in which land or air reinforcements could be sent.[12] Since the German assault on France and the Low Countries had been launched six days previously the ODC's reaction can be totally understood, but it was cold comfort in Singapore. So Babington and Bond now had to look again at what little they had, and it was from then on the differences between them began to surface – as so often happens when resources are too few. While Bond was prepared to agree that the whole of Malaya must be defended he contended that the wider task was for the RAF to undertake, since his regular troops would have to concentrate on the close defence of Singapore, and with both commanders referring their problems increasingly to their own Service Ministries the Acting Governor (in Shenton Thomas's absence) felt compelled to raise the issue with the Chiefs of Staff.

In his paper of 27 June he summarised the position.[13] The GOC, he explained, could envisage no reduction or wider deployment of the Singapore garrison, since if the defences were extended and the RAF failed to disperse the enemy attacks the island would be in grave danger. So apart from providing one battalion near the key northern airfield at Alor Star, Bond was determined to keep his regulars in Singapore and south Johore, leaving local volunteer forces to cover the rest of the mainland, including airfield defence (this was in fact contrary to an earlier appreciation in which Bond had seemed to accept responsibility for various other airfields and possible invasion beaches). The AOC, on the other hand, saw the arrival of air reinforcements and the safeguarding of the airfields as the determining factors, and was insistent upon their being guarded by the ground forces. While sympathising with Bond's wish to concentrate his defences to ensure against failure by the RAF, the Acting Governor pointed out that this could lead to the loss of all facilities for air operations outside the Singapore area, exposing the air and other defences of the Naval Base to land-based air attack – with dire consequences. The weaknesses, in his view, were so fundamental that the only hope lay in strong reinforcements.

A New Situation

By now the whole strategic picture had altered. France had been defeated and the United Kingdom was under direct threat; Italy had entered the war; and the balance of naval power had totally changed, with the British Fleet in the Mediterranean now needed to contain the Italians. All this boded ill for the reinforcement of Singapore. On the other hand, as the Chiefs of Staff recognised in their appreciation of Far East strategy on 28 June,[14] there were signs that Japan might well try to turn the new situation to her advantage; the fall of France had left her possessions in Indo-China dangerously exposed, and the German occupation of the Netherlands had increased the risk to the Dutch East Indies. It followed, despite the pressing demands of the European war, that some way would have to be found to strengthen the defences of Singapore – though as far as aircraft were concerned this would take some time, depending on the progress of the European war, the rate of aircraft production in the Commonwealth, and the supply of aircraft from the USA.

The urgency was soon even more apparent, for on 16 July the comparatively moderate Japanese government resigned under military pressure and was quickly replaced by one in which General Tojo was appointed Minister of War. As the Air Ministry Intelligence Summary observed, everything pointed to the new government being more pro-Axis and adopting a more aggressive attitude towards British interests. It went on to forecast Japanese intentions as to finish the China war, obtain control of Indo-China and possibly secure a footing in Siam so as to facilitate an eventual attack on Singapore; and it then reported that Hanoi was already largely under Japanese control[15] (Map 2).

In the short term very little could be done in response to the Acting Governor's plea at the end of June, but the Colonial Office did ask Australia if she could help, and the arrival of a Wirraway squadron and two Hudson squadrons of the Royal Australian Air Force in July and August provided a most welcome addition to Babington's strength.[16] The single-engined Wirraway, though designed as a fighter bomber (it was in fact a licence-built Harvard), could hardly be regarded as more than an advanced training aircraft, but it would provide invaluable experience for its crews of operating in Malayan conditions. The Hudson, on the other hand, was a modern aircraft, suitable for several roles as it was already proving in the Battle of the Atlantic, and would eventually give a very good account of itself.

For the longer term, however, much more was obviously required, and on 16 August the Chiefs of Staff produced their proposals. There could no longer be any question, they said, of concentrating on the defence of Singapore; the prospect of being threatened from bases in Indo-China and possibly Siam would now necessitate holding the whole peninsula. When to the RAF share of this was added its other responsibilities, namely to deny the use of air bases in British Borneo and to protect the main trade routes in the eastern Indian Ocean, it was estimated that 22 squadrons would be required, comprising 336 front-line aircraft. These would consist of 96 bombers, 32 torpedo bombers, 126 general reconnaissance aircraft, 18 flying boats and 64 fighters.[17] It is often thought that the much-quoted figure of 336 was the stated requirement for the defence of Malaya and Singapore, whereas in fact no fewer than 56 of these were postulated for the Indian Ocean and 76 for Borneo. On the other hand, had the 336 all been available in December 1941, most would undoubtedly have been drawn into the main theatre of operations. The chances of their actually being provided were, however, remote; the Chiefs recognised that the figure of 336 could not be achieved until the end of 1941 at the earliest.

The scheme for Far Eastern defence of which the above formed a part was almost immediately approved by the War Cabinet and on 28 August the three commanders in Singapore were asked to prepare a full tactical appreciation based upon it; we shall turn to this in a moment. First, however, we must remind ourselves that these deliberations in London were taking place at the height of the Battle of Britain, when it must have been exceedingly difficult for those concerned to address their minds to far less pressing problems on the other side of the world. Even so, some of Churchill's observations at this time make strange reading. On 11 August he wrote to the Australian and New Zealand Prime Ministers: 'If attacked, which is unlikely, Singapore ought to stand a long siege'.[18] On 10 September he minuted General Ismay: 'The prime defence of Singapore is the Fleet ... its defence must be based upon a strong local garrison and the general potentialities of sea-power. The idea of trying to defend the Malay peninsula ... cannot be entertained.'[19]

Such a statement hardly accorded with the instructions which had been sent to Singapore only a few days before – and it made no reference to air power.

The Far East commanders – all three of them now – quickly set to work, amid increasingly worrying reports of Japanese activities which culminated in their invasion of the northern part of French Indo-China on 22 September and the signature of the tripartite pact with Germany and Italy five days later. Admittedly the intelligence reports were stressing that their main objective in Indo-China seemed to be the acquisition of air bases for use against the Burma Road, the vital route across the mountains by which most military supplies were reaching China (Map 2), but there were also indications that the tempo of their southward aggression was increasing and on 16 October Singapore was mentioned as a possible objective.[20]

It was on the same day that the commanders produced their appreciation, based on the assumption that, in the absence of a fleet, air power would be the main weapon of defence.[21] Recognising the likelihood of attack from Siam, from where Singapore would be in range for heavy bombers, they urged the need for a British advance into it once the enemy landed. The RAF would then be required to repel attacks at sea and during the landings, and to attack advancing troops or landing grounds or bases. The Army role would be the close defence of the naval and air bases and the defeat of Japanese forces which might gain a footing. This was the forward strategy, clearly spelt out, and according closely with the views of Babington and of the Secretary of Defence, Mr Vlieland; as Louis Allen observes, 'the possibility that Singapore might be approached overland from the north was envisaged in almost the same way as the invasion actually took place in 1941'.[22]

But it was one thing for those in Singapore to have reached broadly the right conclusions about the way the Japanese would attack and to have decided on a reasonable strategy to counter them; it was quite another to persuade the authorities back at home that their assessments were sound and that they must be provided with the wherewithal. For the RAF they judged they needed far more than the 336 aircraft proposed by the Air Staff. In particular they wanted twice as many bombers and fighters, plus 44 army co-operation aircraft (a category not previously considered) in a bid for 31 squadrons, representing 566 front line aircraft.[23] A few days later at a conference in Singapore attended by representatives of India, Burma, Australia and New Zealand, the figure was raised to 582 in order to provide a fighter squadron for Burma.[24] This was a staggering request not only in relation to the number of aircraft it was reasonable to think might be forthcoming at that stage in the war, but also when one considers the immense difficulties of operating and supporting such a quantity in Malayan conditions so far from home, and nobody could really have been surprised at the Chiefs' reaction.

Their reply came on 8 January 1941. While accepting the estimate of 582 aircraft as ideal, they reiterated that their original figure of 336 should give a fair degree of security, bearing in mind experience thus

far in the air war in the United Kingdom, the Middle East and Malta –
where the RAF had always been inferior in numbers. They added that
this target could not be reached before the end of 1941 but the aim
would be to form by then five fighter squadrons. At the same time the
airfield construction programme would be designed to allow two-thirds
of the 336 aircraft to be concentrated in either north or south Malaya
at any one time. The provision of aircraft specifically for army
co-operation was, however, thought to be uneconomic.[25] Disappointing
as this response must have been, it did at least hold promise of the
fighter aircraft that had for so long been conspicuous by their absence,
and before we criticise the Chiefs for not offering more we must remind
ourselves yet again of the pressures elsewhere. Churchill had told the
Dominions Secretary on 15 December of his reluctance to allow 'any
serious dispersion of our forces' to Malaya and Singapore. He certainly
could not send Catalinas at a time of major peril in the North Western
Approaches.[26] His reaction to the Chiefs' statement of 8 January was
in similar tone:

> I do not remember to have given my approval to these very large
> diversions of force … the political situation in the Far East does
> not seem to require, and the strength of our Air Force by no
> means warrants, the maintenance of such large forces in the Far
> East at this time.[27]

The Chiefs, having pointed out that modern flying boats were needed
to locate commerce raiders in the Indian Ocean, sought to explain to
him the need to start the long-term reinforcement plan, but clearly
there were limits to what they could do in the face of such reluctance.
Yet there were now only 11 months to go, and the Far East Air Force
still comprised a mere eight squadrons (two Blenheim, two Vildebeest,
two Hudson, one Wirraway, one Singapore flying boat).[28]

It is worth mentioning here that a document recovered a year later
from a Japanese aircraft that had crashed in China gave 336 as their
estimate of British air strength;[29] almost certainly their information
had been gleaned from Chiefs of Staff documents seized on their way to
Brooke-Popham aboard the British merchant vessel *Automedon*,
intercepted in the Indian Ocean on 11 November 1940 by the German
commerce raider *Atlantis*.[30]

The Command Structure

Meanwhile attention had at last been given to a major weakness in the
higher command structure. The Chiefs of Staff, well aware of the lack
of co-ordination between the Far East commanders, had recommended
the formation of a unified command under a single commander-in-
chief, and Churchill approved the proposal on 13 October 1940.[31] The

Air Chief Marshal Sir Robert Brooke-Popham GCVO KCB CMG DSO AFC,
C-in-C Far East in 1941. He did all he could in an impossible situation. (*AHB*)

broad concept was sound – as would later be demonstrated in
South-East Asia Command under Mountbatten, and again in several
post-war situations overseas. At this juncture, however, the
single-Service loyalties and lines of command were too strong to be
properly overridden, and as constituted the new General Headquarters 'did little more than add another cog to an already somewhat
complex machine', in the view of the official historian.[32]

Its weaknesses were not, however, the fault of the incumbent. Air
Chief Marshal Sir Robert Brooke-Popham had retired from the RAF in
1937 after a distinguished career; he had been the first Commandant
of the RAF Staff College, AOC Iraq and AOC in C Air Defence of Great
Britain, and had also served as Commandant of the Imperial Defence
College and Inspector General of the RAF. Then after becoming
Governor of Kenya he had returned to the active list in 1939. Louis
Allen describes him as a man of varied experience and considerable
shrewdness; the blimpish impression he gave to some observers was

far from justified, for he was physically tough, quick-witted and an astute judge of character.[33] Ian Morrison, a sharp young civil servant who worked in the Far East Bureau of the Ministry of Information and wrote a vivid account of the Malayan campaign shortly afterwards, said 'he was held in considerable esteem as a man who was a hustler despite his seniority'.[34] General Percival, who worked closely alongside him from May 1941 onwards, writes of the very good personal relations they enjoyed.[35] Pilot Officer Cox, the Kallang intelligence officer who afterwards wrote a detailed, perceptive and highly critical report, says that the personnel there never wavered in their confidence in and respect for 'BP'.[36] Unfortunately, like most others, he underestimated the capabilities of the Japanese, but his was under all the circumstances a sound appointment, given that air power was bound to have such an important role.[37]

That said, he was given an impossible hand to play, and he was not even granted the authority to enable him to try to play it properly. He formed his headquarters at the Naval Base on 18 November, his directive making him responsible for the operational control and general direction of training of all British land and air forces, not just in Malaya but also in British Borneo, Burma and Hong Kong, and also for the air forces in Ceylon and the Indian Ocean. He was additionally given wide consultative powers relating to the various governments in the area. On the other hand, the RAF and Army commanders retained all their normal functions and direct links with the single Service ministries in London, and – even worse – he was given no authority at all over naval operations, for which C-in-C China continued to answer directly to the Admiralty.[38] To act as a proper Commander-in-Chief Brooke-Popham would have needed far wider authority than he was given; that he achieved as much as he did was thanks to his ability to persuade and co-ordinate.

To make his task even more difficult he was given a staff of no more than seven officers; repeated pleas for an increase remained unanswered until August 1941, and not all the eight extra posts then authorised had been filled by December. The result of this paucity of staff, as he later pointed out, was overwork which, in conjunction with the Malayan climate, often led to sickness.[39] Such problems were not confined to the staff of GHQ; they applied just as much to the individual Service staffs, and it cannot have helped that Air Vice-Marshal C W H Pulford, who took over from Babington on 20 April, was in poor health even when he arrived in the Far East.[40]

In most other respects, however, Pulford was a good choice. Having started his flying career in the RNAS he had served in the 1920s aboard HMS *Furious*; he had bomber experience; and more recently he had held several important staff appointments connected with the RAF's expansion programme. Most significantly he and Sir Charles

Portal, recently appointed Chief of Air Staff, had been students together at both the Staff College and the Imperial Defence College, and he had later worked for Portal in the Air Ministry. Clearly Portal knew him well and thought highly of him. So did General Percival, who succeeded General Bond as GOC in Singapore on 16 May. Percival and Pulford both lived at Flagstaff House and, as Percival wrote: 'Our close comradeship was not unimportant in fostering the spirit of co-operation between our respective Services both on the Headquarters staffs and in the field units'.[41]

Nevertheless, while a good rapport certainly existed between the two commanders – no doubt assisted by the co-location of their respective headquarters at Sime Road – there had been a long period of poor relations between the RAF and the Army during which jealousy and lack of co-operation, even though provoked by quite sincere differences of opinion, had caused weaknesses in the defence which could not be fully rectified by the time war broke out.[42]

It is worth reminding ourselves, too, that Percival was less impressed by Pulford's staff, who were ill-trained and included only one staff college graduate.[43] The Narrative enlarges on this point, observing that – to the detriment of his health – Pulford felt obliged to keep much of the detail under his personal control. Pilot Officer Cox, who exempted Pulford from his castigations, wrote of AHQ being in the

Air Vice-Marshal C W H Pulford, CB OBE AFC, AOC RAF Far East in 1941, inspects trainees of the Malayan Volunteer Air Force, October 1941. (*AHB*)

hands of 'a happy band of hedonists'.[44] Indeed right across the board, in the expanding headquarters, on the new stations and in the support units, there was a dearth of staffs with any depth of service knowledge and experience; far too many posts had to be filled either locally or from Australia and New Zealand, and enthusiasm on its own was rarely enough.[45] There was, of course, another side to it, as the Australian official historian reminds us. While accepting that the 116 Australian and New Zealand administrative officers had been given very little training before receiving a wide range of duties and higher ranks than were justified, he writes of a time-wasting adherence to peacetime administration and quotes Flight Lieutenant G R F Burlinson, Group Defence Officer, as saying that while the RAF administrative system seemed capable of amazing efficiency in time of peace, coolness and plenty of time, its lack of adaptability to high-speed work in an emergency was immediately obvious.[46]

Others echo the theme. A medical orderly at Seletar compares those who arrived in Singapore in 1941 having been blooded in the United Kingdom with the 'fat cats' who had been there longer, many of whom went to pieces after the shock of the first bombing.[47] An LAC in the marine section was struck when he arrived by the complacency and inexperience of the long-term residents; having been on the south coast of England during the Battle of Britain he was threatened with disciplinary action on one occasion for remaining at work after the sirens had sounded.[48] An officer on 62 Squadron writes of the life of fair luxury and ease at Tengah in 1939/40 and the failure of the CO or squadron commanders to bring home the dangers facing them: only in October 1941 when an intelligence officer visited them at Alor Star did they become aware of the Japanese threat.[49] An electrician with the same squadron describes the conditions at Alor Star in 1941 as 'definitely peacetime Air Force' – they were given no training at all under war conditions.[50] Brooke-Popham would have agreed with much of this. He certainly accepted that there was great ignorance of modern war conditions, and was concerned at the considerable delay in obtaining from the United Kingdom the lessons of recent operations and developments in tactical ideas. He would have welcomed liaison visits from the Air Ministry but they never materialised.[51]

So we see here a staff structure which was very far from ideal, and it should be added that the tradition of ill-feeling between the Army and RAF also had its effect in the earlier part of 1941 on the working of the GHQ, for Bond was reluctant to accept advice from Brooke-Popham – as a senior RAF officer – on matters that would normally be within his own competence. Not surprisingly, on the other hand, the C-in-C took a close personal interest in RAF affairs, and since he was usually consulted on all important issues GHQ became the normal channel of communication between AHQ and the Air Ministry.[52] It took some time for Brooke-Popham to be seen as the impartial joint commander he needed to be. Nor did the separation of the various headquarters help. Brooke-Popham had placed himself at the Naval Base so that he could keep in close touch with the Navy, which proved a good thing insofar as his relations with Admiral Layton were friendly throughout, but from most points of view GHQ should have been alongside the Army and RAF at Sime Road. Not until mid-December 1941 did this move take place.[53]

Intelligence

The Naval Base did, however, offer Brooke-Popham one other advantage: it was the home of the Far East Combined Bureau which handled all intelligence matters. Being under Admiralty control and very largely Navy staffed it tended to concentrate on naval material, but for most purposes it was the only clearly identifiable intelligence organisation in the theatre, and while the RAF did attempt to set up its own structure it was never adequately developed.[54] Cox, who found that the former AHQ intelligence section had been handed over to FECB and blamed Babington for deciding that a separate RAF organisation was now unnecessary, was scathing about FECB: it was dilatory and unreliable; indeed 'as a collector, collator and assessor of news relative to the intentions, dispositions, forces and capacity of the enemy it was morally bankrupt'.[55]

While on the subject of intelligence it is worth devoting some attention to the vexed subject of Japanese capabilities, for as Brooke-Popham later wrote, 'the strength of the Japanese Air Force came as a complete surprise – in quality, performance, mobility and experience of its personnel'.[56] There had certainly been a general assumption that the Japanese fighting abilities and the quality of their equipment were inferior to those of the British, and this had been fostered by most of the few intelligence reports that filtered through. In February 1940, for example, a report of three Japanese bombers being shot down in a raid on Chengtu three months previously drew attention to the crews' use of parachutes, contrary to the Japanese ethical code; from this came the surprising deduction that Japanese morale was suffering owing to the strain and losses of the past few months.[57] Three months later came a further slanted interpretation. Having reported that a neutral and reliable source had formed a high opinion of Japanese formation flying and their ability to find the target (their formations were tight and undisturbed by fighter attacks), the writer commented:

> Whilst the foregoing agrees with previous reports of Japanese flying efficiency it must be remembered that as regards fighter attacks the Japanese have never been obliged to face more than

very occasional interception by small and mostly ineffective Chinese fighter formations.[58]

In August 1940 we read of Japan's continued weakness in aircraft design being illustrated by Mitsubishi's failure to get a contract to supply commercial aircraft to a South American country – they could not produce an adequate design.[59] 'Continued weakness' is the revealing phrase. Two months later we find a report of a visit to Yokosuka by the Commandant of the Central Thai Flying School, who had formerly served in the RAF and was therefore considered competent to express a valid opinion. He formed a very poor impression of Japanese aircraft, which he considered obsolete by Western standards – they probably included the latest types of fighters and bombers in general service with the Japanese Naval Air Force.[60] An even more damning assessment appeared in February 1941:

> Recent information tends to confirm the belief, hitherto held, that the operational value of the Japanese Air Forces is less than that implied by their numerical strength ... estimates must be approximate, but it can be safely assumed the correct figure lies between 2,000 and 2,500 (538 shipborne) ... the performances of Japanese aircraft are much below those of equivalent RAF types. There are good grounds for believing that, allowing for the probable superiority of Italian pilots over their Japanese allies, the operational value of the Japanese air arm is less than that of the Italians.[61]

That the author of this priceless observation was perceived to have gone too far may be inferred from the more balanced comment that appeared two weeks later:

> There was reference recently to the low operational effectiveness of the Japanese Air Forces as compared with British standards. This is due not only to inferiority of performance but also to the probability that some first-line squadrons are equipped with obsolescent aircraft. For the initiation of offensive operations southward, however, it may be safely assumed that Japan would have sufficient of her modern types.[62]

Here at last was a note of realism, and it was accompanied by brief details of one of the 'modern types', the TO SSF, a new aircraft first identified in China about the middle of 1940 of which so far only a very limited number were available in operational squadrons. Its maximum speed was quoted as 345 mph, its ceiling 34,000 ft, its endurance seven hours, its armament 2 × 20 mm cannon and 2 × 7.7 mm machine guns.

This was not the performance of an aircraft 'much below' its RAF equivalents and it should have been clear from at least now on that a fighter such as the Hurricane would be needed to counter it. Yet Sir Archibald Sinclair, Secretary of State for Air, was to tell the Defence Committee on 9 April that to send Hurricanes to Singapore 'would be a mistake'.[63]

The new fighter, soon to be referred to simply as the Zero,[64] continued to arouse attention. In March the Japanese were said to be attaching much importance to its performance,[65] and several later reports spoke of successful operations in China, notably one on 14 March when 12 Zeros engaged 24 Russian-made fighters and shot down 14 (later amended to 20),[66] and another on 11 August against an aerodrome at Chengtu, when seven squadrons (63 aircraft) were employed.[67] The evidence was accumulating, but being unpalatable – as so often to the recipients of intelligence – was given too little weight. Minds long conditioned to a belief in Japanese inferiority were not to be so readily changed. Indeed the performance data about the Zero, although received by FECB, was not circulated to stations; apparently a senior officer strongly denied the possibility of the Japanese possessing such an aircraft and took no action.[68] Consequently some of the Buffalo pilots did not even know that they would meet monoplane fighters.[69] One might add here that a full description of the Zero appeared on 31 December under the heading 'A formidable Japanese fighter'. Among its characteristics was an unusually large fuel load; if the wing tanks and a drop tank were used 'a maximum range of 1,900 miles should be attainable'.[70] The long-range Mustang so much acclaimed in Europe (and indeed in Burma) later in the war could manage 1,710.

It was the same story for the bombers. While there were ample reports of the construction of bases on Hainan island and later in Indo-China few had much respect for the capabilities of the aircraft that might be based there. Despite the great deal of experience already obtained in the long-running war in China, the conventional British view was exemplified in a report of April 1941 which spoke of the 'low standard of efficiency of Japanese bombing'.[71] Nevertheless it was recognised by the middle of the year that the heavy bombers, operating from southern Indo-China, did have the range to cover the 750 miles to Singapore. A report in late July gave a fairly realistic statement of the strength of the Japanese air forces and indicated that, after allowing for their many other commitments, they should be able to concentrate a striking force of up to 150 shore-based aircraft for operations against Malaya or the Netherlands East Indies. Of these some 50 would be heavy bombers, naval or army, but it seemed improbable, in view of the likely high wastage rates, that the initial scale of attack could be long maintained.[72] This was not the kind of assessment that was likely to cause overmuch anxiety.

243 Squadron's Buffaloes over Malaya. (*C G Hutchings*)

The Aircraft

Set against this view of the capabilities of the Japanese air forces we must now turn to those which the RAF managed to put in place during the final months before the enemy assault. The target, as we have seen, was 336; in the event only half that number were provided, some of them very far from modern, and very few up to the operational standards that would be needed.

The major step required was to introduce some fighter squadrons, but in early 1941, such was the situation in the United Kingdom and the Middle East, there was no prospect of sparing Spitfires or even Hurricanes – even if it had been felt that such aircraft were necessary. It so happened, however, that an American-built machine was available, the Brewster Buffalo. This was a small, mid-wing aircraft first produced in 1938 for the United States Navy, and armed with four 0.5″ Browning guns, two fitted in the wings and two firing through the propeller arc. Having entered service in 1939 it was then ordered by the British Purchasing Commission as a land fighter, and deliveries to the RAF in the United Kingdom started in September 1940. The trials that were immediately carried out by 71 Squadron (the first 'Eagle' squadron) at Church Fenton resulted, however, in its being rejected as a first-line fighter for use in Europe,[73] where on the evidence of the air war thus far it would be hopelessly outclassed. For the Far East, however, it appeared to be the answer for at least the time being. Consequently the entire shipment of 170 aircraft (167 actually arrived) was consigned to Singapore, where deliveries began in February 1941. The first two squadrons, Nos 67 and 243, were formed in March at Kallang, the civil airport just east of Singapore City, and two more (453 RAAF and 488 RNZAF) were formed in October, at the same time as 21 Squadron RAAF converted from the Wirraway.[74] With the departure of 67 Squadron for Burma, also in October, there were thus four Buffalo squadrons in Singapore and Malaya when the attack came, representing a front line of 67 aircraft.

Just as important as the numbers were factors such as performance, pilot proficiency and serviceability, and here too it was a sorry tale. In Brooke-Popham's despatch the performance of the Buffalo, as reported in an A & AEE test report from Boscombe Down dated 3 July 1941, was compared with the intelligence figures of the Zero as follows:

	Zero	*Buffalo*
Rate of climb to 13,000 ft	4.3 minutes	6.1 minutes
Speed at 10,000 ft	315 mph	270 mph
Speed at 20,000 ft	295 mph	292 mph[75]

The despatch goes on to say that 292 mph could not be obtained in Malaya, and 280 mph, the maximum speed according to one of the fitters,[76] was probably about right. In summary the Buffalo was heavy, underpowered and had a poor rate of climb, whereas the Zero seemed to have sacrificed armour and armament for performance.[77] Even so the two 7.7 mm guns and two 22 mm cannon with which the Zero was fitted were hardly inadequate.[78]

Turning to the pilots we might reasonably expect many of them to have had combat experience in Europe, but this applied in fact to very few. While most of the squadron commanders and some of the flight commanders did come from the United Kingdom, a high proportion of the pilots – particularly for the later squadrons to be formed – came straight from flying training schools in Australia and New Zealand; the rest were transferred from other units already in Malaya, mainly the Blenheim squadrons.[79] The FTS men were mostly excellent material, but in the absence of a reasonable proportion of pilots with practical war experience who could set a standard there was insufficient time to make them ready. Nor was there a proper Operational Training Unit – the Air Ministry refused to authorise it – and although a 'do it yourself' one formed at Kluang in September and did valuable work it was all happening too late. Weapons training, too, was inadequate; a school was set up at Kuantan in October, but only the two longer established squadrons were able to complete the course, and the others had not been passed operationally fit when the war started.[80]

Aircraft maintenance caused fewer problems; the aircraft had arrived in huge packing cases (very useful subsequently for constructing dispersal huts and rest-rooms)[81] and were fairly easy to assemble and service; moreover there were plenty of tradesmen to do the work. Serious shortages of spare parts, however, often led to cannibalisation and even to theft from the MU; so there was ample scope for the use of personal initiative.[82] Airmen who were there at the time can recall other problems, such as the difficulties of inertia starting when rapid take-off was required, poor visibility when taxying, which led to frequent accidents,[83] and faulty undercarriages.

Despite all these deficiencies, many of which would become apparent only when fighting started, the arrival of the Buffalo force was widely acclaimed. A then LAC remembers an American film unit visiting Kallang in April 1941 to make a documentary about Singapore's defences:

Our few aircraft were filmed on the ground and in the air from all directions and angles. The film (The March of Time) when edited and released made us look formidable indeed as the same aircraft were used in such a way as to make the skies above Singapore look impregnable.[84]

In an island that had never before seen a fighter aircraft the Buffaloes conveyed a sense of security that entirely fitted the mood of the inhabitants. Ian Morrison describes the scene:

Singapore, alone of the cities of the Far East, gave its inhabitants the illusion of security. Aeroplanes droned overhead during the day. The little Buffalo fighters looked beautifully speedy and manoeuvrable. There was hardly an hour of the day when one looked up into the sky and failed to see an aeroplane of some description – a Blenheim bomber, a Wirraway, a Catalina flying boat, a torpedo-carrying Vildebeest.[85]

Even Brooke-Popham was not immune to the general feeling, and his correspondence on the subject with the Air Ministry indicates his gratitude that at last Singapore was actually being given a fighter defence; there is no hint of complaint about its quality.[86] Whatever doubts he may have had it would have been inconceivable to voice them publicly, and Morrison remembers him saying at a press conference a few weeks before the war started that, although Britain's fighter planes in Malaya were not the fastest in the world, he believed them adequate to deal with anything the Japanese could produce.[87] At about the same time he told the Advisory War Council in Australia that the Buffaloes were superior to the Japanese fighters and well suited to operations in Malaya.[88] As events would show, however, the truth was that the fighter defence was quite unsuitable to the task,[89] and Morrison calls it 'a bitter disappointment'.

Fighter defence was not just about aircraft; it was also about control and reporting as the Battle of Britain had shown. So it was clear in early 1941 that a radio direction finding system[90] was needed to complement the Buffaloes. The plan provided for a main air defence

A Vildebeest of 36 Squadron over Singapore. (*RAF Staff College*)

operations room and southern filter room at Katong, in Singapore city, and a further operations room at Kuala Lumpur, each linked to ten radars, but there were no illusions about how long the system would take to construct and become operationally effective. There were few suitably qualified personnel – though many would soon arrive, bringing their experience of the home system as it had worked in 1940; the ground communications were almost totally inadequate,[91] and the ground-to-air links nearly as bad. Moreover the Buffaloes could be controlled only to 20 miles distance. Nevertheless, considering the timescale and continual difficulties over the works services, much progress was made; for example the two coastal radars were linked to the filter room by means of WT or VHF RT sets installed on the top floor of the Cathay Building, whence the reports were sent on by telephone, and the arrangements 'worked faultlessly to the end'.[92] During two fighter exercises in August and September information from these two radars was successfully filtered at Katong.[93] This was one of those situations in which well trained and experienced RAF tradesmen overcame many problems such as lack of equipment by using their initiative.[94] One such tradesman, AC1 J Hall, was in 250 Mobile Radar Unit. All the 20 or so radar people there had served in the UK, half of them during the Battle of Britain, and knew what they were doing, but the mobile radars – the receiver and transmitter were each mounted in a Crossley truck – were not as effective as the CH and CHL units back at home. As for the operations room at Katong, only just completed in time,

The crews of 100 Squadron admire their new Beaufort torpedo-bombers, due to replace their Vildebeests – they have arrived too late. (*AHB*)

its plotting table was built by the gifted amateurs of 250 MRU, just one example of the improvisation that was inevitable all along the line. 'Everything was third rate' suggests Hall, though he recognises that the Far East was at the bottom of the priority list.[95] Nevertheless by December 1941 two MRUs were operational, at Tanah Merah Besar near Changi, and at Mersing, together with three Chain Overseas Low radars. A further radar, at Kota Bharu, was about to be installed, but the invasion came just too soon.[96] Nevertheless, at least Singapore itself would now be able to receive 30 minutes' warning of air attack – if the system worked.

We must turn now more briefly to the other components of the air force that would face the Japanese. The most antiquated were the two squadrons of Vildebeests. This long obsolete aircraft was a biplane of 49 ft wing span with a divided undercarriage enabling it to carry one torpedo or a small bomb load; its range was 630 miles, its maximum speed 156 mph.[97] On the other hand the squadrons had been a long time in the Far East, they knew the local conditions, and their training and experience had made them highly efficient. A wireless and electrical mechanic who flew as an air gunner in 100 Squadron remembers his crew being despatched on 22 February 1941 to look for a Japanese submarine reported to be in the vicinity of Johore Shoal

Buoy; they searched for an hour, working closely with the Royal Navy. While they found nothing 'morale was still sky high, despite their now antiquated equipment'.[98] Six months earlier they had heard with delight that CAS had ruled the Vildebeest obsolete and when two Blenheims joined 100 Squadron in August 1941 to convert the pilots to twin-engined aircraft, they realised that re-equipment with the modern Bristol Beaufort lay not far ahead.[99] The aircraft they were to receive were being manufactured in Australia and should have started to appear in the middle of the year but sadly, thanks to delays in obtaining raw materials and specific parts in England and the USA, the first six arrived at Seletar just two days before the outbreak of war. Neither the aircraft nor the crews were ready for operations and since there was no prospect of making them so in Singapore once the Japanese attacked all but one were sent back to Australia a few days later, the sixth being retained for photographic reconnaissance.[100] There was no choice but to keep the Vildebeests of 36 and 100 Squadrons in the front line.

Fortunately the other ancient aircraft on the inventory, the four Singapore flying boats of 205 Squadron, had been replaced in time, in this case by Catalinas. Several of these already well-proven long-range maritime aircraft were prised away from the Battle of the Atlantic in August 1941 and by December the necessary extra crews had been trained. There were, however, no longer any Sunderlands, 230 Squadron having moved to Ceylon to help deal with the German U-boat threat in the Indian Ocean.

The remaining elements of the force comprised the two RAAF Hudson squadrons that had arrived in 1940 and were well trained and

Catalinas of 205 Squadron operating off the coast. (*AHB*)

equipped for reconnaissance work and for bombing, and four squadrons of Blenheims. One of these (No 27) was trained in the night fighter role and the other three (34, 60 and 62) primarily for bombing. 60 Squadron, though based in Burma, happened to be in Malaya when the war started. An air observer who served with 62 Squadron from September 1939 onwards gives us a good example of their limitations. Thanks to the lack of replacement spares each crew was restricted in 1939/40 to seven hours' flying each month, far too few to allow them to work up to any proper operational standard, and nobody thought to involve them in ground training so as to incorporate the lessons of the European war. The events of mid-1940 made little difference, and even in 1941, when based at Alor Star, he flew no more than 11 hours per month.[101] Comment would be superfluous. Altogether these six squadrons of Hudsons and Blenheims provided 66 aircraft on 7 December – a fair striking force if it could be properly protected, but lacking the range to reach the main enemy-held airfields in Indo-China. Brooke-Popham pressed continually for long-range bombers – at least one airfield, Gong Kedah, had been designed with these in mind – but without success.[102] Other gaps of which Brooke-Popham was painfully aware included aircraft for photo-graphic reconnaissance, army co-operation and air transport – all of them remarkable omissions.

So to summarise the situation on 7 December 1941, the air strength in Malaya and Singapore amounted to just 181 serviceable aircraft:

Hudsons of the Royal Australian Air Force on patrol. (*AHB*)

79 Buffaloes, 50 Blenheims, 18 Hudsons, 31 Vildebeests and three Catalinas. Of these 167 were in the operational squadrons (see Appendix A). In addition there were 84 unserviceable, plus the one Beaufort, plus a few Swordfish of the Fleet Air Arm, plus a few light aircraft of the Malayan Volunteer Air Force which would come in particularly useful for communications purposes.[103] General Percival summarises the position reasonably enough: there was no really effective air striking force, there were none of the aircraft needed by an army, and the fighters could not give effective support to the bombers or take their proper place in defence. But he goes on to make it absolutely clear that it was not Pulford's fault: he had repeatedly represented the situation to higher authority. Nor could responsibility be laid at the door of the C-in-C or even the present government. It went back, in Percival's view, to the pre-war days when the nation's leaders would not face the dangers that threatened.[104] Ultimately he was right, but we must not ignore the way in which the War Cabinet and Chiefs of Staff addressed the questions of priorities that constantly assailed them. It can undoubtedly be argued that more should have been done in 1941, and almost certainly it would have been but for the German attack on the Soviet Union on 22 June and the decision to send to the Russians as many spare aircraft as possible, especially Hurricanes. It was at the end of August that Churchill promised Stalin 200 Hurricanes on top of the 40 already sent, plus another 200 American aircraft. 'They constituted a painful sacrifice on our part' he wrote on 5 September.[105] While he was not referring specifically to the Far East, there would otherwise almost certainly have been Hurricane squadrons in Singapore by December. Sir Maurice Dean agrees, telling us that 'the bulk of the aircraft reinforcements earmarked for Malaya – over 300 aircraft – was diverted to help Britain's newly found and hard pressed ally, Russia'.[106] Whether Sir Archibald Southby was right when he spoke in the House of Commons after the fall of Singapore is another matter, but it is worth reminding ourselves of what he said: 'One month's supply of the aircraft sent to Russia would have saved Malaya'.[107]

Support

So much for the aircraft: it remains to consider all the supporting work that went on in those final months in an effort to make the RAF ready to fight. The biggest task was to continue to develop the pre-war airfields and increase their number; if 336 operational aircraft were to be accommodated and be capable of strategic concentration in any threatened area, altogether 27 airfields were required, 12 more than had been available in 1939.[108] Up to the end of 1940 work was concentrated on improving the existing ones, but in 1941 the volume of work greatly expanded to the point at which it exceeded the capacity of the country, having regard to the civil, army and naval projects also in hand. To add to the task it was now recognised that grass airfields were unsuitable for modern aircraft in such a wet climate and by December a number of hard runways were either finished or under construction.[109] From the middle of the year onwards, too, no new airfields were sited or planned without the aid of the Army staff. There remained, however, great problems. As Air Vice-Marshal Maltby later pointed out, the acquisition of land entailed negotiations with 11 separate provincial governments in Malaya; mechanical plant was short and in poor condition, with few qualified operators; most of the sites were remote and hard to reach; supplies of materials were inadequate; labour was scarce. The arrival of a New Zealand airfield construction unit in October was therefore highly welcome and it did valuable work in the short time left.[110]

By December, therefore, and to the great credit of the hard-pressed works staff, the 27 airfields needed all existed, but many were still very basic and their ground defences were inadequate or non-existent.[111] Unfortunately some of the older and better appointed airfields, notably Alor Star and Kota Bharu, were ill-designed for wartime use and had no form of camouflage, and it was these that found themselves at the centre of the action. In fact only nine of the 27 airfields were occupied when the war started; a few more were used briefly; the rest were merely a liability. Yet the construction work had had to be done on the assumption that the planned numbers of aircraft would materialise.[112]

Another major requirement for this expansion was to build up the maintenance organisation. While 153 MU eventually opened at Kuala Lumpur in June 1941 and 152 MU formed as an equipment depot at Bukit Panjang two months later, it was 151 MU at Seletar (formerly the Aircraft Depot) that carried the main burden, and its task was made no easier by the failure to set up a maintenance group or even to appoint a chief maintenance officer at AHQ. Skilled manpower was another problem; while many Asiatic tradesmen were employed (from August 1940 they began to be mobilised into a Special Technical Corps), there were never enough skilled tradesmen with experience of modern RAF methods, and excessive man-hours had to be spent on crude improvisation. Moreover, in every department of the unit there was a dearth of space, spares and equipment. The range of work was huge. For example all the Buffaloes had to be erected there on arrival and the first few were done without guidance or data; each needed detailed inspection and many modifications were required. Blenheims and Hudsons too had to be assembled, flying boats overhauled, dummy aircraft built. Such work was not helped by shortcomings of the equipment organisation (several thousands of packing cases lay unopened at the end of 1941), and by an Air Ministry instruction in

August stating that only equipment not available from the Commonwealth was to be demanded from the UK. On the other hand, the arrival of a Repair and Salvage Unit, to be based on the small airfield at Kluang in south Johore, was a sign of more positive thinking.[113]

It is hard to exaggerate the importance of Seletar during these years. Not only did it provide most of the support for the whole Command, but it was also a main airfield and flying boat base – a classic case of too many eggs in one basket. As its historian says, it was 'an immense station with every facility',[114] a view with which Flight Lieutenant R P Bulcock, an RAAF equipment officer, would have agreed. His view of its accounting system was less complimentary: 'For a peacetime system it was undoubtedly a perfect method of preventing loss or pilfering, but how would it work in war? The answer was that it didn't'.[115] And even the superb resources of Seletar were stretched in 1941 when a hutted and tented camp outside its bounds, intended for emergency use in the event of bombing, had to be turned into a transit camp for the great number of new arrivals from the UK.[116] An airman who spent some time there remembers the facilities as barely adequate – they slept on shelves in attap huts.[117] Many of these new arrivals were also struck by the attitude of the local British population. A flight rigger remembers the disdain with which non-commissioned servicemen, British or Australian, were treated by people who dismissed all thought that war might occur.[118] Another airman says that the Europeans were the 'high society'; British servicemen were not in the same world.[119] Squadron Leader Carter, who had been there since February 1941, recognised that British civilians were driven by the overriding need to make hard currency for the Empire by exporting tin and rubber, with which nothing must interfere. The British officers, far more heavily taxed, could not afford to join their clubs and there was no social contact; the Services were tolerated but not welcomed.[120]

The Approach of War

It remains to consider briefly the main course of events during 1941, whose early months were marked by Brooke-Popham's attempts to build up some sort of common front in the hope of providing a more effective deterrent. Already, in November 1940, conversations had taken place in Singapore with Dutch representatives, when it was agreed that in the event of attack on Malaya, Borneo or the Dutch East Indies, the Dutch would send 27 aircraft to Malaya and the RAF would operate four reinforcing squadrons from Sumatra. The Australians were brought into the next series of discussions in February, when the Anglo-Dutch undertakings were confirmed and the Australians agreed to provide an air striking force at Darwin. Then in April, with the USA,

New Zealand and India also represented, it was agreed among other things that, while the main strategy should be defensive, preparations should be made for air operations from China and the Philippines against Japanese-occupied territory and Japan herself. This ADB report, summarised in Brooke-Popham's despatch, at least gave welcome evidence of the intention to think constructively, and by November a detailed plan had been drawn up for the employment of the naval and air forces of Great Britain, the Netherlands and the USA. The subsequent joint Anglo-Dutch air operations were conducted in the context of this plan, but the American participation was largely ruled out by the consequences of Pearl Harbor.[121]

In the meantime, after a period when she had seemed largely preoccupied with the war in China, Japan persuaded the Vichy government on 11 March to agree to her using the French military facilities in southern Indo-China. A month later she signed a Neutrality Pact with the Soviet Union and when this was followed by the German attack on 22 June the restraining influence on Japan's northern flank was effectively removed. The way was now clear for Japan to realise her dreams of empire, as Kirby puts it, and on 24 July she marched into southern Indo-China. From now on British policy was to be determined by the overriding need to keep in step with the USA (which had immediately frozen all Japanese assets), since if it came to war the British could hope for American support, and the Chiefs of Staff met on 12 August to consider immediate reinforcement plans. Strangely they devoted more attention to the Navy than the Air Force, and eventually these discussions would lead to the despatch of HMS *Prince of Wales* and HMS *Repulse*. At about the same time came the proposal to replace Brooke-Popham by a younger officer with more up-to-date experience, though Churchill did not agree this until November.[122]

In Singapore, Brooke-Popham and his colleagues were uncomfortably aware that the threat they had long feared was now real, and for the RAF there was a new sense of urgency. The squadrons were informed, not before time, of their operational roles and new training instructions were issued. Night flying arrangements were at last co-ordinated.[123] A general reconnaissance plan for the Hudsons and Catalinas was drawn up. The first airfield defence exercises were held. Preparations were started for American and Dutch air reinforcements.[124] And in some quarters there was optimism; at a joint staff conference in August Group Captain L Darvall is alleged to have stated that the RAF would destroy 70 per cent of the ships of an invading force before it landed.[125] The fundamental weaknesses, however, remained all too apparent, certainly to Brooke-Popham, who told the Chiefs of Staff on 20 August, when supporting Percival's plea for Army reinforcements, that the Allied defences were deplorably weak against the likely pattern of Japanese attack, and the small air striking force would soon be reduced by normal attrition to a state that would greatly increase the possibility of enemy landings.[126] At the same time he commended to them a plan to be known as Operation MATADOR, which would aim at seizing the port and airfields at Singora, in southern Siam, and thus denying to the Japanese the base whose capture would give them the key to Malaya and Singapore. The RAF contribution to this would need to be at least four bomber and two fighter squadrons.[127]

Two months later, on 16 October, the Japanese Premier resigned, to be replaced by General Tojo, and it was soon clear that the pro-war party now had the upper hand. By late November Zeros were reported moving into southern Indo-China and increasingly Japanese reconnaissance aircraft were flying high over northern Malaya. A detachment of Buffaloes was therefore sent to Alor Star, though they clearly had little chance of intercepting.[128] Sadly Brooke-Popham's pleas to the Air Ministry for comparable high altitude PR aircraft had been refused,[129] as was his request to General MacArthur for a B-17, so the RAF was denied the 'eyes' that could have made all the difference to the divining of Japanese intentions. The locally organised PRU, equipped with two (later four) Buffaloes, performed valiantly but the aircraft lacked the performance needed. Nevertheless orders were issued on 22 November for the guarding of vital points, and certain RAF units were put to battle stations. War could not now be far away.

3   The Paper Fortress

The Opening Round

It was on 22 November that Brooke-Popham told Percival and Pulford that war was virtually certain: the arrival of a Japanese bomber force in southern Indo-China pointed strongly towards a sudden attack on Siam, north Malaya or even Singapore itself. At the same time he signalled the Chiefs of Staff, requesting authority to implement Operation MATADOR so as to pre-empt a Japanese landing at Singora. The Chiefs of Staff refused to commit themselves – nothing must be done that might provoke hostilities – but assuming that MATADOR would have to be carried out Brooke-Popham ordered Pulford to move the Blenheims of 34 Squadron and the Buffaloes of 21 Squadron north where they joined 62 and 27 Squadrons at Alor Star and Sungei Patani respectively. At the same time the Buffalo detachment at Alor Star was switched to Kota Bharu where it joined the Hudsons of 1 Squadron RAAF.[1] The full Air Force deployment at the beginning of December is at Appendix A.

The urgent need now was for reconnaissance, and on 29 November the Hudsons began daily sorties from Kota Bharu. The full plan, which included 8 Squadron RAAF from Kuantan, was ordered on 3 December and provided cover as far as the southern tip of Indo-China but not in the Gulf of Siam, there being too few aircraft.[2] Then at last, on the 5th, the War Cabinet authorised Brooke-Popham to order MATADOR – provided he had good information that a Japanese expedition was advancing with the apparent intention of landing on the Kra Isthmus. 'They've now made you responsible for declaring war', observed his Chief of Staff.[3] It was already too late.

The initial sightings came on the 6th. The bad weather which had hidden the invasion fleet as it rounded Cape Cambodia (Map 2) lifted and at 1212 a Hudson of 1 Squadron spotted the first Japanese ships. Two further sightings quickly followed, making it clear that a large force was heading west. Three hours later 'No 1 Degree of Readiness' was ordered, and Seletar was instructed to despatch nine Vildebeests and the one Beaufort of 100 Squadron to Kota Bharu, and to send a Catalina of 205 Squadron to try to shadow the Japanese convoys overnight. This took off at 1830 and returned to base at 0800 on the 7th; a second Catalina had taken off at 0200 and at 0830 it acknowledged a signal from Seletar. Then, according to Japanese records, it sighted the convoys sailing north along the Cambodian coast, dived to attack the fighter escort and was shot down.[4] Louis Allen tells it differently, stating that it was first engaged by a Japanese reconnaissance aircraft before succumbing to the fighters, which may explain why no message was received.[5]

For the rest of that day bad weather hindered the continued efforts of the Hudsons and the solitary Beaufort, operating from the overcrowded airfield at Kota Bharu,[6] and it was not until 1750 that a Hudson sighted and was fired on by a cruiser only 112 miles to the north. A further sighting north of Patani an hour later seemed to confirm that an invasion was in prospect and at 2100 Brooke-Popham decided not to order MATADOR, since it could not possibly succeed in the time now likely to be left. Further reconnaissance missions were ordered for first light.[7] Air Vice-Marshal Maltby (p. 55), who claims that Pulford would have agreed with him, considers that more of the reconnaissance effort on that critical day, 7 December, should have been directed into the Gulf of Siam, where the previous day's sightings had indicated the main Japanese convoys to be, and less to searching for another possible expedition against Malaya.[8] Percival comments also: the failure of air reconnaissance to contact the main invasion forces was a classic example of the dangers of relying on visual sighting from aircraft in such climatic conditions.[9] As a result the Japanese – assisted by the weather – achieved tactical surprise, and the chance of attacking their main force when it was most vulnerable, ie. while landing at Singora, was lost. We shall return to this.

The questions were soon answered. At 0030 on 8 December the beach defences at Kota Bharu (Map 1) told AHQ that three ships were lying off-shore; half an hour later OC 1 Squadron reported gunfire, at 0115 landing craft were stated to be approaching the beach, and at 0120 1 Squadron was ordered to attack the barges and transports. No matter that its crews were already tired after their reconnaissance efforts; eight Hudsons were airborne just after 0200 (at precisely the time when other Japanese forces were attacking Pearl Harbor)[10] and by 0500 17 sorties had been flown, refuelling being unnecessary. This rapid RAAF response was highly successful: transports, warships and barges were all hit by bombs and machine gun fire, with one merchant ship being destroyed, two others seriously damaged and 24 landing barges sunk.[11] Some 3,000 enemy soldiers were estimated killed, and the Japanese themselves subsequently paid tribute to the effectiveness of the attack. Yet it was not enough. Despite the bombing and the determined resistance of the ground defences, sufficient of the enemy were ashore by early morning to establish their beachhead and allow their fleet to withdraw. As a result there was little that the other squadrons which Pulford had ordered into the attack could do. 8 and 60 Squadrons from Kuantan could not get there quickly enough to contribute significantly; 36 Squadron from Gong Kedah mounted an unsuccessful torpedo attack in poor weather on one of the cruisers; 34 Squadron from Tengah and 27 Squadron from Sungei Patani arrived too late.

For 62 Squadron at Alor Star the story was different. Ordered to 'seek and destroy' and finding no targets off Kota Bharu they eventually located and bombed the enemy fleet landing troops at Patani, but without observed results; Flight Lieutenant Reynolds, who flew on this raid, remembers being briefed not to overfly Siamese territory since Siam was not theoretically involved.[12] Ridiculous as this now appears, Brooke-Popham still felt constrained by the repeated pleas from the British Ambassador for Britain not to be the first to break Siam's neutrality. The fact remains that the one slender chance the RAF might ever have had of crippling the invasion was lost in those early hours of 8 December, when most of the striking force was sent to Kota Bharu and not to Singora and Patani. When 100 Squadron's PR Beaufort staggered back to base at 0915 with the photographs that at last revealed the landings at Patani[13] the RAF had run out of time. As Maltby commented subsequently, it was not realised until too late that this was the enemy's main effort, although Singora had long been recognised as the area in which a Japanese expedition against Malaya was likely to land.[14] Yet even had its effort been better directed at that critical moment the RAF was not strong enough to do more than impose a slight delay, though the damage caused at Kota Bharu indicates what a total force of 336 aircraft might have achieved. As Ian Morrison observes: 'If we had had 250 fighters in Malaya, there never would have been any campaign at all, for the enemy would never have been able to set foot on Kota Bharu'.[15]

Louis Allen's conclusion is hard to fault:

> If one remembers the havoc wrought on the Japanese landing vessels off Kota Bharu by the pitifully few Hudsons flying from local airfields on 8 December, it seems likely that air forces provided on the scale requested, and approved by the Chiefs of Staff, might well have wrecked a seaborne invasion, and altered the course of history.[16]

We must now move to Singapore. In the Combined Operations Room at Sime Road, continuously engaged since 0030 in directing operations to the north, a telephone call at 0330 came as an unpleasant shock. The radar at Mersing had detected a large formation of aircraft over the South China Sea, and these had subsequently been plotted by the two

COL stations and the Changi MRU; the filter officer at Katong had labelled them Unidentified, since war had not been declared, but having no doubt that they were hostile he informed his customers accordingly.[17] The radar system had done its job. Sadly, however, as the enemy formation approached Singapore the city lights stayed on (not that it made much difference on a moonlit night) and the warning sirens were not sounded until Pulford had telephoned the Governor, who was attending a meeting with Admiral Phillips and others at the Naval Base. The events of this night gave ample demonstration of the poor level of co-operation between the Service and civilian authorities. Nor did they reflect well on the RAF command. In the absence of night fighters AHQ had decided that night air defence should be left to the anti-aircraft guns, yet three Buffaloes of 453 Squadron at Sembawang were in fact ready for take-off and the squadron commander's repeated requests to be allowed to have a go were refused; had the radar warning time been exploited they could probably have reached the necessary height in time to inflict at least some losses on such a clear night. The bombs started falling on the city centre at 0408, and Seletar and Tengah too were hit, although suffering only slight damage.[18] Singapore had suffered its baptism of fire and the RAF had been able to do little about it.

Nevertheless, the time had now come to issue the long-prepared Order of the Day to all the forces in the Far East. It was full of fine words: 'We are ready ... our preparations are made and tested ... we are confident ... our defences are strong and our weapons efficient'. Brooke-Popham wrote later that he believed it had the effect he meant it to, and at the time it seems to have done so in Singapore itself, but the Services thought differently. As the senior operations officer at Seletar declared, 'It would have been better if this speech had never been made'. At the same time a message of encouragement was circulated from the CAS, which at least recognised the limits of his Service's resources.[19]

The urgent questions were now to be asked in the north. With the Japanese ashore, what could the RAF do to assist the Army, and would the enemy air forces decide to give top priority to a counter-air programme? The answers were painfully soon apparent; indeed after the first day the RAF virtually ceased to exist as a means of defence.

While the initial operations so far described had cost nine aircraft destroyed and others severely damaged, most aircraft had returned to their bases intact, but the need to refuel and rearm gave the Japanese their opportunity. Starting at 0700 and continuing all day some 150 aircraft of 7th Air Brigade, two thirds of them long-range fighters, launched attacks from their bases in southern Indo-China against the seven northern airfields.[20] They concentrated on aircraft on the ground (often when they were taking off or landing)[21]and airfield installations, while trying to avoid damaging the airstrips which they themselves planned to use, and their fighters gave an excellent demonstration of ground attack operations. Three of the airfields attacked were empty – Machang, Gong Kedah and Penang – but elsewhere it was different. Two raids on Sungei Patani left 21 and 27 Squadrons with only four serviceable aircraft apiece; 21 Squadron's 12 Buffaloes had even been conveniently lined up near the standby hut. Butterworth, organised only for care and maintenance, found itself under attack at the moment 34 Squadron's Blenheims were diverted there after their attempt to intervene at Kota Bharu; only two remained serviceable, and the situation worsened when aircraft evacuated there from Sungei Patani were also struck.[22] At Alor Star, where the 'Singapore traitor', Captain Patrick Heenan, was serving as an intelligence officer,[23] four of 62 Squadron's Blenheims were destroyed and the fuel dump and much of the accommodation set alight. Finally Kota Bharu, where a grim struggle was taking place on the ground, was skilfully attacked by fighters no less than seven times, and at 1600 the ground situation compelled the AOC to order 1 Squadron's five remaining Hudsons to leave for Kuantan. The decision to evacuate the airfield soon followed, and although considerable demolition took place there was too little time for a thorough job.

The net result of this disastrous day was the destruction of 40 aircraft (including the nine lost in the night operations) and the serious damage of 20 more. Having started the day with 110 operational aircraft in north Malaya, only 50 remained serviceable at the end – a reduction of 55 per cent. The Japanese counter-air programme had already done its job; they now possessed the air superiority they needed for the rest of their campaign, even though the staffs in Singapore had not yet had the time to realise it. As Brooke-Popham said in his signal to London that afternoon appealing for reinforcements, 'should Japan gain air superiority the situation would be very difficult'.

Despite its losses, for the RAF tomorrow was another day. With the true value of Singora and Patani to the enemy at last clear, thanks in part to some valuable reconnaissance by 21 Squadron's Buffaloes, on 9 December AHQ ordered a force of six Blenheims from Tengah to join those of 62 and 34 Squadrons which were still serviceable at Butterworth for an attack on the airfield at Songkla, near Singora.[24] Sadly the hoped for fighter escort from 21 Squadron failed to materialise, and while the Tengah force pressed on and bombed the heavily defended target, three were shot down, including one piloted by Sergeant A M Johnstone, who would spend the rest of his war as a prisoner (see p. 308). Of the Butterworth force all but one were destroyed or damaged by a well-timed Japanese raid while they were about to take off. Just one aircraft was airborne; the pilot decided to carry on alone. Reaching Singora, despite repeated fighter attacks, he bombed his target but was then seriously wounded. Assisted on the return flight by his navigator, Sergeant Calder, he eventually made an emergency landing near Alor Star, where he was rushed to hospital. His wife, a nurse there, prepared to provide a blood transfusion but it was too late.[25] The Victoria Cross awarded posthumously five years later to Squadron Leader Alan Scarf, of 62 Squadron, was to be the only one received by a member of the Royal Air Force in the Far East war. The citation is at Appendix B. His sortie had been part of a valiant attempt to show that the Blenheims could still hit back, but the lesson was clear: without fighter escort such missions were doomed, and AHQ ordered no more.

Force Z

It was not only unescorted bombers that were at high risk in this situation, but warships too, and here we must turn to the air aspects of one of the Royal Navy's greatest disasters, the sinking of Force Z. *Prince of Wales* and *Repulse* had been sent east at Churchill's insistence in the hope that their presence in Singapore would help deter a Japanese attack, but with little thought of what they should do if deterrence failed. Moreover the aircraft carrier *Indomitable*, intended to accompany them, had been delayed by an accident in the West Indies, so the two ships lacked their own air support. On 8 December, however, there was no doubt in the mind of Admiral Sir Tom Phillips that the Navy had to do something. As Roskill puts it, 'it was unthinkable for the navies to abandon the land and air forces to carry on the unequal fight alone'.[26] So Phillips decided that, given fighter support and surprise, his ships had a good chance of smashing the Japanese landings at Singora and Kota Bharu. Force Z would therefore attack on the 10th.[27] His final decision was, however, taken aboard *Prince of Wales* without representation from Brooke-Popham's Headquarters or from AHQ. How much better, as Middlebrook suggests,[28] had Brooke-Popham been in overall command and able to make Phillips wait. Surely Brooke-Popham would not have countenanced underestimation of the air threat to the unescorted capital ships.

The decision to sail, however, was for Phillips alone to make, and he asked the AOC for three things:

(a). Reconnaissance to the north of the force from daylight 9 December.
(b). Reconnaissance to Singora and beyond, ten miles from the coast, from first light on 10 December.
(c). Fighter protection off Singora at daylight 10 December.

Pulford said tentatively he could provide (a), hoped to provide (b), but could not provide (c). Later that evening after Phillips had sailed, Pulford confirmed this by signal.[29] Events that day in the north, especially at Kota Bharu, had precluded his providing air protection. Phillips now knew that reconnaissance was feasible but he also knew he would have no air cover off Singora. Maltby points out that Pulford's signal did not specify Singora in relation to fighter protection[30] and Louis Allen therefore speculates that Phillips may have thought it ruled out fighter cover anywhere, which might account for his later failure to break radio silence.[31] This is hard to accept, however, since 453 Squadron at Sembawang had already been designated the Fleet Defence Squadron and its CO had arranged R/T procedures with *Prince of Wales*. AHQ was trying to arrange other support, too, including a bombing raid on Singora to coincide with Phillips' attack and also an American raid on the south Indo-China airfields, but none proved possible.[32]

Force Z sailed north on 9 December while Catalinas, Vildebeests and Hudsons supported with reconnaissance. But the enemy too were busy, and a sighting report from a Japanese submarine during the afternoon was sufficient to alert the 22nd Air Flotilla with its 88 bombers based near Saigon. Soon afterwards three reconnaissance aircraft, assumed to be enemy, were seen by *Prince of Wales* and Phillips, convinced that surprise was now lost, decided to turn back.[33] Having done so he then received shortly before midnight a signal from his Chief of Staff, Admiral Palliser, who had remained in Singapore to represent him and co-ordinate with the other Services, reporting a Japanese landing at Kuantan. The airfield there had already been bombed that day, leading to a premature decision to evacuate its aircraft, which were followed by almost all its personnel.[34] Then when an Army report of an enemy landing nearby was received at 2200 a small force of Vildebeests and Hudsons was hurriedly put together from Seletar and Sembawang and sent on a fruitless mission, for they found nothing.[35] The Hudsons in fact arrived over the area at 0530, not long before Force Z approached to investigate – and at the same time as three Blenheims of 34 Squadron were conscientiously carrying out the agreed reconnaissance mission off Singora![36] Finding all quiet at Kuantan, Force Z now moved away; at 1020 a shadowing aircraft was spotted, followed at 1100 by the first elements of the 85-strong Japanese striking force. The tragic events that followed have often been recounted; for our purposes we need merely record that the first signal to Singapore indicating what was happening was not sent until 1150 – and not from the flagship but from *Repulse*. By the time 453 Squadron arrived, both ships had gone.[37]

Why, we must ask, was 453 not summoned until it was too late?

Clearly, as long as he was headed for Singora, Phillips was justified in maintaining radio silence; the success of his mission depended on surprise. Then on turning back and deciding to divert to Kuantan, he seems to have considered that Palliser would read his mind, expect him to go straight there, and arrange fighter cover; there was therefore no need to signal his intention and thus throw away the chance of surprise. Roskill, who quotes one of Phillips' staff, Captain Goodenough, for this explanation, considers that it demanded of the officers in Singapore too high a degree of insight.[38] Nevertheless, had the naval and air staffs been monitoring the situation together in a well-tried working relationship, might they not have decided to move 453 Squadron that morning to Kuantan, damaged though the airfield was? Maltby thinks they might.[39] The faulty command structure must take some of the blame.

Yet even without that, there was still time if the necessary signal had been sent at 1020, when Phillips had no further possible reason for trying to maintain secrecy. Corelli Barnett quotes Pound, the First Sea Lord, as finding his omission inexplicable, though accepting that Phillips might have thought that nothing the RAF could have sent would have been much good. But as Barnett then comments, anything would have been better than nothing.[40] As it was, exactly 90 minutes elapsed between *Repulse*'s signal and 453's arrival – the AOC received the message at 1219 and the 11 Buffaloes were airborne six minutes later (incredibly it was not until 1312 that Palliser made a formal request for fighter cover).[41] Those 90 minutes, starting at 1020, would have put the squadron over Force Z at 1150, coincident with the first torpedo attack. Flight Lieutenant Vigors, a former Battle of Britain pilot who was leading the squadron, reasonably enough believes that – despite their shortcomings – his aircraft could have prevented many of the strikes by the unescorted, heavily laden torpedo bombers.[42] We can imagine his thoughts when he did arrive, seeing many hundreds of men clinging to the wreckage. Hardly surprisingly there were few cheers for the RAF from the survivors, either then or later; indeed there was considerable animosity towards the RAF in general, for they could not know that their Admiral had been determined to go it alone. Why?

Vigors himself gives us a clue. He had discussed air defence problems with *Prince of Wales'* air liaison officer before she sailed and undertaken to keep a standing patrol of six aircraft over the Fleet in daylight up to 60 miles off the coast beyond Kota Bharu, but Phillips had declined the offer for it would limit his freedom of action.[43] Ultimately, however, it perhaps came down to the refusal of a fine but very traditional naval officer to believe, as Slessor said, that an aeroplane could be of any real threat to a man-of-war[44] – and despite what his own Fleet Air Arm had done to the *Bismarck* and to the Italian Fleet at Taranto. Sir Arthur Harris, who had worked closely with him in London, recalls his parting words to Phillips: 'Tom, you've never believed in air. Never get out from under the air umbrella; if you do, you'll be for it'.[45]

Yet when all is said and done, the air umbrella that was available – however well directed – was probably too small to have made all that much difference to the fate of Force Z.

Withdrawal

Nor could the RAF now do much to help the Army's two divisions battling it out in the north, for not only had it suffered heavy losses but its own frontline bases were about to be overrun. Alor Star, whose personnel had had virtually no training under war conditions[46] and had not started to gear up for the war until about a week before, was largely evacuated on the 9th; an armourer on the demolition party that stayed behind remembers that holes originally built in the runway made it fairly easy to place the explosives and believes the job was well done.[47] Yet the Japanese account of the capture of Alor Star indicated that they were soon able to operate from the airfield, making use of thousands of drums of high octane spirit which had not been destroyed.[48] It was a similar story at Butterworth and Sungei Patani, where hasty departure led among other things to unserviceable aircraft being abandoned together with large stocks of fuel. Unfortunately, however, the sight of fires and sounds of explosions at Alor Star so demoralised the troops fighting nearby that the GOC had to forbid the blowing up of buildings and the firing of fuel supplies:[49] clearly it was hard to reconcile this with the effective destruction of the airfields when time was so short.

There has been much justified criticism of the RAF over these and other airfield evacuations, including that at Kuantan. As the meagre strength of the air force was reduced by well-timed attacks on the forward airfields, the war was brought home in no uncertain fashion to flying and ground personnel alike and without doubt morale deteriorated rapidly, leading to their premature evacuation.[50] Maltby supports this, adding as factors the pernicious effect of rumours and the defection of local labour. A court of inquiry was convened in January 1942; no record of this survives, but the chairman, Group Captain J P McCauley RAAF, recalled after the war its general findings:

> While the planning and control of the evacuation was not up to the desired standard and there was lack of co-ordination between

squadron and station commanders, the evidence revealed no instance where disciplinary action was called for.[51]

Brooke-Popham had already been much more critical, telling all units through the AOC on 24 December that he deplored the disorganised evacuation. Some airfields had been abandoned in a state approaching panic, valuable stores had been left behind, a general state of chaos had been evident, and airfields had usually been vacated while still out of range of enemy forces. This was, he said, utterly opposed to all the traditions of the air force.[52] The reasons, of course, were deep rooted as we have already seen: lack of resources, a shortage of experienced leadership, failure to appreciate and prepare for a situation that had appeared, seemingly, out of the blue. Many who were there at the time have bitter memories; as a flight sergeant on 62 Squadron at Alor Star writes, there was no cohesive centre and certainly no one person nor any plan of action around which personnel could form or rally. 'It was pathetic to be uninstructed as to where to go or what role to play'.[53]

Yet in saying that let us remember that most men did whatever they could. The local medical officer believes much of the criticism was unfair, pointing out that Wing Commander Keegan's party of 100 men remained at Alor Star for three days until the enemy were only five miles away.[54] The demolition party itself took six weeks to get back to Singapore, stopping en route at seven airfields or dumps to blow up runways, destroy buildings and unserviceable aircraft, burn fuel stocks, and lay booby traps. While such demolitions often bore the stamp of hasty and disorganised preparation,[55] our armourer reminds us that no one out there had any experience of this type of work; under the circumstances he believes they did a good job.[56] In all this discussion we must remember the virtual impossibility of rendering an airfield unusable for any length of time. As a later intelligence assessment stated, reports from Malaya showed that airfields 'blown up' were usually operational again within a week (never more than two weeks), and the repaired airfields were made to accommodate at least double the number of aircraft they were designed for.[57]

Whatever our conclusions on this vexed subject, the fact remains, as Colonel Tsuji writes, that the Japanese had rapidly come into possession of four large military aerodromes which could be quickly repaired and were provided with abundant equipment, ammunition, fuel and provisions:

> Possession of twofold numerical air strength was one reason for our air superiority over the Malayan theatre of operations, but the decisive factor was that we were able to take immediate advantage of the captured 'Churchill aerodromes'.[58]

We must turn next to the attempts of the RAF to recover from its early disasters and provide at least some assistance to the Army as it tried to halt the Japanese advance down the western side of the peninsula. Such had been its losses, however, that the Air Force could initially undertake little more than reconnaissance, and with reports of a large enemy fleet heading southwards a substantial striking force had to be held in readiness in case it should turn west for a landing near Singapore. Only when it invaded Borneo on the 16th was that particular threat removed (p. 65). Meanwhile on the 11th, with the Japanese starting to bomb Penang and the Army trying to hold its first major defensive line at Jitra, air defence, tactical reconnaissance and close support had become all-important and Pulford ordered 453 Squadron and a detachment from 243 north to Ipoh. Most arrived safely on the 13th and were immediately in action, their efforts doing much to restore local morale, but that night only 13 out of 19 remained. More Buffaloes were sent on the 15th, this time to try to restore 21 Squadron to strength, but with Ipoh now under enemy air attack operating conditions were fast becoming impossible, and on the 18th evacuation was ordered. The surviving five aircraft of 453 Squadron departed for Kuala Lumpur; the remaining 12 (all unserviceable in some respect) were flown back to Sembawang.[59] By this time on the ground the battle of Jitra, 18 miles south of the Siamese border and just north of Alor Star, had been fought and lost, the enemy had then penetrated the position at Gurun, and by the 16th the battered remnants of 11 Division had withdrawn south of the river Muda, whereupon it was decided to evacuate Penang and concentrate around Taiping. The fighter force had done all it could to help in face of almost overwhelming air superiority, but now only 51 Buffaloes remained operational (15 of them Dutch) in the whole of Malaya and Singapore.[60]

There was to be no respite. With the Japanese Army moving into central Malaya, Kuala Lumpur was their air force's next major target and on the 18th 453 Squadron, back to full strength, faced the first onslaught – with some success. The next day ten Buffaloes met the enemy's initial attack – the first occasion on which a reasonably strong force of Buffaloes had been able to meet the enemy in the air. In this and the subsequent engagement three enemy aircraft were claimed as destroyed, with seven 'probables', but of 15 Buffaloes that had started that fateful day only four were operationally serviceable by evening. The crews had fought courageously against a vastly superior enemy but were engaged in a losing battle against better equipment and equally determined opponents. Losses on this scale could be replaced only by seriously weakening the defences of Singapore itself, and AHQ had no choice but to order withdrawal from the north. So on the 23rd – at the same time as Ipoh airfield was effectively destroyed – 453's seven surviving aircraft were back in Singapore. To quote the Narrators:

> The fighter force had not been driven from northern Malaya – rather they had been wiped out as they fought, reeling from one improvised station to another until finally, above the capital of the Federated States, they were so reduced and broken that they could fight no longer.[61]

Given all the weaknesses of the Buffalo as described in Chapter 2, its pilots – and their groundcrews – had acquitted themselves well. As General Percival put it, 'the aircrews lived up to the highest traditions of their Service'.[62] Colonel Tsuji too recognised their qualities: 'The enemy's fighter planes were vigorously aggressive and quick to take advantage of any gap in our air superiority'.[63]

Reinforcement

So by the end of December both the bomber and the fighter force had been severely depleted, leaving Pulford with only his reconnaissance and torpedo bomber squadrons largely intact, the latter being conserved in case of even more dire emergency. Could anything be done by way of reinforcement? Brooke-Popham's initial request for help had included night fighters and long-range bombers, the latter to attack Japanese bases, thus compelling the enemy to divert fighters for their protection. The immediate Air Ministry response was to promise initially 50 Kittyhawks, plus more Blenheims, Hudsons and Catalinas, but Portal, mindful of the needs of other theatres and of the threat now posed to other parts of the Far East including India, Ceylon and Burma, thought this premature and insisted on deeper thought. It was not therefore until 17 December that the reinforcement plan (which included India) was signalled to Singapore. It provided for four Catalinas, 18 Blenheims, 52 Hudsons, 32 crated Kittyhawks (possibly – they never came) and 51 crated Hurricanes.[64]

What would arrive and when? 205 Squadron had already received three Catalinas from the Dutch on the 12th and four more later reached Singapore from Gibraltar. Of 12 (not 18) Blenheims despatched from Egypt, only seven made it to 34 Squadron at Tengah, taking 10 – 18 days en route. The others crashed, force-landed or got lost. As for the Hudsons, 10 reached 1 and 8 Squadrons from Australia on the 23rd, but of the 52 promised from the UK only 36 were eventually got away (mostly flown by experienced Coastal Command crews who could be ill-spared from the Battle of the Atlantic) and just 15 arrived, to become 62 Squadron.[65] So much, then, for the so-called 'Singapore reinforcement plan', originally propounded by Trenchard in

1926 (p. 3). While the route existed only two squadrons had used it –
in 1939 and in slow time – whereas had it been kept in constant use by
periodical flights, even of token numbers, the experience gained and
recorded might well have been used to great advantage when the final
emergency arose. The experience of a WOp/AG who had been flying in
Coastal Command was typical. His squadron was taken off operations
at St Eval on 12 December, they left Portreath in new aircraft on the
29th, and he himself reached Tengah on 17 January after 22 stops.[66] In
fairness one of the staging posts – Victoria Point in southern Burma –
had already been seized by the enemy, and a diversion had had to be
organised via Sabang (Map 2).

Last but not least came the 51 Hurricanes, originally destined with
their crews for Iraq, and diverted on 17 December while at sea off
South Africa. They duly reached Singapore in their crates on 13
January; within four days 21 had been assembled, and 232 Squadron –
its pilots quite unaccustomed to the local conditions – went into action
on the 20th. While it has to be said that not much had been done to
prepare for their arrival, full credit must go to the ground crews at
Seletar, many with no experience of the Hurricane, who worked round
the clock amid frequent air raids to assemble them; a then sergeant
particularly remembers how long it took to remove the liberal
protective coating of grease.[67] A week later came the first part – and
last – of the second wave of reinforcements, 15 Hurricanes of 258
Squadron which flew in via Java and Sumatra from the carrier
Indomitable.[68] By now others also were on their way, but it was all
much too late. As Mr Bowden, the Australian Representative in
Singapore, had already told his government, the measures for
reinforcement were 'little more than gestures'.[69] When it really
mattered, in the early and critical stages of the campaign, the Far East
had been given meagre and insufficient help, though it is hard to see
how the many deficiencies of the earlier years could possibly have been
remedied once the attack began.

So the net result of all this effort, apart from temporarily
strengthening the fighter defence, was merely to replace the losses of
the two Hudson squadrons, one of the Blenheim squadrons and the
Catalina squadron, and while it had been going on the Japanese
advance through central Malaya had compelled the RAF to
concentrate its remaining resources on the four main airfields on
Singapore Island or increasingly in Sumatra, thought to be safe from
enemy attack. We shall consider the events in the Dutch East Indies in
Chapter 4; for the moment our attention must focus on Singapore,
where in the words of the GHQ instruction issued on 27 December[70]
the overriding need was to protect the convoys which were due to
deliver the Army's main reinforcements. The first duly appeared on 3
January, covered by every available aircraft, and at the expense of

providing support for the retreating land forces. The security had been good and the Japanese did not intervene. Bad weather assisted the even stronger air defences when the second convoy also arrived safely on the 13th. They were indeed fortunate, for the Japanese had 81 bombers and 20 Zeros ready to attack.[71] Three further convoys in later January called for similar effort.

The Losing Fight

If that was a success story little else was. Having started to bring the RAF's former bases in northern Malaya into use, the Japanese had resumed their bombing of Singapore on 30 December, their chief targets to begin with being the airfields.[72] Initially they came mainly at night, but once a daylight attack on Tengah on 12 January indicated the weaknesses of the air defence they switched mainly to daytime operations, coming over usually in formations of 27 aircraft and bombing on the instructions of the leader. Often they even announced their raids beforehand over the radio.[73] From now onwards the weight of Japanese attack was averaging some 120 sorties a day,[74] and while the two Buffalo air defence squadrons based at Kallang did their best – 'the pilots showed terrific guts in getting stuck in' writes one witness[75] – they were taking heavy losses. On 3 January there had been 46 serviceable Buffaloes in the front line; by the 18th there were only 24.[76] Moreover, while the radars continued to provide their full 30 minutes' warning until 25 January, when 243 AMES had to pull out from Mersing,[77] it was taking the fighters all that time to climb to 25,000 ft, the bombers' normal height, and without VHF they could not be kept informed of the raiders' movements. Nor did it help that the two squadrons at Sembawang, having been earmarked for Army support, were not under the control of the air defence commander and could not retaliate even when their station was under attack.[77] The enemy air attacks took their toll, too, of aircraft on the ground – and indeed the sea, when three Catalinas were machine gunned at their moorings at Seletar.[79] The net result of these losses, coupled with those incurred in offensive operations, was that a front line of 127 operational aircraft at the beginning of January had been reduced to 71 a fortnight later.[80]

It is to these offensive operations in support of the Army that we must now turn, while remembering that throughout this period the RAF had to give priority to the air defence of Singapore, the protection of the convoys, and reconnaissance over the South China Sea – a constant task for the Catalinas and Hudsons. The key to Percival's land strategy in the earlier part of January was to try to prevent the Japanese acquiring the airfields in central Malaya from which they could so easily attack the essential reinforcement convoys; the longer he could hold on there the better his chances of mounting a successful defence in the south.[81] 11 Division had therefore withdrawn across the Perak river and by late December had taken up a strong defensive position at Kampar, while 9 Division was guarding its flank and trying to restrict the enemy advance through the mountains and down the east coast. In early January, however, critical battles were lost first at Kampar and then at Slim River, and it did not help that the soldiers were having to fight virtually without air support and under constant air attack from the Japanese. The effect on their morale was predictable, though Percival refused to blame the RAF for he knew how slender were its resources.[82] Some of its efforts were – as ever with supporting air operations – way out of sight of the troops. Sungei Patani, where 100 enemy aircraft were based, was twice bombed at night by Blenheims from Tengah at the end of December, and Catalinas, each carrying eight 500 lb bombs slung under the wings, attacked Sungei Patani and Gong Kedah.[83] Then, taking advantage of several advance landing grounds which had been opened up in south Johore, operations against the northern airfields and against shipping were intensified from 8 January, with Vildebeests and Dutch Glenn Martin bombers taking a hand alongside the Blenheims, Hudsons and Catalinas. All units were doing what they could, including the two stripped down Buffaloes of the invaluable Photographic Reconnaissance Unit, and the men of the Malayan Volunteer Air Force, whose light aircraft were invaluable in maintaining communications, providing reconnaissance and helping in jungle rescue.[84] All their efforts, however, were on much too small a scale to affect the issue in face of the enemy's massive air superiority. Kuala Lumpur fell on 11 January, its airfield having been demolished the previous day, and on the 14th the Japanese crossed into northern Johore.[85]

The enemy were now barely 100 miles from Singapore and with the second convoy safely arrived the RAF could at last offer some direct help to the land forces; on the 16th occurred the one properly concentrated air action of the campaign designed to support an ambush being laid by Australian troops at Gemas. A force of 15 Buffaloes carried out ground strafing, and other Buffaloes escorted Tengah's nine operational Blenheims and Sembawang's six Dutch Glenn Martins as they bombed the enemy positions. To quote Percival 'the RAF co-operated gallantly' in an operation which cost the enemy several hundred lives.[86] The all-out effort was continued for several more days: enemy landings on the west coast were attacked; Vildebeests, Blenheims and Hudsons bombed the airfields at Kuala Lumpur and Kuantan by night, and as the Japanese advance closed in on the approaches to Singapore just about everything that could fly was pressed into service. The air support of the retreating land forces, though diminishing in weight, was lacking nothing in determination;

whenever attacks could be mounted they were pressed home in the same resolute spirit which was to inspire the final tragic action over Endau.[87]

Higher Command

We shall come to this episode in a moment, but first we must examine some major changes in the higher command. To begin with, on 27 December, Brooke-Popham was replaced by Lieutenant General Sir Henry Pownall.[88] Churchill had originally arranged for the C-in-C to receive a baronetcy on his retirement but Sinclair advised its postponement:

> The House of Commons is very concerned about recent events in the Far East, and the immediate prospect is gloomy. Brooke-Popham made an unfortunate speech in Australia in which he gave a number of forecasts which have been falsified by the event. No doubt his object was to put up a bold front against the Japanese when it was still doubtful whether they could enter the war. All the same, the effect of conferring a baronetcy on Brooke-Popham in the New Year Honours would, I am afraid, be to make him the subject of public controversy.[89]

So to save embarrassing both the government and Brooke-Popham, he said, Sinclair proposed to postpone the conferment. In fact nothing was ever done; Brooke-Popham, for all his endeavours, had to pay the price of being in the wrong place at the wrong time.

A week after his departure another senior RAF officer arrived, Air Vice-Marshal P C Maltby, designated as Pownall's Chief of Staff. Then, following a decision at the Washington Conference in mid-December, a new American, British, Dutch and Australian Command (ABDACOM) was formed on 15 January to cover all the theatres of operation in the Far East as distinct from the Pacific, and General Sir Archibald Wavell took over the unenviable post, forming his Headquarters in Java; Pownall became his Chief of Staff.[90] Soon afterwards Air Marshal Sir Richard Peirse, previously C-in-C Bomber Command, arrived to command all the Allied air forces. Their responsibilities ranged far wider than Singapore, as we shall see later, and there was nothing they could do to retrieve the immediate situation, but Maltby was to play an important role.

An officer with a distinguished operational record in the First World War, Maltby had just spent a year as AOC 71 (Army Cooperation) Group, having previously been AOC Malta and AOC 24 (Training) Group. Immediately on reaching Singapore he had been instructed to investigate the air situation and found that Pulford, while handling his squadrons ably, was a very tired man, overwhelmed with work. The shortage of officers with the necessary training and experience had led him to use his SASO and two other senior staff officers to run the three watches in the Operations Room, leaving Pulford himself to direct all aspects of policy and administration. The burden in this highly centralised system, as Maltby tells us, was being carried by a few capable individuals, in particular by the AOC himself. The immediate need, Maltby decided, was for a Deputy AOC, and although he was the senior and could have taken over he felt that Pulford was handling the operational situation satisfactorily and ought to carry on. Otherwise Pulford would have seen himself a failure and been a broken man. So with Pownall's agreement, Maltby installed himself as Deputy AOC on 12 January, while telling Pulford that, as the senior, he would accept ultimate responsibility for all that might happen from then on.[91]

The Hurricanes Join In

The convoy bringing the Hurricanes was due in the next day, and in recording the tension that prevailed during its approach and the exultation that greeted its safe arrival Maltby goes on to say that it was confidently expected the new aircraft would sweep the Japanese from the sky.[92] These expectations, shared by civilians and armed forces alike, were after a successful first day to prove unjustified. It was immediately discovered that all the aircraft were fitted with desert sand air-intake filters which were integral to the engine cowling and could not be replaced;[93] these according to Maltby reduced their speed by 30 mph. Then there were shortages of tools, spare parts, glycol, oxygen, and oil for the hydraulics, and the R/T was inefficient.[94] Moreover, while AHQ had intended to allow the pilots time to adjust to the local conditions, for they had originally been destined for south Russia and had had a very long sea voyage,[95] this was out of the question, and the aircraft had to be sent into action immediately they were erected and tested. So from 20 January onwards 232 Squadron was constantly engaged alongside the remaining Buffaloes against raiding forces often over a hundred strong, and it was quickly recognised that while the Hurricane had the advantage in speed and rate of climb above 20,000 ft and could dive at higher speeds, the Zero was the more manoeuvrable. So dog-fighting did not pay off and rapid 'in and out' tactics had to be used instead. Ultimately, however, it was numbers that mattered: during the first week of operations only 16 aircraft were on average operational each day, and by the end of the week one-third of the initial 51 had been destroyed. No criticism attaches to the pilots, who as Maltby says achieved in the face of overwhelming numbers results which stood greatly to their credit; while they took their share of the enemy with them (26 aircraft were claimed destroyed) they were never in with a chance.[96] The Hurricanes were, nevertheless, briefly able to deliver a warning of things to come when, as Tsuji tells us, their intrepid pilots flew low over the rubber forests in south Johore machine-gunning the roads, shooting up motor transport and blocking traffic:

> Until then our mobile corps had been advancing on the paved roads in broad daylight taking no precautions against enemy raids. While the Hurricanes were flying even single cars moved off the road into the cover of the jungle, and all convoys had to move off the road and get out of sight at the first alarm.[97]

We can only speculate on what an adequate force of Hurricanes might have achieved.

The Final Disasters

The increasing weight of air attack on Singapore was coinciding with the inexorable advance of the enemy land forces across Johore, and on the 21st those on the east coast reached Endau. Five days later, at 0745, two Hudsons sighted a further invasion force 20 miles to the north-east consisting of two large transports and a substantial naval and air escort.[98] Jamming of the W/T prevented the news of this new and direct threat to Singapore reaching AHQ until the aircraft had returned to base, but nobody doubted that it must be countered by all means available. While a number of Hudsons and Blenheims were usable, some of them now based in Sumatra, the only force that was still relatively intact comprised the Vildebeests of 36 and 100 Squadrons, which though far from inactive had hitherto been employed mainly at night. They were now to be committed in daylight against a landing force that had air cover, and armed with bombs rather than their more familiar torpedoes. Apparently it was thought that the water in the estuary was too shallow, yet it was deep enough to float a 10,000 ton ship.[99] Kirby says the decision to use bombs was taken only with great reluctance after careful consideration by Pulford and with the agreement of both squadron commanders,[100] but the crews were well practised in dive bombing[101] and the real question is not the method of attack but the decision to commit the aircraft in a daylight operation. Maltby, so frank on most matters, makes no comment.

It was early afternoon before the first wave of 12 Vildebeests, mainly from 100 Squadron, took off from Seletar, their departure delayed by the need to load up with bombs and refuel after the previous night's operations. Padre A S Giles comments:

I saw the squadron setting out on that last raid on Endau – their actions were more than the normal fulfilment of duty, for flying Vildebeest aircraft on a daylight raid they knew they had little chance of coming through unscathed.[102]

Together with nine Hudsons and escorted by 15 Buffaloes and nine Hurricanes they set course at 90 knots, and the first attack went in at 1505. Despite encountering intense fighter and AA opposition they hit several of the enemy vessels but five of the Vildebeests were shot down. The second wave at 1730 fared even worse. Of the nine Vildebeests and three Albacores (naval aircraft which had been transferred to 36 Squadron), eight did not return, nor did two of 62 Squadron's six Hudsons. While two enemy transports, a cruiser and two destroyers were later seen to be stationary and high out of the water, most of their troops were already ashore, and as the Japanese said in summing up the operation, 'nearly all of the remaining enemy air force in Singapore, which had been hiding until now, was destroyed'.[103]

It had been a tragic episode, costing 12 Vildebeests (10 shot down, two written off) and two Albacores, together with 38 of their aircrew including both squadron commanders, plus two Hudsons and a Hurricane and more aircraft damaged.[104] The AOC, while convinced at that stage that the attack had been reasonably successful, told the survivors they would not be sent again on a similar operation. The Narrators continue:

These two squadrons, except for 205 Squadron, were the oldest RAF units in Singapore. Many years of training had brought them to a peak of proficiency in their task of torpedo dropping. Yet when ultimately they were involved in war their aircraft were so antiquated that they stood no chance against modern weapons … and when the critical time arrived the attack was not delivered with the well-practised torpedo but with small bombs against ships emptied of invading troops. Their sacrifice was in vain.[105]

There was a sad postscript. A few days later, after another unfortunate incident, the station commander at Tengah, Group Captain F E – 'Poppa' – Watts, was summoned to AHQ to explain why his Hurricanes were failing in their escort duties. The historian of 100 Squadron goes on:

For a man who, like many others, had argued in vain against complacency and had been forced to watch his squadrons destroyed and his station's morale deteriorate, it was the last straw. He had a final drink with his remaining crews, bade everyone goodnight, and retired quietly to his room where he shot himself.[106]

But there was another side to it. A 36 Squadron pilot on that dreadful day remembers the shock of seeing many of his comrades 'fry' in petrol, yet that evening he went to a friend's bungalow and got very drunk on his whisky – a far better therapy in his view than the 'mental treatment' nowadays demanded by those engaged in war.[107]

It would be surprising if morale had not deteriorated. An electrician who arrived back after a long trip to Alor Star, servicing Blenheims en route, recalls the airmen at Tengah 'not being very happy'.[108] A flight rigger, who remembers Tengah as a perfect station pre-war, with very good morale, writes of the punctuality of the Japanese air attacks and wondered why the aircraft were so often caught on the ground; yet not knowing the full situation he always thought things would get better.[109] An aircrew flight sergeant, on the other hand, writes of fear being manifest at almost every level, encouraged by excellent Japanese propaganda, though nerves were calmed when the station commander walked around apparently unconcerned. The overwhelming factor was 'the complete lack of positive, informative, encouraging and courageous direction'.[110] A flight mechanic, who had been at Kota Bharu with the Buffalo detachment and noticed when he got back to Kallang how the previously aloof attitude of the European community had changed, speaks of waning confidence in the high command after the loss of Force Z; only from the censored reports in the *Straits Times* could they find out what was happening up-country, and the lack of communication did nothing to help morale.[111] And when Terence Kelly, a pilot with 258 Squadron, flew his Hurricane into Seletar on 29 January, he considered that 'the pall of defeatism was so thick you could have cut it with a knife'.[112]

His reaction was no more than one would expect. Seletar had been under attack for a month, suffering casualties and much damage to its aircraft and facilities; its men had worked flat out on the Hurricanes only to see their high hopes dashed; they had watched their two torpedo bomber squadrons all but wiped out; and now on the 29th the Japanese were approaching the Straits of Johore and the surviving Catalinas and Vildebeests were under orders to depart for Java. Moreover, while all this was happening, attempts were being made to move long-accumulated stores and maintenance equipment to Java in an exodus the like of which had never before been seen in the RAF.[114] How welcome would have been a fleet of air transports; in their absence everything had to go via docks that were increasingly congested, under growing air attack, and lacking most of their civilian labour.

The decision to move all but the fighter squadrons away from Singapore to either Sumatra or Java had been taken on the 14th, when it became clear that the RAF would henceforth be confined to the island's four airfields, and by the 31st – the day the Causeway was blown – only the fighters remained, together with four naval Swordfish which had been resurrected by 151 MU.[114] Wavell and Peirse had visited Singapore the previous day and in view of the great difficulty of maintaining serviceable landing strips on the island in face of the constant bombing they approved the transfer to Sumatra of all the fighters as well, except for a token force of eight Hurricanes and eight Buffaloes.[115] The force by now on the island included 15 Hurricanes of 258 Squadron which reached Seletar on 28 January, and nine more two days later; all had been flown from the carrier *Indomitable* via Java and Sumatra. It took several days to strip, clean, test and harmonise their guns, which had been packed with grease, and their first combat patrol on 1 February coincided with the evacuation order.[116] Churchill, who had been following the air situation in consultation with Portal,[117] queried this decision the next day, saying it appeared to indicate despair of holding Singapore. Wavell, explaining the dangers of leaving fighters on exposed airfields, felt his dispositions were correct, but Churchill's reply on the 4th indicated he was not totally convinced; he wanted all the fighters left in the island to be Hurricanes and said 90 more were on their way.[118] But it was all too late; by the 5th Singapore's air defence rested on the shoulders of 232 Squadron's 14 serviceable Hurricanes (plus the Swordfish).

That day, with a number of the AHQ staff having already moved to Sumatra and Java, Pulford decided shortly to depart for Batavia, leaving Maltby to follow after supervising the further evacuation; Maltby would then take over. Peirse, however, had doubts about AHQ leaving Singapore at that stage, and despite Pulford and Maltby arguing that AHQ could now function to better purpose in Batavia he signalled that he did not take so gloomy a view of the possibilities: 'Please impress on everybody that we intend to stop the enemy'. Maltby believed – though he did not then realise it and did not think it was intended – that Pulford took this as a personal and public rebuke, administered for suggesting that he and his HQ should abandon the Army HQ in Singapore. Thereafter, says Maltby, nothing would move him from his determination to remain in Singapore until the end, supported by his personal friendship for Percival and his early training as a naval officer that he should be the last to leave the sinking ship.[119] Three days later, on 8/9 February, the Japanese were ashore, and on the 10th, Pulford still refusing to leave, Maltby departed on Wavell's instructions to take over all the British Commonwealth air forces in Java and Sumatra.[120]

Meanwhile the surviving Blenheims and Hudsons that had been moved to Sumatra, joined by more such aircraft beginning to arrive from elsewhere, had been attempting to disrupt Japanese air operations by attacking their airfields, assisted on occasion by a few B-17s of the USAAF based in Java. Alor Star, Singora and Kluang featured particularly but the scale of attack was too small to be significant, and it is to the final efforts of the Hurricanes that we must now turn. By the 5th, as we have seen, these numbered just 14, and with Tengah, Seletar and Sembawang coming under shellfire, directed from an observation balloon, only Kallang remained in remotely usable state. So the final four days of the air defence of Singapore were conducted from a single landing strip of 700 yards, pitted with bomb craters and under constant enemy bombing. Yet despite its CO being killed on the 6th, 232 Squadron was becoming more accustomed to the enemy tactics and making frequent interceptions.

Finally on the 9th, with the enemy ashore in the north of the island, the squadron fought continuously against appalling odds in an action bearing comparison with the most epic achievements of the RAF.[121] The day began with eight aircraft twice engaging 84 of the enemy and continued in like manner. Ian Morrison was at Kallang that day:

Never have I admired people more than I admired those boys. They were tired out ... flying infinitely longer hours than fighter pilots were supposed to fly. The strain was all too evident. They stuck grimly to their task ... harrying the dive bombers who were giving our ground troops such hell ... a young wing commander was in charge; he cannot have been more than 23 ... I came away feeling I had been among heroes.[122]

They could, of course, have done nothing without the magnificent and untiring efforts of the ground crews, men who without prior experience of the Hurricane and lacking special tools and spare parts had patched and wired their aircraft together to keep them 100 per cent serviceable. It was indeed a day for pride.

It could not continue. That evening Maltby visited the squadron, realised the hopelessness of the situation, and ordered them to depart for Palembang at first light. The air battle of Malaya and Singapore was over. The RAF had lost almost its entire original air strength, and in terms of fighters the cost was 122 Buffaloes and 45 Hurricanes. Japanese sources give their losses from all causes during the whole campaign as 512.[123] Theirs had not been a cheap victory.

It remained to try to deny to the Japanese the airfields and the great quantities of equipment held on the island, and to evacuate the thousands of personnel still there. While much was done by way of destruction,[124] including ploughing the airfield surfaces, there was far too little time for a thorough job, and evacuation was a confused and difficult affair. The radar stations, for example, had been progressively destroyed and when on the 13th Pulford was allocated space for RAF personnel in a flotilla of small vessels all 250 of the radar staff moved in small parties to the docks under continuous bombing and shelling.[125] Those at Tanah Merah Besar, who had half expected to be caught up in land fighting, were warned by the AOC on the 12th to keep a good look-out, and later that day as the situation rapidly worsened were instructed to get out as fast as possible. They destroyed their equipment, made a nightmare journey to the docks, were accused by the military police of being deserters, and eventually talked their way aboard a river boat.[126] At AHQ the evacuation of the operations room, with destruction of the signals equipment and manuals, was ordered on the 11th; one of the airmen recalls the courageous leadership of a wing commander who tore around detailing duties and giving a morale boost to dazed personnel. Eventually 200 or so were herded into trucks and moved to the docks through bombed streets filled with streams of Chinese clutching children and anything else they could salvage.[127] The roads were choked with cars trying to reach the docks and newly arrived army vehicles trying to leave them.[128]

It was amid such conditions that the great majority of RAF men reached the chaos of the docks and eventually found themselves aboard ships of all shapes and sizes. Many were on the *Empire Star*, a frozen meat transporter whose captain appealed for volunteers to man guns that had been installed in Australia. Although the ship was bombed and set on fire the next day with consequent heavy casualties, three aircraft were shot down and the ship made it to Java.[129] Others were on smaller boats, some getting to Sumatra rather than Java, some reaching smaller islands, and others disappearing without trace, falling victim either to Japanese attack or to the natural elements. Of those who did reach land, some still did not survive, most notably Pulford himself.

Having sent most of his staff away from the doomed island, Pulford was at last persuaded by Percival to go himself on the 13th. The launch carrying him and Rear Admiral Spooner, with some 40 others, was attacked by Japanese aircraft and stranded on a small uninhabited island north of Banka. Two months later disease and starvation had taken their toll and the survivors had to surrender. Pulford and Spooner were not among them.[130] We can imagine Pulford's thoughts in those final days as he reflected on the disaster; Percival records his parting words: 'I suppose you and I will be held responsible for this, but God knows we did our best with what little we had been given'.[131]

So as our hearts go out to a man who quite literally gave his all to one of the most thankless tasks ever allotted to a senior RAF commander, we have to ask if he was right. Many who were there will echo the thoughts of Squadron Leader Carter, who had no doubt that when Pulford arrived in Singapore he believed that Japan intended to attack, and that he did everything in his power to prepare the air defences of the Far East. The Australian historian agrees. 'Throughout the campaign he had striven selflessly and earnestly to fulfil the heavy responsibilities that had rested on him'.[132]

On the other hand, Pulford was not given the strongest of teams to lead. Understandably perhaps, the best of the RAF's middle ranking commanders and staff officers were being kept in Europe during 1941 and the new blood that was ordered to the Far East after the Japanese attack arrived too late.[133] Certainly there were failures of leadership under the sudden and intense pressures of war, and Pulford's centralised structure – though partly forced on him by staff limitations – tied him too much to the Air Headquarters.[134] So when we consider the causes of the poor morale that definitely existed at the time, inadequate leadership must be included. What the flight sergeant with 62 Squadron wrote about his own unit had wide application: in his view there was no intentional planned process of erasing the peacetime ethos and changing it into one of war, and there was hardly any sensible officer-led direction which would have counteracted the sense of isolation and impunity.[135] Portal himself was aware of the problem, minuting the Prime Minister on 17 February:

> With the closing of the Staff College for over two years it had been impossible to find really good staff officers for all the commands and naturally the Far East did not get the pick of those we had.[136]

Yet however inspired the leadership, it would have been hard-pressed to counter the effects of the early disasters, and especially the loss of Force Z, after which few had much real confidence in the high command. Ultimately it was all a matter of 'too little and too late', but in fairness many who were there accept that under all the circumstances of the time Britain was right to give priority to the dangers nearer home. Ian Morrison, while referring to 'pathetic weakness', says it would be difficult to argue that Malaya in 1940/41 should have taken precedence over Great Britain, the Middle East or Russia.[137] To quote Hilary Saunders, 'the loss of Singapore was part of the price paid for the incurable habit of the English of allowing their armed forces in times of peace to fall far below the lowest level of safety'.[138]

Nevertheless it would be wrong to conclude this sad tale without a reminder of the heroism and devotion to duty shown by so many airmen, both in the air and on the ground, under almost totally adverse circumstances. They, like their AOC, had done all they could, and a lesson had been learnt for the future – just as the Germans had taught a similar lesson in France in the summer of 1940. To quote Ian Morrison just once more: 'The campaign demonstrated above all things the importance of the aerial arm in modern warfare, especially when it is used in close conjunction with the naval and military arms'.[139]

Herein lay the chief hope for the future, he went on to say. Events would prove him right.

4   The Chain of Disaster

Hong Kong

With Singapore gone our main story moves on to the Dutch East Indies
and to Burma, both now under Japanese attack. First, however, we
must refer briefly to events in Hong Kong, where a mere handful of
RAF men had been able to make virtually no effective contribution
whatsoever.

The single air base in the colony, Kai Tak, dated back to 1927, since
when its main role had been to provide for visiting aircraft of the Fleet
Air Arm.[1] No significant number of aircraft had ever been based there.
The Chiefs of Staff had recognised in 1938 that the colony could not be
held indefinitely against major attack, and while there could be no
question of demilitarising it the sole reason for its defence was to deny
the harbour for as long as possible.[2] In August 1940 they again stated
that it must be regarded as an outpost,[3] and although Brooke-Popham
at one stage argued that it might be able to withstand attack if
adequately reinforced the Chiefs remained adamant. When we bear in
mind the RAF's parlous situation in Malaya it is hardly surprising that
nothing could be spared for Hong Kong, whose defence had to be left
largely to the Army. Admittedly some local planning was done in 1941
in case a Buffalo squadron could be spared – it would certainly have
been valuable for civilian morale[4] – and sites were selected for radars
and a sector control room, but in December the RAF strength consisted
of just three Vildebeests and two Walruses.[5]

Hardly surprisingly therefore, General Maltby, the GOC (and the
brother of Air Vice-Marshal Maltby), directed that since these obsolete
aircraft would be no match for the enemy fighters none was to take off
unless the torpedo bombers had a chance of attacking a heavy
warship,[6] and the two Walruses and one Vildebeest, together with a
number of civil aircraft, were destroyed in the opening attack on Kai
Tak on 8 December by 36 Japanese aircraft. Two days later, the
Japanese Army having broken through the main defence line in the
New Territories, the evacuation of Kai Tak was ordered and the
remaining two Vildebeests were destroyed. Their crews had pleaded to
be allowed to fly to a Nationalist-held airfield, bombing Japanese

airfields en route, but the GOC refused since it could lead to unnecessary reprisals.[7] So on the 10th most personnel departed by launch for Hong Kong Island, from where they did all they could to assist the Army in its defence up to the surrender on Christmas Day. Courageous and determined as was the Army's fight, 'from the outset a dominant factor was the British inability to dispute the Japanese command of the air.'[8] Moreover, just as in Malaya, the performance of the Japanese Air Forces came as a revelation to men who had earlier been briefed that the Japanese aircraft were mostly obsolete and their pilots myopic and thus unable to dive-bomb.[9]

British Borneo

The surrender of Hong Kong coincided with the loss of another outpost of the British Empire which had been long recognised as indefensible, British Borneo (Map 2). Here there was a small airfield at Kuching and a reasonably equipped base at Sinkawang, just across the border in Dutch Borneo, and since this was only 350 miles from Singapore it was thought necessary to try to protect its approaches.[10] The Dutch had allocated Sinkawang for up to four RAF bomber squadrons and by December it was ready for use.[11] In the event, however, only a handful of Dutch Glenn Martins and Buffaloes which had been placed under RAF command were able to operate from it.[12]

The enemy invasion fleet was first reported off Indo-China on 13 December (p. 50) and the first landings occurred in and around Brunei on the 16th. Over the next few days the Glenn Martins tried several times to attack the invasion force off North Borneo; then on the 23rd Sinkawang was heavily bombed and its aircraft were evacuated to Sumatra. The next day five Blenheims from 34 Squadron at Tengah unsuccessfully attacked enemy ships approaching Kuching and by the 26th the town and airfield were in enemy hands. Although it was another month before Sinkawang itself was captured, its Punjabi defenders having been supplied by an air drop from three Blenheims on 30 December,[13] the way was clear for the next stage of the main Japanese advance into the heart of the Dutch East Indies.

Sumatra

The Chiefs of Staff had already advised Brooke-Popham to consult the Dutch about land and air reinforcements for Java and Sumatra both under present conditions and in the event of a Japanese occupation of Singapore,[14] and as early as 16 December an AHQ team had been sent to reconnoitre the airfields in Sumatra (Map 2). At that stage their value was seen largely in relation to the reinforcement route, and plans were made to stock Sabang, Medan and Pakan Baroe with supplies and to deploy handling parties, but on the 27th Pulford was instructed to prepare facilities to enable 'substantial bomber forces' to operate from the island. Despite the many difficulties of communications, supply, maintenance and so forth, it was recognised that the need to disperse the bomber force, including its reinforcements, could well prove paramount, and on 4 January the Chiefs of Staff endorsed Sumatra's importance as a base for future operations. By now its airfields had again been inspected after consultation with the Dutch authorities and it was decided that Palembang offered the best site for the new headquarters – even though it would probably be the focal point of the initial Japanese attack. It had two airfields nearby, one of them secret; it had a good port with road and rail links to the south; and it had an oilfield and a high octane refinery. Work to prepare the airfields began on 31 December.[15]

There was to be little time. Within a fortnight, with the Japanese entering Johore, dispersal was becoming imperative, and on 16 January Maltby ordered the formation of 225 (Bomber) Group, which moved to Palembang on the 18th and was taken over on the 30th by Air Commodore H J F Hunter, newly arrived from the UK.[16] By then most of his aircraft had also arrived from Singapore, the Hudsons of 1 and 8 RAAF Squadrons and of 62 Squadron, and the Blenheims of 27 and 34 Squadrons. In addition two more squadrons of Blenheims (they had already seen service in the Greek campaign), Nos 84 and 211, were on the two-week trip from the Middle East, the first five aircraft arriving on the 23rd; of the 46 aircraft despatched 11 failed to complete the journey, and the 35 that did lacked their own ground support, for the servicing parties reached Oosthaven only on 14 February, whence they had to depart immediately for Java. To make matters worse, on 23 January came the first Japanese bombing attack, which led to a decision to concentrate all the bombers other than those of 84 and 211 Squadrons at the secret airfield (known as P2). The Hurricanes of the newly formed 226 (Fighter) Group under Air Commodore S F Vincent would be based at the civil airfield (P1). He, like Hunter, had appeared from the UK unbeknown to Pulford.[17]

Notwithstanding what Maltby describes as 'magnificent assistance' from the Dutch, the conditions they found were primitive in the extreme. They were on a hot equatorial island a thousand miles long, with a mountain range along the west coast and the rest of it a low-lying expanse of unhealthy jungle and swamp. The wet monsoon was in progress, its constant cycle of torrential thunderstorms both by day and night making flying exceptionally hazardous. On the ground road and rail communications were poor and the limited radio telephone service was open and insecure.[18] As for the airfields, P1 had been developed for civil use with two hard runways but had limited dispersal facilities and sparse accommodation, and P2 was little more than a large natural clearing some 40 miles further inland. The one bonus was that aircraft could be easily dispersed under the trees – up to 100 were there at one point – and despite frequent reconnaissance the Japanese failed to find it. Clearly much work was needed to make these bases fit for bomber operations and not only was there insufficient time but the equipment needed had had to be packed, loaded and shipped from Singapore amid ever mounting confusion, compounded by enemy air attack;[19] as a result practically all equipment destined for Sumatra went astray.[20] When one adds to this a dearth of transport, which made life particularly difficult at P2, inadequate cooking facilities, poor telephone links, to mention just a few of the deficiencies,[21] one can appreciate the multitude of problems being faced by men most of whom had made the dangerous trip by sea from the mounting carnage of Singapore. To make matters worse, far more airmen eventually reached Palembang than could either be accommodated or properly employed; by early February there were 1,500 at P2, which could 'accommodate' 250, and 2,500 were housed in schools and cinemas in Palembang town.[22] Altogether about 5,000 airmen arrived, usually as a mass of individuals, hungry, exhausted and in a low state of morale.[23] Then, there being no work for them, many had to be moved on by train to Oosthaven and Java.[24]

Given these circumstances it is remarkable what was achieved over the period of just three weeks when the RAF operated in Sumatra. A bomber force consisting at its peak on 5 February of 32 Hudsons and 28 Blenheims[25] joined in the Endau operation, covered the Singapore reinforcement convoys and undertook night attacks on airfields and ports as far distant as Singora. They flew under appalling difficulties, navigating long distances over mountainous jungle in the inky blackness of a moonless tropical night, when thunderstorms of great violence and magnitude were frequent.[26] Moreover not all the aircrew of the reinforcing squadrons were up to the standard of night flying required, particularly without radio aids to navigation, but those that were – like the crews that had been in Singapore – showed outstanding determination and skill.[27]

Meanwhile the fighter force was being built up at P1. Some 40 Hurricanes, mostly those flown off HMS *Indomitable* on 25 January, were there by early February; the survivors from Singapore arrived on the 10th, and 17 more appeared on the 12th and 13th from Batavia.[28] Thanks to losses in action and through accidents, however, never did the strength exceed two squadrons. Moreover few of the pilots had operational experience, many having come straight from the OTUs; servicing was difficult in the absence of toolkits and had to be done for most of the time by ground crews from former Buffalo squadrons; and in the absence of radars warning of attack depended on a group of observer posts. To improve their performance, four of each aircraft's 12

Browning guns were removed; eight were thought sufficient against the unarmoured Japanese aircraft.[29]

It was not long before Japanese intentions became clear, initially with photographic reconnaissance flights, then with heavy attacks on P1 on 6, 7 and 8 February. With the advantage of surprise the first two raids caused considerable damage, especially on the 7th, when, in addition to several Blenheims, three Hurricanes were destroyed and nine damaged on the ground, and three more shot down in what was accepted as a crippling attack.[30] Clearly, as Terence Kelly says, the Japanese were trying to wipe out the fighter opposition, yet they succeeded only in reducing its scale – essentially because they had not discovered P2. So at least some Hurricanes remained for use against the invasion force which had been spotted by a Hudson on the 6th assembling off the Anamba Islands. Then on the 13th, a day when P1 was again attacked just as some new Hurricanes were landing, reconnaissance showed a concentration of Japanese shipping north of Banka Island.[31] The date is significant. Back in Singapore the enemy were closing in on the city and a host of people were trying to get away from the doomed island, many of them in small boats and headed towards Sumatra. Kelly describes the situation as they found themselves amid the enemy and quotes Air Commodore C O F Modin, Pulford's AOA:

> The enemy appeared to have achieved complete surprise in closing the Banka Strait just when the final and heaviest flow of evacuation craft from Singapore might be expected to pass ... I doubt whether the capture of so many surface craft has ever been achieved with greater ease.[32]

Many, of course, were not captured; they were sunk or damaged with heavy loss of life then or subsequently, and Pulford was just one of many airmen who failed to survive. Others did, however, some to be taken prisoner and others, after further adventures, to escape.[33]

So it was that on the morning of 14 February all the available Hudsons and Blenheims, escorted by 14 Hurricanes (the largest number ever assembled for a single operation, says Kelly), set course towards the enemy convoy at the entrance to the Banka Straits. An attempted strike on the previous evening had met with little success, but now, despite strong fighter defence and heavy AA fire, the attack was pressed home with great determination and despite heavy losses one transport was sunk and five more set on fire. As a result the convoy was scattered and the seaborne landing planned for that day had to be postponed.[34] The RAF now had problems, however, back at base.

At 0800, soon after the Hurricanes had taken off, a Japanese bomber force was reported heading for Palembang; attempts to recall the fighters failed and P1 was heavily attacked. Then an hour later some 20-30 transport aircraft looking remarkably like Hudsons (they were in fact Hudsons bought from Lockheed or manufactured under licence, says Kelly), disgorged about 300 paratroops in two groups near the airfield. Confronting them were 150 British soldiers manning the anti-aircraft batteries that had been sent to Palembang on Wavell's instructions, 110 Netherlands soldiers drawn from the Sumatra garrison, and three officers and 72 men of the RAF ground defence unit. These latter were ground tradesmen who had been trained at Seletar for this role; experience of the earlier part of the war, and notably of the German airborne landings in Crete, had shown that the RAF needed to be able to take some responsibility for airfield defence, and these precursors of the RAF Regiment – admittedly not fully trained – had just arrived at Palembang.[35]

The enemy fairly quickly established a road block and engaged the AA batteries, but having taken heavy casualties could not capture the airfield itself, whose defence was in the capable hands of Wing Commander H G Maguire, recently arrived to command the Hurricane Wing. Consequently when some of 232 Squadron's aircraft landed it was still possible to refuel them and send them to P2. Thereafter, while the situation at P1 seemed to be under control, worrying reports were coming from the oil refinery, where other paratroops had dropped, and from Palembang town, and it was decided to evacuate the two Group HQs to P2, together with most of the support personnel. The situation during the afternoon was one of stalemate, with Maguire's men holding the airfield but short of water, food and ammunition, and the road blocked. Then he was advised (wrongly it appears) of a further Japanese landing 15 miles away and bearing in mind the difficulties the Dutch troops were likely to have in clearing the area he decided to pull out.[36]

Meanwhile all the remaining aircraft – 22 Hurricanes, 35 Blenheims and three Hudsons[37] – had been concentrated at the still undiscovered P2, commanded by Group Captain McCauley; unfortunately the initial news from P1 had led Hunter to order P2's evacuation and the preparatory destruction was already in hand when more optimistic tidings from P1 caused the order to be countermanded, but what Kelly describes as a 'reasonably efficient station' had already been seriously damaged.[38] Nevertheless, with the general situation still uncertain and the main invasion force not yet ashore, everyone got down to working all night to enable their aircraft to fly again the next morning, the 15th, and the Blenheims, mostly flown by crews from 84 and 211 Squadrons, mounted their first attack on Japanese landing craft in the Moesi river at first light. It was to be a strenuous day, say the Narrators:

There was a constant stream of Blenheims and Hurricanes between P2 and the river. Refuelling and rearming as quickly as possible, aircrews turned round and set off again. Japanese fighter opposition had ceased after the first attack, and transport and landing barges were shot up by the Hurricanes and low-flying Blenheims after their bombs had gone. By late afternoon all movement of shipping in the river had ceased.[39]

Maltby, accepting the difficulty of assessing the damage done, talks of thousands of troops in barges being caught in the open by machine gun fire, particularly by the Hurricanes, and speaks of very heavy casualties. Then, as a fitting finale, a number of Zeros were located on a beach landing strip and destroyed. The Japanese had been punished heavily for their failure to locate P2, but there were no troops or light naval craft available in the area to take advantage of the situation.[40]

The airmen could do nothing more on their own, and that night Wavell ordered the evacuation of Sumatra, having decided to concentrate all remaining forces in Java, the one place where an effective stand might still be made. The surviving aircraft were therefore flown out on the 16th and apart from the care and maintenance parties on the northern airfields, most of whom got away to India, the RAF ground personnel were evacuated via Oosthaven. Here there was quite unnecessary haste; the enemy were nowhere near, yet great quantities of valuable equipment – including the newly arrived stores for the Hurricane Wing – were ordered by the British Military Embarkation Commandant to be destroyed or abandoned. So incensed were many of the airmen that two days later Group Captain G E Nicholetts gathered a party of volunteers and returned in HMAS *Ballarat* to collect as much equipment as the ship could carry – and in the process to destroy some of the harbour facilities.[41] This spirited initiative did at least something to redeem a disgraceful episode.

The brief Sumatra story leaves us with a sense of wondering what might have been. It included the gallant defence of an airfield under paratroop assault which might well have been prolonged had a little more outside support been quickly forthcoming, and there was a demonstration of just what could be achieved by the Air Force in low-level attack provided the circumstances were not too unfavourable. Nothing like it had been seen in the Malaya campaign – which, by coincidence, ended on that self-same day with the surrender of Singapore. It was undoubtedly a major success for the RAF and their RAAF colleagues, made possible by the determination not only of the aircrews but also of the groundcrews who had improvised unceasingly to keep their aircraft flying. Could it have been better exploited? Terence Kelly thinks the RAF could have continued to operate against the invasion force from P2 and points out that land reinforcements and many essential supplies had already reached Oosthaven, making possible a much longer resistance which could have imposed a major delay on the Java campaign.[42] He has a point, and certainly the evacuation was premature, but when one recalls the chain of disaster thus far and the strength being demonstrated by the Japanese on every front it was probably asking too much of those in command to provide the positive leadership needed at this particular moment. For the RAF, however, these few days had at least shown there was hope for the future.

Java

The stage was now set for the culmination of the battle for the East Indies, the Japanese assault on the island of Java (Map 3). This was the prosperous heart of the Dutch empire, more heavily populated and developed than the rest, and up to now there were hopes that it might be successfully defended. Wavell had set up his Allied Headquarters there on 15 January, thus boosting Dutch confidence, some reinforcements had arrived and more were on their way, and the longer Singapore held out the better would be Java's chances. On 3 February Wavell signalled the Chiefs of Staff: 'My impression is Japanese air force very stretched and if once we can get upper hand they will go down fairly fast'.[43] Such forced optimism could not last. Several of Java's virtually undefended airfields were attacked on that and subsequent days[44] and with the enemy having overrun the Philippines and established themselves in Borneo and Celebes it was clear they would soon be poised to attack Java itself. Then, with Singapore and Sumatra gone, Churchill answered the Dutch appeal for stubborn resistance: 'Any question of abandoning Java without a fight is unthinkable. All forces in the island whatever nationality should resist to the end. There should be no withdrawal and no surrender'.[45] Yet the Prime Minister was already well aware of the hopelessness of the situation. Wavell had just pointed out the scale of the expected enemy attack, which would include 400-500 fighters and 300-400 bombers, and the very limited naval, land and air forces at his disposal. Without naval and air superiority – most unlikely to be obtainable – he could not prevent their seizing the island's main bases; he concluded that it should not be reinforced and its loss be accepted.[46] Churchill agreed, telling Wavell on the 20th that Java would be fought for with the existing forces and some that were en route, but the main reinforcements would be diverted to Burma and India.[47] There was thus no justification for retaining Wavell's Headquarters in Bandoeng, and on 22 February the dissolution of ABDACOM was approved.

The land forces in Java now consisted of some 25,000 Dutch regular troops, a 40,000 strong 'home guard', two well trained Australian

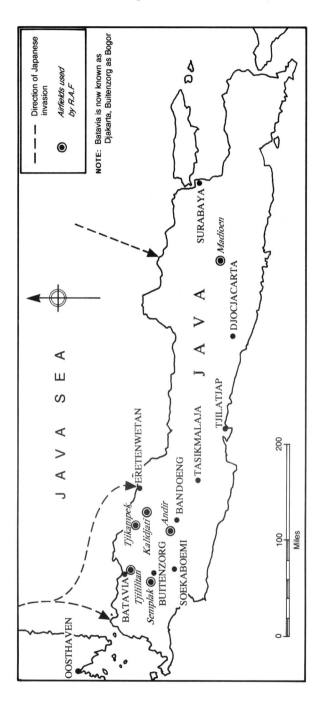

Map 3   Java

battalions, five British AA regiments and a squadron of light tanks, and an American artillery regiment.[48] All these, together with the naval and air forces, were placed under Dutch command and before departing for India on the 25th Wavell told Air Vice-Marshal Maltby that, as senior British officer, he was to be the channel of communication on all policy matters affecting more than one Service. Maltby, who had arrived in Java on the 14th and then organised the RAF HQ at Soekaboemi, now moved it to Bandoeng and under the authority of the Dutch AOC took over operational control of all RAF units. His tasks, as ordered by Wavell, were to continue the fight to defend Java as long as aircraft and equipment could be maintained, and to do everything possible to evacuate surplus units and personnel, giving high priority to such tradesmen as could contribute to the defence.[49] Churchill signalled him the next day:

> I send you and all ranks of the British forces who have stayed behind in Java my best wishes for success and honour in the great fight that confronts you. Every day gained is precious, and I know that you will do everything humanly possible to prolong the battle.[50]

RAF units had been moving into Java for some time. 153 MU had been ordered there from Seletar as early as 4 January and started work at Djocjacarta on the 15th.[51] 151 MU and Base Accounts and Records had followed later in the month,[52] and on 5 February Pulford had sent his SASO, Air Commodore B J Silly, to command the new Rear Base in Batavia. Its main task was to organise the reception, sorting, posting and evacuation of the many RAF personnel arriving on the island, and the six transit camps it established eventually handled 12,000 men,[53] 10,000 of them arriving between the 12th and 18th in great disorder. Maltby describes the chaos as refugees of all sorts from Singapore, together with reinforcements, reached Batavia: the congestion in the harbour and its approaches; the problems of unloading; the quays, warehouses and access roads crammed with an inextricable confusion of merchandise, equipment, MT, abandoned cars and goods of every description; the city itself grossly overcrowded.[54] Not surprisingly those who were there remember how lost and demoralised they felt. Many were given little if any briefing or information; their accommodation was improvised in schools or barracks; those who were given jobs were often used as general labourers at the docks or airfields; others had nothing worthwhile to do at all.[55] For all the efforts of those in command, who had themselves only just arrived, there was far too little time to get things properly organised.

Meanwhile all the remaining aircraft had arrived. 205 Squadron's four Catalinas had reached Batavia on 1 February and most had spent the next fortnight operating from Oosthaven within the Allied Reconnaissance Group before transferring to Tjilatjap; the nine surviving Vildebeests and one Albacore had appeared at the same time and were based as 36 Squadron at Tjikampek; 26 Hudsons (12 operationally serviceable) reorganised as 1 Squadron RAAF were at Semplak; and 26 Blenheims – most having come straight from Palembang and with only six serviceable – were at the well-established Dutch base of Kalidjati as 84 Squadron. Finally there were 25 Hurricanes, 18 serviceable, in 232, 242 and 605 Squadrons at Tjililitan,[56] just outside Batavia. Hopefully 605 Squadron would shortly be re-equipped with 40 Kittyhawks (P-40s) being shipped from Australia aboard the US carrier *Langley*, but this was sunk. So the air defence rested on the shoulders of a small force of Hurricanes operating within Air Commodore Vincent's reconstituted 226 Group and supported by two radar units, a reasonable control and reporting system, and a fighter operations room – all set up with invaluable assistance from the Dutch.[57] The Dutch themselves still had five bomber, three fighter and two observation squadrons, all much depleted, and the Americans some B-17s and P-40s in eastern Java. Such was the Allied air strength on 18 February: effectively they were going to be outnumbered by about 10:1.

During the next week the land forces prepared to resist the expected invasion. The main Dutch strength was concentrated in the west, with a smaller force in the east around Surabaya, the British AA units were deployed to defend Batavia and the main airfields, and the other British and Australian units near Buitenzorg were formed into a mobile striking force to become known as 'Blackforce'.[58] Meanwhile the RAF's Blenheims tried to interfere with the enemy build-up at Palembang and the Japanese used P1 to mount attacks on Semplak and knocked out all but six of the Hudson force; these had to be moved to Kalidjati, where two more were lost.[59] Then on the 25th a large enemy convoy was spotted off east Borneo, and when on the 27th it was seen heading towards the coast north of Surabaya Admiral Doorman led the Allied fleet into action. There could be no air support, and even had there been its scale could hardly have affected the outcome. The loss of all five cruisers on that and the next day in the Battle of the Java Sea ended any hope there might have been of saving the island.

The invasion convoy did not, however, come through unscathed. 36 Squadron, operating temporarily from Madioen and escorted by Dutch Buffaloes, joined a number of American B-17s and P-40s in attacking a large group of transports five miles off the coast on the night of 28 February/1 March, and the Americans credited the RAF with sinking eight ships. Having said that three of the nine aircraft were lost, including that of the CO, Maltby goes on: 'Each aircrew of this squadron, operating from a strange aerodrome, thus carried out two night attacks in 24 hours, involving over 15 hours' flying in open cockpits – a magnificent achievement'.[60] Simultaneously two further convoys were approaching the coast east and west of Batavia, and at dusk the Blenheims and Hudsons set out in bad weather from the barely serviceable airfield at Kalidjati. Altogether 32 sorties were carried out that night as landings were under way at Eretenwetan, with some crews attacking three times, and at least three ships were sunk.[61]

Now disaster struck. The airmen had been either operating at high pressure or on standby for 36 hours and desperately needed rest; moreover their aircraft were at great risk from the Zeros if operating in cloudless morning conditions. The crews were therefore stood down until the afternoon and the aircraft dispersed, the Dutch AOC having asked for them to remain at Kalidjati rather than being withdrawn further inland. Then at 1030 the Japanese tanks and infantry which had landed at Eretenwetan, 40 miles away, only ten hours earlier overran the airfield. The four remaining Hudsons were able to take off under fire and escape, but all the 21 dispersed Blenheims – just eight of them still serviceable – were captured. This was a tragic ending to the saga of the Blenheim squadrons; despite many setbacks they had flown throughout the Malayan and East Indies campaigns with great gallantry and determination, and there was still fight left in them. Not unreasonably, therefore, there were questions about the incident and despite the now desperate situation on the island time was made for a joint Army/RAF court of inquiry. In essence this found that the inability of the Dutch troops to halt the Japanese advance had not been communicated to the RAF by the Dutch AOC – despite his ordering the Dutch squadrons to withdraw in time. There had been serious failures of communication between the Dutch and British commands and by the time OC 84 Squadron found out what was happening the enemy had arrived. The local defence parties, Army, RAF and Dutch, did all they could; the Japanese later testified to their gallant and protracted defence, and Maltby believed there were no survivors. There was therefore much anger when Field Marshal Dill signalled the GOC from Washington about a Dutch intelligence report accusing the British of deserting the aerodrome. The Dutch C-in-C immediately set the record straight: the accusation arose from a mistranslation, and all British ·forces under his command had fought throughout with the greatest bravery and daring.[62]

The Hurricanes too had been making their contribution. Up to 27 February they had operated continuously in the defence of Batavia and its nearby airfields, and though hopelessly outnumbered had given good account of themselves. Terence Kelly, one of the pilots, reflects:

The Japanese fighters, although of a quality which surprised the

Allies, were not machine for machine superior to the Hurricane when flown by pilots who had learnt their craft against the Navy O ... this was up to 20,000 ft slightly faster and had a definite advantage in manoeuvrability, but it was unarmoured, its fire power was less, its ceiling was apparently lower, and above all it lacked the astonishing ability of the Hurricane to absorb punishment.[63]

Kelly is convinced that a force of suitable size, flown by experienced pilots and properly controlled, could have wrought the most dreadful havoc, and believes Wing Commander Maguire was right in pressing for the Hurricane Wing to be built up into a coherent force for the defence of Java rather than thrown piecemeal into the battle and inevitably destroyed. Portal had minuted Churchill along precisely these lines a few days previously:

> We have had a good deal of evidence during the war of the indifferent performance of hurried collections of pilots and aircraft without unit esprit de corps and a period of collective training. But in the Far East emergency there was nothing to be done except try to get what pilots and aircraft we could to Singapore in time.[64]

So on the morning of 1 March, the critical day, 242 Squadron (into which the other squadrons had been merged) could put just 12 aircraft into the air against the enemy forces landing at Eretenwetan.[65] Attacking at low level in the face of intense AA fire, they inflicted severe losses on troops in barges and on land, and intensive air defence and ground attack operations continued on the 2nd and 3rd, when their base at Tjililitan came under threat and they were moved back to Andir. Then, with Batavia now declared an open city, they lost their control system. Yet for four more days they went on attacking captured airfields, trying to slow the enemy advance, and defending their own base, but by the 7th only five Hurricanes were still serviceable and after a final operation on the 8th the remaining aircraft were destroyed.[66] Maltby had already highly commended the work of the squadron in Malaya and in Java, calling it a 'magnificent and sustained performance against greatly superior opposition'.[67] His post-war tribute also deserves recording:

> This unit under the leadership of the late Squadron Leader R E P Brooker DSO DFC was in constant action from the time it arrived in Singapore until fighting ceased in Java. It inflicted severe casualties on the enemy in the air, in landing craft and on the ground. It volunteered to remain in Java as the last fighter

squadron. Great credit is due to all ranks of a magnificent squadron.[68]

Meanwhile the surviving Catalinas of 205 Squadron, which had continued their reconnaissance and anti-submarine patrols throughout, left their final base at Tjilatjap on the 3rd, one bound for Ceylon and two for Australia, where both were strafed by Zeros on arrival at Broome.[69] The next day the last three Hudsons also departed for Australia. As for the Vildebeests, whose remaining crews maintained their bombing of enemy-held airfields until the 6th, just two were left to attempt to escape on the 7th.[70] As one of the pilots, Squadron Leader Allanson, recalls, they intended to fly as far as possible up the west coast of Sumatra, ditch, and then get away by sea, but having ended up near Bencoolen he and his crew were soon captured. The other aircraft was lost at sea. Like their Blenheim counterparts, the Vildebeest crews had done everything asked of them in the fight against the Japanese and paid the price.

So within a week of the enemy landings all the RAF's aircraft were gone, but what of its men? After the tremendous influx in mid-February every effort was made to evacuate all who could be spared; Batavia was used until it was closed on the 23rd, many men leaving for Ceylon aboard the P & O liner *Orcades*;[71] thereafter all had to make their way, often by self-help, to the south coast port of Tjilatjap where amid much disorganisation the lucky ones got away. But for the sinking of the large transport vessel *City of Manchester* by a Japanese submarine most might have done so; in the event it was the grossly overcrowded tramp steamer *Kota Gede* that carried the majority of the lucky ones to Ceylon. With up to 2,500 men of all three Services on board – many in poor physical state – the conditions were 'less than spartan', with an almost total absence of military discipline, and little seemed to have been done in Colombo to prepare for their arrival a week later on 7 March.[72] Many of the airmen then went on to Karachi, where the then LAC Barkus remembers their reception:

We were humiliated, verbally abused and given every kind of fatigues, pickets, guards etc by the permanent staff. Most of us had chronic dysentery, yet day by day in a searing 100 degrees were paraded and insulted by such words as 'you are a disgrace to the British Empire'.[73]

Perhaps it was asking too much of those remote from the chain of disaster to understand that these men had done all they could in an impossible situation, but surely higher command could have anticipated the problems.

Yet Barkus and his comrades were in reality the fortunate ones.

While altogether some 7,000 airmen had got away from Sumatra and Java (though not all reached their destinations), about 5,000 were still in Java at the beginning of March, many of them unarmed and including a lot of skilled tradesmen.[74] Just a few would escape by their own efforts, most notably Wing Commander Jeudwine, the redoubtable CO of 84 Squadron, who with 11 others discovered a derelict ship's lifeboat at Tjilatjap and spent the next 47 days sailing it to Australia.[75] On the 5th Maltby and the GOC, General Sitwell, attended a conference called by the Dutch C-in-C in Bandoeng. He indicated that the city would not be defended and his headquarters would surrender, though local resistance was to continue elsewhere if possible. Accepting that AHQ and Andir airfield must now be given up, Maltby agreed with Sitwell that Blackforce and all other British units except those waiting near Tjilatjap should be ordered into an area near Tasikmalaja which was thought suitable for protracted defence. In effect this meant some 8,000 men, 2,000 of them RAF, and by the morning of the 8th the move was under way.[76]

Then, to Maltby's consternation, he heard at 0900 a broadcast from the C-in-C to the effect that all organised resistance was to cease forthwith. Five hours later, after frantic efforts to confirm the Dutch intentions, Maltby and Sitwell decided they had no choice. While resistance was certainly possible it would be for days, not weeks; there were few supplies and no medical facilities, the jointly-staffed Australian Field Hospital having to remain in Bandoeng, and the native population might well prove hostile. Moreover, since the C-in-C's statement had referred to the Allied forces, not just the Dutch, it seemed that continued resistance might well put the British soldiers and airmen outside the protection of international law if captured. Surrender was therefore agreed and a signal sent to the Air Ministry. It never arrived.[77]

Two days later Maltby met the Japanese commander, Lieutenant General Maruyama, who implied that prisoners would be treated according to the Geneva Convention, and when the formal surrender terms were signed on the 12th they included the following: 'All troops will obey absolutely any orders of the Japanese troops, subject to their rights as prisoners of war, vide the Geneva Convention of 1929'.

Maltby tried to insert the word 'lawful' before 'orders', but Maruyama insisted this was unnecessary since the prisoners were being given the protection of the Convention.[78] According to Colonel Dunlop, the Commandant of the Allied hospital, Maltby was also given a letter from Maruyama promising to observe the Hague Convention on prisoners of war.[79] When a few days later an order for all prisoners to march the 150 miles to Batavia in eight days was rescinded, Maltby believed Maruyama's influence had been decisive. Such a march, forbidden by the Geneva Convention, would have caused many deaths.

There were already, however, abundant indications that the Convention would be honoured far more in the breach than the observance. On the 20th Air Commodore Staton and Group Captain Bishop, among others, were imprisoned for a month for refusal to answer questions under interrogation; aircrews from 242 and 1 (RAAF) Squadrons were brutally treated in the unsuccessful attempt to extract information; and, as Maltby concluded, the later treatment of prisoners of war, with little regard to the terms of the Geneva Convention which had been accorded to them on surrendering, was too well known to need further elaboration.[80]

This is not the place for a detailed description of the dreadful things that befell those who became captives of the Japanese, some of whom were told on capture that they were bandits and were to be executed on the spot.[81] Many remained in Java for much of the time, living in humiliating conditions, enduring ill-treatment, undernourishment and disease, and often required to serve as slave labour. Others went to camps on neighbouring islands where conditions were even worse. A few RAF men caught in Malaya and Sumatra eventually found themselves working on the infamous railway of death in Siam. Others, including Maltby and other senior officers, were later transported to Japan. All who survived ended up shadows of their former selves and would never forget; indeed few would ever forgive. Nor would they ever forget – and nor should we – the many who did not survive. Of 5,102 RAF men captured by the Japanese during the entire war, most of them in Java, 1,714 died in captivity – almost exactly one third. This figure may be contrasted with the 152 out of 9,879 who died while in German hands.[82]

Yet amid the tribulations were many triumphs of the human spirit. Let two tributes encapsulate them. An Australian pilot officer wrote:

> During our imprisonment the personnel of our Squadron acted in a manner which was of the highest merit, and throughout the period of brutality, shortage of food, etc, their conduct made me very proud to be a member of 84 Squadron. (The senior NCOs) set an example by their work, interest and demeanour which helped tremendously in keeping the men's morale high, and infusing in them a condition of cheerfulness which the Japanese could never understand or overcome.[83]

Now the AOC, Air Vice-Marshal Maltby, who as Sir Maurice Dean reminds us was responsible for the prisoners and 'fought their battles with the Japanese camp commandants to the end with exemplary dedication':[84]

I wish to express my appreciation for the great fortitude of those

Air Vice-Marshal P C Maltby CB DSO AFC, AOC in Java in 1942 and the most
senior RAF officer to be taken prisoner, is greeted on arrival in India following
his release from prison camp in Japan, 3 September 1945. (*AHB*)

who became prisoners of war in Japanese hands. There were
many who at great risk to themselves constantly minimised the
assistance they were forced to give their captors. Others refused
to divulge information in spite of brutal treatment. There were
also those who constantly worked for the welfare of their
comrades, often at considerable sacrifice to themselves. The
credit due to them for the services they rendered during three and
a half years of captivity, often in extreme circumstances, is very
great indeed.[85]

5 India Under Threat

The First Burma Campaign

So far we have concentrated on the tale of almost unmitigated disaster for the RAF that accompanied the Japanese advance through Malaya and Singapore into the East Indies, but this was far from the whole story. To the west lay Burma, through which passed the one supply road leading from the outside world to beleaguered China, and beyond Burma was India. As early as 21 January Churchill had asked the Chiefs of Staff to consider whether Singapore should be abandoned so that all available resources could be concentrated on defending Burma and keeping open the Burma Road.[1] Taking the widest view, he felt 'Burma was more important than Singapore'.[2] Politically, however, such a course was quite unacceptable, and it was only after the fall of Singapore that the Defence Committee decided to bite what remained of the bullet: Java would not be reinforced and all resources would be devoted to the defence of Australia, Burma, India and Ceylon.[3] For Burma it was already too late.

A country of 17 million people, Burma had been politically separate from India since 1937, and while its defence was of obvious importance to India in the event of attack from the east no real threat was perceived until July 1941 when the Japanese took over Indo-China. Consequently very little had been done by way of defensive preparations, even after Burma had been brought into Far East Command in October 1940. Nevertheless the Singapore Defence Conference held that month (p. 19) recognised the value of its economic resources, the significance of its air communications with Singapore, and the enormous importance of Rangoon and the Burma Road in the delivery of supplies to China; a limited scale of air defence was therefore recommended, consisting of five squadrons (two bomber, one fighter, one GR, one army co-operation). All were within the 582 aircraft postulated by Far East Command, and some would have to be provided by switching squadrons from Malaya if necessary.[4]

The siting of the operational airfields was also considered, and a brief description of the geography of Burma, where so much of the action we shall be describing in this book took place, may be helpful at

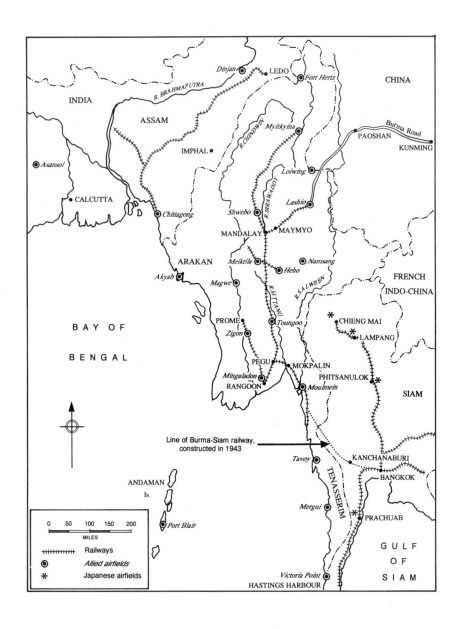

Map 4   Burma 1941/42

this point (Map 4). In the heart of the country, watered by the four main rivers flowing from north to south, lived most of the people, and the lines of communication lay in the same direction, all leading towards Rangoon. This central region was surrounded by jungle-covered mountain barriers which – apart from the Burma Road from Lashio to Kunming – could be traversed only by tracks that were often impassable. To the west was the coastal strip of the Arakan and to the south the long fringe of Tenasserim, pointing towards Malaya. As Louis Allen describes it, Burma was a country of immense topographical contrasts: high jungles, swampy coastal plains, alluvial deltas, a central plain with a dry triangle (Mandalay-Magwe-Toungoo), the whole walled in by high mountains separating it from India in the west, China in the north, and Siam in the east. From mid-May to mid-October the south-west monsoon turned vast areas into swamp and quagmire, whereas from October to March the climate was delightful. Malaria was endemic, and the jungles teemed with wildlife.[5]

The airfield plan, apart from Akyab on the Arakan coast, followed the north-south alignment of Burma's topography. Intended to counter possible attacks through China and northern Siam, sites were to be developed at Lashio, Namsang, Heho and Toungoo, fairly close to the eastern border; Mingaladon would serve the defence of Rangoon; and a chain from Moulmein through Tavoy and Mergui to Victoria Point would also provide the transit route to Malaya.[6] These selections were designed to ensure maximum operational mobility, but as Air Vice-Marshal Stevenson – AOC during the 1942 campaign – would later observe, the northern ones were placed too far forward in the Sittang valley where no radar warning was possible. They should have been in the Irrawaddy and Chindwin valleys, allowing radar units to be located to the east.[7] General Slim, who arrived in Burma as Corps Commander in March 1942, echoed this view; the airfields had been well built by the Burma Public Works Department for all-weather use, but they were indefensible without an efficient warning system.[8] We must remember that the planning in late 1940 and early 1941 was directed from Singapore where Burma took low priority; while 221 Group was formed in April 1941 in Rangoon for the specific purpose of organising airfields for emergency use, it was very small and headed only by a group captain.[9] The real mistake was to locate Burma within Far East Command rather than under C-in-C India, whose AOC-in-C would probably have recognised that the air defence of Burma was in effect the first line of protection for eastern India and sited his airfields accordingly. While control was eventually transferred it was only after the Japanese attack. Later when ABDACOM was formed control passed to Wavell in Java,[10] and not until Java was about to fall did responsibility for the defence of Burma revert to where it should have been all along. Wavell himself took this view, and for air defence purposes Burma and north-east India, with its vital ports and industries, certainly ought to have been treated as one.[11] Instead, when it really mattered in 1941, Burma was a poor relation. As Slim wrote: 'Burma was last on the priority list for aircraft, as for everything else, and in December 1941 the air forces in Burma were almost negligible'.[12]

Admittedly much work had been done in building the airfields and preparing them for occupation, in constructing a new joint-service HQ in Rangoon, in developing an air defence system, but few of the aircraft needed were forthcoming. Most of the Blenheims of 60 Squadron, which had arrived in February, were at Kuantan for armament training in November and stayed there, and the recently built-up 67 Squadron, equipped with Buffaloes, was the only RAF flying unit in Burma when the war began. They were, however, supported by the 11 Tiger Moths of the Burma Volunteer Air Force which did valuable work ferrying personnel and mail, and co-operating with AA batteries and the civil defence,[13] and by a squadron of the American Volunteer Group which was to play an indispensable part in the subsequent air operations. The AVG had been formed by Major Chennault, a retired US Army Air Corps officer who since 1937 had been Air Adviser to the Chinese, to combat the increasingly heavy Japanese air attack on the Burma Road; he had enrolled 100 experienced pilots and 200 ground staff, acquired 100 Tomahawk (P-40) fighters, and transported them to Burma. Using RAF facilities they were trained at Toungoo when the war started and one of his three squadrons was allocated to the defence of Rangoon. Serving willingly under the AOC and co-operating closely with the RAF, these American volunteers were to play a major role in winning the critical battle for air superiority.[14]

So when Air Vice-Marshal Stevenson[15] reached Rangoon on 1 January 1942 he found just 21 Tomahawks and 16 Buffaloes at his disposal, though he had been promised 11 reinforcing squadrons.[16] Having rapidly surveyed the scene he submitted his appreciation of the air situation on the 14th. Given Burma's potential as an Allied base for offensive operations in South-East Asia and for the supply of China he believed that Japan was bound to try to occupy the country, and before the onset of the monsoon in May. Therefore, even at the cost of action at home or in the Middle East, sufficient air and land forces must be provided for Burma's defence, and resources built up for an offensive. Assuming that the enemy would attempt a knock-out air blow against Rangoon followed by a seaborne attack, and that they would eventually be able to mount 600 sorties per day, he estimated his requirement as 14 fighter squadrons (224 aircraft, a mix of Hurricanes, Tomahawks and Beaufighters), with a similar number in other roles.[17] Yet he must have known that practice was bound to be very different from theory.

In the event his fighter force comprised no more than 67 Squadron's

Buffaloes, three squadrons of Hurricanes (most of which arrived in late January from Egypt), and the AVG squadron. Some of the Hurricanes were obsolescent, worn-out Mark 1s; as Stevenson reported to Peirse on 5 February, he had carried out a test the moment the Hurricanes arrived, and found their radius of action little more than 135 miles from base. The alternative of using long-range tanks had been carefully investigated but they were non-self-sealing, only a lash-up fitting – impracticable to fight with.[18] In practice never could more than 30 of these aircraft be sent into action at one time and their strength fell away rapidly due to lack of reinforcing aircraft, proper operational facilities and shortage of spares. Indeed there were virtually no spares for Hurricane IIs, few tools, and no proper organisation for repair and salvage.[19] By 15 February only 15 Hurricanes were serviceable and two further squadrons earlier promised by DCAS were diverted for the air defence of Ceylon, thought by the Chiefs of Staff to merit higher priority.[20] So with the Buffaloes outclassed and having to be withdrawn in late January the air defence depended on a small and diminishing force of Hurricanes and the AVG's average of 15 serviceable Tomahawks. To make matters worse, instead of the planned seven radars there was just one, 517 AMES, equipped with a COL set; this was moved early on from Moulmein to Rangoon, where despite total lack of spares it was kept operational until withdrawal. But there were limits to what one set could do. As Stevenson wrote: 'The lack of adequate RDF equipment exerted a critical influence on the air battle in Burma'.[21]

It was a similar tale with the bombers. Of seven Blenheim squadrons he had been originally promised,[22] Stevenson was told on 2 February to expect three immediately, yet he never received more than one

A Lysander of 28 Squadron, used for army co-operation work in Burma, early 1942. (*Group Captain A S Mann*)

squadron's worth of aircraft, enough to provide six available for operations on an average day.[23] The rest of his force consisted of a handful of Wapiti and Audax aircraft of the Indian Air Force (later replaced by Blenheims) used for general reconnaissance, and 28 Squadron and 1 Squadron IAF, both equipped with Lysanders for army co-operation. Having flown initially to Lashio and Namsang in late January these subsequently operated from and near Mingaladon, Stevenson having unsuccessfully urged their re-equipment with modern aircraft.[24]

Confronting this minuscule force in the early stages were some 180 Japanese aircraft based in Siam, but by mid-March the enemy had been able to redeploy some of their units from further south and their strength had almost doubled.[25] Stevenson describes the opposition he faced, drawing particular attention to the performance of the Navy 'O' compared with that of the older Japanese fighters, to the 500 mile radius of action all these could achieve with the use of drop tanks, and to the 700 mile radius of action and one and a half ton bomb load of the Army 97 bombers. This was a force which could strike at considerable distance and against which a good warning system and effective ground defence were essential. He sums up as follows:

> Thus we were much inferior to the enemy in numbers, in the vital factor of restricted range in our fighters, in range, bomb lifts and speed of our bombers. The enemy, on the other hand, suffered the grave disadvantage of not having armour and self-sealing tanks, while the Hurricane II was a much superior fighter to the Army 97, slightly superior to the Navy 'O' and quite decisive against such ill-defended bombers as the Army 97. The P-40 was comparable to the Hurricane II, particularly in medium altitude fighting.[26]

The first significant air action had in fact occurred before Stevenson's arrival. On 23 and 25 December 70 to 80 escorted Japanese bombers attacked the city of Rangoon and Mingaladon airfield, causing substantial damage together with heavy casualties among the civilian population, many of whom were standing in the streets watching. The AVG and 67 Squadron had, however, been warned, and 36 enemy aircraft were claimed destroyed.[27] This was a severe setback to the Japanese, and for the next month their bombers returned their attention to Malaya. On land, however, it was another story. Despite the arrival in Burma of British Army reinforcements the southern airfields of Mergui and Tavoy were lost on 19 January (Victoria Point had been taken earlier), and Moulmein followed on the 30th. Then during February the Army was forced back towards the River Sittang, where the bridge was blown on the 23rd, leaving substantial forces on the wrong side.

During these two months the RAF did all it could to support the Army, operations being planned by Stevenson and General Hutton, the GOC. at their daily staff conferences in Rangoon.[28] Most of the work was done by the Blenheims of 113 Squadron, which attacked Japanese shipping and docks at Bangkok the night after their arrival on 7 January and subsequently concentrated on airfields, harbours and ground support. Then in February the Lysanders joined in, each carrying 2 x 250 lb bombs, and mainly attacking enemy communications. Altogether that month 202 Blenheim and 63 Lysander sorties were flown, all requiring escort by the sorely pressed fighters whose primary task was to defend Rangoon:[29] a puny effort maybe but Kirby acknowledges the value to 17 Division of the daily reconnaissances,[30] and attacks on troop concentrations, motor transport, river traffic and enemy-occupied airfields.[31] Unfortunately, however, the air forces had been unable to interfere when the Japanese were advancing through thick forest, and Stevenson describes the virtual impossibility of pinpointing targets or distinguishing between friend and foe in close jungle country.[32]

The occasional 'friendly fire' incident was therefore almost inevitable. On 20 February while the break-out of a surrounded battalion was being covered by the RAF some of its men were mistaken for the enemy, and the following day several columns at Mokpalin were bombed and machine-gunned, first by Japanese aircraft and then by aircraft with Allied markings. Heavy damage and casualties were inflicted and morale suffered. According to Kirby air reconnaissance had falsely reported an enemy column of 300 vehicles moving along a particular road and all available aircraft, RAF and AVG, had been ordered into the attack.[33] Stevenson carried out an extensive enquiry and could not reach a firm conclusion: he thought the Japanese might have used captured Blenheims or that their bombers might have been mistaken for Blenheims; the silhouettes were similar. He did, however, accept – writing later in 1942 – the probability that some crews had bombed the wrong objective.[34] As with other such incidents in the Second World War – and indeed more recently – the price that the Army had to pay for close air support was the risk that occasionally something would go wrong.

While Stevenson set much store on helping the Army, he rightly saw his primary task as the air defence of Rangoon, through which all the much needed reinforcements must come, with its base facilities and its airfields. For most of January the enemy bombing was restricted to small scale night attacks; then from 23 – 29 January a force of some 200 aircraft attempted to overwhelm the defences, and in continuous day fighting the 40 Tomahawks and Hurricanes claimed some 50 Japanese bombers and fighters destroyed. A month later, on 24 and 25 February, the enemy put about 170 aircraft into their third major attempt to win air superiority, this time with 37 aircraft claimed destroyed.[35] These were high losses and the Japanese made no further attacks before the deteriorating state of the land battle compelled Rangoon's evacuation.

This was indeed a fine achievement. In the first place, as Stevenson says, the warning was good: the Burma Observer Corps was highly efficient, and the radar which had been moved from Moulmein to Rangoon on 15 January achieved a high rate of detection.[36] The operations of the AVG and the Hurricanes were well co-ordinated and controlled, thus taking full advantage of the considerable experience of the American pilots and of such of the Hurricane pilots as had fought against the Luftwaffe. The tactics were those generally used in Europe, except that on account of the Japanese fighters' manoeuvrability the best method of attack was a dive, taking advantage of height and sun. By night, on the other hand, little could be done, although Hurricanes did achieve the occasional interception.[37] The ground crews too worked under intense strain in the heat of the 'dry season' sun, striving to make do with what equipment and tools they had and constantly improvising; stimulated by the success of the fighters their morale was high.[38]

Wing Commander (later Group Captain) Frank Carey brings his experience of the Battle of Britain to the air campaign in Burma, early 1942. Seen here with a member of the American Volunteer Group and, in the background, a Tomahawk. (*AHB*)

It was, nevertheless, a narrow margin. On 27 February the combined fighter strength of the RAF and AVG was down to ten, mainly owing to the number damaged and temporarily unserviceable for lack of spares. The pilots, the ground crews, the operational staff and many more had won a significant victory against the odds and well deserved the personal congratulations sent to 67, 17 and 135 Squadrons and the AVG by the Secretary of State for Air and General Wavell.[39] Rightly observing that most of the enemy had fallen to the AVG, Slim later summed up the significance of the two-month air battle:

> It was thus possible for the last convoys of reinforcements to enter Rangoon and for the demolition and final evacuation to be completed without serious air interference. At the same time P-40s and Buffaloes – the range was too great for Hurricanes – attacked any enemy airfield within reach, and our few bombers ranged far into Siam. Rarely can so small an air force have battled so gallantly and so effectively against the odds.[40]

General Alexander too recognised the value of what had been achieved. Having taken over as GOC on 5 March he had to order Rangoon to be evacuated on the 7th and as his troops moved to the north they were seriously held up by a Japanese road block. Japanese air attack, he states in his despatch, would at this stage have had disastrous consequences; that it did not occur was due to the complete air ascendancy established by the RAF and the AVG. For the same reason not one ship was lost during the seaborne evacuation.[41] The post-war American survey of air operations put it another way, commenting that the few RAF Hurricanes and AVG P-40s 'rendered a service to the Allied forces in India-Burma comparable to the Dunkirk evacuation in Europe'.[42]

The air situation was, however, much too good to last. Not only had the loss of Rangoon cost China the one seaport through which she could be supplied from the outside world and deprived the Allies of Burma's many valuable exports, but it had also cut off the Army and the remaining air forces from outside assistance, except for the trickle of reinforcements and supplies that might be brought in by air. At the same time the enemy now had the use of Rangoon for their further operations.[43] Stevenson had been considering for some time his best course of action should Rangoon fall. As far back as 12 February he had sought ABDACOM's view on whether the RAF should accompany the Army north towards China or withdraw to India to concentrate on the defence of Calcutta and NE India. He had little doubt that in Burma and China his force would be wide open to attack and quietly waste away, whereas from Indian bases it could not only provide strong local defence but also build up a proper level of support for the Army in northern Burma. Six days later he added a third option, namely to leave a small mixed force of aircraft in Burma while moving everything else to India. Neither of his messages was acknowledged by ABDACOM, but AHQ India told him on the 19th that a plan had been prepared for withdrawal to India and the next day he and Hutton agreed to work on option three.[44]

It was now clear that the Army intended to retire northwards along the line of the Irrawaddy through Prome and not along the valley of the Sittang where the main railway and the chain of airfields were situated. On the Prome route there was only one airfield remotely suitable for operating modern fighters and bombers with high wing loading, namely Magwe, a small civil airport which lacked accommodation, pens and dispersals; an MT driver described it as a levelled earth strip with a relatively small hangar/workshop, and no storage for petrol or bombs, little more in fact than the flying fields in the early days of aviation.[45] It was, however, covered by two sets of observer corps telephone lines; since it could eventually receive the radar from Rangoon it was selected as the future base and a rear headquarters was opened on the 23rd. The mixed wing to be based there would comprise a Hurricane squadron, a Blenheim squadron and half an army co-operation squadron, together with the AVG, the size of force being determined by the amount of maintenance available, and to enable the fighters to support the Army to the south a series of landing strips was prepared for forward operations, their locations as far as possible kept secret. A second mixed wing was to be established at Akyab, and both wings would be directed and supported from Stevenson's new base organisation in India.[46] General Slim, who would take over as Corps Commander on 19 March, later reflected on this structure. A convinced believer in the necessity of land and air headquarters being co-located, he was dismayed to find that the Air Headquarters was in Calcutta, 500 miles from his HQ at Maymyo and unconnected by land, and that even the local Wing HQ at Magwe was 200 miles away. He accepted that paucity of resources made it inevitable, but his general point is important: 'Until 1945 this pull between the defence of Calcutta and the Burma campaign continued ... it hampered the free movement of air support in the area, and air commanders were compelled to keep looking over their shoulders'.[47]

Thus from late February onwards the RAF was preparing for the worst. On the 20th air transport was requested from India to fly most personnel to Akyab, whence they would continue by sea to India, and by early March 3,000 airmen had departed, most by air, some by sea.[48] The radar unit transferred to Magwe on 2 March, and on the 7th the headquarters known as 'X' Wing which had been controlling the air operations in defence of Rangoon was moved to Zigon, one of the temporary strips 60 miles south of Prome. The necessary demolitions at Mingaladon and the former headquarters were then carried out and before moving on to Magwe on the 11th 'X' Wing continued to patrol the area through which the Army was withdrawing. The units at Magwe[49] were now formed into Burwing and placed under General Alexander's operational control, while those at Akyab became Akwing.[50] Meanwhile AOC-in-C India (now Sir Richard Peirse) had met Stevenson and issued him his directive, and on 17 March Stevenson arrived in Calcutta to re-form his 221 Group Headquarters. He was now responsible not just for the two mixed wings but also for bombing and other operations in support of the Army in Burma and for the air defence of north-east India.[51]

So far so good. Rangoon had been safely evacuated without enemy air interference; the Army was withdrawing north unhindered; the fighters were providing the necessary protection despite the poor operating surfaces (at Zigon, for example, the Hurricane tail units gave way on one in every five landings); the bombers were attacking enemy troop concentrations, airfields and communications; constant reconnaissance was being undertaken; there was little enemy air activity. On the 20th, however, 50 Japanese aircraft (out of a total of 260 now available in Burma[52]) were reported at Mingaladon and Burwing asked to be allowed to attack them. Nine Blenheims of 45 Squadron and 10 Hurricanes of 17 Squadron took off next morning and despite a running battle with the Zeros (five were claimed shot down with four

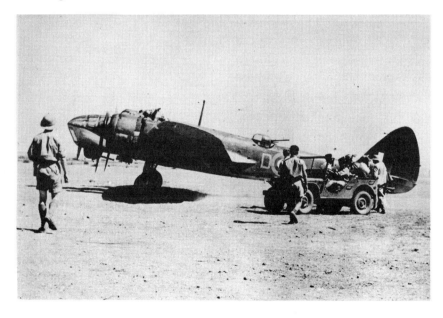

A Blenheim of 45/113 Squadron operating in Burma, early 1942. (*AHB*)

more probables) achieved considerable success against runways and parked aircraft for the loss of only two Hurricanes, though most attacking aircraft were damaged. A repeat raid was ordered for the afternoon.[53]

Now disaster struck. The Japanese had been uncertain about which airfields the RAF were using after the fall of Rangoon and also of the Allied air strength, and when after considerable photographic reconnaissance effort they realised the significance of Magwe they prepared to attack it at full strength.[54] The first raid, by 21 bombers escorted by 10 fighters, came in at 1330 – not as a reprisal but as the initial stage of a carefully planned assault. By 1430 two more waves, making 59 bombers and 24 fighters in all, had appeared. While the first wave had been detected, enabling four Hurricanes and six Tomahawks to intercept, the later ones could not be countered and six Blenheims and a Hurricane were destroyed on the ground. Desperate repair work continued all night but next morning two further waves attacked with virtually no opposition. Altogether, having mounted 113 bomber and 44 fighter sorties, the Japanese had destroyed nine Blenheims and damaged five more beyond quick repair. The remaining six, though operationally unserviceable, were still flyable and together with the 11 surviving Hurricanes (only three combat-worthy) had to be flown out to Akyab, while the last three Tomahawks went to Lashio. A final attack that afternoon completed the destruction of the already heavily damaged airfield. The report subsequently produced by the CO makes it clear that Magwe was unsuitable as an operational base – though more could have been done to make it so had there not been increasing difficulty in obtaining labour. As for early warning, the observer posts did all they could but amid growing confusion and damage to communications the system could not cope, and the radar not only suffered from a very low state of serviceability but was incorrectly sited. Essentially, however, under such a weight of carefully planned attack Magwe was always going to be overwhelmed; the Hurricanes and Tomahawks which had done so well over Rangoon could do no more.[55]

But while the decision to fly out the remaining aircraft was fully justifiable there are questions about the accompanying evacuation of the base itself. Plans for the move had been prepared in advance, but when Stevenson heard on the 23rd that the main parties had already started out for Lashio he ordered some of them, including the radar unit, to turn back. With the Army still engaging the enemy near Prome, 90 miles to the south, it seemed possible that the airfield might be repaired and returned to operational use; in any case it was needed for transport aircraft and there was much armament and equipment to salvage.[56] In practice, however, not much could now be done, and as Slim says, 'some hard things were said by the angry soldiery about the speed and disorder of the abandonment of Magwe'.[57] He himself had arrived there by air a few evenings earlier and been unimpressed at finding the airfield and its aircraft completely deserted. On eventually reaching the Wing HQ some miles away, he 'found everyone in good heart and cheer'. On suggesting that it was a bit rash to leave so many aeroplanes on a deserted airfield in the midst of a not too reliable population, he was told it was the Army's business to look after their safety.[58] Given such an atmosphere of complacency it may not be surprising that the immediate reaction to the Japanese attacks was to get out fast, but the decision is hard to justify. Almost certainly much more might have been done if the RAF had stayed longer, both for the restoration of the airfield and salvage of equipment, and charges of disorganised and premature evacuation would never have arisen.[59]

Yet quite a lot was in fact done. Corporal Ransom's experience as an MT driver both at Magwe and over the next six months reminds us not just of a unique episode in RAF history but also of the usually unsung contributions made by those who do not fly the aeroplanes. On 2 April he and nine other drivers were ordered to return from Lashio to Magwe to retrieve as many bombs, tail fins and long distance tanks as they could. That task complete they returned to try to move aviation fuel and ended up as the Army's only means of transport between Magwe and the fighting front. By 18 April – Magwe having fallen – they were back at Lashio, where they were ordered to try to shuttle bombs along the congested Burma Road. In early May they crossed into China, finding the Chinese lorry drivers a bigger menace than the enemy; they experienced the Japanese bombing of Paoshan; one of their number – an RAF policeman acting as a volunteer driver – was killed by a Chinese soldier; and when approaching the flimsy suspension bridge across the River Salween they watched radio vehicles too big to pass under an overhanging rock being pushed to the valley floor.[60] Their journey along the appalling roads continued via Kunming to Chengtu where they were to support the Chinese Air Force; eventually, after a long expedition to Lanchou, in north China, to collect aviation fuel, they returned to Kunming and were flown out to India in November 1942. They – like many other airmen from Burma – had coped with most unusual and difficult circumstances, and not least had done all their own vehicle maintenance – contrary to everything they had been told at the RAF driving schools about leaving the servicing to the mechanics.[61]

For Burwing, then, the destruction of Magwe marked the end for most practical purposes, some 350 of its survivors making their way to China and the rest being flown out to India. The enemy now turned their attention to Akwing, carrying out heavy raids on Akyab on 23, 24 and 27 March; in the last of these most of the Hurricanes were caught on the ground and destroyed, giving Stevenson no choice but to withdraw the Wing to Chittagong, while leaving behind a refuelling party to enable GR aircraft to use the airfield.[62] So within three weeks of the loss of Rangoon the Allied air force in Burma had been wiped out. In the absence of an effective warning system the large air striking force which the enemy had been able to move into Burma from Malaya had proved overwhelmingly superior,[63] and the RAF had been treated to yet another exhibition of the flexibility of Japanese air power. Yet strangely the enemy failed to exploit this air victory by turning their attention to the ground forces: instead they delivered a series of devastating attacks against the towns and cities in order to disrupt the public services.[64] While these certainly hindered the Army's withdrawal they did not stop it, and Alexander's forces suffered less from the absence of RAF support than they might have expected. As Slim says, the actual casualties inflicted by the enemy air force were surprisingly small, and he recognised that Wavell and Stevenson had had no choice but to withdraw, but in consequence, 'The Army in Burma must struggle on without an air force. There is no doubt that this was a right decision. But it was cold comfort to us'.[65]

Wavell, well aware of the situation, told the Prime Minister on 1 April that the Japanese complete command of the air was setting the commanders in Burma an extremely difficult task. Yet he felt obliged to tell Alexander that he had to conserve his resources for the air defence of north-east India, and the Chiefs of Staff supported him.[66] Nevertheless throughout April and May, by the end of which the Army had after heavy fighting extricated itself from Burma, the RAF in eastern India did what it could to help. Known from 20 April as Bengal Command (Stevenson now had 221 and 224 Groups under him, the former comprising the bombers, the latter the air defence fighters),[67] it mounted bomber operations whenever possible, and its attached transport squadron began to demonstrate many of the roles that would eventually prove so crucial to Burma's reconquest.

The Blenheims of 113 Squadron at Asansol could carry out a mere 40 ground support sorties in April but on 3 – 5 May they responded to Alexander's request for strikes on enemy vessels moving up the Irrawaddy and considerably delayed the Japanese advance at a critical stage.[68] The rest of the month saw a heartening increase in RAF activities (120 sorties), with the first Wellington squadron to arrive in India, No 215, making its initial contribution both in night bombing and supply dropping. The aircraft were elderly, the tarmac runway at Asansol was too short for take-off with full fuel and bomb loads, there were no good maps or modern navigation aids, the briefings were poor. Squadron Leader Archbold recalls that for an attack on Rangoon the briefing officer discovered the round trip was impossible and advised them to get back as far as possible and then ditch; the Navy would pick them up! Needless to say the mission was cancelled.[69] Among the targets they did attack were Magwe and Akyab (which had been evacuated on 4 May); operating alongside the Blenheims and a few USAAF B-17s they were already giving the Japanese some slight indication that they would no longer have everything their own way, and B-25s of the newly formed 3 PRU were also beginning to keep an eye on their activities with photographic reconnaissance,[70] whose total lack had hitherto been one of Slim's great regrets.[71]

Air transport, in which the USAAF shared, was for the RAF mainly the responsibility of 31 Squadron, a unit with a long tradition of service on the North-West Frontier. Equipped with DC-2s and DC-3s which had been donated by American businessmen, it had already contributed much to the Burma campaign, ferrying supplies and assisting with the evacuation, and by mid-April when the squadron began to operate from Dinjan, only five aircraft were serviceable. For the first fortnight they were able to operate to the northern airfield of Myitkyina, carrying supplies and personnel, and on 5 May a record 520 personnel, 367 of them casualties, were brought out. The next day, however, after several Dakotas were caught on the ground by enemy dive bombers and three destroyed, the airfield had to be abandoned; air evacuation was at an end.[72] As Kirby observes:

> After the fall of Mandalay, British and American aircrews defied every normal limit of payload in their endeavours to rescue as many as possible of the sick, wounded and refugees before the Japanese Army could close in upon the few airfields still remaining in Allied hands. In all, by the close of the campaign, 8,600 people, including 2,600 wounded, had been flown out by the Allied air forces.[73]

Now the task switched to supply dropping, partly to help the pitiable columns of refugees making their way to Assam along almost impassable mountain tracks. Since there were no special containers and few parachutes, some supplies were lost or damaged, but the all-out effort continued – on 13 May just two Dakotas were serviceable; they carried out seven sorties.[74] Louis Allen illustrates their value. Describing the experiences of a small British party trying to escape across the mountains he writes:

> The tiredness began to tell, the food to grow short, until they began to disbelieve the rumours of the RAF dropping rations. But they found new energy from the sound of large aircraft flying low over a village with a large open clearing ... for three days they fed a pitiful breadline of hundreds of Indians, including mothers with babies and young children: rice, condensed milk, tinned fruit, corned beef, packets of figs and dried apricots.[75]

Scenes like this are now commonplace; in May 1942 they were unheard of.

So air supply was beginning to demonstrate its potential, and over the next three years Burma would prove just what it could achieve. Of all the lessons of the first campaign in Burma this was the greatest, namely the possibility of air supply for an Army cut off from all other means of support.[76]

Danger in the Indian Ocean

We must turn now to the maritime scene, where the enemy had been presenting a very different kind of threat. By the end of February the damage inflicted on the Allied navies at Pearl Harbor, off Malaya and in the Java Sea had given the Japanese virtual naval supremacy, and the Chiefs of Staff realised that the Indian Ocean now lay open. Were the enemy to capture Ceylon they could imperil the sea communications not only to Australia and India but also to the Middle East, where Rommel was forcing the 8th Army back towards the Egyptian frontier.[77] With Malta under incessant air attack and a new German offensive likely in Russia this was a desperate time, and after the war Churchill was to call the prospect of a Japanese assault on Ceylon 'the most dangerous moment of the war'.[78] It was on 28 March, five days after the enemy had occupied the Andaman Islands and established an air base there, that intelligence gave warning that Admiral Nagumo's First Air Fleet – already so successful at Pearl Harbor – was headed towards Ceylon and would probably launch an air attack on 1 April.[79] Its intentions, as we now know, were limited, namely to knock out the Eastern Fleet and prevent its interference with the Burma operations, and to provide a demonstration of Japanese invincibility to the Indians at a time when Anglo-Indian political relations were far from easy,[80] but from the Allied side the potential dangers appeared much more far-reaching. Ever since the loss of Singapore the Chiefs of Staff had been exercised about the threat to Ceylon, though Wavell – the man on the spot – had tried to persuade them to concentrate the main defensive effort in north-east India; in his view Ceylon was unlikely to face anything more than hit-and-run attacks. The Chiefs, however, were insistent: the Eastern Fleet was to be built up (albeit largely with out-of-date ships), land forces were to be assembled, and a strong fighter force provided.[81]

Time, however, was desperately short, and not least for the RAF. Before the war little had been done other than start to build a permanent airfield at China Bay, on the north-east coast near the naval base at Trincomalee (Map 5),[82] and not until April 1941 was a local headquarters established in Colombo, its purpose to set up a number of island refuelling bases and to direct flying boat operations to

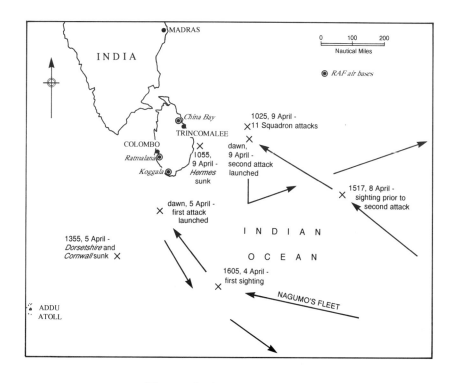

Map 5   Ceylon: April 1942

protect shipping against German commerce raiders. It was hoped eventually to provide four squadrons, but the two Catalinas of 205 Squadron that arrived soon afterwards at Koggala, a land-locked lagoon on the SW coast, were not reinforced until March 1942.[83] These apart, the RAF had nothing other than 273 Squadron's handful of aged biplanes, mainly Vildebeests – even though in September 1941 it had been given its own Group HQ, No 222.[84]

Virtually all the RAF aircraft needed to counter the Japanese threat therefore had to be brought in at short notice. First to arrive, on 23 February, were eight Hurricanes which had been erected in Karachi and were to re-form 258 Squadron. Then Pilot Officer Conway recalls how green were most of the pilots; most of the experienced men from his Wing, originally destined for south Russia, had gone on to Singapore, Java and Burma, leaving him and his colleagues in the Middle East awaiting aircraft.[85] Two more Hurricane squadrons, Nos 30 and 261, were flown off HMS *Indomitable* on 6 and 7 March, and the Chiefs of Staff told Wavell that all must remain there; they thought it right to issue definite instructions on this point in view of the fact that essential interests outside his Command were involved in the security of the island.[86] This injunction applied too to the Catalinas, including 205 Squadron's one survivor and the reinforcements beginning to arrive from Gibraltar and the UK. To complete the line-up were the Blenheim IVs of 11 Squadron which flew from the Middle East, but apart from a few Swordfish of the Fleet Air Arm these represented the only striking force; an urgent appeal for Beaufort torpedo bombers was turned down by the Chiefs of Staff.

So at the end of March the newly appointed AOC, Air Vice-Marshal J H D'Albiac, had just 50 serviceable Hurricanes, 14 Blenheims, six Catalinas and a few Fulmars. There were also two FAA Fulmar squadrons on the island.[87] They would face an attacking force of some 300 carrier-borne aircraft, yet even had more been available they could hardly have been accommodated. Apart from China Bay the only other usable airfield was the civil airport at Ratmalana, seven miles south of Colombo, and to provide an extra base nearby an airstrip was constructed across the city racecourse – entailing the demolition of several houses including that of the Chief Justice.[88] Used by 258 and 11 Squadrons it was never attacked, for the enemy were unaware of its existence. The other prime requirement was a radar system, about which Churchill himself requested a briefing. Portal replied on 27 February that eight sets were needed, all of which should be there by the end of March, though not all could be operational.[89] Squadron Leader Carter, who had escaped from Singapore, remembers the reality. Finding the dockside at Colombo jammed with stores and equipment that had been shipped from the UK intended for the Middle East, he was tasked with collecting the necessary items and using ex-Singapore radar personnel (there were none in Ceylon or India) to set up an MRU at Trincomalee. They succeeded – just – but a second installation at Colombo could not be made operational in time.[90]

March was indeed a busy month, not just for the RAF, and the effort was assisted when Admiral Layton – who having learnt the lessons of Singapore had urged the need for a single, all-powerful, central command[91] – was appointed Commander-in-Chief Ceylon, with all naval, military, air and civil authorities subject to his direction. For the first time the principle of unified command was being applied in an operational theatre, although – understandably under the circumstances – the single-service commanders remained under India Command for administrative purposes.[92] It was a great step forward.

The scene was now set for the Japanese attack (Map 5). This is not the place to discuss the naval operations in detail; suffice it to say that Admiral Somerville, who took over from Layton on 27 March, was under firm orders not to expose the Eastern Fleet to the risk of destruction. With but three carriers, all equipped with out-dated aircraft, and five battleships (four of them elderly) he could not face direct engagement with Nagumo's five fleet carriers and four modern battleships, nor must he be caught in harbour in Ceylon. If, however, he could use his Swordfish and Albacores by night he had a chance of successfully attacking the enemy. What he needed, therefore, was information about Nagumo's movements, something which only the Catalinas from Koggala could provide.[93] With no more than three of the six able to operate at any one time, the likely areas of approach were patrolled on 31 March and 1 April, when the attack was expected, but nothing was seen then or on the next two days. The Fleet now made for its island base at Addu Atoll,[94] arriving on the 4th, and given the course of subsequent events in and near Ceylon Somerville eventually decided to withdraw westwards.

The critical sighting was made at 1605 on the 4th by a Catalina of 413 Squadron that had reached Koggala from Pembroke Dock only two days before. The essential message could be only partly transmitted before the aircraft was attacked, and Squadron Leader L J Birchall and his crew spent the rest of their war as guests of the enemy.[95] They had, however, done their job – and it was to them that Churchill referred when speaking of his 'most dangerous moment':

> We were saved from this disaster by an airman on reconnaissance who spotted the Japanese Fleet and, though shot down, was able to get a message through to Ceylon ... he had made one of the most important single contributions to victory.[96]

An overstatement maybe, as we look back from longer perspective, but let nobody deny credit not just to Birchall and his men but to all their usually unsung colleagues in the world of aerial reconnaissance. Theirs were the eyes that made possible so much else.

Knowing now that the enemy fleet was 360 miles south-east of Ceylon, the AOC immediately ordered further Catalinas to the area, one of which – the survivor from Singapore – disappeared without trace, but although various sightings were reported the messages were confused. Nevertheless it was reasonably certain that the enemy would attack on the morning of the 5th (Easter Sunday, as it happened), and the Hurricanes were at readiness.[97] Unfortunately, however, the radar being installed near Ratmalana was not yet effective, and although the 120-strong enemy force (including 36 escorting Zeros) flew along the coast for half an hour before reaching Colombo no warning was received until they were sighted overhead. Consequently 30 Squadron was able to take off only as its airfield, Ratmalana, was coming under attack. 258 Squadron at the Racecourse was better placed, for its airstrip was unknown to the enemy, and its CO had the doubtful pleasure of telling Fighter Operations in Colombo what was happening. It should have been the other way round; D'Albiac, who having previously commanded in Greece was no stranger to disaster, was devastated at the failure of his communications.[98]

So, although 36 Hurricanes and six FAA Fulmars did get airborne, they were heavily outnumbered and at a tactical disadvantage. There was no co-ordination, the weather was bad, and while a series of low altitude dogfights developed the enemy was in general able to carry out his main attack on the port and city of Colombo methodically and efficiently (fortunately all seaworthy ships had already been got away as a result of Birchall's message, though the cruisers HMS *Dorsetshire* and HMS *Cornwall* were subsequently sunk in a separate attack). As might be expected in such a situation, the losses inflicted on the enemy were heavily exaggerated; altogether 27 aircraft were claimed destroyed by the air and ground defences, yet only three wrecks were found on land and the Japanese admitted to only two more. On the other hand 15 Hurricanes and four Fulmars were lost, and by the evening 30 and 258 Squadrons had only 16 aircraft serviceable.[99] It had not been a good day for the rapidly improvised defences, though the enemy had failed in their main object, namely to inflict a 'Pearl Harbor' on the Eastern Fleet.

Nor had it been a good day for the small striking force. Six FAA Swordfish (flying from China Bay to Ratmalana in preparation for a torpedo attack on the enemy fleet) were all shot down, and 11 Squadron's Blenheims – fortunately based at the Racecourse – were sent on a wild goose chase. A Catalina ordered to shadow the enemy aircraft back to their carriers lacked the speed to keep up, and on the strength of confused reports from other reconnaissance aircraft the squadron was despatched in the wrong direction, eventually having to return without catching a glimpse of the enemy.[100] To Churchill, closely following these events, this failure appeared reprehensible, and Portal – writing several days later – had to point out to him that it was not attributable to the squadron's lack of training or experience in maritime operations but to an SOS message sent in error by a Catalina. He went on to observe that the squadron had located the enemy carriers at its second attempt, on 9 April, losing five of its nine aircraft.[101]

This was the day when Nagumo launched his carrier aircraft against the naval base at Trincomalee and the nearby airfield at China Bay. The Catalina patrols had been continued and when part of the fleet was sighted 400 miles east of the island on the 8th, steering north-west, most of the ships – including the carrier HMS *Hermes* – were ordered to disperse at sea. At dawn on the 9th a Catalina was shot down just after it began transmitting its report, and at 0700 the radar at China Bay (only just operational) detected a large number of aircraft approaching at 90 miles range. There was thus time for 261 Squadron's 17 Hurricanes and 273 Squadron's six Fulmars to get airborne and for some to reach the height needed for the dive and zoom tactics needed to counter the manoeuvrability of the enemy aircraft. They were, of course, hopelessly outnumbered and eight Hurricanes and three Fulmars were lost; nevertheless 24 enemy aircraft were claimed destroyed, and the Japanese accepted that their losses were higher than at Colombo. Once again they inflicted considerable damage on the dockyard and airfield, but most ships escaped.[102]

Hermes, however, did not. She was spotted by enemy aircraft during the morning of the 9th and when the sighting report was intercepted at Colombo she was ordered to return to Trincomalee where fighter cover would be available. Unfortunately, partly as a result of the Japanese assault, communications between Colombo and Trincomalee had broken down and when *Hermes* came under air attack the surviving Hurricanes at China Bay, a mere 60 miles away, were blissfully unaware of the peril. Lacking her own aircraft, which had earlier been transferred ashore, *Hermes* was virtually defenceless. She lasted a mere 20 minutes.[103]

Meanwhile 11 Squadron had been ordered to try to hit back. This time the enemy fleet's position was known but it was also recognised that the attack would have to be made in daylight, against great odds in the air, and without fighter protection – 261 Squadron was already in action; the other squadrons were too far away. At 1025 the nine Blenheims selected their target, which proved to be Nagumo's flagship *Akagi*. They came in at 11,000 ft, already under attack from the patrolling Zeros, and their bombs straddled the carrier. Sadly they failed to hit her but under such conditions they had done remarkably well to come so close. Just four aircraft, all damaged, limped back to the Racecourse; their crews and the 17 men who did not survive, including the CO Squadron Leader K Ault, had delivered what Churchill called 'a heroic but forlorn attack against overwhelming odds' on Nagumo's Strike Force.[104] That afternoon the enemy departed, never to be seen again in strength in the Indian Ocean.

Theirs had been in many ways a highly successful mission, costing them a mere 17 aircraft,[105] but with Japan's resources now greatly stretched her high command rejected proposals for further westward expansion.[106] From hindsight the threat appears less serious than it did then, but it is not hard to understand why Churchill and his colleagues had been so anxious. For the RAF it was a small-scale affair lasting only a few days, but those who were there can be proud to have played their part at one of the war's great turning points. The main Japanese thrust to the west could go no further, and a mere two months later Nagumo's carriers would meet their end at the Battle of Midway.

6   Priorities and Preparations

Thus far this has been a gloomy tale. In a mere four months the Japanese had reached the doorsteps of India and Australia, and virtually the whole of South-East Asia and the islands of the western Pacific lay under their control. Moreover while all this had been happening there were ill tidings elsewhere. In the Mediterranean, as we have seen, the British forces in Libya were in retreat and Malta was under increasingly heavy attack; in the Battle of the Atlantic heavy shipping losses were being incurred and the escape of the German battle cruisers *Scharnhorst* and *Gneisenau* up the English Channel on 12 February (three days before the fall of Singapore) had severely injured British pride; many ships were being sunk in the Arctic convoys carrying supplies to the hard-pressed Russians; and in the bomber offensive against Germany there was growing evidence that much less damage was being caused than had been thought. These were dark days, and there would be worse as the year advanced. On the other hand, the USA was now in the war, and while this had the immediate disadvantage of reducing the flow of Lend-Lease supplies there was no doubt that eventually the application of America's immense power to the overall war effort would prove overwhelming.

Conflicting Priorities

For the present, however, hard decisions were needed. Portal had already identified the fundamental issue in a note written on 11 December 1941. There were two broad courses of action: (a) to try to reinforce the key points east of India so as to maintain them until sea and air power were re-established, even though this would mean weakening the position at home and in the Middle East, or (b) concentrate everything on the fight against Germany and Italy, ie. to send no reinforcements to the Far East but fight to the last with what was already there. It was too late for (a), so the right course was to accept that the position in the Far East might have to be abandoned and could only be restored after Germany was defeated and with American help. As he saw it:

103

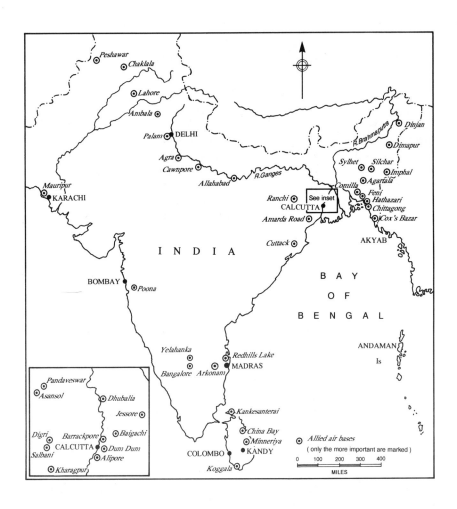

Map 6   India

The greatest danger in the present situation is that by trying to retrieve our position in the Far East we may lose the Middle East and control of the Atlantic and thus, in spite of the assistance of Russia, fail to defeat Germany.[1]

At the same time Portal had realised that political reasons might compel some form of compromise, and we have seen that attempts had to be made to reinforce Singapore, Burma and Ceylon; nevertheless the essential principle was clear and would continue to underlie not only British but also Allied policy. At the Washington Conference, shortly after the Japanese attack, any fears Churchill might have had of an American 'Asia first' strategy were quickly dispelled, the Chiefs of Staff making it clear on 23 December that in their view Germany was the key to victory.[2] It was to be 'Germany first'. So as we turn to the challenges facing the RAF in the aftermath of the Japanese victories let us bear in mind the underlying conviction of the Chief of Air Staff, as stated by his biographer: 'At all times he regarded Japan as an enemy who could be readily beaten once Britain and the United States could bring their full power to bear on her after the defeat of Germany'.[3]

Portal was absolutely right, but he also knew that the Far East war was not going to go away, and during February and March he and the other Chiefs of Staff were much involved in discussions about how to share the responsibility between the Americans and the British. With the pattern of the Japanese advance emphasising the division of the Pacific and Indian Oceans into distinct theatres it made good sense for the USA to take responsibility in the former and the United Kingdom the latter, and on 4 April the boundaries were agreed. For our purposes it will suffice to note that the British operational theatre covered India and the Indian Ocean and extended east to include Burma, Siam, Malaya, Singapore and Sumatra. Everywhere further east – including Australia and New Zealand – was to come under American command.[4]

This division did not, however, include China, whose situation introduced a significant complication in the Anglo-American relationship and was to impose a major constraint on RAF operations. At war with Japan since 1937, China had become increasingly dependent on supplies – mainly American – delivered via Rangoon and the Burma Road (p. 81), and in 1942 Britain and the USA regarded her continued involvement in the war as essential both for her own sake and for the large number of Japanese forces she could tie down. However, once the enemy had seized Rangoon and closed the Burma Road the sole means of maintaining a supply link was by air from India, and only the Americans had any hope of providing the necessary aircraft and their support. So with British agreement the 10th USAAF was assigned to the theatre and on 5 March 1942 General Brereton took command of the American air forces in India, establishing his headquarters in New Delhi. There followed a fairly slow but steady build-up of strength, enabling the new Assam-Burma-China Ferry Command to get the airlift under way, but as we shall see this growing USAAF operation imposed an immense extra strain on India's resources. Moreover the airlift was later extended not only to support General Chennault's new 14th USAAF which operated alongside the Chinese from 1943 onwards, but also in 1944/45 to supply a force of B-29s which would fly via advanced bases in China to attack strategic targets in Manchuria and Japan.[5]

The Americans were thus mainly interested in India as a base both to support the Chinese and for further strategic operations, and the British – especially the RAF – always needed to take their presence and their interests closely into account. On the other hand, while fully supporting the American aims, the British were anxious to try to regain their South-East Asian empire, so the reconquest of Burma was seen also as the necessary preliminary to the invasion of Malaya and the recapture of Singapore. There was a long way to go, however, before this could happen, partly because the needs of the Far East were so far down the priority list, and partly because so much preparation had to be done.

Peirse's Challenge

On the RAF side the responsibility lay on the shoulders of Air Marshal Sir Richard Peirse (Air Chief Marshal from September 1942), one of the RAF's most experienced commanders. A naval airman in the First World War he had held several posts in the Air Ministry, including those of DCAS and VCAS, before taking over Bomber Command in October 1940. During 1941, when his Command's performance inevitably fell short of expectations, Peirse had to bear some of the criticisms;[6] nevertheless Sinclair and Portal had no doubt that he was the right man for the Far East. Minuting Churchill on 10 December Sinclair wrote:

> Peirse possesses not only recent experience in command, but also a wide background of war knowledge and high staff experience. He is loyal, able and hard-working, and would be a strong support to C-in-C India. If you approve this proposal, I suggest he be succeeded in Bomber Command by Air Marshal Harris.[7]

At the same time Sinclair suggested an alternative plot whereby Air Marshal Barratt, currently at Army Co-operation Command, might go to the Far East and Peirse replace Tedder in the Middle East, but he

Air Chief Marshal Sir Richard Peirse, KCB DSO AFC, accompanies the Prime Minister during a meeting in Baghdad in August 1942. (*Air Vice-Marshal Sir Richard Peirse*)

made it clear that his preference for Wavell's staff was Peirse. Churchill was content. Yet soon afterwards the American President urged Peirse's replacement by one of their officers, General Brett, in command of the combined air forces in ABDACOM. Brett himself, however, objected to the unsettling effect of such a drastic change,[8] and Portal – suspecting that this move was connected with the controversy in the USA about the formation of a separate air force – reinforced his support for Peirse in another minute to Churchill, stressing among other things his practical war experience.[9] As it turned out ABDACOM was to be short-lived and on 2 March Peirse arrived in New Delhi from Java to take command of the air forces in India and Ceylon.

The situation he found was depressing in the extreme. As he wrote to Portal in May:

Everything in India is unbelievably primitive – the totally inadequate staff and complete lack of most things essential is quite devastating, and much of the personnel is past praying for – the government of India is an Alice in Wonderland hierarchy.[10]

At the same time he told Sinclair that two months previously there had been no air force in India except a collection of museum pieces and an AHQ headquarters organisation which would have made a loss if it

Sir Richard Peirse in informal conversation with Air Vice-Marshal T M Williams OBE MC (*centre*) and Air Marshal Sir John Baldwin KBE CB DSO, 1943. (*Air Vice-Marshal Sir Richard Peirse*)

had tried to run a perambulator hire service.[11] This Air Headquarters, as he later described it, consisted of a mere 30 officers many of whom had been in India for some years, and was clearly incapable of solving one to say nothing of the incredible number of problems which presented themselves with bewildering rapidity. In contrast the Army Headquarters had more than this number of major-generals and above, supported by countless brigadiers and lower ranks, and few of them even knew where Air Headquarters was. Yet, almost overnight, Peirse went on, the Air Force in India had emerged from an ill-considered trifle – rather less important to the General Staff than a mule transport company – to be a major factor in its defence. It had taken its place beside the sorely tried Royal Navy as their only hope of saving India.[12] The new C-in-C was not a man to pull his punches.

To set the scene we need to look back for a moment. Unlike in other overseas areas such as Iraq and Aden, where the RAF had been made responsible for air control operations between the wars, in India the RAF had always remained subordinate to the Army, its funding met from the Indian military budget and its operations under Army tactical control. These had been entirely concentrated in the area of the North-West Frontier, where a handful of outmoded aircraft had carried out tribal operations in co-operation with land columns, and modernisation was thought unnecessary. Then, when war broke out in 1939 and Russia was being increasingly perceived as a possible attacker, it was too late, for the up-to-date equipment now thought desirable was all required elsewhere. The net result was that the seven squadrons of 1939 (one Blenheim, one Valentia, two Wapiti and three Audax) were still seven in December 1941 (one Mohawk, one Audax, one Lysander, one DC-2, plus three Audax and Lysander squadrons of the Indian Air Force), with the addition of six VR coastal defence flights operating Valentias.[13] By comparison Singapore was well defended.

Admittedly when an attempt had been made in August 1940 to draw up an overall plan for the defence of India against all threats a force of 21 squadrons had been postulated but this was seen as long term. Throughout 1940 India was low on the priority list for aircraft and equipment, and attempts to manufacture aircraft locally came to naught. 1941 was even worse, as the squadrons were forced to watch their machines become increasingly obsolescent and their efficacy as an air striking force grow progressively less.[14] Morale inevitably suffered. Officers and men felt the war was passing them by; they were a forgotten force, unable even to train for modern warfare. The then AOC-in-C, Air Marshal Sir Patrick Playfair, wrote to CAS in June 1941 warning him that while morale in India was not bad he should understand the difficulties likely to arise if units could not be given more definite promises about the prospect of getting modern aircraft and equipment.[15]

The position was no better as regards airfields. In 1939 there were just four reasonable ones, all in the north-west and none possessing a runway longer than 1,100 yards, and despite the urgings of the Air Ministry very little was done until Japan entered the war. Then orders were given for the construction of 25 airfields in the north-east, but progress was slow and in March 1942 only 16 existed with all-weather runways throughout the whole of India.[16] Moreover there was not a single radar unit and no observer posts except in the north-west.[17] As for maintenance and supply, the only unit was in Karachi, once again reflecting the north-western orientation of the RAF's activities. We can sympathise with Peirse as he faced this deplorable state of affairs, knowing that his defences needed to be directed towards the east and well aware from his short time in Java of the enemy's capabilities.

To appreciate the immensity of his task we need to consider briefly the sub-continent from which the RAF must now prepare to operate (Map 6). India was not a highly industrialised nation, her great natural resources were only on the fringe of development, and while she had enormous amounts of unskilled labour there were few men with technical skills.[18] The industrial base essential for the support of a large modern air force did not exist, and although much would in time be done to develop it the RAF's main requirements would mostly have to be imported (not to mention those of the Army). So not only must the airmen come from far afield but also the aircraft, most of the engineering and transport requirements, much of the fuel and many raw materials. Since the Mediterranean and Suez Canal route was effectively closed until late 1943 the much longer Cape route had to be used, and on average it took four months for goods to travel from the USA or UK to the users in India. The Indian build-up therefore depended heavily on the availability of ships, and the heavy losses of Allied merchant vessels in 1942 and early 1943 seriously affected British and American strategy in all theatres. As Churchill wrote: 'Shipping was at once the stranglehold and sole foundation of our war strategy'.[19]

Then there was the matter of internal transportation. India was a huge country – from Karachi to Calcutta, for example, was almost as far as from London to Moscow – and 90% of the internal traffic was carried by the already heavily laden railway system. This was now to be stretched much further, with shortages of rolling stock and especially locomotives the critical factors, and the almost total dependence on the railways was to prove a major constraint on the airfield and other major construction programmes, and on the subsequent supply systems. The problems were particularly acute in the all-important north-eastern area, with its many waterways; the existing communications were very poor, complicated by a different rail gauge and the absence of bridges over the River Brahmaputra, and all routes to the battle areas were long, slow and of limited capacity.[20]

Building the Infrastructure

In this situation airfield construction was bound to be fraught with difficulty, yet it was absolutely essential not just for the future conduct of military operations but also for internal communications, and in March 1942 a plan to build no fewer than 215 airfields at a cost estimated at £50 million was given top priority – subject only to the requirements for concentrating troops and the needs of actual operations. In the absence of an RAF works directorate the construction was directed by the Engineer-in-Chief at GHQ India, usually working through the regional public works departments who employed local civilian contractors. The Army engineers did a magnificent job amidst an administrative nightmare. There were few RAF and Army officers with the qualifications needed to select sites which were suitable both operationally and geologically, vast amounts of materials had to be obtained and transported over access roads which were often extremely bad, the necessary building machinery and

The construction of a new bomber base at Digri in 1942/43 was a
labour-intensive affair. (*Lucian Ercolani*)

mechanical transport were scarce and hard to maintain, there were
few Indian engineers with the skill, experience and drive needed for
such work, and progress was often hindered by the venality of local
contractors. Moreover the inefficiency and lack of enterprise were most
marked in eastern India where the need was greatest.

Yet despite the many difficulties this enormous programme was
carried through largely as planned. While the need for airfields in the
north-east was always paramount many were also envisaged for the
rest of India, some to counter possible threats from the north-west,
some for coastal protection, some to provide internal communications
and permit the redeployment of operational squadrons within the
country, some to cater for training, maintenance and aircraft storage.
As time went on part of the planned construction in the west and
north-west was abandoned, whereas the increasing scale of offensive
operations in the north-east, coupled with the growing needs of the
USAAF,[21] necessitated a larger programme in that area; moreover the
decision to conduct operations throughout the monsoon period meant
that some of the fair-weather airfields had to be developed to

all-weather standards. The net result was that by November 1943 some 140 airfields were complete in all respects, each with two all-weather runways and accommodation for two squadrons, 64 more had one all-weather runway and 71 had fair-weather strips: 275 in all.[22] Given all the circumstances it was a remarkable achievement; at one point over a million men were engaged on it. Inevitably many other projects – military as well as civil – suffered as a result. Nevertheless the concentration of effort on these airfields was of vital importance, for without them air superiority over the Japanese, so necessary for the successful conduct of the war, was unattainable.[23]

Before leaving this subject we must remind ourselves of all the facilities that also had to be built in: electrical power, water supply, operations rooms, communications, aircraft servicing, domestic accommodation, catering, medical, weapons storage, fuel – to mention just a few of the many services essential to the functioning of an operational base. All needed to be provided even though often at the most basic level. None was more important than the supply of aviation fuel, most of which had to come from Abadan, in the Persian Gulf, by tanker and then by rail or eventually by pipeline to bulk fuel installations, each sited so that it could supply a number of airfields.[24] Other services too required their support organisations, to which we must now turn.

Up to 1942 the RAF Depot at Karachi had met the main needs of the small force in NW India: aircraft erection and storage, airframe, engine and ancillary repairs, and equipment supply. Now, however, this was far too small and in the wrong place, and a new main supply unit – subsequently 320 MU – was opened at Allahabad, half way between Delhi and Calcutta. At the same time base repair facilities were expanded first by drawing in existing RAF units at Lahore and Ambala and then by taking over several Indian railway workshops. This local organisation for third-line repair and maintenance was gradually expanded until in late 1943 there were four RAF and seven civilian MUs, the latter having RAF supervisors on their staff. Aircraft erection and storage was another expanding task; many aircraft arrived by sea badly corroded, most had to be parked in the open where they were exposed to the extremes of heat and humidity, and much modification had to be done – most notably on the Vultee Vengeance which needed extensive work to render it suitable for tropical use. The many airmen who beavered away in these units in often very exhausting conditions deserve their tribute: by the end of 1943 they were serving some 60 squadrons and looking after 500 non-operational aircraft, and thanks in large measure to their efforts aircraft serviceability had risen to almost 80% from the 40% of June 1942.[25] The front line would not have existed without them.

Nor would it have got far without signals facilities; the units in

Bengal in early 1942 had found themselves without the most elementary means of communicating with each other or with higher formations, but by April work was being set in hand. One of the urgent needs was for point-to-point links; the local landline services were rudimentary and virtually useless, despite urgent requests for teleprinters few arrived and they rarely worked, and wireless telegraphy had to provide the primary links between major units, with Air Formation Signals furnishing the local line communications. By September a comprehensive signals plan had been prepared for the whole of India and Ceylon, and W/T links between the various headquarters and airfields remained at the heart of it, though plans were now to be prepared for a defence teleprinter network and a mass of new speech circuits involving the construction of 35,000 miles of twin-wire line and the building of nine communications centres. This was, however, to be a long time coming, and throughout 1943 W/T point-to-point systems continued to bear the brunt of the signals traffic.[26]

Just as important was the need for an air defence system. Squadron Leader Carter, whom we have already met in Singapore and Colombo, found himself in Bombay in early April, sent there on the verbal instructions of the newly arrived Command Radio Officer to set up the Radio Installation and Maintenance Unit. Finding the civilian authorities unwilling to allow a 24-year-old officer the use of three newly built factories and the local army commander unprepared to requisition without written authority from AHQ in Delhi, he used his own temporary status on the AHQ staff to write himself a letter instructing him to ask the authorities to requisition, as a matter of urgency, the necessary accommodation. This was unorthodox staffwork to say the least but he got away with it. A convoy carrying radar equipment and 500 personnel arrived a few days later, a COL unit was quickly erected just in case the Japanese fleet should appear off Bombay, and the RIMU began the task it would continue for the rest of the war of preparing radars for the operational areas and designing and manufacturing tropical modifications.[27] In this particular episode – as with so many others in those early days in India – initiative, improvisation and rule-bending were the keys to success.

The outcome was that 52 radars were operational in India and Ceylon by the end of 1942, together with seven filter rooms to co-ordinate their plots. At the same time operations rooms were being set up at Calcutta and in Ceylon, and combined operations and intelligence centres at AHQ and the operational groups. Thus with the addition of an Indian Observer Corps network around Calcutta and the neighbouring industrial areas a proper system of plotting and recording the tracks of enemy aircraft was well in hand, and coincidentally fighter control was being improved. Initially only HF equipment had been available but by December 1942 VHF was appearing, being fitted first to the Hurricanes defending Calcutta. Development continued apace throughout 1943 and by December wireless communication and radar equipment, both air and ground, was approaching the standard of other theatres.[28] A bland statement this, concealing a vast amount of work, often highly skilled, under usually very difficult circumstances.

It is worth reminding ourselves of just what the conditions were like in India at this time, as the work we have been describing was being set under way. The months of early 1942 were the hottest for many years; work on the airfields was impossible after 10.0 am; seven airmen died out of 200 taken ill from heat exhaustion at Allahabad; in the air at 1,000 feet it was even hotter; and all were rendered less efficient by the torture of prickly heat and auxiliary torments such as the myriad flies, foot rot and dhobi's itch. Then came the monsoon at the end of May – a grey-blue horizon marching across the Gangetic plain, becoming grey-black and each moment growing darker until the wind mounted to a gale. Yet the storm, when it came, brought no respite from the heat.

In this and in the coming monsoons which the men were to endure in India and Burma, they would find that the period June to October was one of prolonged misery and discomfort for newcomers, the type of misery that comes from working in stinging downpours with inadequate tools, and then, on going to bed dog-tired, finding camp-beds and blankets as wet as the air they breathe. For months on end the men bore these conditions – inevitably shortages worsened, extending to armour, aircraft tools, spares, men, to everything in fact except the men's sense of humour. At the outposts there were neither books to read nor hurricane lamps to read them by in the long nights. So men lay sweating under their mosquito nets, talking across the tent until there was nothing left to talk about.

For the survivors of the Burma retreat and of Malaya, as well as those who were fresh from Britain and the temperate Empire, these conditions might have combined with the general atmosphere of defeat to form a mood of unbearable depression, yet it was never like that.

From each smallest unit the reports were similar – too much to do and too few men with whom to do it, too little equipment, not enough to drink or to eat or to smoke, not enough of anything except heat and rain and dysentery, dengue and malaria. And yet, they said, it would be all right. The men would see it was all right.[29]

It was Squadron Leader Stephen, who went through Singapore and Java and then flew Hurricanes with 146 Squadron in India, who first drew my attention to these extracts from *Wings of the Phoenix*, stating that he thought its appreciation of the men's attitude and morale at that time was about right. In his view two factors contributed: the forward rush of the Japanese armed forces had run out of steam, at least temporarily, and the essential reinforcements for the build-up of the RAF were now to be seen in both hardware and personnel. We have considered some of the many types of support that were included in these reinforcements; it is time now to turn to the front line.

Expanding the Front Line

Notwithstanding the 'Germany first' policy, the Chiefs of Staff were in no doubt that India Command must be greatly strengthened both for the defence of India and Ceylon and for the eventual reconquest of Burma, and in March 1942 they set the RAF target as 64 squadrons, plus one transport squadron (note: only one!) and a PRU; later in the year the figure was raised to 83.[30] On the other hand it was soon clear that Peirse's force would be nowhere near the front of the queue in terms of quality, and certainly not as far as bombers were concerned. Yet there were those in London who were sceptical about the concentration of so much RAF effort on the bombing of Germany: on 25 February, for example, the Dominions Secretary, anxious about the Indian Ocean situation and doubtless aware of the criticisms of Bomber Command's performance, asked the Prime Minister for heavy bombers to be sent to India and Ceylon, expressing the view that the Air Ministry were inclined to be too rigidly devoted to the policy of bombing Germany.[31] Portal, while pointing out the value of the offensive against Germany (Harris had just been appointed to direct it), indicated the immense problems of operating heavy bombers in such a theatre and stressed the value of the smaller bombers being sent.[32] Then in April, stung into action by the recent events in Ceylon, Wavell entered the fray:

> It certainly gives us furiously to think when, after trying with less than 20 light bombers to meet an attack which has cost us three important warships and several others and nearly 100,000 tons of merchant shipping, we see that over 200 heavy bombers attacked one town in Germany.[33]

Churchill too believed there was a need for heavy bombers and told Roosevelt on the 15th that while Britain was sending every suitable aircraft to the East which could be efficiently serviced out there, this would be insufficient without American reinforcements of their 14

B-17s already in India.[34] However, when Attlee went so far as to propose the transfer of Bomber Command to India and the Middle East, he replied that it would be 'no use flying out squadrons which would sit helpless and useless when they arrived. We have built up a great plan here for bombing Germany, which is the only way in our power of helping Russia. One has to be sure that we do not ruin our punch here without getting any proportionate advantage elsewhere.'[35]

Yet the Prime Minister was still somewhat ambivalent. Two days later he sent Portal a paper which had been written at his request by Admiral Lyster of the Naval Staff and which set out the steps that would be needed to establish a force of Halifaxes and Stirlings to attack Japanese warships, transports and other shipping in the Bay of Bengal and to the south and west of India. Mindful not only of the needs of Bomber Command but also of the ever-mounting pressures of the Battle of the Atlantic, Portal minced no words in his reply. Stressing the formidable difficulties and observing that it would take seven months to fit 200 aircraft with ASV radar or to modify them for torpedo-carrying, he went on: 'It is extremely uneconomical to introduce drastic modifications urgently into existing types of aircraft. The whole flow of production is held up and large numbers of aircraft prevented from taking an active part in the war'.[36] Totally impracticable as such ideas were they demonstrate the deep anxiety felt about the Far East situation in the early months of 1942 and the need for Portal and his staff to keep cool heads. Responding to the pressure from India, where on 14 April Wavell, Somerville and Peirse had sent an urgent joint demand for air reinforcements, the Chiefs indicated on the 16th that some heavy bombers, ie. Liberators, were being sent, together with Wellington medium bombers, but there would be no Halifaxes.[37]

So India Command would for a long time have to make do, as far as heavy bombers were concerned, with one squadron of Liberators (No 159), which arrived at Salbani, west of Calcutta, in September 1942. They first operated over Burma two months later but could not be used in quantity for lack of spares and ground equipment. The heavy bomber needed a well developed industrial hinterland more than any other type of aircraft, and not until 1944, when a complex supply system with second and third line servicing echelons had been established, did the employment of heavy bombers on the Burma front on any scale become a practicable proposition.[38] How right Portal had been in 1942.

Meanwhile a small force of Wellingtons was built up for night bomber operations; although the mainstay of Bomber Command in 1941/42 the Wellington was now gradually being superseded in Europe, but having shown its value in North Africa it clearly had a role also in the Far East. The first squadron (215) arrived in April 1942, followed

In 1943 the RAF depended largely on the Wellington for bomber operations: this one, at Digri, belonged to 99 Squadron. (*Lucian Ercolani*)

by 99 Squadron six months later, and in 1943 they became 175 Wing at Jessore, north-east of Calcutta, where their Mark 1c aircraft were later replaced by more powerful versions.

The rest of the bomber force in 1942/43 comprised a handful of squadrons of the Far East's faithful Blenheims. The two squadrons that had emerged from Burma, re-equipped with the Mark IV, constituted the main strike force and with the addition of some Bisleys (Blenheim derivatives) there were five squadrons by April 1943. Then came a most important change, prompted by a shortage of Blenheims and the availability of a substantial reserve of Hurricanes, namely the conversion of these squadrons to Hurricane fighter bombers.[39] As already well proven in the Western Desert, the Hurricane in this role, coupled with ground strafing, was a good weapon for army support and would quickly demonstrate its value. Alongside it would be a new type of light bomber, the American-built Vengeance. Substantial numbers of these arrived in 1942 but as we have seen they needed a long procession of trials and modifications, including re-design of the fuel systems, to bring them up to operational standard. Consequently, while Vengeance squadrons were being formed in late 1942 it was another year before the first three were able to join the front line. For the next year or so the Vengeance was the standard light bomber in the Command and could claim the highest serviceability rate of any operational aircraft.[40] A sergeant who served with 45 Squadron as a wireless and electrical mechanic recalls the Vengeance as the RAF's first purpose-built dive bomber, capable of operating in a vertical dive and thus extremely robust; it had a crew of two and carried three pairs of .30 guns and up to 2,000 lbs of bombs.[41]

A Vengeance squadron of the Royal Indian Air Force. (*IAF over Burma*)

Turning to the fighter defences, the critical north-eastern area hitherto looked after solely by 5 Squadron's Mohawks was quickly reinforced by six squadrons of Hurricanes, including three that had been re-equipped after fighting in Burma – one of them 67 Squadron from Singapore. By the end of 1942 there were three more, plus a second Mohawk squadron, all 11 located around Calcutta or further east along the forward defence line to the north of Chittagong.[42] Together with the three squadrons still based in Ceylon this was a fair-sized force, and even before the start of the monsoon in May their build-up had been spared interference by the Japanese. This had been a trying time for the pilots as they sweltered in the heat waiting for the 'scramble' warnings that never came and then endured the trials of the monsoon months, but those summer months had witnessed an air force renaissance in Calcutta as men arrived from all over the world to man the depleted squadrons. Moreover as the newcomers from home – including those experienced in combat with the Luftwaffe – listened to the talk of the old-timers from Singapore, Palembang, Java and Burma,

they gained a deep respect for the qualities of Japanese airmen. They hated them for their arrogance, their atrocities and calculated brutalities ... but they admired their fighting ability. Japanese airmen possessed none of the caricaturists' attributes

... their aircraft were more manoeuvrable ... they were not unoriginal; their tactics were excellent. While their aircraft lacked self-sealing tanks and carried no protective armour for their crews, they compensated by having little regard for their own lives.[43]

There was thus emerging a more accurate appreciation of Japanese qualities in the air; the dividends would start to appear when the action resumed, and even more so when in October 1943 the last Mohawks were withdrawn and the first Spitfires appeared – undoubtedly the greatest single step in the modernisation of the air forces in India.[44]

These were not in fact the first Spitfires to arrive in the Far East. Back in June 1942, prompted by several Japanese air attacks on Darwin, in north Australia, arrangements had been put in hand to send a Spitfire squadron to assist in its air defence, and from December 1942 until the end of the war 54 Squadron operated with the RAAF, joining in the interception of the continuing enemy raids and later helping to take the offensive. Thus was provided some recognition of the fact that the RAAF, while providing a massive contribution alongside the RAF in the European war, had home defence problems of its own.

Meanwhile in India the build-up of the day fighter force was accompanied in January 1943 by the arrival from the Middle East of a flight of AI Beaufighters (soon to become 176 Squadron) to take over the night fighter defence of Calcutta. Hitherto this had been provided by Hurricanes, but the better speed, ceiling and technical equipment of the Beaufighters, combined with the greatly improved warning system that had been installed, brought the city's air defence up to a standard comparable in quality, if not in quantity, with that of the United Kingdom. Another Beaufighter squadron (No 27), equipped for low-level strike operations against enemy lines of communications, appeared at the same time, followed in September by 177 Squadron, and as their strength built up and they gained experience they would play a major role in the war of attrition.[45]

For maritime air operations and photographic reconnaissance, too, there were great improvements. The Catalina force, required to patrol the vast areas of ocean extending from the Arabian Sea to the Andaman Islands, was built up by mid-1943 to six squadrons including one Dutch (No 321) and one Canadian (No 413); Hudson squadrons carried out the task of general reconnaissance over the Bay of Bengal until switched to transport duties in later 1943; a Beaufort squadron (No 217) became operational as a torpedo and reconnaissance unit in June 1942, replacing the unsuitable Blenheims; and in February 1943 the first GR Liberators of 160 Squadron arrived, followed by a

Wellington GR squadron (No 203). As for PR, 681 Squadron's long-range work was initially done by Mitchells taken over from the Dutch and its short-range operations by Hurricanes; then in November 1942 came the first PR Spitfires, followed nine months later by Mosquitos,[46] at which point 684 Squadron was formed for the long-range tasks.

Last but not least we come to air transport, more important than in any other theatre of war owing to the huge distances involved and the great problems of land communications. From the RAF viewpoint, nothing contributed more towards making India a base for offensive operations than the development of an organisation capable of handling large numbers of transport aircraft, unless it was the building up of the squadrons themselves. Moreover, unlike all the other uses of air power where there was already a great body of practical experience to draw upon, air transport was the role in which India Command would have to work things out largely for itself. In essence there were three tasks: to provide air supply in support of the land operations on the India-Burma border, to move mail, important persons and urgent freight throughout India, and to enable the operational squadrons to be rapidly reinforced. The build-up was, however, to be seriously delayed by the lack of transport aircraft, all of which had to come ultimately from the USA since British aircraft production was entirely concentrated on combat types. In November 1942 General Irwin, GOC India, appreciating that the future of the war in Burma lay with transport aircraft, urged Wavell to press for a force of 150 such planes, to which Wavell replied:

> I only wish I could get you more. They do not appear to be making any at all at home and we are entirely dependent on the Americans, who also appear to be in short supply; at any rate they are not producing many for us, and the prospect is not encouraging.[47]

Indeed it was not; a year later there were still only five squadrons. The critical air supply task over the Burma front remained the preserve of 31 Squadron's Dakotas, whose original worn-out aircraft had flown to their limits during the Burma retreat and evacuation; and the internal air services which had first been provided by the Hudsons of 194 Squadron were now handled by 353 Squadron, the route mileage having risen from 5,000 per week in December 1942 to 37,000 a year later. An airman who regularly flew in a Hudson as a 'flying fitter' remembers carrying supplies round every part of India, often using very primitive landing grounds, and – in liberal interpretation of the rule book – using his own initiative to make repairs and keep his aircraft flyable.[48] The other three transport squadrons, all flying

Dakotas, were engaged on airborne training in north-west India, organised as 177 Wing and preparing to move forward together once their training was complete. The third transport role, aircraft reinforcement, was the responsibility of 179 Ferry Wing based at Karachi, which organised the flow of all aircraft within the Command.[49]

Altogether by November 1943 India Command had 2,820 aircraft on its books, compared with 426 in April 1942.[50] Of these many were being erected or were in transit or were under repair, and many more were in non-operational flying units, so the front-line strength of 52 squadrons at the end of the year (Appendix C) actually comprised 672 aircraft, most of them reasonably modern. To complete the picture the 10th USAAF now had 18 squadrons in India comprising four B-24 (Liberator equivalent), four B-25 (Mitchell), two C-47 (Dakota) and eight fighter.[51]

One other component of the air forces in India needs a mention here, namely the Royal Indian Air Force, which at the end of 1943 provided one of the operational Hurricane squadrons and several more (Vengeance and Hurricane) which were still working up. Unlike the Indian Army the small Indian Air Force (it became 'Royal' on 1 April 1943) had always been completely Indian: no European could hold a commission in it and although up to early 1942 RAF officers had commanded IAF units from then on this practice ceased. Unfortunately, however, there were few Indian officers suitable for important commands and with serious problems of recruiting and training it proved very difficult to bring the RIAF squadrons up to modern operational standards, even though they were often given a stiffening of RAF personnel. Nevertheless it was hoped that the RIAF would be able to take a proper part in the campaign that lay ahead.[52]

All this – the construction of the airfields, the development of the supply and maintenance organisation, the provision of communications, the installation of the radar system, the building up and modernisation of the front line – took place over a period of little more than 18 months; it amounted to the creation of a whole operational air force virtually from scratch, at the end of long and vulnerable supply lines, during a period when the competition for resources nearer home was almost overwhelming. The demands of the Battle of the Atlantic were never more pressing than in early 1943; the campaign to clear the Axis from North Africa was a dominant feature of the same period and was followed by the invasion of Sicily and Italy; the build-up of the combined bomber offensive against Germany was attracting high priority; and underlying all else were the immensely complex preparations for the eventual assault on north-west Europe. It was against this background that Peirse and his staff – all too often largely forgotten back in the United Kingdom – had to labour, and theirs was no mean achievement.

The Command Structure

One of Peirse's earliest tasks was to devise a new and expanded command structure (Appendix E). Up to March 1942 there had been only two Group Headquarters, No 222 at Colombo (p. 98) and No 1 (Indian) at Peshawar, controlling operations on the North-West Frontier. While these continued, the latter becoming 223 Group, another operational group, No 225, was formed at Bangalore to take charge of the whole of peninsular India – probably the largest land area covered by any group in the world, and at that time possessing fewer aircraft than any other. Two support groups were also established: No 227 Group at Lahore became responsible for all training in the Command, including that of the IAF, and 226 Group at Karachi took over all the supply and maintenance tasks.[53]

The critical area, however, was in the north-east, where Stevenson had re-formed HQ 221 Group from Rangoon in March. Soon afterwards 221 Group was assigned responsibility for the bomber and general reconnaissance operations and a new 224 Group took over fighter operations, but Peirse and Stevenson quickly realised how difficult it would be to control these two groups from the main headquarters in Delhi, 850 miles away. Given the dreadful state of the communications it seemed essential that the direct control of the operational groups should be exercised from an advanced headquarters in Calcutta, located alongside the local army, naval and civilian authorities.[54] On 19 April AHQ Delhi therefore announced the formation of AHQ Bengal. The Air Ministry, which had not been consulted over this unorthodox innovation, objected strongly, informing the AOC-in-C that his new organisation was unnecessary for a force of the present size.[55] The subsequent exchanges are worth summarising, for they indicate clearly how wide was the gap in thinking between London and Delhi and just how much Peirse knew he had to do – and how determined he was to do it.

On 4 May he signalled the Air Ministry pointing out that he was trying to create an air force and a defence system in an area four-and-a-half times the size of Great Britain, and at the same time to resist an enemy who was on the doorstep. By 1 August he would have 25 squadrons and his group organisation was the minimum needed to meet an exceptional and grave situation. London remained adamant and on the 17th Peirse again signalled, insisting on his freedom to organise his forces in the manner he and his staff considered would offer the best prospect of creating a fighting organisation. He went on:

Since, however, it seems clear that Air Ministry is in better position to judge the defence needs of India than I am, it is plain that the alternatives are either to withdraw me and conduct matters from Whitehall or to relieve me by someone possessing a modicum of operational ability.

The reply from VCAS (Air Chief Marshal Sir Wilfrid Freeman) was couched in even sharper language and indicated that the Inspector General (Air Chief Marshal Sir Edgar Ludlow-Hewitt) was being asked to adjudicate. Peirse now decided to write direct to Portal and remind him of just what he and his staff were trying to do. They were attempting to evolve a fighting organisation in north-east India out of little or nothing in order to support the Army being driven out of Burma, to provide a miniature 'air defence of Great Britain', to build up land and maritime strike forces, to reduce the enemy scale of attack, to provide a new airfield layout and a proper control organisation, to absorb, train and operate new units, and to provide a single commander in Calcutta alongside the military, naval and civil authorities. He felt he had no choice but to fight his case.[56]

A month later Portal told the Secretary of State that the matter had been settled as Peirse wished; Ludlow-Hewitt, an officer of great experience and wisdom, had taken a good look at the situation on the spot and declared that the formation of the two groups, Nos 221 and 224, at Calcutta was fully justified as also was the formation of AHQ Bengal.[57] Altogether his visit had paid great dividends, drawing to the attention of the distant Air Ministry a host of matters ranging from the special difficulties of operating aircraft in the Far East to organisation, training, administration, welfare, medical facilities: little escaped his eye. An observation to AMSO in a minute about personnel establishments showed how strongly he felt: 'What India wants, and should be allowed to have, is to be free to organise itself to meet the Japanese menace, without restrictions and interferences from Whitehall.'[58] Peirse had received just the support he needed, and in reply to an emollient letter from Portal he wrote that Ludlow-Hewitt's visit had been of the greatest value and was already bearing fruit.[59] What, we may wonder, might have been the outcome had the Inspector General been sent a year earlier to visit Brooke-Popham and Pulford?

From now on relations improved, though for some time Peirse would have preferred for family reasons to return home. Wavell, referring to this in January 1943, told Portal how sorry he would be to lose him,[60] and in February Peirse wrote to Portal that he was now ready to stay; the problems facing the air forces were difficult and onerous, and he would prefer to see them through himself.[61] He had already made one significant change in the earlier command structure, converting 221 and 224 Groups from their functional roles into composite formations. The former thus controlled from Calcutta all the bomber, fighter and coastal squadrons based in western Bengal, while the latter moved its headquarters forward to Chittagong in order to direct all the offensive and defensive fighter and light bomber squadrons that were spread along the Burma front.[62] This made much better sense in terms of both control and communication and of liaison with the ground forces engaging the Japanese; the way was now clear for both groups to develop into the tactical formations that would work so closely and effectively with the Army for the rest of the war.

One more aspect of the expansion is worth comment. When Peirse arrived in March 1942 the Air Staff in New Delhi comprised just 10 officers, with 35 others to cover all the support roles; there were none elsewhere apart from 222 Group at Colombo. By the end of 1943 his own staff numbered 90 in all, and the AHQ and seven Group Headquarters staffs added another 104.[63] A total officer staff of some 200 does not appear unduly generous given the immense task being undertaken, but the quality was good – far better than in Singapore – both in training and in range of experience. Moreover in his Deputy Cs-in-C, first Air Marshal Sir John Baldwin and then Air Marshal Sir Guy Garrod, Peirse had men of proved ability. Baldwin had commanded 3 Group, Bomber Command's Wellington force, for the first three years of the war, while Garrod had been Air Member for Training, largely responsible for developing the Empire Air Training Scheme. They presided over a force numbering by September 1943 almost 80,000 men, 9 per cent of the RAF's total strength (compared with less than 50,000 (6 per cent) a year earlier and a mere 11,600 (2 per cent) in the Far East in September 1941).[64] By the end of 1943 India Command was well prepared to take its part in the great battles of the next two years.

To conclude this chapter it is appropriate to mention briefly the situation facing the land forces alongside whom the RAF had to operate. Most belonged to the long-established Indian Army, which consisted of Indian soldiers under British leadership. Although almost a million strong at the end of 1941, some 300,000 were serving in the Middle East, Iraq and Malaya, and many more were committed in India to internal security duties and guarding the North-West Frontier. Then, after playing major roles in the fighting retreats through Malaya and Burma, the rest found themselves in mid-1942 facing a possible invasion of north-east India. To make matters worse, in August they were confronted with a major civil disturbance campaign following the Congress Party's demands for Indian independence and the arrest of its leader, Mahatma Gandhi. When one considers that General Irwin also had to face vast organisational, administrative, training and equipment problems similar in many ways to those confronting the RAF, it is small wonder that the Army too was ill-placed to embark on major offensive operations before the end of 1943.

7 Hopes Deferred

Despite all these difficulties, during the later part of 1942 and most of 1943 Wavell and his senior commanders, strongly encouraged by Churchill, were determined to use what forces they had to try to seize the initiative, and while most of their plans came to naught they are essential to an understanding of what actually took place.

Plans

In June 1942, with the retreat from Burma complete and the monsoon precluding further land operations before the autumn, Wavell's initial thoughts were directed towards an advance into northern Burma in early 1943 in order to re-establish a combined front with the Chinese and to boost morale in India.[1] The Prime Minister, however, had already been contemplating a bolder offensive aimed at recapturing Rangoon, for which he promised to gather landing craft and air reinforcements 'to the utmost limit permissible by other needs',[2] and on 12 June – keen to exploit the American success in the Battle of Midway – he cabled Wavell urging that preparations go forward to capture Rangoon and Moulmein and thereafter strike at Bangkok.[3] While he recognised that such an operation could take place only if all went well in Russia and the Middle East (which of course it did not), the whole idea betrayed a deep misunderstanding of the parlous situation in India and the amount of time and effort needed before anything worthwhile could be attempted – never mind such an ambitious project as a seaborne assault on Rangoon.

In response the C-in-C told Churchill that his pressing need was an effective air striking force, including long-range fighters.[4] Currently the air force in India was not only inadequate for an offensive against Burma but also for the defence of the sub-continent against seaborne attack: 'it was deficient in numbers, in reserves, in range, in hitting power and in training'.[5] Wavell and Peirse were quite rightly pulling no punches, for both knew that air superiority was the prerequisite for all else. Nevertheless, against the hope that the resources might be forthcoming, planning for such an operation – code-named ANAKIM – was put in hand; its air force requirements were assessed at 1,150 first-line aircraft. By the end of August, however, with the Germans advancing into the Caucasus and Rommel at the gates of Egypt, it was clear to all that ANAKIM would be impracticable until at least the end of 1943.[6]

Wavell was also keen to take some action in northern Burma, and various plans for joint action with the Chinese were discussed at meetings with General Stilwell[7] and others from October 1942 onwards. The complexities of these are outside the scope of this account; suffice it to say that by early 1943 it was clear that no major action intended to reopen land communications with China could take place before the end of the 1943 monsoon. At a major conference in Delhi in February it was therefore agreed that for the rest of the current dry season land operations would be largely local and limited, while air operations would be directed against enemy communications, airfields and aircraft, ports and shipping. Then in the dry season of 1943/44 there would be a major joint offensive with the Chinese in the north, further assaults in the Arakan, and finally an attack on Rangoon. This ambitious project, intended to lead to the reconquest of Burma by mid-1944, was much in line with the conclusions of the Allied conference at Casablanca the previous month, when ANAKIM had been firmly endorsed for late 1943.[8]

Nevertheless it remained clear that such plans would only be practicable given the necessary reinforcements for all three Services – including on the air side some 200 transport aircraft, 240 fighters and 215 bombers – and when Wavell, Somerville and Peirse began to consider ANAKIM in detail they recognised that a large naval task force approaching Rangoon would have to operate for some time without land-based air cover and within easy range of strong Japanese air forces based on conveniently located airfields. Since there was little chance of preventing their intervention, ANAKIM would be a gamble.[9] At home, too, despite Churchill's accusation that the Indian commanders were making excessive demands,[10] there was growing uneasiness and in April Wavell and his two colleagues came to London to meet the Chiefs of Staff. The decision was inevitable. The necessary naval strength could not be spared from the Mediterranean; a direct assault on Rangoon would almost certainly fail; ANAKIM was not essential to the defeat of Japan; even if it succeeded it would be 1945 before the Burma Road could be reopened to full capacity. ANAKIM was dead. For the next dry season the main effort would be devoted to increasing the flow of airborne supplies to China and the 14th USAAF now based there, and to intensifying the air offensive against the Japanese in Burma.[11]

Churchill, previously so keen on a major amphibious operation against the enemy in Burma, had completely changed his mind; the best way to defeat the Japanese, in his view, was by bombing Japan from bases in Russia and China, but this would not be possible until after the defeat of Germany. Meanwhile the Allies should concentrate on the support of China by the largest possible air transport service, and also find the most favourable locality for attacking the Japanese 'by-passing Burma and making full use of our sea power'.[12] A concept along these lines had already been floated by Wavell in a note to his staff on 16 February, when he suggested a combined Anglo-American assault on Sumatra and Java in the area of the Sunda Strait, and Operation CULVERIN was strongly advocated by Churchill at the Quebec Conference in August. The Chiefs of Staff, however, believed that whereas the necessary land and air forces could be found the naval element would still be a problem; moreover while the operation would provide a valuable base for the strategic air forces, nobody could effectively answer the question of how any immediate success might be exploited. Singapore, the obvious next target, could hardly be attacked quickly enough to prevent the Japanese preparing adequate defences. Nor could the British overcome the basic American objections that CULVERIN would divert resources from the more important aim of reopening communications with China, and that it offered too indirect a route to the ultimate objective, Japan itself.[13]

So by autumn 1943 a number of elaborate schemes had been propounded, debated and largely discarded; the reality was that the resources had been too limited, the competing priorities too great, the local infrastructure too undeveloped, to allow of more than a very modest range of offensive operations. It is to these, and particularly the RAF's contribution to them, that we shall shortly turn, but first we must consider the fight for air superiority.

Air Superiority

We saw in Chapter 6 how the air defence force, consisting largely of Hurricanes, was built up to 12 squadrons by the end of 1942 and deployed on airfields around Calcutta and north of Chittagong. The aircraft were mostly old; an aero engine fitter at Alipore with 67 Squadron, re-equipped with Hurricanes after its tribulations with Buffaloes in Burma, describes them as 'clapped out rubbish from the desert war' and tells what he and his comrades did:

> No one writes a fighter squadron off until it writes itself off. We increased our efforts, changing engines and cylinder blocks, adjusting propeller pitches and replacing radiators, sweating and straining until 15 aircraft continually stood at serviceable state. We were an efficient unit again and returned to operational status.

This was the work of men who on reaching India had been ill-received, finding themselves on nobody's ration strength, possessing only Burmese money which no-one wanted, lacking much of their kit, and generally having to scrounge and fend for themselves until they were eventually reunited with their squadron. As a much respected squadron warrant officer told them when bidding farewell:

> You might not be God's gift to the Grenadier Guards and I can't think of anyone who would want to see you lot marching down the Mall, but a crowd who can keep 15 aeroplanes constantly on a flight line can't be all bad. You're a great bunch of lads, I'm glad to have met you and proud to have served with you.[14]

Another squadron based for a while at Alipore, on the outskirts of Calcutta, was 136; Gordon Conway, a pilot, remembers the routine. Before dawn they would drive to satellite strips where the aircraft had been dispersed overnight, fly to the main base, spend most of the day at various states of readiness, practise battle formation, interceptions and combat, and then disperse again. Later it was decided that they should operate from Red Road, a highway running parallel to the main street in the centre of the city; better warning could be obtained and it was good for local morale. As Conway says, the road was short, narrow and heavily cambered, which tended to cause the fighters to drift into the bordering balustrades. Exceptional piloting was needed.[15]

Yet throughout the summer months there was no sign of the enemy, and by the time they did appear over Calcutta in December the warning system was at least partly in place and the pilots had become well versed in the tactics most likely to succeed against the more manoeuvrable Japanese fighters. In the event, however, the enemy did not try to come by day; instead on five nights late in the month a few unescorted bombers, never more than nine in number, bombed a wide diversity of targets. Both damage and casualties were light, but the raids caused a substantial exodus of civilians, mainly low caste workers, which led to considerable disruption of public services. The Hurricanes did what they could but without night fighter equipment had to rely on visual sighting; only one bomber was definitely destroyed. Clearly the threat to civilian morale of even this small scale of attack was substantial and Peirse sent an urgent request for night fighters.[16]

Within a fortnight they had arrived, and none too soon, for with the approach of another moon period and under the influence of Japanese propaganda thousands of people were fleeing the city. The next attack, by three bombers, came on the night of 15/16 January; one of 176 Squadron's Beaufighters piloted by Flight Sergeant Pring intercepted and shot down all three. 'Pring Prangs Three' was the headline in the squadron's news sheet. Five nights later four more bombers arrived, two of which were destroyed, and that was it.[17] The enemy, attributing their losses partly to the bombers' faulty exhaust flame dampers,[18] abandoned the operation and Calcutta returned to normal. The four Beaufighters had more than earned their keep; their presence had effectively denied the enemy the right to bomb the most important strategic target in India.[19] It would be another year before they reappeared.

Elsewhere, however, it was a different story. The Japanese now had up to 200 front-line aircraft at their disposal in Burma, and once the monsoon was over their fighters and light bombers operating from airfields such as Maymyo, Meiktila, Heho and Toungoo (Map 4) posed a considerable threat. Their offensive began in October 1942 with several attacks on airfields in Assam which were being used by the Americans for the supply route to China; they caused considerable damage and the defending USAAF fighters suffered substantial losses. To the south enemy fighters attacked Chittagong airfield on 26 October, achieving surprise but little success, and it was not until December that regular attacks began on the airfields at Chittagong and Feni. Some of these were by day, others by night; despite the poor warning system interceptions were made and losses inflicted, but the battle for air superiority over the battle area remained wide open at the end of the year. On the other hand the Japanese air effort was not reaching the level that had been expected, and their keenness to conserve their aircraft and crews suggested that reinforcement was uncertain.[20]

The inconclusive struggle continued in early 1943, when most of the Japanese operations were carried out in direct or indirect support of the land battle which Wavell had just launched (p. 133) in the Arakan. Airfields, docks and ground forces were the main targets, with the daylight raids normally on a scale of 10 to 20 aircraft, and while the enemy usually achieved little the RAF fighters were unable to inflict serious losses.[21] Then in mid-March the enemy stepped up his offensive, seeking first to prevent the RAF fighters interfering with his land operations and then to disrupt communications, and at last the Hurricanes began to obtain better results. Conway, whose 136 Squadron was now operating from the Chittagong area alongside 67 Squadron, tells of the excitement as both sides fought to establish air superiority:

We took part in several offensive sweeps and on other days were busy scrambling to intercept Jap raids. Our airfields at Ramu, Feni, Dohazari and Chittagong were all bombed or ground-strafed once or more, and our success was limited by poor early warning, the lack of precise radars, and the comparatively poor performance of the Hurricane at the height the Zeros chose to fight. One of our difficulties was our inability to get to height in time to intercept Japanese high-flying recces; they would fly with impunity over our bases providing the target material for the next raids.[22]

Meanwhile for the airmen on the ground keeping the aircraft flying was the only thing that mattered:

Everyone worked from dawn till dusk, changing cylinder blocks, changing engines, stripping carburettors, patching fabric, changing brake shoes and tyres, rearming, refuelling, cursing and swearing as mosquitoes nipped our ankles or spanners slipped and knuckles got crunched.[23]

The main enemy offensive continued until 11 April; over the four weeks it lasted some 600 sorties were mounted, mostly by light bombers and fighters, and 23 aircraft were claimed destroyed, with 20 probables. RAF losses were 14 fighters destroyed and 12 damaged. Sporadic attacks continued until June, and in late May better warning enabled the Hurricanes to inflict heavy losses on two raids on Chittagong.[24] Conway, who calls May a good month, mentions a further factor: his squadron had at last been re-equipped with the Mk IIC, fitted with 20 mm cannon and VHF radio. Now, however, the monsoon arrived. Our engine fitter describes it:

The wind screamed up to gale force, trees tottered and fell, the rain lashed down ... the water poured in rivers through the tents ... we were all bedded down on rush mats in part finished huts ... the CO stood the squadron down for a day and everyone gave a hand cleaning up the mess. The rain continued to pour down in torrents, monsoon covers were erected over the aircraft and we worked away under these ... we were incessantly soaking wet and steaming ... it seemed to go on for ever.[25]

But the weather was no respecter of sides. As the Narrators succinctly put it: 'As was their usual wont the Japanese Air Force retired for the monsoon'.[26]

The dry season had witnessed an important stage in the battle for air superiority, largely but not entirely fought out in the skies over the Arakan. Most of it had been directed by a new commander, Air Vice-Marshal T M ('Bill') Williams, who after serving in France with the Advanced Air Striking Force and then with 2 Group had reached India in March 1942, following a brief spell in Java. He succeeded Stevenson as AOC Bengal in January 1943, and Slim, whose XV Corps

HQ at Barrackpore was co-located with his, speaks of the close and friendly co-operation that was quickly established:

> Williams was an inspiring commander for his own Service and an understanding and unselfish colleague to us ... he was the man who laid the foundations of the air supremacy we later gained, and on which everything else was built.[27]

Slim makes a crucial point: victory in this battle was indeed the key to all else. The enemy was not, however, yet ready to concede it; he would be back at the end of the year. All one can say of the events of the first half of 1943 is that the honours were even. The Allied fighter force was defending a 700-mile front with limited strength and an inadequate warning system, and the performance of its principal aircraft, the Hurricane, placed it at a tactical disadvantage. Yet the enemy – still convinced that airfields were the best targets for attack – failed to knock any of them out and largely ignored the tempting strategic targets further afield.[28] Admittedly they lacked an effective long-range bomber, but more imaginative use of their medium bombers might have posed the RAF and USAAF defences serious problems at this critical stage of the Allied build-up in India. As it was, by concentrating their efforts mainly on counter-air and to a lesser extent on tactical operations they showed an inflexibility of thought which boded ill for the future. So by mid-1943 the RAF defences were giving as good as they got, and by October when the Japanese air offensive resumed the situation was about to be radically changed with the advent of the Spitfire.

Meanwhile there had already been attempts to take the offensive, both on the ground and in the air.

The First Arakan Campaign

When it became clear that ANAKIM was impracticable in the dry season of early 1943, the planners' attention was switched to a more limited operation, namely the recapture of Akyab. Its significance, as Louis Allen reminds us, lay in its airfields, for without them land-based cover would be impracticable for any future operations against Rangoon and southern Burma.[29] Their capture would also reduce the air threat to Calcutta, and a successful offensive would have a considerable moral effect in India.[30] By now, after several months of complete inactivity by the Japanese air forces in Burma, air reconnaissance was revealing a substantial airfield construction programme, and in response to Peirse's urgings the Air Ministry increased his supply of aircraft to enable him to build up the size of striking force that would be necessary.[31]

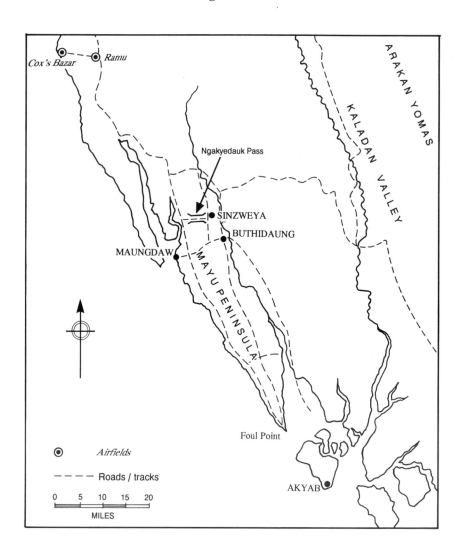

Map 7   The Arakan 1942/44

Wavell's plan was for 14 Indian Division to advance rapidly down the Arakan coast to the end of the Mayu peninsula and then launch a short-range ship-borne assault on Akyab (Map 7). Speed was of the essence if the small Japanese forces were not to be reinforced, but the very difficult terrain and virtual absence of roads were bound to cause problems and the few transport aircraft available in the theatre were all committed elsewhere. Air support was to be provided by HQ 224 Group at Chittagong, equipped with five Hurricane squadrons, a Mohawk squadron, three Blenheim squadrons and a Lysander flight; all were based on airfields around Chittagong and the fighters were also charged with air defence, as we have just seen.[32]

It was a disappointing campaign, marked by an initial rapid advance down the peninsula in late December 1942, an unfortunate delay of 10 days which gave the enemy time to construct defences which could not be breached, and then a full-scale attack on the now reinforced Japanese in February. When this failed an enemy counter offensive in March led to bitter fighting with heavy losses, and by the start of the monsoon the Army was back where it had started. It was a campaign whose principal value lay in the lessons it taught, and not least for the RAF.

In the earlier phases the Blenheims operated at maximum effort against Akyab town and villages in the Mayu peninsula, while the Hurricanes – in addition to intercepting the Japanese raids – carried out ground strafing and attacked communications, especially the rivercraft so important to the Japanese. The Blenheims were also called on by the Army to attack troop concentrations in the jungle, targets which they could not see and had to be indicated to them by pinpoint positions or smoke shells fired by the ground forces. The Blenheim was not really suitable for this work, for it could not bomb accurately enough to destroy the enemy's dug-in positions, and when some Vengeances were brought in during March in the attempt to do better they soon had to be withdrawn for technical reasons.[33] Another role was the dangerous business of tactical reconnaissance, carried out first by the Lysanders and then the Hurricanes of 28 Squadron, flying from a forward airstrip right alongside the Divisional HQ at Maungdaw and usually operating in pairs for mutual protection. The pilots found visual reconnaissance over the jungle particularly difficult and unrewarding and the best results were obtained from vertical and oblique photography.[34]

Then in March the entire strength of 224 Group was at critical moments deployed in direct ground support,[35] and as the fighting intensified the air operations were extended in the attempt to interrupt the enemy's main supply route between central Burma and Akyab, culminating in a major offensive from 18 to 20 May. Wellingtons from 221 Group and B-17s from the USAAF contributed to the day and night assault on supply bases, shipping and rivercraft, bridges and road and rail transport, and 224 Group's Hurricanes were joined by Beaufighters in their attacks on the waterways. This was the first concerted air operation on a significant scale in the Burma campaign and General Irwin congratulated the RAF and USAAF:

> Ground intelligence reports confirm result in Japanese casualties most effective and whole effort appears definitely to have restricted further forward movements of enemy in any numbers and to have seriously upset their supply arrangements.[36]

Reflecting later on the RAF's support in the overall campaign, Slim (who had taken command of all troops in Arakan on 14 August) wrote of the great debt to 224 Group, which had achieved marvels of sustained effort to cover the recent withdrawals. 'More than once the troops could not have extricated themselves without this cover'.[37]

Altogether some 5,000 sorties had been flown in direct and indirect support of the land battle as well as 700 in defence of airfields and other installations,[38] and despite the failure of the operation as a whole it marked the origins of joint air/ground warfare on the India-Burma frontier, with the aircraft for close support being satisfactorily controlled by an Army Air Support Control (AASC) working alongside the Divisional HQ.[39] Without the right sort of aircraft and more experience of jungle conditions, however, it was impossible to achieve the accuracy necessary to bring the bomb line close enough to the troops on the ground to enable them to take immediate advantage of the bombing. Japanese troops could therefore recover from the effects long before a ground assault was launched.[40] On the other hand, when friendly troops were withdrawing, bombing could and did keep the enemy immobile and enable them to escape. So while the Blenheims had done all they could in indirect support together with the Hurricanes, it was clear that better aircraft were essential, and more of them, before the RAF could give the Army the kind of help it really needed.

The First Chindit Campaign[41]

Further north another quite different operation was under way, one which – for all the controversy that still surrounds it – was well worth its effort in terms of both its effect on morale and its demonstration of the potential of air supply. Lieutenant Colonel Orde Wingate, a proven if unorthodox leader of guerilla operations in Palestine and Abyssinia, had been sent to India in early 1942 in the hope that his methods might be applicable in Burma, and it was not long before Wavell accepted his proposal to use a specially organised and trained brigade to penetrate deep into enemy-held territory and operate there by means of air supply. This would not only disrupt enemy communications but also provide detailed air intelligence, thus assisting the direction of the strategic air offensive.[42] As Louis Allen observes, the basis of Wingate's ideas was air power:

> British defeat in Malaya and Burma had been at the hands of numerically inferior forces because the British were road-bound. If their line of communication was cut – a standard, reiterated Japanese ploy – they seemed incapable of fighting back. In an age of air transport Wingate saw that this could change radically. Most of what lorries could bring up aircraft could carry in or, if they could not land, drop by parachute ... the only requisite was an efficient wireless system to signal dropping points with accuracy. When surrounded ... the soldier could stay and fight it out on the spot.[43]

The 77th Brigade was accordingly formed in July 1942; it comprised some 3,000 men divided eventually into seven columns, each equipped with mortars, machine guns and a wireless set, and relying on pack animals for their transport.[44] The radio, a 1082/83 RAF set, was bulky and cumbersome, its heaviest part weighing over 200 lbs,[45] and to use the equipment in order to arrange supply dropping and control air strikes each column included an RAF section comprising one officer pilot and four wireless operators. Commanded by Squadron Leader (later Sir) Robert Thompson, they underwent all the rigorous jungle training designed to prepare Wingate's men for the extreme hardships they would face – they knew, for example, that sick or wounded men would have to be abandoned.[46]

The intensive training was accompanied by a few supply dropping exercises by Lysanders, but only in January 1943, at the insistence of the newly appointed AOC, Bill Williams, was a realistic exercise carried out. This and several more trials confirmed that supplies could be dropped by night (day drops were thought unsafe) so allaying the doubts of many of Wingate's men. At the same time Williams provided his best operational airfield, Agartala, for the transport aircraft of 31 and 194 Squadrons allotted to the Chindits; it was a measure of their scarcity at this stage in the war that hardly ever did the detachment exceed three Dakotas and three Hudsons.[47] Supporting them was an Army staff with a section of expert packers and a three months' reserve of supplies.

On 6 February Wavell ordered Wingate to go ahead. The abandonment of larger scale operations in conjunction with the Chinese in northern Burma had left his brigade (or long-range penetration group, as it was now known) without a strategic aim, but they were ready to go and it was sensible to test the feasibility of their type of operation and generally make life difficult for the enemy by disrupting his communications.[48] Four months later 2,182 of the 3,000 men who had entered Burma were back, each having marched at least 1,000 miles. They had penetrated beyond the Irrawaddy in the area north of Mandalay and caused much destruction, most notably by cutting the main north-south railway in many places. In their support the RAF had flown 178 sorties, 19 of them abortive, and dropped 300 tons of supplies; not all were collected safely, especially early on, but techniques improved with practice. While large paddy fields made the best dropping zones, jungle clearings were also used, and on occasion daylight deliveries proved possible. Much was learnt too about the best ways of indicating DZs; the procedures laid down by AHQ were often found too elaborate.[49]

There were, of course, criticisms; some considered that RAF convenience was studied to the detriment of the men on the ground, and inevitably there were unfortunate incidents. On 15 February, for example, a pilot who could not find his DZ decided to jettison his load rather than try to return with it over the hills in bad weather; when the Japanese retrieved it they found it included the complete mail of the northern force, thus making them a present of the order of battle. Then on 13 March Wingate decided to cancel a delivery since enemy forces were nearby but the message failed to arrive and when the aircraft appeared poor signalling procedures made it impossible to arrange the drop. Conversely there was the occasion when a party unable to cross a swiftly moving river received several dinghies in an emergency delivery, and on 28 April Flying Officer Vlasto managed to land his Dakota in a jungle clearing and take off again with 17 sick and wounded men on board. No praise could be too great at that moment.[50]

As well as calling for air supply the RAF sections could request air strikes, but in fact only eight took place. There had been no training for these with 77 Brigade, no RAF formation was allotted to the role until late in the operation, and no air plan existed. Nor did the RAF sections in the field have the ability to communicate with support aircraft and direct them on to targets. Such attacks as were made resulted from intelligence passed by the columns, and were generally on troop concentrations in particular villages.[51] Clearly there was much scope for improvement.

A tribute is due here to the men of the RAF sections. They had to cope with bulky, unwieldy equipment which was liable to breakdown, they often had little information about the aircraft being sent to help them, and they were subject to the same physical and mental stresses as their Army comrades. Their presence, as evidence of RAF co-operation, was nevertheless essential, and the RAF officer was seen as the authentic voice of his Service by all concerned. Afterwards AHQ urged that pilots were too valuable elsewhere: better to select and train Army officers for this particular duty.[52] Wingate, however, was adamant that the operational experience of the pilot was fundamental to the task and the transport pilots agreed. Undoubtedly the RAF men had acquitted themselves well; indeed Wingate considered some of the officers capable of commanding columns themselves. He singled out two in his report:

> These two indefatigable and devoted RAF officers viewed every problem simply from one point of view – the defeat of the enemy. I am afraid both have lost their lives, one in trying to save Gurkhas from drowning in the Irrawaddy and the other in sticking by his wounded Colonel after all hope of getting him back to India had been abandoned.[53]

So what was achieved? In terms of damage and casualties inflicted on the enemy, not much. But as Slim tells us:

> Skilfully handled, the press of the Allied world took up the tale, and everywhere the story ran that we had beaten the Japanese at their own game. This not only distracted attention from the failure in Arakan, but was important in itself for our own people at home, for our allies, and above all for our troops on the Burma front.[54]

It was in fact the first good news to come for the British from the Far East war and it was rightly exploited, despite the dangers of reading too much into it; Churchill was certainly not immune from this, unwisely telling the Chiefs of Staff in July that Wingate should command the Army against Burma.[55] Apart from its value for publicity purposes, the most significant accomplishment was, to quote Brigadier Fergusson, who led No 5 Column: 'We proved that it was feasible to maintain a force by supply dropping alone'.[56] Louis Allen amplifies the point:

> The RAF officers who marched with the columns and shared all their hardships put into practice an effective way of taking the British Army off the roads and into the air ... the hard fact was that Wingate had changed the nature of jungle campaigning for good.[57]

We might add that the campaign also demonstrated the need for some method of evacuating the sick and wounded. What a Dakota had done once could be done again more often, and if light aircraft were also available casualty evacuation – so essential to morale – could be properly organised.[58]

Yet in saying all this we must not forget, as the Commander of IV Corps, General Scoones, pointed out, that during the entire operation enemy air opposition was not once encountered and the RAF was fortunate not to lose a single aircraft from any cause.[59] The General appreciated the fundamental truth, all too easy to lose sight of, that for air supply to be effective there could be no thought of serious enemy interference, and that air superiority was the prerequisite.

Finally there was an unforeseen consequence. The enemy, believing it too difficult to move across the grain of the country along the Assam border, had so far adopted an entirely defensive policy in Burma. Having now received a demonstration that such movement was possible and realising that the British might try to repeat their operation on a larger scale a year later, they resolved to take the offensive themselves in 1944. This new policy, leading to the battles of Imphal and Kohima, was according to Kirby the outstanding result of Wingate's first campaign.[60]

Other Offensive Operations over Burma

We must now turn more briefly to the RAF's other activities in this period when it still had so few resources and so little experience, and first to the work of the small bomber force, Blenheims, Wellingtons and a handful of Liberators (p. 116–117).

Plagued with very low serviceability, caused by shortage of tools and equipment, the poor living conditions at Asansol, the difficulties of the monsoon, and a defeatist attitude engendered by the retreat from Burma, the Blenheims could operate only in very small numbers to begin with; while the refuelling and rearming parties established at the forward airfields of Agartala and Chittagong enabled them to reach as far as central Burma, there was much wasteful flying.[61] Nevertheless from October 1942 onwards the conditions were better and the attacks on airfields, though causing little actual damage, persuaded the enemy to station his own bombers out of range in Malaya and Siam, bringing them forward only for operations.[62] While most aircraft operated by day with fighter escort, 34 Squadron was trained for night bombing and joined the Wellingtons and Liberators in attacks on the more distant airfields, dumps and communications. The overall effort was small: 942 sorties and 473 tons of bombs dropped in nine months, together with 299 sorties (413 tons) by USAAF heavy bombers reaching as far as Rangoon, Mandalay and Bangkok.[63]

This pattern continued in the drier months of early 1943. Rangoon, through which all Japanese military supplies and reinforcements for Burma had to come, was considered the key target but, being out of range of all but the heavy bombers, was left largely to the USAAF. For the RAF's bomber force the primary objective continued to be the enemy airfields, with communications the secondary objective, though the Blenheims had to devote much of their time to tactical operations. The scale of effort remained limited: average availability was a mere four Liberators and 13 Wellingtons for night operations, and 50 Blenheims, and over the six months to June only 3,054 sorties were flown, 477 by the heavier bombers, and 18 aircraft were lost. That the enemy did not take the threat too seriously is indicated by their poor attempts at interception, especially by night. Later in the year, however, they began devoting more attention to air defence, for the Allied bomber effort – now directed mainly towards their rail, river and road communications and continuing through the monsoon – was having its effect on their build-up for the land offensives being planned for 1944.[64]

Compared with the great bombing campaign building up in Europe the operations in Burma during 1943 were puny in scale; moreover – apart from the heavy bombers, mostly USAAF – the aircraft available were obsolescent. The Blenheims were no longer suitable for the European war: 'so old were these aircraft now, and so excellent the squadron spirit, that it was said the Blenheims flew on happiness alone'.[65] The Wellingtons too were aged and had a poor record of serviceability under tropical conditions – indeed Ludlow-Hewitt had described them as 'not very satisfactory in the East' as far back as June 1942.[66] Yet on 15/16 November the RAF night bombers mounted their biggest raid so far, against the enemy camp and railway station at Pegu. The force comprised six Liberators and 21 Wellingtons – by European standards almost negligible, but a signal achievement for the RAF in India, and not least when one remembers that the radio aids to navigation were still almost non-existent.

By this time newer types of aircraft were joining in the action. In May 1943 the first Vengeances became operational in the Arakan and in October 45 and 110 Squadrons brought their Vengeances into the front line near Imphal; with the Army increasing its patrol activity the dive bombers were now enabled to prove themselves. After a 'friendly fire' incident had shown the dangers of providing close support they concentrated their efforts on clearly defined targets on lines of communication, dumps and troop concentrations immediately behind the battle line, and very quickly they were proving the accuracy of their bombing.[67]

Beaufighters too arrived on the scene in 1943. Fitted with two radial engines which coped well with the tropical conditions, armed with four 20mm cannon and six machine guns, the Beaufighter had an operational radius of action of 500 miles, much greater than that of the Hurricane even when fitted with long-range tanks. From their bases at Agartala and Feni 27 and 177 Squadrons could reach across the intervening mountain range into central Burma more easily than the

Blenheims, and in September, the first month when both squadrons were engaged, roads, rivers and railways were searched, locomotives and steamers, rivercraft and rolling stock riddled with cannon and machine gun fire, factories and oil tanks left in flames. Significantly the monsoon barely interrupted their activities, though they often had to fight their way through dense cloud and storms, and their speed, allied with their low-level tactics, prevented the enemy anti-aircraft batteries – and mortar and small arms fire as well – from inflicting much damage. In the first eight months of operations some 400 sorties were carried out for a loss of only five aircraft.[68]

A train on the central Burmese plain, photographed by an attacking Beaufighter. (*Group Captain P H Baldwin*)

27 Squadron, commanded from August 1943 by Wing Commander J B Nicolson, the Battle of Britain VC, received recognition at this time from a most unusual but highly perceptive quarter. They were visited in January 1944 by Wing Commander Roland Winfield, a medical officer who had qualified as a pilot and became one of the great pioneers of aviation medicine at Farnborough, where he specialised in the problems facing operational aircrew. In his book *The Sky Belongs to Them*, he described 7 Squadron (it flew Stirlings) and 27 Squadron as the finest he ever flew with.

I admired Nicolson because he had moulded his squadron into the finest instrument of war I ever came across in India ... he inspired a loyalty in the members of his squadron through the example he set them. I admired him even more when I discovered what it was that had driven him first to create and then to command its spirit of complete operational efficiency. He was haunted by the doubt of whether or not he was really worth the Victoria Cross he had won. He said to me, 'Doc, I shall never know if I should have done what I did if I'd had the time to weigh up the pros and cons in cold blood. If you're given a decoration that you cannot refuse and yet are not sure that you've deserved, then the only thing to do is to shape your life so that what's left of it is an honest attempt to show yourself and the rest of the RAF that at least you've tried to earn it!'.[69]

The enemy too, who called the Beaufighter 'Whispering Death' because of its silent approach, respected the bravery of the airmen, 'men who were prepared to fly into trees rather than be shot down', but the crews themselves knew that 'if you had to crash land in Burma, then it would be advisable to do so as far away as you could possibly make it from the target area. The intensity of our formidable fire power had become self-evident. We knew that we were not popular with the Japanese'.[70]

We might observe here that all aircrew had a fair idea of their likely fate should they fall into enemy hands, and their ground crews knew it too. There were plenty of stories around, and clear inferences could be drawn from intelligence reports. One of these, a quotation from the Japanese Inspector-General's 'Rules of Conduct for Aircrews', appeared in June 1943:

Under no circumstances should you cling to life by accepting defeat, nor should you forget the dignity of our Imperial forces to the extent of enduring the disgrace of being taken prisoner.[71]

Alan Fox, who earned the DFM as an airman flying many sorties with 681 Squadron as a Mitchell camera operator and recently wrote an excellent account of his experiences, records in starkly simple words what happened when one of his squadron's Spitfires was shot down: 'The pilot was captured by the Japanese, tortured, mutilated, and then burnt to death'.[72]

By the end of 1943 the Beaufighters had established themselves as an essential part of the RAF's armoury, capable not only of long-range strike and interdiction but also of visual and photographic reconnaissance, since each carried a camera which yielded invaluable information from low level to supplement that obtained by the high level PR aircraft of 681 Squadron. Based at Alipore, and using forward airfields when necessary, this squadron's Hurricanes and Spitfires concentrated their efforts on central Burma, and in particular the enemy supply lines, but the Hurricanes were too slow and it was fortunate that the enemy did not try to interfere with them. The Mitchells, supplemented later by the first Mosquitos, ranged further afield, covering Rangoon, Moulmein, the construction of the infamous Siam-Burma railway, and the Andaman Islands. Such were the distances involved, however, that the sole way of reaching the more distant areas in which the Allies were interested, such as Sumatra and Malaya, was to use the Liberators of 160 Squadron, based in Ceylon, but these were too slow and three were shot down in late 1943. The only answer was the longer range Mosquito which was not yet available.[73]

The Indian Ocean

Reconnaissance was also an important task of the maritime aircraft operating over the great expanses of the Indian Ocean. Despite the withdrawal of the enemy carrier force after the attacks on Ceylon in early April 1942 (Ch. 5) the possibility of a further incursion by Japanese surface vessels could not be totally discounted, and there was the inevitable submarine threat. Since almost the whole build-up in India, as we have seen, depended on seaborne supplies arriving from the Persian Gulf or via either the Cape or Australia, the protection of these routes was an essential task for the Navy and Air Force. Fortunately in 1942/43 the enemy made little attempt to interfere and no conflict developed that was remotely comparable to the Battle of the Atlantic, yet it might so easily have been very different.

One important step was taken early on after Hudsons operating from Dum Dum, near Calcutta, discovered some 13 enemy flying boats at Port Blair, in the Andaman Islands. There were also indications that the local airfield was being developed together with fighter defences. Clearly a threat was building up to the sea route leading to Calcutta, and while there was no possibility of recapturing the islands it was essential to restrict the enemy's use of them, not least for reconnaissance. So on 14 April 1942 two Hudsons of 62 Squadron flew via Akyab, which although it had been evacuated still housed a small refuelling party,[74] and attacked the flying boats at low level; moored in lines they were an easy target and all were destroyed or damaged. A repeat attack four days later destroyed several more, and although this time one of the Hudsons was shot down the two small raids had done much to reduce the scale of Japanese reconnaissance over the Bay of Bengal at a critical time.[75]

Another measure deemed necessary to protect the sea communications was to seize the Vichy French naval and air base at Diego

Suarez in order to pre-empt any Japanese attempt to establish themselves in Madagascar; the landing took place on 5 May and six months later the whole island was in British hands [76] (Map 9). While the RAF was not involved in these operations, air support having been provided by the Fleet Air Arm, it was an undoubted beneficiary: from now on all the bases that might be needed for effective patrolling of the Indian Ocean were secure. In the event the aircraft involved – Catalinas from Ceylon, Madras and Karachi, and Hudsons from Bengal – encountered little enemy activity for the rest of 1942 as they carried out their unspectacular work covering convoys and unescorted vessels, and guiding rescue craft when occasionally a ship was torpedoed. These operations apart, the Catalinas started a regular air service from Ceylon to Australia – a non-stop distance of 2,650 miles – and in December three of them bombed harbour installations at Sabang, in Sumatra, by night in an attempt to simulate a carrier-borne attack; hopefully this would convince the enemy that the Eastern Fleet was still a potent force at the time when the Americans were about to take the offensive in the south-west Pacific.[77]

It was much the same story for 1943. The main task for the slowly expanding force of maritime aircraft continued to be the patrolling of the shipping lanes and the protection of convoys; in February a particularly important one which included the *Queen Mary, Aquitania* and *Ile de France* was escorted by Catalinas, some of them operating from Addu Atoll and Diego Garcia, but the enemy never appeared.[78] Coastal shipping was also watched first by Hudsons operating from Dhubalia over the Bay of Bengal, and then by Wellingtons, and these operations were extended to include the routes used by enemy shipping along the Arakan coast. Their success, in conjunction with the Navy's submarines, was such that – according to the Japanese – not even one third of the supplies needed by their air and ground forces could be transported: 'the difficulties of sea transportation seriously affected the maintenance of our fighting power'.[79]

In the early days there was little effective co-ordination of the maritime air effort, but by mid-1943 it was at last recognised that the immense area to be covered by the small number of aircraft available required some form of central control, and in July AOC 222 Group (Air Vice-Marshal Lees), based in Ceylon, was given operational control of all GR aircraft in the theatre (other than those in Bengal). Under him a new operations room at Bombay, working alongside the Navy, was given responsibilities as far west as the Persian Gulf, and a similar operations room was set up at Madras.[80]

Yet for all their efforts the maritime aircraft could claim few positive results in terms of enemy ships destroyed; theirs was a professionally demanding but boring business, as a Catalina crew member with 240 Squadron recalls. Based for 18 months in primitive, unhealthy conditions at Redhills Lake, near Madras, they flew 85 operational sorties, each averaging 11 hours and some much longer; the occasional alert, when radar blips indicated something, often turned out to be a whale or oil drum and only once did they find and attack a submarine – at night and without success.[81] Their experience was typical, but let there be no doubt that alongside their naval colleagues they were helping to ensure that all the necessary materials for war would reach their destination in India – truly a vital task.

Air Supply

Just as vital – and far better remembered – was the work of the transport aircraft. The handful of DC-2s and DC-3s of 31 Squadron had already demonstrated their potential in the retreat from Burma (p. 95), flying 36 sorties in May 1942, but not until the Wingate expedition in February 1943 would this scale of effort be repeated. Partly this was because of the monsoon conditions, but mainly owing to the shortage of aircraft and the many operational and organisational difficulties in north-east India. 1943 was a different story, with the air supply effort building up steadily almost regardless of the monsoon. Consequently, compared with 543 sorties (10 per cent of them abortive) carried out between April and December 1942, 1,913 (12 per cent abortive) took place between January and November 1943.[82]

Most of this effort was devoted to supplying Army units in forward positions in the Chin and Naga hills and in north Burma. Some of these units were in direct contact with the enemy and at times needed urgent help; others had to be assisted when the weather cut their normal lines of communication. There was too a steadily increasing chain of RAF-manned wireless observer units and radars in the Arakan, the Chin Hills and further north, providing the warning system for Bengal and Assam – their work was among the most solitary that the RAF was required to do anywhere in the world,[83] and they also often needed air supply.

A smaller but regular commitment for 31 Squadron was generated by the small garrison at Fort Hertz (Map 4). Situated north of Myitkyina and possessed of an airstrip, this isolated post had no land route to the west and on 13 June 1942, with the Japanese reported to be moving towards it, a Dakota had managed to land and evacuate a party of 23 Britons. Then, when reconnaissance showed that the enemy had not moved in, it was decided to try to reoccupy it and after a group of parachutists had been dropped in August the landing ground was reopened and a garrison installed.[84]

Apart from its value for possible operations in northern Burma, Fort Hertz was particularly important since it provided the only emergency landing ground on the India-China aerial lifeline.[85] This route, forever

known as 'The Hump', had first been flown by Lieutenant Colonel W D
Old, USAAF, in April and the transport flights were now being steadily
built up. They were, and would remain, very largely an American
operation, usually taking priority over other commitments and making
immense demands upon the Allied resources in north-east India, but
the RAF was not entirely left out; from 1 September 1942 a weekly
service was flown, primarily to supply the signals detachment in China
(p. 93, note 60). The Narrators' description of the hazards is worth
quoting, not just as a reminder of the conditions faced by the American
and British transport crews but also as an indication of what so many
other airmen had to contend with while flying piston-engined,
unpressurised aircraft in a part of the world where aviation had
hitherto hardly penetrated:

> As flying terrain, the air route was considered one of the most
> difficult in the world. Much of the country was uncharted,
> ice-capped peaks rising to 20,000 feet and dense jungles covering
> the valleys below. The weather was unusually bad and about 50
> per cent of the flying over the route had to be carried out on
> instruments. At first wireless aids to navigation were almost
> non-existent but later great efforts were made to safeguard
> aircraft in an area where the most turbulent weather in the world
> was experienced. Incredible air currents threatened the transport
> aircraft, jagged peaks 'lined the clouds with rocks' and Japanese
> fighters in the earlier days were constantly trying to intercept the
> unarmed aircraft making the crossing. Flying over other
> mountainous regions of the world was considered by pilots of the
> 'Hump' route as mild compared with the lonely and awesome
> snow peaks, the terrific down drifts and powerful cross winds,
> and the seemingly endless square miles of jungle, without a
> single spot for a landing, which marked the towering barrier
> between India and hard-pressed China.[86]

Most of the RAF's transport aircraft did not, of course, have to cross
the Hump; their task was usually to drop supplies, and here too we
must remember what was entailed. First there was the joint
Army/RAF base organisation to ensure the goods were available,
sorted and packed in accordance with the requirements signalled by
the intended recipients. Then the parachutes had to be packed, the
loads prepared, the missions planned, the aircraft loaded, the crews
briefed. There is nothing unusual today about such activities; in 1942/43
in India they all had to be organised from scratch. The crews
themselves – pilot, navigator, two wireless operators and sometimes
an extra man to help the others eject the supplies – often flew nine or
more hours a day and might complete three separate missions. Flying

over the jungle-clad hills was always difficult owing to the peculiar atmospheric conditions, for the sharp contours gave rise to considerable air turbulence, a factor intensified by the onset of the rains. Aircraft were pitched and tossed unpredictably; on one occasion a Dakota was seen to emerge from cloud upside down. Moreover much of the work was done at night; there were no wireless or radar aids such as were usual in Europe, maps were 'unbelievably skimpy and inaccurate', and the pinpoints almost intolerably vague. Then when the DZ was found, by night or day, the right moment for the drop had to be chosen, several circuits might be necessary, the crew would be involved in 'rough and exacting labour' inside an extremely hot aircraft flying at 50 or 100 feet, and all the time there was the risk of enemy action, particularly small arms fire.[87]

It was under such conditions that 31 Squadron, flying from Agartala and Dinjan, and assisted at times by 62 and 194 Squadrons, operated from mid-1942 to the end of 1943. General Giffard, who had succeeded General Irwin as GOC-in-C Eastern Army, paid them tribute:

> Without the maintenance of supply by air the Army could not have held throughout the monsoon the positions in which it had entrenched itself at the end of the campaigning season in May. Owing to the efforts of 31 Squadron none of his troops had ever gone hungry.[88]

Incredibly, throughout this whole period, only three transport aircraft (two Hudsons and one Dakota) had been lost by enemy action. While 195 other aircraft had been shot down, including 90 Hurricanes, 33 Blenheims, 19 Beaufighters, 14 Mohawks and nine Wellingtons,[89] the Japanese had failed to appreciate the significance of air transport, perhaps because they themselves had never seen the need for it. Had they learnt that lesson 1944 could have turned out very differently.

8 Towards the Offensive

A New Command Structure

As the build-up in India progressed during 1943 and minds concentrated on the strategy for the following year it was becoming clear that the command structure, adequate for the defensive phase of the war, was no longer suitable. Up to now the C-in-C (Wavell) had doubled as the Viceroy's military adviser and head of the fighting services, and on all major matters of defence policy he was the normal channel of communication with the authorities in the United Kingdom. Peirse was therefore answerable to him and not in theory supposed to communicate directly with the Air Ministry, so for all practical purposes C-in-C India was the supreme authority in the sphere of air and military policy.[1] Such a system was not, however, going to lend itself easily to the waging of offensive war in Burma and further afield, and not least since air power was bound to play an all-important role. Moreover, with United States air forces operating on an increasing scale alongside the RAF, some means of joint control of Allied air operations had to be devised; this would be even more essential as the main areas of military operations moved away from India and when eventually, after the defeat of Germany, the full weight of the Anglo-American air forces would be concentrated against Japan. The need for a South-East Asian equivalent of the already proven Mediterranean Allied Air Command was becoming clear. The air forces could not possibly do their job properly if their every act was to go on being controlled by C-in-C India.[2]

The command problems were not, of course, limited to the air forces, and as early as February Wavell had started discussing them with the Viceroy. In April the latter had suggested to the Secretary of State for India, Leo Amery, the appointment of a C-in-C Asia (or Far East), and in May Wavell personally urged on Churchill the need for a South-East Asia command separate from C-in-C India.[3] These ideas were informally discussed with the Americans at the subsequent Washington Conference and on 15 June Churchill – distressed by what he saw as a lack of drive in the Far Eastern theatre[4] – issued a memorandum to the Chiefs of Staff. This advocated an organisation headed by a British

Supreme Commander, with an American deputy and an Allied staff, who would be responsible for the conduct of all operations against Japan in South-East Asia; C-in-C India would remain in charge of internal security, the maintenance of the Indian Army, and the running of the base. A few days later General Auchinleck, who had been relieved by Churchill of his post as C-in-C Middle East, returned to his old appointment in India as C-in-C, Wavell becoming Viceroy. This was to prove a very fruitful change, with the two working closely together to support the war in Burma.[5]

Portal reacted quickly to Churchill's memorandum, advising the Secretary of State for Air that the Prime Minister was keen to give the supreme command to an air force officer: 'It would please the Air everywhere and recognise that the major part of the war against Japan will be an air war'. Of the three possible choices, he went on, Tedder was indispensable in the Mediterranean, and Douglas would be better than Coningham.[6] Douglas's name was accordingly put forward to the Americans but rejected by them since he had no experience of inter-Allied command,[7] and Churchill next suggested Admiral Lord Louis Mountbatten, whose experience as Head of Combined Operations was deemed particularly appropriate to South-East Asia. As he wrote to Attlee, 'there is no doubt of the need of a young and vigorous mind in this lethargic and stagnant Indian scene.'[8] Roosevelt accepted the proposal, Mountbatten's appointment was announced on 25 August and he assumed command on 16 November.

Meanwhile there had been much discussion about the new structure, and Peirse – initially sceptical about the need for a Supreme Commander[9] – was particularly worried about the intention implied in Churchill's memorandum to place the RAF support organisation under a separate AOC India. He felt strongly that, as in other overseas theatres, the Air Commander must direct and control his own maintenance and training – though it was also arguable that the local situation was more akin to that in the UK, where separate commands provided the many support services. At the back of his mind, however, 'weighing like a millstone around his neck, was a constant dread of the obstructive effect on all his plans of the ponderous, cumbersome and antipathetic Government of India machine'.[10] Throughout July, therefore, while the complex staffwork was underway between London and the authorities in India, Peirse maintained his position that the operational capability of his air forces could not be divorced from the maintenance and training organisation, and the Air Ministry – accepting his case – decided that the rest of the administration must also come under him. On 9 August, the Indian Government's arguments having been overruled, it was agreed that the Air C-in-C would have complete control of the air forces. Only the administration of the Indian Air Force and the control of certain units in the north-west were left to the AOC India. So now, for the first time, all RAF units were to be placed on the normal Imperial as opposed to the Indian establishment.[11]

A further factor also had to be taken into account: the status of the United States air forces in the theatre, which were taken over on 20 August by General Stratemeyer.[12] While the Americans needed support from the Indian Government they were in no way answerable to it, yet if the concept of integrated command was to mean anything means had to be found to bring them within the new air command structure, something which became much more practicable once the RAF units had won their independence. Portal had addressed the basic problem early on, pointing out to the Prime Minister on 18 June the relative operational strengths of the two air forces. While the RAF combat strength outnumbered the American by 7:1, he said, the transport aircraft were almost exclusively American, so the USA ought to be asked to agree that the Air Commander should be British and his deputy American.[13] It was to be a while, however, before the final relationship was worked out. Soon after the Quebec Conference in August the principal senior commanders were named, including Peirse as C-in-C Air Forces, South-East Asia Command (his Headquarters would now be known as Air Command South-East Asia – ACSEA), but the Americans were reluctant to place Stratemeyer's air forces under him. These fighters, bombers and transport aircraft were intended primarily for the support of China, not for the campaigns in South-East Asia, and the Americans therefore wanted Stratemeyer to remain answerable to General Stilwell – who while becoming Mountbatten's Deputy Supreme Commander retained his independent role in relation to China.[14]

This was far from an ideal situation. It had its roots in the Americans' long-running policy to support China and develop it as a base for strategic air operations against Japan, and understandably they were reluctant to see that purpose constrained by commitments to any operations in Burma which were not directly linked to it. They were happy to co-operate with the British air forces in the area – indeed in their view relations between them and the RAF were more harmonious than between the RAF and the British land forces[15] – and, as Arnold told Stratemeyer, the success of this complicated command set-up depended in great measure on personalities; if a true spirit of co-operation was engendered it would work.[16] They were, however, anxious not to jeopardise their primary task by actually placing their forces under the British air commander. To Peirse and his staff, on the other hand, it seemed essential to move towards a structure comparable with that which was already proving itself in the Mediterranean. Since one of Mountbatten's two primary tasks was to be the maintenance and broadening of contacts with China, American commitments there now had to be built into the general scheme of Allied operations in South-East Asia, and the many operational arguments for the unified control of all the air assets in the theatre seemed to apply. Yet despite much negotiation during October between Peirse and Stratemeyer the latter felt there would have to be two parallel commands, not one.[17]

It was now that Mountbatten, newly arrived in Delhi, took a hand. The position, as he saw it, was that 'a subordinate air commander in my theatre was responsible to me for his air operations through a senior officer other than my Air Commander-in-Chief.' This could entail overlapping of effort, possible gaps in air defence, and lack of co-ordination: in a crisis the consequences could be very serious.[18] So on 28 October he chaired a meeting of those principally concerned at which they worked out what they thought would be the ideal integrated structure, yet the Americans remained unable to support it since it conflicted with their own directives, and when Mountbatten took over on 16 November the American and British air organisations were still independent of each other. He had already, however, written to the Combined Chiefs of Staff telling them of his decision to integrate the air forces, and in informal talks at Cairo with Portal, General Marshall and General Arnold he obtained their unofficial backing. Then on 12 December he issued the necessary directive, but Stilwell and Stratemeyer, while agreeing to carry it out, felt obliged to ask for their objections to be passed to the American Chiefs.[19] Mountbatten accordingly did so, forwarding their arguments together with his own rebuttal. He noted in his diary: 'It is time we had a showdown ... as to who is in command of this party'.[20] On the 22nd he updated Portal:

> The situation was truly electric after Stilwell and Stratemeyer had threatened to telegraph to Washington rather than carry out my orders to integrate ... I read the Riot Act to both ... I absolutely had to integrate ... the two Air Forces were running in watertight compartments with friction which occasionally came to a head.[21]

The answer he wanted came on 4 January in a letter from General Marshall heartily approving his action – though reserving the right to transfer units from the 10th to the 14th Air Force if necessary. Mountbatten had won what he considered an all-important battle. What may surprise us is that it needed to be fought at all. His orders had actually been implemented on 16 December, when 10th Air Force was placed under Peirse's command and Stratemeyer became his deputy. Mountbatten immediately welcomed Stratemeyer, confident that he would throw himself enthusiastically into the new set-up, and his trust was to be amply rewarded.[22]

So Peirse was now in command of all the Allied Air Forces. Mountbatten had already shown confidence in him; they had exchanged welcoming letters in September,[23] Peirse had backed him loyally since his arrival, and as Mountbatten later wrote in his Personalities Report: 'I could always rely on his support for determined and vigorous policies'.[24] Sadly, however, Mountbatten was also aware of a developing affair between Peirse and Lady Auchinleck – 'the eternal triangle' as he called it in a private letter to Portal on 13 October. Keen to try to avoid any scandal and anxious not to lose his air commander at this stage, Mountbatten went on to suggest that he might be moved elsewhere once he had completed a two year tour in India, ie. early 1944.[25] Three months later, however, a further letter to Portal made no reference to the affair; clearly he and Peirse were getting on well: 'Peirse has been good to work with, most co-operative and helpful, and a great support in times of trouble, both with the Americans and other non-co-operators'.[26]

It remains to consider at this point the structure of ACSEA, the new joint command (Appendix D). Since the main operational focus of the RAF and USAAF was in eastern India a new formation was established to oversee all the air forces in that area; titled Eastern Air Command (EAC) and located initially in Delhi alongside the main HQ it was led by Stratemeyer himself, who thus combined the role with that of deputy to Peirse. Into EAC came the units of Bengal Command and the 10th AF, which were divided by role into four subordinate formations:

(a) The Strategic Air Force, commanded by Brigadier General Davidson, USAAF, comprised the heavy and medium bombers, including the RAF's Liberator and Wellington squadrons, now controlled by a new 231 Group.

(b) The Third Tactical Air Force, effectively the successor to Bengal Command, comprised the fighter and light bomber squadrons of 221 Group at Imphal supporting IV Corps, 224 Group at Chittagong supporting XV Corps, and the Northern Air Sector Force, USAAF, at Dinjan supporting Stilwell's Chinese. The fighter squadrons of 293 Wing defending Calcutta were also included but were later placed under 3 TAF's direct control. 3 TAF was commanded by Air Marshal Baldwin, while Air Vice-Marshal Williams, his very able predecessor at Bengal Command, became Stratemeyer's deputy.[27] Baldwin's HQ was located at Comilla, alongside Slim's 14th Army HQ, and Slim comments on how they worked to a considerable extent as a joint headquarters, pooling intelligence, planning together and – most important – living together. Requests for help from other formations were usually routed through Baldwin, who became in effect his opposite number. Slim wrote: 'we grew into a very close brotherhood, depending on one another, trusting one another, and taking as much pride in each other's triumphs as we did in our own. The difficulties overcome and the successes obtained on the Burma front were a joint achievement'.[28]

(c) Troop Carrier Command, commanded by Brigadier General Old and also located at Comilla, initially controlled all the transport squadrons in Burma and Assam, except for those belonging to US Air Transport Command, but as its tasks grew and the pressure increased it became too inflexible and in June 1944 transport operations in support of 14th Army and XV Corps passed under the direct control of 3 TAF.

(d) The Photographic Reconnaissance Force, commanded by Group Captain S G Wise, was set up at Calcutta in February 1944 under the direct control of Eastern Air Command.[29]

Stratemeyer would later write of Eastern Air Command:

The various obstacles which might be expected to arise as a result of combining USAAF and RAF units have been overcome by integration of (the Headquarters staffs). Such a revolutionary change in staff organisation might well have produced many difficulties and misunderstandings, but such has not been the case and we have undoubtedly derived mutual benefit ... in the tactical operating of air forces.[30]

Elsewhere the existing RAF Groups (p. 122) continued, supplemented by two more, Nos 229 (Transport) and 230 (Maintenance). The former, at Delhi, co-operated with the recently formed RAF Transport Command and co-ordinated the internal air services and ferrying; the latter, at Calcutta, handled all RAF maintenance in the EAC area. In addition 222 Group's responsibilities were broadened to match the extended boundaries of the Naval C-in-C's command; effectively – as well as looking after Ceylon's air defence – the Group was now responsible for all air operations in the Indian Ocean from East Africa and Aden as far as the Japanese perimeter.[31] It also had a new AOC. In January Mountbatten, telling Portal how worried he and Peirse were about shipping losses, had requested some up to date experts from the Battle of the Atlantic, and Portal was able to promise him that Air Vice-Marshal Durston, currently Slessor's SASO at Coastal Command, would shortly be on his way.[32]

Durston arrived in March and was soon to find himself with new neighbours. While Mountbatten had no choice initially but to establish his headquarters in Delhi, where everybody else was, he disliked the social and political atmosphere and the generally negative attitude, and felt it important that his staff should stand on their own feet. Since he was keen at this stage to adopt a maritime strategy rather than have his forces bogged down in the jungles of Burma, Ceylon seemed the obvious place from which to exercise operational control, and Kandy – 'probably the most beautiful spot in the world and a delightful place in which to work' as he described it – was selected. Not surprisingly Admiral Somerville, his Naval C-in-C, was delighted; General Giffard, the Army C-in-C, on the other hand was strongly opposed – he needed the close assistance of Auchinleck's GHQ in Delhi, and Ceylon was even farther from the battle front in Burma – and Peirse, though feeling less strongly about it, also had his doubts, as did the Americans. Mountbatten was, however, not to be denied, and his move took place in April 1944.[33] Peirse, like Giffard, was unable to depart in such a hurry and therefore sent his RAF deputy, Garrod, to represent him. At the same time Peirse agreed that it was time for Stratemeyer to go forward to HQ EAC in Calcutta – a sound move in terms of co-ordinating the Allied air forces in the east. On the other hand the main headquarters were now hopelessly scattered – a situation hardly conducive to operational or administrative efficiency. So, for example, Mountbatten at Kandy was responsible for air policy through Peirse at Delhi, while Stratemeyer at Calcutta was responsible for fighting the air war over Burma. Consequently if Stratemeyer wanted a high level decision from the Supreme Commander a request had to go from Calcutta via Delhi to Kandy and return by the same circuitous route. Not until the autumn was this situation resolved, when the Air C-in-C moved his HQ to Kandy.[34]

Planning for 1944

As we turn now to the strategic questions that Mountbatten and his staff had to address, it is worth reminding ourselves of the wider war situation into which all their hopes and plans had perforce to fit. By the time of the Quebec Conference in August 1943, when Mountbatten was appointed, the Battle of the Atlantic was essentially won, the foundations for air superiority in Europe were being laid, the surrender of Italy was imminent, the Russians were driving the German armies back, Operation OVERLORD was at the detailed planning stage, and in the Pacific the Americans and Australians had seized the initiative. In South-East Asia, on the other hand, the position was one of stalemate, and with the climax of the war against Germany fast approaching it was inevitable that Europe would continue to take priority. As Mountbatten later wrote: 'This overriding factor condemned our strategy to being planned against a background of continued uncertainty about higher policy'.[35] This lack of clear purpose communicated itself to the British troops and airmen, confirming their impression that they were forgotten. In fact, as Ehrman observes, their affairs were being discussed more than those of any other theatre of war, but it was a complex, uncertain debate, marked by much hypothetical argument and conducted often in an air of unreality by men who had already borne heavy responsibilities for four years of war and were simultaneously preoccupied with the anxieties of invasion and victory in Europe.[36] Moreover, the 5,000 miles between London and India precluded the frequent personal contact so valuable elsewhere and largely restricted discussion to the signal and the letter. Slim quotes a poem composed by one of the planners:

> Plan followed plan in swift procession,
> Commanders went; commanders came,
> While telegrams in quick succession
> Arrived to douse or fan the flame.[37]

We can follow the actual debate only briefly. Mountbatten's October directive required him first to engage the enemy as closely and continuously as possible so as to wear down his forces – especially the air – and thus compel him to divert forces from the Pacific, and second (but equally important) to maintain and extend the links with China. In pursuit of the first objective he was to use the air and sea power that would be at his disposal to carry out some form of amphibious operation.[38] Churchill had already urged on him the potentialities of CULVERIN (p. 127) but it was soon clear that such an ambitious plan was far beyond the resources he could be allocated, and in November the Supreme Commander proposed a more modest seaborne operation to recapture the Andaman Islands – Operation BUCCANEER. This would deprive the Japanese of a useful forward base, enable shore-based fighters to cover the approaches to Calcutta, extend the range of the RAF reconnaissance aircraft, and enable Allied bombers to operate as far afield as Malaya and Indo-China. Though initially approved by the British and American Chiefs of Staff, it soon became clear that BUCCANEER too was over-ambitious, not least since the necessary landing craft would probably be needed for forthcoming operations in the Mediterranean connected with the Normandy invasion. Yet another amphibious assault was then considered – a landing near Akyab in conjunction with a land attack by XV Corps from the north – but in January this also had to be abandoned.[39] Until at least late 1944, it was clear, the needs of the European war would remain paramount. Then, once Germany was beaten, the entire Allied effort would be concentrated on Japan – including the might of the USSR, which had just undertaken to join in the assault when that happened.

So for the present Mountbatten would have to be content to pursue the relatively modest land/air operations on the Burma front which had been under discussion for much of 1943 – though, as we shall see later, more ambitious long-term plans remained under consideration. His directive of 14 January specified the operations now to be undertaken by Stilwell's Chinese forces in the north, by IV Corps from Imphal, by XV Corps in the Arakan, and by Wingate's LRP brigades behind the enemy lines.[40]

The Air Contribution

Support for these operations would be the task of Stratemeyer's new Eastern Air Command, whose men he addressed on 15 December in ringing tones:

> A resourceful, able and wily enemy must be blasted from the jungles of Burma and driven from its skies. His lines of communication must be obliterated, his shipping destroyed, his will to resist crushed ... our lifeline to China must be strengthened and protected. Every ounce of energy of every man of this Command will be required to accomplish this purpose. We must merge into one unified force neither British nor American, with the faults of neither and the virtues of both. I greet the forces of Bengal Command and their Commander, Air Marshal Baldwin, as comrades in battle and brothers in the air. A standard of co-operation which we must strive to surpass has been set by the striking example of joint achievement of our colleagues in the Northwest African Air Force. We must establish in Asia a record of Allied air victory of which we can all be proud in the years to come. Let us write it now in the skies over Burma.[41]

To do the job he had 11 heavy and medium bomber squadrons (seven of them American) and in 3TAF 26 squadrons of aircraft (19 of them RAF) for air defence and tactical strike operations. The Blenheims had gone, their squadrons converted either to Vengeance light bombers or Hurricane fighter bombers, and air defence was now largely in the hands of Beaufighters and – most important – Spitfires. In addition he had four PR squadrons (two USAAF), and three transport squadrons (two USAAF); significantly, while the total force would be much the same size six months later, there would by then be 11 Dakota squadrons (seven USAAF) operational.[42] As Peirse states, this was a more modern, powerful, and numerically stronger air force than had hitherto been available in this theatre, and much had been achieved during the monsoon to give it greater striking power.[43] On the other hand, 'as far as aircraft types were concerned, the RAF in South-East Asia was at least a year behind other theatres'.[44]

Peirse goes on in his Despatch to provide salutary reminder of the multiplicity of activities so essential to the RAF's operations. The vast programme of airfield development was continuing throughout India and Ceylon, with five airfields west of Calcutta being prepared for use by American B-29 bombers, and the construction of advanced landing grounds was giving the short-range aircraft greater radius of action. Aircrew training was now a major task, much of it to familiarise newly arriving reinforcements with the Command's aircraft and to convert existing crews to the new types with which their squadrons were starting to re-equip – notably Mosquitos, Liberators and Thunderbolts. There was also continuation training, notably at the Air Fighting Training Unit run by Group Captain Frank Carey, one of the Battle of Britain pilots who had later flown with great distinction in Burma and the Arakan; here experienced pilots and gunnery leaders were taught advanced air fighting tactics and gunnery.[45] The weapons posed great challenges to the all-too-small armament staff as well, especially with the arrival of 40mm cannon, rocket projectiles and larger capacity bombs.

Then there were the aircraft storage units and reserve pools, dispersed over much of India, together with the repair and salvage organisation: the 'fundamental and ineradicable shortcomings of the transport system' (Peirse's words) were making recovery so difficult that an airborne salvage section was formed in November 1943, using one of its own salvaged Dakotas to reach otherwise inaccessible crash sites.[46] The whole task of aircraft repair and maintenance presented enormous problems: the service tradesmen could not turn to reliable civilian contractors as they would at home; distance and transport difficulties made spares slow to arrive; manpower was below establishment, especially in some key trades; sickness rates were often high. Local manufacturing too was often unsatisfactory: for example the production of drop tanks to enable fighters to operate at longer range met interminable difficulties. On the other hand local industry coped well with simple types of equipment such as parachutes. Silk was scarce and to meet the high demand for supply dropping simple canopies were designed to be made from jute. Though not safe enough for men, these 'parajutes' were adequate for ordinary supplies and enormous quantities were produced costing just £1 each, as opposed to £20 for normal parachutes.[47]

Communications, too, continued to present major problems, with shortage of personnel the greatest single limiting factor in the expansion of signals facilities. Fortunately, in this as in many other areas, there was a high degree of co-operation and exchange of technical information with the Americans; in building up the much needed air traffic control system the two air forces worked closely together, and the same applied in the sphere of radar, where the warning and GCI units covered the bases of both. All signals planning for future operations was undertaken with mobility the keynote; when the Army advanced to Maungdaw, in January 1944, to quote just one early example, an early warning radar was anchored offshore, where together with a GCI and MRU sited on land it did invaluable work.

The warning system comprised more than just the radars, whose low cover was limited by the 'clutter' from the forests, especially when wet. The many gaps were filled by the wireless observer units (WOUs), which being portable could use good sites inaccessible to the vehicle-mounted radars. Bob Mitchell, who commanded one such unit, recalls having a number of posts spaced roughly 12 miles apart along a north-south ridge to the east of Chittagong, their supply base. Goods and personnel had to come by river boat, a week's journey, and then finally on foot along jungle tracks. The posts themselves, built of bamboo, comprised an observation tower where portable W/T equipment was installed, and the most basic domestic facilities; each had a corporal in charge, enough observers and wireless operators to cover daylight hours, and a mechanic who doubled as cook. Mitchell himself remembers visiting all his posts, travelling by river and on foot, and carrying an imprest account to pay the airmen and the village headmen for portering services: it was a 270 mile hike, mainly in monsoon rain.[48] The work of such men, and they were many, was a lonely, unspectacular but demanding job.

Moreover, like the men manning the radars, they were often well in advance of the front line and within range of the enemy's guns and night patrols, and it fell to the RAF Regiment to defend them and ensure they could carry on their tasks. The Regiment, never up to the strength required to defend adequately all the RAF's airfields and radars in the more forward areas, was now doing sterling and much appreciated work; as Baldwin wrote of them in late 1944:

They have proved themselves of the greatest value in this campaign of which the insecurity of airfields and warning establishments in forward areas has been a feature ... it has proved quite unsound to rely on the Army maintaining troops for local defence in times of crisis when the land situation deteriorates. This is the time when they are really needed by us, but this is the time when they are inevitably withdrawn to take part in the land battle.[49]

And so we could go on. The RAF and Army staff at the highly secure

Wireless Experimental Centre in New Delhi applied themselves to breaking, translating and evaluating the Japanese Army Air Force signals and thus contributing to the intelligence picture so vital for the Allied air operations.[50] The processing and interpretation of aerial photographs was a continuing, urgent and skilled task. The reporting and forecasting of the weather, so important for air operations, was never more difficult than under the climatic conditions of South-East Asia. There was the work of air-sea rescue, carried out by aircraft and launches off the Arakan coast, as well as around the shores of India and Ceylon.[51] Nor must we forget the men themselves, who needed to be accommodated, fed, clothed and equipped, paid, kept healthy and provided with welfare amenities. The many specialist services – administrators, caterers, suppliers, accountants, doctors, dentists, educators, chaplains and so on – all had their part to play. So when we turn shortly to the operations of Eastern Air Command in the challenging months of early 1944 let us not forget the extensive support organisation on which they all depended.

The Enemy Air Forces

First, however, we need to consider the opposition that EAC was facing, and a contemporary intelligence assessment of the fighting value of the Japanese air forces is worth some attention. Suggesting that the speed of their advance had taken them by surprise and that they had failed to appreciate the scale on which their replacements of men and material would be required, the report pointed out that their limited air resources were spread around a very extensive perimeter (including of course the south-west Pacific) rather than concentrated at a few strategic points from which powerful blows might be struck. When organised for attack and encountering only slight Allied opposition, their air forces had shown great persistence and energy, but now that they were on the defensive they were showing little ability to consolidate and hit back. Their former tactic of assembling units at rear bases, mounting a series of rapid attacks from forward bases and then abruptly withdrawing to the rear was no longer sound in face of the constant surveillance being maintained by Allied PR aircraft.

Moreover, the report continued, the Japanese still seemed preoccupied with the value of attacking airfields; they consistently neglected Allied lines of communication such as the supply route to China, they had almost entirely ignored the potential of strategic bombing against the inadequately defended towns and cities of Bengal in 1942, and they rarely tried to give their ground troops close air support. As for air defence, the frequency with which their aircraft were being caught on the ground suggested that their warning system was far from perfect. Pilot shortage was also mentioned; the Japanese honour code had often led to unnecessary loss of skilled, experienced men, the reluctance to fit armour protection had caused unnecessarily high casualties, and the training machine had not provided enough replacements. While their fighting spirit was excellent (Stratemeyer later called them experienced and resourceful – a courageous and worthy foe[52]), the aircrew were allowed to exercise little initiative, and other shortcomings included poor navigational skills, especially at night.[53] An earlier report based on a prisoner-of-war interrogation had drawn attention to the limitations of their training: fighter pilots were taught to keep out of clouds, given no instruction on blind landings, and possessed no air-to-ground communications.[54]

This was not the picture of an air force which could effectively counter the stronger Allied forces being gathered against it, though it would still be able to mount very considerable opposition. In South-East Asia this was represented at the end of 1943 by some 740 aircraft of all types, spread across Burma, Siam, Indo-China, Malaya and Sumatra. Of these it was the 370 aircraft of the 5th Air Division, based in Burma and Siam, that constituted the threat to EAC; 200 were fighters, 110 light and medium bombers and 60 reconnaissance aircraft. With the addition of 50 naval aircraft the total came to 420, whereas EAC had 719 aircraft of all types in north-east India.[55] Moreover, while Allied air strength would steadily increase during early 1944 that of the enemy would decline through attrition and withdrawals to other theatres.[56] Nevertheless, the balance did not yet weigh heavily in the Allied favour, for much effort still had to be devoted to the defence of the Hump route and eastern Bengal, and to protecting and co-operating with the land forces; moreover the enemy had the advantage of interior lines of communication. Nor was the Allied task made easier by gaps in the radar warning chain occasioned by some of the intervening mountains.[57]

So as 1943 drew to a close and the battles of 1944 beckoned, each air force realised that it was essential to try to neutralise the other. The fight for air superiority had so far proved inconclusive; now either Eastern Air Command or 5th Air Division had to win it.

Air Superiority the Key

The battle began on 20 October with Japanese attacks on the docks at Chittagong, and over the next few weeks their bombers, with fighter escort, went for a variety of targets, particularly airfields, in the Arakan, the Imphal plain and further back. They seemed to be following no systematic plan, which made it difficult to anticipate their moves, and the Hurricanes and Mohawks that attempted to intercept were still unable to achieve marked success.[58] At long last, however, the aircraft for which the fighter squadrons had been hoping were on their way. The high-performance Spitfire Mark VIII, with a maximum speed of 408 mph as compared to the 342 mph of the Hurricane II, had for some time been seen as the answer to the Japanese Zeros and Oscars, and was soon to be despatched in quantity. Initially, however, the Mark V was sent to hold the fort[59] and in October – a red letter day, Maurice Dean calls it[60] – three Hurricane squadrons were re-equipped. The first of them, No 615, reached Chittagong early in November and almost immediately shot down a formation of four Dinah reconnaissance aircraft which had hitherto been able to operate with impunity at heights and speeds which the Hurricanes could not match.[61] This spectacular success was enthusiastically greeted throughout ACSEA and from then on, as the Japanese admitted, their reconnaissance became much more difficult and experienced pilots were lost in large numbers.[62]

It was to be a while, however, before the Spitfires could really prove their mettle against the Japanese fighters. By the end of November 607 and 136 Squadrons had joined 615 in the Arakan and were seeking to intercept the enemy offensive sweeps that were being sent to test them, but on 5 December they could do little about a major Japanese attack on Calcutta. Alerted by reconnaissance to the presence of some 60 major vessels in the harbour, the enemy launched 27 bombers with strong fighter escort against the docks;[63] their route took them well south of Chittagong and although they were plotted the force of 65 Spitfires and Hurricanes sent from Chittagong to intercept lacked the range to reach them. Just one Spitfire pilot made contact; he shot down one bomber and then force-landed on a sandbank, out of fuel. So it was left to the Hurricanes of the newly arrived 67 and 146 Squadrons to try to tackle the raid over Calcutta itself, but they were unable to cope with the escorting fighters. Then when a second raid arrived 45 minutes later they were on the ground refuelling and only the night fighters were able to scramble. Both groups of bombers therefore attacked without loss, and the vain attempts to reach them cost eight Hurricanes. Two of the Spitfire squadrons tried to get to them on the way back but again without success.[64] It had been an unhappy episode for the RAF and a tactical coup for the Japanese, who had not expected to get off so lightly;[65] while their bomb loads were small owing to the distance of the mission, they succeeded in damaging three merchantmen and a naval vessel, setting fire to 15 barges, hitting several dock buildings, and causing 500 civilian casualties which were immediately followed by an exodus from the local area. The risks of repetition were obvious and some of the Spitfires were immediately sent back to Calcutta.[66] Soon afterwards 81 and 152 Squadrons, equipped with just arrived Mark VIIIs, became operational for its defence, but instead of trying to repeat the operation – as surely they should have done – the enemy switched their efforts to the main

The Supreme Commander was highly regarded, his frequent informal visits to the front line doing much to boost morale. Here he talks to Corporal E A Davey on a forward Hurribomber strip, February 1945. (*AHB*)

airfields being used by the Americans for the India-China air route, including Kunming, and not until late in the month did the Spitfires have the opportunity they were waiting for.

By now their new Supremo was out and about, paying frequent visits to the fighting forces of all nationalities, addressing many tens of thousands, and speaking personally to many of the officers:

> I told them I was convinced of the superiority of our forces – man for man and unit by unit – over the Japanese. I said there would be no more retreating, since any units cut off by Japanese infiltration would, in future, be supplied by air; and that it was my intention to fight for, and maintain, the high degree of air superiority necessary for the successful and uninterrupted operation of air supply. I told them we would fight on and fly on throughout the monsoon, giving the enemy no respite.[67]

His biographer records his call on 607 Squadron on the 16th, when he had to abandon his speech owing to the constant coming and going of aircraft: 'I was only trying to convince you that we will eventually have enough resources to ensure our victory, and the sight we see today on this airfield is better proof of that than anything I could tell you'.[68]

That such visits paid handsome dividends in their effect on morale brooks no argument in the view of the men who were there – quite contrary to the views of some latter-day critics.

Ten days later the enemy returned to Chittagong with an escorted force of 20 bombers; while three bombers and two fighters were destroyed, the Spitfire and Hurricane pilots were far from happy. Altogether 80 of them had been airborne, enough to give them a handsome victory had they been properly controlled; in fact, as an unco-ordinated collection of aircraft in groups varying from three to 12, they presented no problem to a compact enemy force.[69] Clearly it was not enough to have Spitfires; there were still lessons to be learnt from the European war about the way they should be used.

The turning point came on New Year's Eve. A naval force which had been carrying out a coastal bombardment was attacked by 14 Sally bombers and 15 Oscars, which in turn were intercepted by 136 Squadron's 12 Spitfires. Breaking through the fighter screen they picked off the bombers one by one and then took toll of the fighters. Altogether at least 13 were destroyed and most of the others damaged – huge losses the Japanese called them.[70] Just one Spitfire was lost, its pilot being machine-gunned after baling out but escaping when the enemy pilot crashed into the ground. Soon afterwards, Peirse tells us: 'The Secretary of State for Air signalled his congratulations and commented that the newly arrived Spitfires had come into good hands'.[71]

They had a further chance to demonstrate their superiority on 15 January, when the enemy mounted three fighter sweeps over the Arakan battle zone, each with 12 to 15 aircraft. In the surprising absence of top cover the Spitfires were able to position themselves above, and altogether at least 16 of the enemy fighters were destroyed at a cost of two. Most of the action occurred in sight of the Army's forward troops – an excellent fillip to morale. Five days later the score was seven for two when 24 Spitfires engaged another sweep of 35 fighters;[72] at last the RAF had achieved the superiority in air-to-air combat that had so long been denied, and when the enemy later introduced the better Tojo fighter and changed their tactics the Spitfire VIII was on hand to counter it and retain the advantage.

Wings of the Phoenix reminds us of some of the factors in the victory and not least of the work of Carey's AFTU, whose courses produced some of the most ingenious fighter pilots of the war: 'in Burma it was said that a remarkable proportion of enemy fighters brought down were destroyed by pilots listening to the echo of Carey's voice and obeying his teaching'. It also reminds us that the ground crews must share the backstage glory – up every night, at work under the stars, most were still the old campaigners who had gone out east at the beginning.[73]

There was, however, more to air superiority than this. What the Spitfires had done in the south was to prevent the enemy making significant daylight use of their bombers and stop their fighters making deep penetrations. On the other hand the attacks on Calcutta and the Hump airfields showed the existence in Burma of a relatively strong and aggressive enemy force that – able to attack anywhere over a 900-mile front which could never be given a really effective defence system – could still seriously interfere with Allied plans.[74] So the fight would have to be taken to the enemy with a counter-air campaign – just as the Japanese themselves had done earlier in the war. There was nothing new about this: experience in Europe as well as in the Far East had shown that fighters relegated to the passivity of routine patrols above ground held by their own troops would often fail conspicuously; indeed Trenchard had long urged the importance of taking the offensive against hostile aircraft over their own territory, and as far back as 1914 Churchill had stated in relation to the threat to London that the greatest defence against the aerial menace was to attack aircraft as near as possible to their point of departure.[75] This time-honoured principle of air power now had to be applied in South-East Asia. But how?

One method would be to use heavy and medium bombers – and at times these were employed, but they were also required for many other purposes, particularly the interdiction of the enemy supply system. In any case the Japanese were able to use so many airfields and airstrips, and were so adept at runway repair, aircraft dispersal and switching units between locations that bombing was rarely effective.[76] The answer had to be the long-range fighter. The need for such aircraft had long been recognised. Peirse had told Sinclair as early as May 1942 that the defence of India required an air striking force, including long-range fighters,[77] and Ludlow-Hewitt had subsequently supported him. Observing that the value of the comparatively long range of the Zero had impressed everybody and that the long range of the Mohawk had been invaluable, he went on: 'long-range fighters of superior performance would be of value for destroying enemy aircraft on their aerodromes ... and would contribute considerably to the task of obtaining air superiority in Burma'.[78] It was one thing for a far-sighted Inspector General to present the case; it was quite another for the Air Ministry to provide the aircraft. The nearest Peirse got in 1943 was his Beaufighter squadrons, and these were particularly suited, as we have seen, to interdiction. Then when he at last got his Spitfires they were needed very largely for defensive work in co-operation with the ground forces. So it was that the counter-air operations of early 1944 fell mainly to the lot of recently arrived American squadrons equipped with the really long-range P-51 (Mustang) and P-38 (Lightning).

The campaign lasted three months from March to May, and

coincided with the many other air operations connected with the major land battles of early 1944; these will be described in Chapter 9. The P-51s of 530 Squadron and the Air Commando Force were based in Assam, while 459 Squadron's P-38s were at Chittagong under 224 Group. Joined on occasion by RAF Spitfires and Beaufighters, and by USAAF P-40s and B-25s, they repeatedly bombed and strafed enemy airfields and aircraft spread right across Burma, their operations greatly assisted by the work of Y Service units which listened in to the enemy radio transmissions; according to Peirse 81 Japanese aircraft were destroyed in seven weeks thanks to their briefing information.[79] There were many successful days, perhaps most notably 4 April, when 25 aircraft were claimed destroyed at Aungban (Map 10) and the airfield was almost completely burnt out, while the American losses were minimal.[80] Magwe had been avenged, with interest.

It is not practicable to isolate the aircraft losses associated with the counter-air campaign from those connected with the many other air operations going on at the same time, but the 'bag' over the three month period, according to the Americans, was 309 aircraft destroyed (including 38 by the RAF), with 56 (21) probables and 193 (75) damaged, and special tribute is due to 459 Squadron's P-38s, which alone accounted for 125 of the 'definites' for a loss of only 10 of their own.[81] The RAF lost 96 fighters over the same period, but most of these were engaged in air defence operations,[82] and total Allied losses of all types of aircraft came to 230 – out of a vastly greater effort.

The real test of what was achieved, however, lay in the fact that by June 1944 the enemy air strength in Burma had been reduced to some 125 aircraft.[83] Admittedly Burma was receiving a lower priority for increasingly scarce Japanese resources than it had possessed six months earlier – which has led to suggestions in some quarters that the Allies won air superiority in Burma almost by default[84] – but the fact remains that they did now hold it, and it would remain theirs for the rest of the war. Moreover, just as important, the long-range fighters had prevented the Japanese air forces providing anything like the degree of air support that their land forces had expected when they took the offensive in the Arakan and at Kohima and Imphal. It is to these battles, and the coincidental Chindit operations, that we must now turn.

9   The Battle Joined

By the start of the 1944 campaigning season, as we have seen, it was clear that operations directed towards the reconquest of Burma would have to be conducted by land, without the aid of amphibious operations. The European war was still dictating the priorities, and with the Normandy invasion a mere five months away Mountbatten must make do with what he had. Four main operations were therefore planned. In the Arakan XV Corps was to secure the Maungdaw-Buthidaung area and prepare the way for the possible recapture of Akyab; IV Corps centred in the Imphal plain was to push forward towards the Chindwin in the attempt to engage and pin down as many Japanese forces as possible; in the north Stilwell's Chinese divisions of Northern Combat Area Command (NCAC) were to advance towards Mogaung and Myitkyina so as to protect the construction of the Ledo road to China and secure the air route; and Wingate's LRP Brigades were to assist the more northerly operations by disorganising the enemy forces opposing them and preventing their reinforcement and supply.[1]

These operations thus had the general aim of bringing the Japanese forces to battle, while at the same time reopening the land route to China, and to help matters, as Mountbatten says, 'the Japanese High Command played into our hands'.[2] They themselves had been planning a two-pronged offensive. Operation HA-GO was intended to destroy the British forces in the Arakan or at least draw off their reserves and prevent them being used elsewhere; Operation U-GO, a month later, was designed to capture the bases of Imphal and Kohima.[3] Success in these campaigns, which on previous experience they regarded as a foregone conclusion, would lead to the capture of Chittagong and open up the routes into Bengal, with incalculable consequences not just for the all-important Allied base areas, including the airfields, but also for India itself. What the Japanese totally failed to appreciate was that their advantage in interior land and river lines of communication could be counterbalanced by the Allied use of air supply. They knew that substantial numbers of transport aircraft were available but could not conceive – given all the hazards – that a major force, once isolated, could be properly supplied for long enough to affect the outcome.[4] No longer would the British troops have to retreat when cut off; now they could stay and fight. Moreover, as Mountbatten and his land and air commanders discerned, the Army would be fighting on their own ground, near their own bases and well within range of the vital transport aircraft.[5]

Battle was first joined in the Arakan, and then for the first half of 1944 – with minds at home largely concentrated on the preparations for D-Day – several bitter campaigns were fought in parallel, each having its effects on the others and all heavily dependent on air power. Support for the NCAC offensive was essentially a USAAF commitment and we shall concentrate here on the three campaigns involving the RAF.

The Second Arakan Campaign

After the abortive battles of early 1943 the Japanese had been left firmly in control of not just Akyab but also the area to the north as far as the important east-west road across the Mayu hills between Maungdaw and Buthidaung (Map 7), and by the end of the year this route had been heavily fortified. So when in November General Christison's Corps began its southward advance from Cox's Bazar across very difficult jungle and swamp terrain, they faced no easy task. The plan was for 5 and 7 Divisions to move down the Mayu peninsula and for 81 (West African) Division to guard their eastern flank in the Kaladan Valley, where it would rely totally on air supply. Supporting them was Air Commodore Gray's 224 Group which at the end of December (apart from the three air defence Spitfire squadrons) had six squadrons of Hurricanes (mainly IIc and later on increased to eight squadrons), an RIAF tactical reconnaissance squadron (Hurricane IIb), and two Vengeance squadrons. They were based in the areas of Chittagong, Comilla and Agartala, from where they assisted the earlier stages of XV Corps' advance, but in January most were able to move forward to fair weather strips from where they could operate at short range to support the assaults on the main fortified positions.[6]

The two Vengeance squadrons, Nos 8 (RIAF) and 82, were heavily employed, carrying out no fewer than 552 dive-bombing sorties in 28 attacks during January, but the results were disappointing; only a direct hit had much effect on a small bunker hidden deep in the jungle, and rarely could the target be accurately pinpointed.[7] The strategic bombers – 16 B-24s and seven B-25s – joined them on the 26th against a strongly fortified hill east of Maungdaw, and the artillery followed up: 'To the observer it did not seem possible that there could be a single survivor ... the tanks closed in ... behind came the infantry ... to run into a merciless hail of small arms and mortar fire'.[8] There was a lesson here. As Mountbatten put it, the depth of the dug-outs and the

The Hurricane, first used in the battle of Singapore, remained operational until the end of the war, later on mainly in the ground support role. Here a 'Hurribomber' is being bombed up for operations in Burma. (*AHB*)

nature of the terrain made air bombardment relatively ineffective, and heavy bombers in particular – operating in small numbers over great distances and often in poor weather – were not suited to this type of operation. On the other hand he recognised that with experience pilots of light and fighter bombers who knew the country and the enemy tactics could achieve the necessary accuracy – as would be proved time and again as the war moved on.[9]

So despite the combined efforts of XV Corps and 224 Group the battle for the Maungdaw – Buthidaung road remained undecided by early February and on the 4th the enemy launched HA-GO. As Patrick Turnbull tells us, 'the concept was based on lessons learnt in early 1943, boiling down to the principle that should XV Corps find its communications severed there would be panic British retreat or surrender'.[10] Using infiltration tactics the main Japanese thrust was accordingly directed through 7 Division's positions north of Buthidaung and thence turning west to attack the Division from the rear. Another thrust from the south then linked up with it near Ngakyedauk Pass, so cutting the only route that linked 7 Division with 5 Division to the west of the hills. 7 Division was thus encircled, its Headquarters was disrupted and most of its units were under attack.

According to all precedents from the Malayan campaign onwards, the land forces would now have beaten a hasty retreat, but in fact nothing of the sort occurred.[11] Instead all were ordered to hold firm and the Battle of the Ngakyedauk Pass was on. Popularly known as the Battle of the Box – the Administrative Box at Sinzweya around which General Messervy now concentrated his men – this witnessed some of the bitterest, cruellest fighting of the Burma war, with the Japanese sparing nothing (Slim's words) in the attempt to destroy 7 Division.[12]

Whether they would succeed depended on the RAF, and first and foremost on the fighter pilots. The enemy had mobilised a strong fighter force and with sweeps of 60 or more aircraft appearing over the battle area the great anxiety was to maintain air superiority for, as Mountbatten says, supply dropping would have been impossible without it. He goes on quite simply: 'the air battle was fought by the three forward squadrons of Spitfires, for which Hurricanes provided airfield cover while they refuelled and re-armed.'[13] The balance sheet came to 65 Japanese aircraft destroyed, probably destroyed or damaged during the first 13 critical days, for a loss of three Spitfires; to quote Louis Allen 'the Japanese were pushed out of the skies'.[14]

Yet to begin with it looked as though the Dakotas might have problems. Certainly they and their support organisation were ready; to back up his general instructions to 14th Army that forward units were to stand fast and rely on air supply, unless given specific orders to withdraw, Slim had told his administrative staff to prepare and stock the supply units at Agartala and Comilla,[15] and when on 8 February he asked for General Old's Troop Carrier Command to take over the supply of 7 Division he made only one attempt to interfere with the planning. He felt it would be a good idea to put a case of rum in every fourth or fifth plane to make sure that the men on the ground would search for everything dropped to them. 'Sir', replied General Snelling, his principal administrative staff officer, 'I have already given orders for a case to be put in every plane'.[16]

The task fell initially to the Dakotas of 31 Squadron, for the only other RAF transport aircraft available at that moment belonged to 62 Squadron, which had been fully committed to the support of 81 Division in the Kaladan Valley for the past month.[17] The first sortie that tried to reach the dropping zone on the 8th had to turn back to avoid enemy fighters and General Old led the second sortie himself. This time nine of the 16 aircraft got through to make their drops, but a precious Dakota had been shot down, and the next day several more were forced by light anti-aircraft fire to abandon their sorties and some were badly damaged.[18] Very soon, however, 194 Squadron – just arrived in Bengal from its training area in the Punjab – was joining in the operation, and over the following days as the battle raged on the ground the transport crews gained the measure of their task. The danger from enemy aircraft and small arms fire led to some of the deliveries being made at night, but the DZ for the 'box' itself was overlooked by the enemy and could only be supplied by day, so special circuits had to be devised to keep the aircraft as far as possible out of range of enemy fire.[19] It was a hazardous business. Douglas Williams, a wireless operator/air gunner with 194 Squadron, known throughout the theatre as 'The Friendly Firm', describes it:

On 14 February we arrived over the DZ at 1630 hours and did a normal run in to idcntify ourselves to the Allied troops, and spotted huge puffs of smoke in the jungle and fields below which indicated that the battle was still in progress at that spot. We began our drop at 500 feet and had to pass over enemy lines on each circuit. On either the third or fourth run we heard gunfire over the roar of the engines. We must have been incredibly low, but Joe Curtis excelled at low flying. Suddenly black smoke gushed past the loading door as Jimmy Howe and Ian Darnley stood with me steadying the bales on the static lines ready for the next drop. I rushed to the cockpit as the aircraft lurched, to be told by Joe that the port engine had been hit and he had feathered it. There was still quite a load on board and it was difficult to maintain height on one engine. We were now very low and the trees were flashing by. I thought a crash landing was inevitable and wondered if it would happen over enemy or friendly territory.

It didn't. They got rid of the rest of the load, gained enough height to climb over the Chin Hills, and two hours later made a perfect landing at Agartala – where the pilot, instead of receiving the DFC his crew believed he deserved, was reprimanded for not landing at the first satellite strip on the way home.[20]

Williams's Dakota, like many others, had shown a remarkable ability to take punishment, and incredibly, thanks to the skill of their crews, the tactics devised, and the protection provided by the escorting Hurricanes, the only casualty in the whole episode was the one aircraft lost on the first day. By the 20th the enemy were in difficulties, having failed to capture the supplies which they had planned on and increasingly concerned at what their Chief of Staff was calling 'the cylinder position operation' of the British. As Louis Allen explains it: 'down into Sinzweya, like liquid through a cylinder or funnel, poured the munitions of war'.[21] Three days later the Japanese were in retreat, and the next day 7 Division regained contact with 5 Division. The siege was over. With 26 and 36 Divisions pressing in from the north the enemy was beaten and XV Corps was able to resume its offensive in early March.

Without doubt the massive intervention of the transport aircraft, amounting altogether to over 700 sorties, had a decisive effect, yet it was a close-run thing. By the end of February the entire RAF element of Troop Carrier Command was committed in the Arakan, including a fourth squadron, No 117, which arrived from the Mediterranean and began supply dropping on the 24th. Between them they were supplying two divisions totally and two more partly, and since the American squadrons were fully employed in the north Troop Carrier Command was stretched to the limit.[22] Moreover transport aircraft were about to be urgently required for the fly-in of Wingate's LRP brigades, and if this were not to be abandoned reinforcements seemed essential. The only aircraft that might quickly be made available, however, were those of US Air Transport Command operating the air route to China, aircraft which could not be diverted without the authority of the Combined Chiefs of Staff. Arguing that the LRP operations were largely intended to help protect the Hump route, Mountbatten therefore requested the necessary permission, and on 24 February he was given the use of 25 C-46 Commando aircraft which operated in the Arakan until land communications were fully reopened in mid-March.[23]

The RAF's contribution in the Arakan battle was not limited to the transport aircraft. The Hurricanes have already been mentioned; it was they who bore the burden of escort, patrol and offensive fighter operations, the latter directed particularly against Japanese communications leading into the battle zone.[24] The Vengeances, which in one week alone flew 269 sorties, harried the enemy's moves by bombing reported troop concentrations and bunkers; while target identification remained difficult, the Army recognised the value of their support in physical terms and in the effect not only on their morale but also on that of the enemy.[25] The Wellingtons and American B-25s tried to help as well but remained relatively ineffective against the kind of targets offered. It became increasingly clear both during the Battle of the Box and in the subsequent fighting in the Arakan that close support bombing was a task for the smaller aircraft operating in rapid response to requests from the ground. Smoke shells were of some help, but the real answer lay in R/T communications, which made a modest start in the Arakan. Coupled with this was the need for greater contact and understanding between the airmen and the soldiers so that each became aware of the other's problems, and for a system of control that was responsive to the Army's needs. To this end an Army Air Support Control (AASC) under a wing commander was set up alongside XV Corps HQ at Cox's Bazar. The system did not work terribly well, but these were early days.[26]

Another important role was tactical reconnaissance, carried out mainly by the Hurricanes of 6 (RIAF) Squadron. Operating usually in pairs, they flew at about 50 ft in open country and 100-150 ft over the jungle, heights at which they could achieve surprise and actually see something; as the pilots gained experience they learnt how to look into the jungle rather than at it, and when opportunity offered they would use their weapons.[27] Slim makes a point of saying how impressed he was by the work of this particular squadron.[28] Unfortunately neither their cameras nor the ground equipment for photographic processing were anything like up to date, and despite all their efforts – backed up by the activities of the PR force – the results at this stage failed to match the requirements of the Army and the tactical squadrons.[29] Another task of 6 (RIAF) Squadron to begin with was artillery observation but in January 1944 the Austers of 656 (Air Observation Post) Squadron, flown by army pilots, arrived to take over the role and during the rest of the campaign they operated from close alongside XV Corps Headquarters.[30]

One further air contribution requires mention here: casualty evacuation. Slim, who well understood the overriding need in the jungle war to win the battle of health and insisted that great effort be devoted to it, wrote: 'Air evacuation, in the long run, probably made the greatest difference of all to the wounded and sick'.[31]

While Dakotas which had air-landed supplies could obviously be used at times there were many situations where only light aircraft could operate, and in the Arakan this was an improvised affair. The Americans provided some L-5 Sentinel aircraft for a short time to fly 200 seriously wounded men out of the Box,[32] but most of the effort was provided by RAF Fox Moths and Tiger Moths, the latter specially modified to carry stretcher cases – one per aircraft. Altogether light

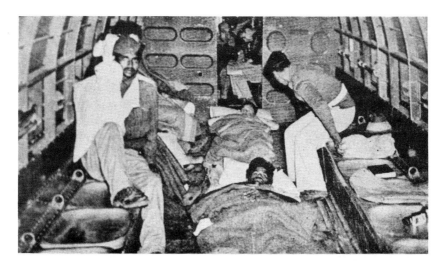

The casualties were brought back. (*Air Transport Operations on the Burma Front*)

aircraft evacuated over 1,000 casualties in the Mayu and Kaladan areas; their devotion and their ability to land their aircraft in small jungle clearings undoubtedly saved a great many lives besides relieving army units of the embarrassment of carrying wounded and sick men.[33] Backing them up at the forward airfields were the Dakotas. Theirs too was an improvised service, fitted in when possible with their supply missions; nevertheless during the Arakan campaign they took over 6,000 casualties back to the base hospitals in India.

That the second Arakan campaign, and in particular the Battle of the Box, was a highly significant achievement brooks no argument. Patrick Turnbull goes so far as to call it 'one of the decisive turning points in World War II', comparing it with the Battle of Britain, Stalingrad and Midway, and pointing out that for the first time in history a Japanese army had been defeated on level terms in the jungle it had made its own; thereafter they would never win a major victory.[34] When we reflect on the European war and the far greater scale of the operations being carried out against the Japanese in the Pacific, this may seem to be overdoing it; the Battle of the Box was fought by just one Japanese division and involved only four British. For the Burma war, however, it was certainly seen by those who were there as 'the turning point'. Slim so described it,[35] as did Mountbatten. Paying tribute to the preliminary training and reorganisation carried out in India under Auchinleck, Giffard and Peirse, and to the timely preparations which had been made, he went on:

> Mainly it was the fact that we were able to supply the troops by air, as they had been promised, which gave them the certainty that they would eventually be reinforced, and that the tide would turn in their favour.[36]

So it was by its effect on morale, Mountbatten believed, that the significance of the victory was to be judged. As Louis Allen observes, the British had used their material superiority in tanks and aircraft with intelligence and skill, and their victory was also – at last – one of morale and ideas.[37] In effect, therefore, the Battle of the Box witnessed the successful proving of a new weapon. According to Turnbull, 'without in any way detracting from the fighting qualities of the British and Indian soldiers who between them smashed the Japanese legend for invincibility ... they might well have succumbed but for this new weapon.'[38]

Note the term: transport aircraft are not always thought of as weapons of war. But in Burma they were now firmly recognised as such, and thanks to their flexibility were about to be switched to meet other equally pressing demands.

The Second Chindit Campaign

For the decision to mount another LRP operation we must go back to the Quebec Conference in August 1943, when Wingate – brought along by Churchill – so impressed the Combined Chiefs of Staff that they agreed to give full backing to an expedition into northern Burma. The Americans were particularly keen on this, since by interfering with Japanese communications and distracting their forces it would assist the advance of Stilwell's army towards Myitkyina and thus further their strategic objective of reopening a land route to China. So as the planning and preparation proceeded in late 1943 and early 1944 there was strong American backing, and the final concept was for most of Wingate's six brigades not only to be supplied by air but also to be delivered by the same means. Rapidly constructed 1,200 yard airstrips would then be used for air-landing supplies and reinforcements and for casualty evacuation, and the surrounds would be turned into well defended strongholds (Wingate's term) serving as bases from which individual columns would operate in the adjacent areas.[39]

Air power was therefore critical, in terms both of air transport and of air superiority, and to Wingate's delight General Arnold, Commanding General of the USAAF, decided on his own initiative to present him with a private air force, soon to be entitled the Air Commando Force (ACF).[40] Commanded by Colonel Cochran and comprising 12 B-25 bombers, 30 P-51 fighters, 25 transport aircraft, 100 L-1s/L-5s, four helicopters and 150 gliders, this was an invaluable asset, though not everyone was enamoured of it. The RAF staffs in London and India who had begun working out how best to meet Wingate's requirements were not exactly amused when told of its formation and there was anxiety about command and control: for Wingate to be given an air force dedicated solely to his campaign flew in the face of the conventional wisdom that all air forces in a theatre should operate under the single direction of an air commander working in close collaboration with his army opposite number. Eventually it was agreed that it should come under Baldwin's control, as Air Commander 3 TAF, so that its activities could be properly co-ordinated with those of other RAF and USAAF formations, but throughout its existence it retained its separate identity and operated only in support of the LRP brigades.[41]

The direct RAF contribution to the operation was therefore limited. 221 Group lent a hand occasionally with its Vengeances and Spitfires but was too deeply committed elsewhere to do more, and the four transport squadrons joined their American colleagues in the initial airlift (apart from glider-towing) and the subsequent supply operations. There was, however, another critical role. Having proved their value with Wingate's columns a year before, the RAF ground parties were now needed in greater strength, and – despite reluctance in some quarters to spare them – the case for having experienced airmen on the ground to direct the air support won the day, though this time not all the aircrew officers sent were pilots. Altogether the RAF Component Special Force comprised 60 officers and 162 airmen, all of whom again shared the rigorous training and the many tribulations that followed.[42] Their primary role, as devised by Squadron Leader Thompson, is described by Shelford Bidwell:

> When direct air support was called for they could 'talk down' the supporting aircraft so that they were able to bring their tremendous fire-power to bear on the Japanese even when they were locked in combat with the columns. The Chindits learned to trust their accuracy implicitly.[43]

By early February 1944 the broad planning was complete. The first three of Wingate's brigades were to converge on the area of Burma within 40 miles radius of Indaw (Map 8), thus cutting the communications of the enemy troops opposing IV Corps and the Ledo sector; 16 Brigade, supplied by air, would move in from the north overland, and 77 and 111 Brigades would be inserted by air in a six-day operation, Operation THURSDAY, starting on the night of 5 March – a date determined by the moon period. Three landing areas were chosen, code-named Broadway, Piccadilly and Chowringhee.[44] Then, as the detailed planning continued, the air transport force found itself totally committed in the Arakan, and it was the end of the month before it could be switched back to prepare for the new task.

Nevertheless on 5 March all was ready. 80 gliders were lined up at Lalaghat, the mounting base; 52 were to be used on the initial 200-mile sortie to Broadway and Piccadilly, two towed by each ACF tug, and 12 RAF and 10 American aircraft would drop supplies. Then at 1710, 30 minutes before take-off time, there arrived photographs of the landing areas just taken by a B-25, showing that Piccadilly had been obstructed by tree trunks, though Broadway was clear. Wingate, convinced says Slim that the whole plan had been betrayed, wanted to call it off. Slim, however, remembering that Piccadilly had been used by Wingate's men in 1943 and that a photograph of it featuring a Dakota had appeared in *Life* Magazine, thought this could have caused the enemy to blockade it; betrayal would surely have led to all three areas being obstructed. He and Baldwin, the responsible air commander, therefore decided that the operation should continue. The plans were rapidly changed so that Broadway alone should be used that night, and take-offs commenced at 1812 hours.[45]

Not much went according to the hurriedly rearranged plan. Of the 52 gliders 17 failed to reach Broadway, most because the tow ropes broke (double tows were thereafter forbidden), and several of them deposited their loads near Japanese headquarters thereby creating several invaluable unplanned deceptions. Of the 35 that did arrive most crashed on landing, partly thanks to the unexpectedly rough ground, partly to faulty loading.[46] The last-minute change of plan had clearly not helped, and it needs to be said that Wingate, anxious not to give the game away, had forbidden low-level air reconnaissance over the landing areas during the previous week. Nor had the specialist PR squadrons operating at high level been asked to maintain discreet surveillance, as they could easily have done. It was Cochran who had ordered the last-minute B-25 sortie on his own initiative.[47]

In fact it was not the Japanese who had blockaded Piccadilly but a group of local foresters. Operation THURSDAY had not been betrayed and during the critical day following the initial landings at Broadway there was no Japanese interference. Despite the initial chaos, coupled with the failure of the first supply drops, 'what had been a few hours earlier an unfrequented forest glade was now a busy airfield, strewn with wrecked gliders, in which men were erecting defences, sorting equipment and organising a camp',[48] and by evening the airstrip was ready to take Dakotas. There followed that night 65 sorties bringing men, mules and equipment, 38 of them flown from Hailakandi by the RAF. One of them, piloted by Group Captain G F K Donaldson, the commander of the Dakota wing, brought in Baldwin, who wrote later:

Nobody has seen a transport operation until he has … …watched Dakotas coming in and taking off in opposite directions on a single strip all night long at the rate of one landing or one take-off every three minutes.[49]

That same night 12 glider sorties were made to the other selected landing area, Chowringhee, and again after initial difficulties the first few Dakotas managed to land on a 900-yd strip 24 hours later. The full-length strip was ready by 8-9 March, when 78 Dakotas came in.[50] Aboard an RAF one was Richard Rhodes-James, a cipher officer with 111 Brigade:

I will always remember that first sight of Chowringhee – a brilliantly lit flare path cutting a long, narrow path through the jungle clearing – we circled for 30 minutes as other planes came in – and were then skilfully deposited behind the Japanese lines. The pilot departed – he had another trip that night.[51]

Altogether on the 8-9th 160 sorties were flown to the two strips each entailing a round trip of some 500 miles, and by the time the initial fly-in was complete, the night of 11 March, the tally amounted to 660,

331 flown by the four RAF squadrons and 329 by the Americans. They had carried 9,000 men, 1,350 animals and 250 tons of stores,[52] a remarkable achievement made possible among other things by a high degree of air superiority, enemy ignorance of what was happening, favourable weather, great night-flying skills, and – as Bidwell reminds us – 'a tour de force of staffwork'.[53] The result was the acquisition of a valuable defended airfield – Broadway – deep behind enemy lines. The second – Chowringhee – had already been abandoned; nearer the enemy and more exposed, it had served its purpose in providing a lodgement for 111 Brigade and distracted the enemy from the more important Broadway, and hardly had the Brigade moved out on the 10th than it came under enemy attack.[54]

Three days later 15 Japanese Oscars found Broadway but since Air Commodore Vincent, recently appointed AOC 221 Group, had already responded to a request from Wingate, they were intercepted by five of the six Spitfires of 81 Squadron that had been deployed to the airstrip the previous day.[55] While one Spitfire was shot down, the others destroyed several Oscars; then on the 17th 12 Oscars caught the defences by surprise and four of the Spitfires were destroyed, three on the ground. The light radar set had already been knocked out; adequate warning was impracticable; so the remaining Spitfire was withdrawn. It had been a gallant effort but to little avail. Yet the enemy failed to capitalise and for nearly two months Broadway's air transport operations continued almost unimpeded.[56]

By now a second 'stronghold' was being established. Code-named Aberdeen, the strip was prepared by 16 Brigade and brought into use on the 23rd; although fairly regularly attacked by enemy aircraft it too remained in use until early May, proving particularly valuable for casualty evacuation. The light aircraft based there would bring them in and on one particular night as many as 200 men were flown out by Dakota.[57] It was, however, much more dangerous than Broadway: a mere 500-600 yards long it was situated in a valley with hills on three sides. So as Deryck Groocock, a 194 Squadron pilot, recalls: 'It could only be approached from one direction and take-off must be in the opposite direction. Once committed to an approach an overshoot was deemed impossible'.[58]

Meanwhile the first real clash with the enemy troops had occurred on 16 March, when 77 Brigade from Broadway attacked their positions near Mawlu and established themselves across the road and railway. This block, soon known as White City, incorporated a light aircraft strip used by L-5s and occasionally by Dakotas, and it too was held until early May. With 16 Brigade then operating further south, near Indaw, Japanese communications to the north were thus effectively cut.

On 24 March, however, with his first brigades now achieving success, the American B-25 carrying Wingate from Imphal to Sylhet

The mules had to go too – with reluctance. (*Wings of the Phoenix*)

crashed in the hills killing all on board. While some accounts state that
the weather was particularly bad, Baldwin, who had just been
conferring with Wingate in Imphal and was flying not far behind,
recalls it as a good flying day on which the isolated storms could be
avoided. The precise cause was never established.[59] The loss of
Wingate was a severe blow; great controversy still surrounds him but
certainly he provided the drive and inspiration for both the Chindit
campaigns. Let it be said quite simply: whatever his shortcomings, for
his vision of what soldiers could achieve with the help of air power in
the conditions of jungle war he deserves our lasting recognition.[60]

Space does not permit detailed description of the subsequent
activities of the LRP brigades, now commanded by Brigadier
Lentaigne. Sufficient to say that in the absence of all-weather airfields
(the one enemy airfield that was captured in April – Indaw West – was
fair-weather only) it would be impracticable to continue operations
once the monsoon arrived, so at the end of April the evacuation began.
First Aberdeen was cleared, entailing 188 Dakota sorties carrying
1,500 men and 68 animals (mules were too valuable to leave behind),
together with weapons and supplies. Then came White City, from
whose short airstrip the weapons, equipment and casualties were all
removed on one night under the noses of the enemy by 37 Dakotas,
whereupon the garrison stole away. Finally, between 1 and 12 May,
183 sorties shifted 2,265 men and 188 mules, plus stores, from
Broadway.[61] All in all, this was another remarkable operation whose

complexities in terms of detailed planning, constant improvisation and sheer skill in night flying must command our admiration. Observing that, except for one aircraft which crashed shortly after take-off due to pilot error, not one aircraft was lost at either Aberdeen or Broadway by accident or from enemy action, Bidwell writes: 'So ended a tour de force of airmanship and staffwork, unnoticed, unsung and unrewarded, as such actions always are when perfectly executed'.[62]

It is worth reflecting for a moment on what this effort entailed. Ever since March the Chindits had had to compete for air transport and supply against the demands of the Imphal battle, which we shall be discussing shortly. One consequence was that no empty sorties were allowed to run into the strongholds, so casualties could be evacuated only on aircraft that had brought supplies. Then when the main evacuation took place in May the Dakota schedules had to be dovetailed into those needed to support the besieged garrisons at Kohima and Imphal, where the battle was at crisis stage.[63] Nor must it be forgotten that throughout the operation not only the strongholds but also the mobile columns had to be supplied, the latter by air drops, the total task requiring some 45 sorties per day. Most of the work was organised at Air Base HQ, Sylhet, to which supply requests were signalled from the field, and the RAF officers with the columns had, among other things, the duty of selecting the DZs and arranging the drops.[64]

Their main task, however, was to advise on and control direct air support, most of which was provided by the B-25s and P-51s of the ACF. Owing to the demands of the Imphal battle it was only the Vengeances of 84 Squadron based at Kumbhirgram that could do much to help, as they did for example by bombing enemy dugouts near White City, but they were based a long way back, needed fighter escort, and could not bomb through low cloud; moreover, equipped with VHF and usually unable to communicate with the men on the ground, they were at a great disadvantage compared with ACF aircraft which were fitted with HF radio and could talk to the ground troops by R/T. The value of the R/T links between the American aircrews and the RAF officers with the columns was soon proved: the crews did not need detailed pre-briefing and could therefore respond more quickly, their targets could be adjusted on arrival, there was close confidence between air and ground, and aircraft could be redirected elsewhere if necessary.[65] Squadron Leader Thompson himself directed the strike aircraft at White City on 19 April 'with devastating results' according to Bidwell,[66] and there were many other successes; altogether they mounted 382 tactical operations in just over three months, amounting to 1,904 sorties.

Hardly surprisingly the Army was loud in its praise not only of the RAF men who marched with them but also of the Air Commando. To

The L-5 was ubiquitous. (*Wings of the Phoenix*)

quote Richard Rhodes-James, 'American air support made the whole operation possible'.[67] He was, of course, referring not just to the B-25s and P-51s, the transports and the gliders but also to the light aircraft, which he called 'the lynchpin of the whole operation – a bigger factor in sustaining morale than anything else'.[68] Peirse too recognised the value of the L-1s and L-5s:

They could land more or less at will even in bad country to convey messages and supplies of small bulk, carry commanders from one unit to another, evacuate casualties and perform a host of miscellaneous services without the risks attendant upon wireless silence or employing heavy aircraft. I consider their widespread use in future comparable operations essential.[69]

He might have added a word about the handful of helicopters which the ACF also put to use, a portent of things to come.[70]

Peirse was less enthusiastic about the Air Commando principle. While accepting that such units had their place as spearheads for airborne and air transit operations, he believed it dangerous to tie down fighter and bomber aircraft permanently and exclusively to one particular Army formation with the consequent risks of duplication and lack of flexibility.[71] So when the 90-day term that General Arnold had given the ACF came to an end at the beginning of May the Air Ministry accepted Peirse's view that it should be disbanded. This was certainly a blow to the Chindits who were still in the field, for they would now have to stand in the same queue for air support as everyone else; the ACF had done them proud – and it must be said had taught valuable lessons about how to apply close support. The real point, however, as urged by the RAF, was that all the aircraft in the theatre needed to be available to the air commander; to earmark some of them exclusively for the support of one formation was fundamentally unsound.[72]

The departure of the ACF in early May coincided with the decision to use the remaining Chindits to assist Stilwell's forces advancing on Mogaung and Myitkyina, and orders were given to establish a new fortified block across the railway north of Pinbaw, soon to be known as Blackpool. Unlike the earlier strongholds, this lay in an area frequented by the enemy, and it took four incident-packed days, with a good many glider and Dakota pile-ups, before the airstrip became properly usable on 13 May.[73] Rhodes-James describes the scene:

> There was always a moment of agony as the aircraft throttled down, whether they had come too low, too high, too fast. One plane bust a tyre, shot off into the paddy and burst into flames – the crew got out (there were no passengers) and walked off. Chesty Jennings (the RAF officer on the spot – he had been a Blenheim and Sunderland air gunner) dived gallantly in to rescue the mail. It was an amazing scene, a continuous roar of engines, huge flashing lights and an organised chaos of men deplaning, stores being offloaded and jeeps running about. Our column RAF officers were controlling and with every pilot wanting to get down and get off it was not an easy task.[74]

For a few days Blackpool held; then on the 20th the monsoon broke. Close support sorties became impossible so the enemy was able to move his guns in and on the 22nd overran the airstrip. With supplies running out the Dakotas forced their way through and

> we were treated to as daring a display of flying as I have ever seen. They came in at 50 feet … the Japs opened up with everything … they were sitting targets … one called 'sorry if my dropping is a bit inaccurate but my rudder controls have been shot away'. Then we watched as most chutes drifted slowly but surely into enemy lines.[75]

Sadly not even the most determined flying could replenish the fast dwindling supplies of food and ammunition.[76] It was time to go. Amid appalling conditions of rain and mud, the exhausted garrison moved out across the hill tracks carrying their wounded with them. Other columns too were on their way north, many of their men sick and some dying. Surely they had done enough.[77]

Yet at this point all were transferred to Stilwell's command, and he – having captured the all-weather airfield at Myitkyina on 17 May amid much publicity and oblivious to their condition – was determined to use them to help complete the destruction of the Japanese forces in north Burma. Thus it was that 77 Brigade, still supplied by air (largely by 117 Squadron) and given tactical air support despite the weather, contributed in June to the capture of Mogaung. Minor actions continued in support of Stilwell's other forces for a further two months before the last elements of the LRP brigades were withdrawn in August.

Throughout these final monsoon months casualty evacuation was a major problem, and one particular episode deserves mention. Many of the survivors from Blackpool made their way to Indawgwi Lake, and with the waterlogged ground rendering land-based operations impossible it was decided to try using a Sunderland to move the sick and wounded. According to Rhodes-James it was Jennings' own idea – received with horror at AHQ and only pushed through by a very senior officer who nearly lost his job.[78] Since Calcutta was too far away, the 230 Squadron aircraft alighted at Dibrugarh on the River Brahmaputra on 31 May, attempted unsuccessfully to reach the lake on the 1st, and made it the next day. By the 6th another Sunderland had arrived, and Gert and Daisy, as the Army nicknamed them, operated in tandem until the 10th. By the time the last trip was made on 4 July, 13 sorties had been flown, each carrying freight out and bringing back up to 40 casualties. They were far from easy – the fast-flowing Brahmaputra presented problems (one of the aircraft eventually foundered at its moorings); flying in monsoon conditions at 11,000 ft in order to clear the mountains was unusual for a Sunderland, to say the least, and several missions had to be aborted; and most of the time there was no fighter escort.[79] Did the evacuation of 506 sick and wounded justify all the effort? In objective terms perhaps not, but the men themselves had no doubts.

So ended the Chindit War. One is bound to conclude that it was all of very questionable military value; it had little effect on the great Imphal battle apart from stretching Allied resources at a critical time, and in strategic terms the reopening of a land route to China was never going to make much difference; in March 1944 no fewer than 350 aircraft of American Air Transport Command were already operating over the Hump.[80] Yet the men who took part deserve great credit for their efforts in what at the time seemed to be an excellent way of exploiting air power to take the war to the enemy.

The Battles of Imphal and Kohima

We must now turn back in time to look at the battles that raged for several months on the central front and – for the first time in the Burma campaign – captured the world's attention (Map 8). An attack by General Mutaguchi's 15th Army had been expected for some while, and the prospect was indeed welcomed by Mountbatten, Slim and the

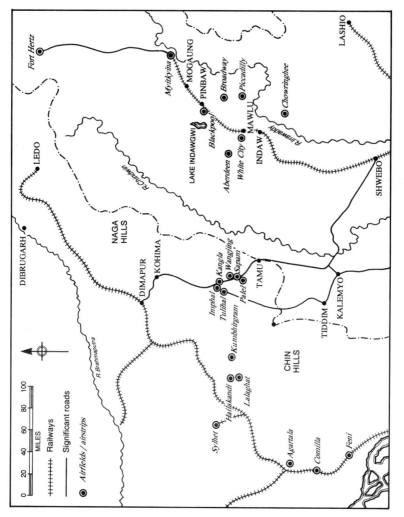

Map 8   North Burma 1944

air commanders. While IV Corps under General Scoones had been preparing to mount a limited offensive across the Chindwin, they recognised that their chances of destroying 15th Army would be much better on ground of their own choosing. At Imphal the enemy would be at the end of long, precarious lines of communication, whereas Slim's men would possess the inestimable bonus of air supply from bases that were relatively near at hand.[81] There were of course risks. In enemy hands the Imphal plain with its airfields and other military installations would pose a serious threat to the rail route through Dimapur to the main air bases in north-east Assam; indeed the whole Allied position in eastern India would be in danger, and with it the American air supply operations to China.

Land transportation was always difficult. The Manipur road to Kohima was a typical 'main road'; many were far worse. (*Norman Franks*)

Many writers have described the beauty of the Imphal plain, some comparing it with Kashmir.[82] 'From the air it was a breath-taking panorama: a beautiful green oasis in an otherwise unbroken stretch of high mountains, so unexpected and out of place that it looked almost artificial, like discovering a bowling green on the other side of Everest'.[83] Some 3,000 ft above sea level, covering 600 square miles and surrounded by jungle-clad mountains, it was accessible from the rest of India by only one proper road leading from Dimapur via Kohima, and transport aircraft had to cope – especially during the monsoon – with a wall of storm clouds over the mountains that often made flying utterly impossible.[84] Yet the valley itself, with its relatively low rainfall, had been recognised since 1942 as the one area where it was possible to construct the forward airfields so essential to support military operations in the Chindwin theatre, and in late 1943 Imphal became the home of 221 Group. By now there were two all-weather airfields at Imphal and Palel, together with four fair-weather strips, and based on them in early 1944 were two Spitfire and five Hurricane squadrons, their early warning provided by radar and a screen of wireless observer posts in the hills to the east. Other 221 Group squadrons, including three Vengeance, were based in north Assam.[85]

It was on 8 March, just three days after the start of Operation THURSDAY (p. 174), that the first Japanese offensive move was spotted – an attempt to cut off 17 Division, located well south of Imphal near Tiddim, from the rest of IV Corps.[86] This move came a week earlier than expected and if – as had been planned – 17 Division was to be pulled back to assist the defence of Imphal, Scoones would now have to use his other forces to help extricate them, thus endangering his position in face of growing pressure further north. Immediately therefore there was a crisis. Reinforcements were essential, but there was disagreement about the degree of urgency and how to move them. General Giffard was according to General Pownall, Mountbatten's Chief of Staff, 'disturbingly complacent', and Pownall thought Slim showed little sense of urgency either.[87] The situation was not helped by Mountbatten being in hospital at the critical time suffering from an eye injury, and it was not until 14 March that Slim and Baldwin could bring him up to date and press for the extra airlift needed to transport 5 Division directly from the Arakan to Imphal. As Baldwin told him, the eight squadrons of Troop Carrier Command, already heavily committed, could not possibly do the job in the necessary timescale. On the 15th Mountbatten therefore signalled the Chiefs of Staff stressing both the dangers and the opportunities of the situation and stating that unless he heard to the contrary he was diverting for a month 30 aircraft from the China ferry route.[88] The Chiefs backed him, Churchill sent Roosevelt a telegram – 'the stakes are pretty high in this battle, and victory would have far-reaching consequences' – and on the 17th the American Chiefs agreed, though refusing Mountbatten's further request for authority to divert such aircraft in future without prior reference.[89] Supreme Commander he might be, but the Americans were not prepared to give him *carte blanche* on matters relating to the airlift to China.

So for the first time in history, as *Wings of the Phoenix* observes, an entire division was moved by air from action on one front to action on another hundreds of miles away. Starting on 19 March the task was accomplished in 758 sorties flown by the Dakotas of 194 Squadron and the 20 C-46 Commandos (the equivalent of 30 Dakotas) diverted from the Hump. It was a remarkable effort; for example

One gunner regiment came out of action in the Maungdaw area in Arakan one day, travelled all the following day to the airfield at Dohazari, spent the night taking its guns to pieces and the next day was airborne. A day later they were in action east of Imphal in the heart of the siege.[90]

Nor was this the whole story. With the enemy also pressing directly towards Imphal and in the direction of Kohima – where they might well not only cut IV Corps' land communications but also threaten Dimapur – a parachute brigade and an Army Air Support Control unit were flown in to Imphal as well, and then units of XXXIII Corps were delivered to Dimapur, some of them by air.

By now it was clear that the transport force faced a major challenge. The 130 RAF and US Dakotas of Troop Carrier Command, supplemented by the 20 Commandos, were already working flat out and could not be driven harder without risking heavy wastage in terms of aircraft and crews. Barely sufficient to meet immediate needs (including those of the Chindits), they could not possibly undertake the massive extra commitment which the fast developing situation around Imphal seemed bound to entail. On 25 March, therefore, Mountbatten appealed to the Chiefs of Staff for a further 70 Dakotas and authority to retain the Commandos. With the Normandy invasion hardly more than two months away there was little the RAF could do on its own, but given the urgency of the situation the Combined Chiefs agreed on the 29th to transfer 64 American and 25 RAF Dakotas temporarily from the Mediterranean[91] – more in fact than Mountbatten had asked for, as Portal reported to the Prime Minister, eliciting the response, 'Good'.[92] By early April most had arrived and begun to operate, though 216 Squadron, the RAF unit involved, could provide only 15 aircraft.

It was just as well they were being sent, for on 29 March the Japanese had severed the main road leading north from Imphal. 17 Division having virtually completed its fighting withdrawal from Tiddim, there were thus four divisions cut off in the area around Imphal, together with HQ 221 Group and its local airfields: a total of some 150,000 men, including 6,000 RAF. Then on 4 April the more northerly Japanese thrust reached Kohima, beginning one of the bloodiest land battles of the Second World War. Slim's 14th Army was now to be put to the critical test, and much would depend on whether the RAF and USAAF Dakotas could keep it supplied and what Vincent's 221 Group could do in its support.

The air supply task was examined at a major land/air conference at Comilla on 17/18 April. Assuming that the siege could well last until late June it was decided that IV Corps and the RAF around Imphal would need on average 540 tons per day, but the detailed plan then worked out quickly began to go awry. The demands of the Chindits, of the West African division in the Kaladan Valley, of unforeseen but urgent troop movements elsewhere: these combined with unexpected bad weather to cause a growing backlog. So in May the ration scales had to be reduced, two hospitals were evacuated westwards, and some 50,000 men whose presence was not essential were taken out. As part of this process 221 Group's strength around Imphal was reduced to six squadrons, with the remainder now operating from further back. At the same time a forward staging depot was established at Kumbhirgram, 50 miles from Imphal, so that Dakotas unable to cross the mountains because of bad weather would not have to carry their loads all the way back to their base airfields.[93]

Even with such measures the supply situation remained critical. On 28 April Mountbatten had been directed to return his Middle East borrowings by mid-May (the European war, with OVERLORD only weeks away, took precedence), and on 1 May he told the Chiefs of Staff how disastrous this would be. No reply came, so on the 4th Peirse warned Giffard and Slim that these aircraft must leave on the 8th. The Army Commanders' reaction was predictable: they would not be responsible for the consequences. Mountbatten's view was unequivocal: the aircraft would not depart without his orders. That evening a telegram arrived from Churchill: 'Let nothing go from the battle that you need for victory. I will not accept denial of this from any quarter, and will back you to the full'.[94]

Even that was not the end of the saga, for initially the loan extended only to 31 May and subsequently – despite protests from the Mediterranean – to 16 June, by when a new cargo group would have arrived from the USA. Moreover, such was the pressure, on 19 May 40 Wellington crews were attached to Troop Carrier Command to help its overworked airmen, and five Wellingtons were used to deliver over 500 x 250lb bombs to the tactical squadrons operating near Imphal.[95]

For all these efforts it was by only a narrow margin that the defenders of Imphal were kept supplied – and it must be remembered that this entailed not just rations but all the wherewithal for defence and attack. While the evacuations had reduced the daily requirements in late May to 412 tons (including 50 for the RAF) average deliveries amounted to only 100 tons early in the month, and 220 later on; and in early June Mountbatten, anxious lest IV Corps' supplies might run out, again signalled his concerns to London. Peirse and Stratemeyer, however, remained confident and rightly so as it turned out, for with an unexpected break in the monsoon, deliveries rose steadily during June to a peak of over 500 tons. This was the more remarkable because the hard strips at Palel and Tulihal (where bituminised hessian had been laid) had broken up and only the single narrow runway at Imphal and the well-drained fair-weather strip at Kangla remained usable. So by the time the siege was lifted on 22 June IV Corps' needs were being met and its reserves being rebuilt. It had been a great achievement, made possible as Kirby reminds us only by Allied air superiority and reflecting enormous credit on all the air and ground crews involved.[96] In broad figures 120,000 British and Empire troops had been wholly supplied by air (RAF and USAAF) for three months, a division had been flown in, and 50,000 administrative personnel and 10,000 sick and wounded had been evacuated[97] – an unprecedented achievement.

Elsewhere, particularly at Kohima, airlanding of supplies was impossible. On 5 April the 2,500 strong Kohima garrison was encircled by some 6,000 enemy troops, in a triangular area measuring 700 x 900 x 1,100 yards, and a fortnight later, when the gallant survivors were relieved, the scene was what Louis Allen describes as 'the nearest thing to a battlefield of the First World War in the whole Burma campaign'.[98] In his graphic account of the siege Arthur Swinson describes the RAF efforts to deliver their supplies. Sometimes, as on the 15th, the howitzer ammunition was dropped right on the gun positions; at other times exhausted men would watch despairingly as some or all the parachutes drifted into the enemy lines, to become what the Japanese called 'Churchill's rations'. Even drinking water had to come by air, dropped in motor-car inner tubes. Then, even though the

Often – as at Kohima – air drop was the only means of delivery. (*Wings of the Phoenix*)

siege itself was lifted, the bitter fighting at Kohima continued for two more months before the road to Imphal could be reopened, and many of the supplies – including water – still had to be air dropped.[99] Deryck Groocock describes one such sortie. Flying at 8,500 ft over unbroken cloud which obscured the 7,000 ft mountain below, he was searching in vain for a gap near his DZ when his aircraft suddenly for no apparent reason went into a spin. He recovered below the cloud at 4,500 ft in a valley, unbelievably spotted the DZ, dropped the load, and did a steep climbing turn out again through the clouds. His was the only one of 12 Dakotas to drop that day; aided by a large slice of luck he had well earned the congratulations sent him by the recipients of his load.[100]

We cannot leave the subject of air supply without briefly considering what was entailed. The transport aircraft had operated hitherto mainly from Comilla and Agartala, near which were two air supply depots; to reach these from Calcutta involved long journeys along congested railways and trans-shipment across the unbridged Brahmaputra, and in early 1944 the whole system was coming under heavy strain. Now Chittagong, Feni and Sylhet were also pressed into use, and a joint-service planning organisation worked out how best to use the available air effort. All sorts of permutations were possible. A Dakota based at Agartala might start its day by dropping supplies in the Kaladan Valley, collecting a load at Chittagong, delivering it to Imphal and then flying out surplus personnel. Another at Sylhet might drop supplies to the Chindits, collect passengers from a jungle airstrip, bring them to Imphal, and evacuate casualties to a base hospital. When one recalls that bad weather, particularly after the onset of the monsoon, could often restrict operations – indeed the daily lift was occasionally down to 10 tons – the ground supply organisation had to be immensely flexible, aircraft maintenance and loading arrangements had to be highly efficient and adaptable, and the aircrew had to be ready to fly to the point of exhaustion. Much of the time they were on instruments, yet with assistance from several fixing stations most of those on the Imphal run got through; in May, the worst month, the abort rate was less than 6 per cent. Then at the receiving end there could be congestion, landing and taxying accidents, unloading difficulties, and problems of organising return loads, not least of casualties. Imphal Ground Control, set up early on and having to do its work close behind the fighting front, played a crucial role.[101]

Nearby was HQ 221 Group, where Vincent had been asked early on by General Scoones if he wished to move his HQ and most of his units from the valley and operate from further back. Vincent was in no mind to do this – having, as he said, done enough retreating from the Japs in the past (p. 66) – and told his men they would be staying put.[102] Their task was to maintain the air cover so essential to the supply operation

The men of the RAF Regiment helped to guard the airstrips. (*Wings of the Phoenix*)

and the land battle, and Imphal was where they must be. So the orders went out: all men were to carry arms and be given extra combat training, emergency radio networks were to be established in case the telephones were cut, at every airstrip defensive 'boxes' were to be created, each self-contained but mutually supporting. The RAF Regiment could and did assist: a sergeant remembers his squadron being flown in from the Arakan as reinforcements and helping to keep one of the airstrips open throughout the three-month siege; he pays special tribute to their cook, Corporal Jones, who used broken biscuits and other scraps to conjure up palatable meals to be sent by mule to the isolated positions.[103] There were countless Corporal Joneses out in the Far East.

For all its efforts, however, the RAF Regiment lacked the strength to take over much of the defence at Imphal – indeed Peirse had recently had to resist Air Ministry attempts to halve its size. So the airmen usually had to provide their own guards and defensive patrols at night, and this proved to be particularly demanding at the more exposed airstrips such as Palel, where the enemy were only two or three miles away.[104] An MT driver who was there with 42 Squadron remembers it vividly:

We drew all aircraft and personnel into a 'box' at night and left
the airstrip exposed to the enemy patrols. Our box was a large
mound at the eastern end of the airstrip with bays dug from it;
from the top it must have looked something like a huge sprocket.
The aircraft were parked in the bays and we camped around them
mostly sleeping in the backs of wagons. The whole box was
surrounded by wire and inside were slit trenches. We all had to do
two hours' guard duty every night. We had nightly attacks from
marauding patrols, some of whom were Sikh deserters. They used
to come up to the wire and shout 'Johnny, Johnny, help me'; if one
of our men was foolish enough to go towards them they would
throw a grenade. Then during the day the enemy disappeared
and flying took place normally.[105]

Vincent, who had issued an Order of the Day when the Dimapur
road was cut and observed that 'Air Force humour would beat the Jap',
wrote later of the high morale that existed throughout the siege: it was
impossible to give the pilots too much flying, and the airmen would
work all day and all night to keep the aircraft flying and to guard them;
they were itching for the Japanese to try to attack their particular
spot, and this applied too at the isolated radar stations. Mountbatten's
informal visits, too, were great morale boosters,[106] just as was the fact
that the airmen could actually witness some of their pilots' air strikes.
Yet it was probably just as well that none of the positions ever came
under serious assault. Very basic living conditions, the arrival of the
monsoon, growing health problems,[107] regularly broken nights,
occasional small-scale air as well as ground attacks (especially at
Palel) combined with the high pressures of the men's normal work to
impose strains that were too much for some and certainly exhausted
many. If aircraft serviceability, however, was the yardstick, the
airmen deserved the highest praise, for a percentage of 85.5 in March
rose to 88.2 in July.[108]

Throughout these months the aircraft operated at high intensity.
Initially the work of the tactical reconnaissance Hurricanes of 1 (RIAF)
and 28 Squadrons in observing the enemy advance was particularly
important, as was the support given by the fighter bombers to 17
Division as it fought its way north from Tiddim.[109] Slim writes:

Had not our fighters maintained continuous cover and given
quick support at call, the withdrawal, if it could have been carried
out at all, would have been a much grimmer and more protracted
affair, with serious consequences to the main battle around
Imphal.[110]

Indirect support by the Vengeances and ground attack Hurricanes against the enemy's forward lines of communication was equally valuable, not least in preventing them using motor transport in daylight. Often there would be rapid response operations, such as on 29 March when a Japanese battalion was spotted by an RAF Hurricane just before nightfall a mere 10 miles from Imphal airfield. Despite having just been stood down for the night 33 Hurricanes managed to get airborne and, using their landing lights for illumination, broke up the enemy attack.[111] A fortnight later, on 13 April, the Japanese were even closer to Imphal, having captured a hilltop only a few miles away, and for one and a half hours Vengeances, Hurricanes and artillery prepared the way for the successful but costly assault that at last removed the danger.[112]

That same day – the 'Black Thirteenth' – the Kohima garrison was in dire straits, and the supply drops were being accompanied by close support whenever possible. Kirby describes how 'in order to fly low enough to ensure accuracy, the airmen risked crashing on the mountain sides or being shot at close range by the enemy occupying them. Added to these risks was the ever present danger of being engulfed in the sudden mists sweeping down from the surrounding mountain tops, or being caught in the violent air pockets – a formidable combination of dangers which needed great skill and courage to overcome'.[113] Five days later – just in time – came the air-supported attack by 2 Division that broke Kohima's siege. As Captain Peter Steyn of the 1st Burma Regiment wrote:

> To the garrison, it seemed unbelievable that the nightmare of the past few weeks could be drawing to a close. Tired eyes watched as fighter bombers of the RAF roared overhead to strafe GPT Ridge and the surrounding areas.[114]

The heavy fighting, however, both at Kohima and Imphal still had over two months to run, and although the RAF and Army staffs were not operating in a joint headquarters a very high level of understanding and co-operation was achieved. Much credit belonged to 23 and 25 Army Air Support Controls, joint-service units which had trained in southern India and were quickly moved in to work alongside IV and XXXIII Corps, respectively. Provided with 'tentacles' at division and brigade headquarters and 'links' at the forward airstrips, the AASCs enabled the Hurricanes and Vengeances to respond rapidly to the Army's requests; a former wireless operator with 25 AASC recalls with pride the work they did, stating – maybe with slight but understandable exaggeration – that not one of the 1,100 requests for close air support his unit received over the eight months it was active during the 1944 campaigns was ever turned down.[115] On one occasion, however, Slim considered cancelling a planned attack on the Japanese 15th Division headquarters since the unenterprising General Sato was one of his 'most-helpful' generals![116]

Detailed description of the intensive ground support operations that continued throughout the battle is quite impracticable; suffice it to say that, as the enemy continued his attempts to infiltrate into the Imphal valley during May, it was the Hurricanes' precision attacks in particular that helped repel them and subsequently became an indispensable part of the regular pattern of the Army's advance. Altogether from March to July they and the other tactical aircraft of 221 Group, mainly Vengeances, flew over 25,000 sorties;[117] their operations – together with those of the strategic bombers against tactical targets – are fully covered in Norman Franks' *The Air Battle of Imphal*.

The Battle of Imphal was crucial. 607 Squadron Spitfires and a USAAF Mitchell are seen here on Imphal Main during the siege. (*Norman Franks*)

Franks also recounts the essential contribution of 221 Group's five Spitfire squadrons engaged in protecting the air corridor to Imphal and in dealing with the attempts of the Oscars to attack the RAF airstrips and intervene in the land fighting. The need to withdraw the radar units from the hills to the east, coupled with the enemy's switch in late April from high to low-level tactics, made interception difficult and the Japanese were able to make some successful attacks. The balance of advantage, however, lay with the defenders: according to Franks 33 Oscars were claimed destroyed during March to July, with 22 probables and 61 damaged, against the loss of 18 Spitfires. Seven of these were to Japanese fighters and two more were destroyed on 3/4 July at Palel, after the Imphal siege had been raised but before the enemy could be driven away to the east. The damage was done when a small patrol penetrated to the dispersal and attached small bombs to these and other aircraft. One further incident deserves a word, for it demonstrated yet again that the Japanese were not the only enemy. 615 Squadron, which had already lost three aircraft in a storm on 15 June, left Palel on 10 August for Baigachi near Calcutta, found themselves totally disorientated in a turbulent monsoon cloud and lost eight of their 16 aircraft, with four of the pilots killed – including their fine CO, Squadron Leader D W McCormack. For a squadron that had acquitted itself with distinction throughout the Imphal battle this was a cruel blow.[118]

Two Burmese pilots who flew with 607 Squadron. (*Norman Franks*)

So by July 1944 the great battles of Kohima and Imphal (relieved on 22 June) were over. The success of the Japanese plan had depended on their ability to capture the Imphal plain and with it the mass of food and stores belonging to the British garrison. When Allied resistance – made possible by air supply – held the enemy at bay, their attempts to bring up reinforcements and supplies were largely thwarted by Allied fighters harassing their communications over a wide area.[119] Moreover the measure and quality of ground support provided by the fighter-bombers and dive bombers in the peculiarly difficult terrain of Burma proved of inestimable value. This is in no way to disparage the achievement of the 14th Army in inflicting what Swinson, echoing Slim, describes as 'the greatest defeat in the history of the Japanese army'.[120] Slim himself, however, had no doubts:

Without the victory of the air forces there could have been no victory for the Army ... the shares of the soldier and the airman were so intermingled that it was a joint victory.[121]

General Giffard too acknowledged the debt:

I am sure no one who watched them is likely to forget the courage, determination and skill of the pilots and crews who have flown through some of the worst weather in the world over appalling country either to attack the enemy in front of the Army and his communications ... or to deliver reinforcements, supplies, ammunition etc. to the troops isolated in the Arakan, Imphal and Central Burma.[122]

Ian Lyall Grant, who fought with 17 Division and has recently published an excellent study of the critical battles on the Tiddim Road, totally concurs: 'Never had an army been so dependent on air support ... the greatest credit is due to the RAF and USAAF for their remarkable achievement in one of the most hostile flying climates in the world'.[123]

The air victory was not won without cost, but this was hardly excessive considering the scale of the operations and the conditions under which they were carried out. Over the seven month period from January to July it was the Hurricanes that took the brunt, losing 97 of their number through enemy action or crashes; 38 Beaufighters were lost too, carrying out their dangerous intruder missions deep behind the enemy lines, together with 15 Vengeances and 34 Spitfires. As for the RAF Dakotas only three were destroyed by enemy action during the main supply operations we have been describing, and the total loss of 32 aircraft must be set against the almost 15,000 supply sorties flown in the seven months – a remarkable tribute to the aircrews, the groundcrews and the air defences.[124]

Yet for all that had been achieved on land and in the air the victory was in the end almost entirely overshadowed by events elsewhere. By the time the siege was raised the Allied armies were ashore in Normandy, and the great battle that ensued was of far more interest to those at home than the activities of a forgotten army and its associated air force in the distant jungles of India and Burma. For the present they would just have to soldier on, their achievements largely ignored.

The Kohima Memorial

We today remember them still. (*Michael Wilcox, 1994*)

10 The Long Arm of Air Power

We shall return later to the jungle war, but first we need to consider the multiplicity of long-range operations which the RAF was now undertaking – all with indirect application to the Burma campaign and some also with much wider implications.

The Ocean War

By the beginning of 1944 major changes were afoot in the Indian Ocean. Thanks to the surrender of the Italian Fleet the previous September it had become possible for the Royal Navy to rebuild the Eastern Fleet, and this was moved from Kenya back to Ceylon in January. The improved situation in the Mediterranean also enabled many of the convoys to India to be re-routed via Suez and the Arabian Sea, thus altering the pattern of naval/air operations required for their protection.[1] At the same time, however, there was a marked increase in enemy submarine activity. In 1942 the Japanese had established a submarine base at Penang and in early 1943 its facilities were opened to the Germans, who were keen not only to extend their U-boat offensive against Allied shipping but also to use submarines as blockade runners. As a result, by March 1944 when the threat reached its peak, there were seven German and seven Japanese U-boats operating in the Indian Ocean. These were small numbers when compared with those that had been engaged in the Battle of the Atlantic, but spread across 13 million square miles of ocean they took some finding, and the losses they inflicted in the first quarter of the year came to almost 200,000 tons – heavier than in any other theatre,[2] and serious indeed in relation to SEAC's urgent needs for the battles we have just described.

To help remedy this state of affairs it was fast becoming clear that means must be found to improve the control of the maritime aircraft operating from different bases in and around the Ocean. Already in December 1943 there had been some improvement when the Chiefs of Staff allotted to Peirse broad control of all the GR aircraft in Aden and East Africa, as well as those in India and Ceylon. This control would be exercised through AOC 222 Group in Ceylon, who would co-operate

There was a war at sea too, against the German and Japanese submarines.
(*AMWIS 310*)

closely with C-in-C Eastern Fleet. In practice, however, the great distances involved and the inadequate communications meant that the local AOCs had to retain operational control; AOC 222 Group could do little more than issue general directives.[3]

On 1 May 1944, however, a more significant advance was made, when a Deputy AOC was appointed at 222 Group and given his own staff in order to organise and supervise the operational effort of all the GR formations throughout the Indian Ocean. Entitled Indian Ocean General Reconnaissance Operations, this staff immediately attracted the ghastly acronym 'IOGROPS'. Their primary function was to travel round the many units involved to advise on and standardise operational procedures, tactics, training, intelligence and signals, and at the same time naval/air operations rooms were set up at the five main centres.[4] At last the proper control machinery was coming into place, and it was possible to start seriously applying some of the lessons of the Battle of the Atlantic. One of these was that air cover should be allotted to shipping in accordance with the degree of risk and the value of the convoy, particularly important in view of the need to conserve the limited force of ageing and hard-worked flying boats. Obvious though such a measure may seem, it had hitherto been impracticable, and the need for it was soon demonstrated by figures showing that in East Africa and 225 Group more than half the flying hours during May had been wasted.[5]

All this was in the future, however, when the enemy submarines stepped up their activities at the turn of the year. What they faced in the air was a loosely controlled force of something like 160 aircraft, half of them land-based, the rest flying boats. The former, consisting of three Liberator, three Wellington, one Bisley and two Beaufort squadrons, were based mainly in Ceylon, India and Aden, and the latter – nine Catalina squadrons and one Sunderland – in Ceylon, India and East Africa (Appendix C, note 3). This, however, is to over-simplify, for there were many forward anchorages and airfields to which aircraft might be deployed as occasion demanded; as Map 9 shows these ranged as far afield as the Seychelles, Madagascar and Mauritius in the south, Kenya and South Africa to the west, and Socotra and Somaliland in the north. So the GR squadrons had to be constantly on the move, for the vast area of the Indian Ocean presented an impossible patrol problem and the aircraft had to be concentrated where enemy submarines were known or suspected to be.[6]

Yet even when a submarine was found positive results were hard to achieve. To take an example from November 1943, a U-boat was sighted and depth-charged in moonlight off Cape Comorin by a 205 Squadron Catalina on convoy escort. Though damaged it got away, and the intensive search that followed over the next five days, until it had to be given up off the Nicobar Islands, entailed 18 Catalina, 11 Liberator and four Beaufort sorties.[7] Such operations were bound to be costly and pose questions of priorities. Similar questions were raised over convoy escorts themselves, as on 12 February 1944 when 222 Group was covering the transit of a floating dock and various Fleet units; partly in consequence no air cover was provided for the incoming troopship *Khedive Ismail*, whose surface escort was deemed sufficient. It was not, for *Khedive Ismail* was sunk by a Japanese submarine with the loss of over 1,000 lives.[8]

When ships were sunk, of course, the aircraft had their work cut out,

Sunderland EJ143 of 230 Squadron, taking off at Diego Garcia. (*AHB*)

and during the early months of 1944 rescue operations were of great importance. One of these began when a message was received on 1 February that survivors from SS *Fort Buckingham*, sunk near the Laccadive Islands a fortnight earlier, were afloat in lifeboats. After initial fruitless searches – and the loss of a Catalina on take-off – 15 survivors were found, followed later by others, and a rescue vessel was guided to the scene. This six-day operation by 205 and 413 Squadrons was carried out no less than 800 miles from their base at Koggala – a quite outstanding achievement.[9] We need to remember in this context that sinkings by Japanese submarines were being increasingly marked by atrocities, a matter about which in April C-in-C Eastern Fleet expressed his concern; this gave added weight to the importance of the rescue service which the RAF and their naval colleagues sought to provide, and was certainly a factor when the P & O liner *Nellore* and the American *Jean Nicolet* were torpedoed by a Japanese submarine in mid-ocean on 29 June and 2 July respectively. There followed a 14-day operation involving 34 long sorties, mainly by Catalinas from Diego Garcia, but including some by Liberators from Addu Atoll and one by a Sunderland, as a result of which 234 of *Nellore*'s 341 passengers and crew were rescued, together with those of the Americans who had not been bayoneted or shot.[10] Such operations – and there were many more – deserve an honoured place in our record. As the Narrators say: 'On no occasion when the RAF was called on for rescue work, and it was feasible to provide it, was it refused'.[11]

Just occasionally the airmen achieved the reward they were really seeking. Two U-boats had been sunk in later 1943, one by two RAF Catalinas from Madagascar and another by a Bisley in the Gulf of Oman,[12] but in 1944 they scored only one success, and that against a very determined opponent. U852, ordered to attack shipping between Aden and Bombay, was sighted on 2 May by a Wellington of 621 Squadron in the Gulf of Aden and damaged by depth charges. Unable now to dive, the captain used anti-aircraft fire to fight off a series of further Wellington attacks, in which 8 Squadron also joined, over the next 24 hours before his vessel finally blew up. Maybe it should have been despatched more quickly; the Narrators' very detailed account implies this. Nevertheless the end result was eminently satisfactory: a dangerous and ruthless enemy, well capable of inflicting heavy losses on Allied shipping, had been successfully disposed of.[13]

A success of a different sort had been achieved in February 1944. The Germans, desperately needing strategic materials and specialist scientific apparatus, were stepping up their attempts to bring them in by U-boat blockade runners operating between Penang and Europe, and critical to their operations (and also important for their submarines' offensive activities) were two oil tankers, the *Charlotte Schliemann* and the *Brake*. These sailed out of Batavia or Penang and were used to refuel U-boats in the unfrequented parts of the southern Indian Ocean. An attempt to intercept some of the blockade runners was made in January by three Catalinas sent to the forward base at Tombeau Bay, Mauritius, in January, but bad weather foiled their efforts. Then on 11 February, with seven Catalinas patrolling from Mauritius in co-operation with surface vessels, one of 259 Squadron's aircraft, piloted by Flight Lieutenant Bob Dutton, sighted the *Schliemann* 900 miles to the east and enabled HMS *Relentless* to intercept and destroy her. A month later another joint air/sea search was launched from Mauritius in order to find the *Brake*; several Catalinas again took part but this time it was a carrier-borne aircraft that made the essential sighting.[14] The loss of both his tankers threw Admiral Dönitz's U-boat plans into confusion and contributed in large measure to the ending of his offensive in the Indian Ocean.

Even so the enemy did not give up. With the arrival of more U-boats there were still five at large in the Indian Ocean by the end of May, and in July German and Japanese submarines sank five Allied merchant ships, followed by seven in August – a total of over 100,000 tons. Thereafter the U-boat threat fell away, partly since the Japanese needed their remaining submarines in the Pacific, and partly thanks to a remarkable operation by the strategic bombers to which we shall turn in a moment. Before doing so, however, we should recall two naval tributes to the maritime squadrons which had ceaselessly patrolled the Indian Ocean ever since 1942. Admiral Somerville, the Naval C-in-C, writing to Peirse in August 1944 just before departing, praised the co-operation between 222 Group and others in protecting the sea communications. They had not had much luck in killing submarines but the immediate appearance of aircraft when submarines were reported, together with their continuous patrolling of sea lanes near focal points, had contributed greatly to reducing the losses which would otherwise have occurred owing to so many ships having to run independently without escorts.[15] Later the naval historian wrote:

> The air escorts provided by the RAF commands in the theatre, from Aden and East Africa to India and Ceylon, though never large in numbers by Atlantic standards, undoubtedly contributed to the discomfiture of the U-boats and to the safe arrival of the thousands of fighting men and the vast quantities of supplies needed by the Allied land forces in India and Burma.[16]

One further measure was necessary to complete this discomfiture; it was taken on 27 October 1944 by Liberators of the Strategic Air Force. Their objective was the harbour at Penang (Map 9). This was not only a key point in the Japanese supply and fuel transport system that fed the Burma front but also, as we have seen, the main base of the

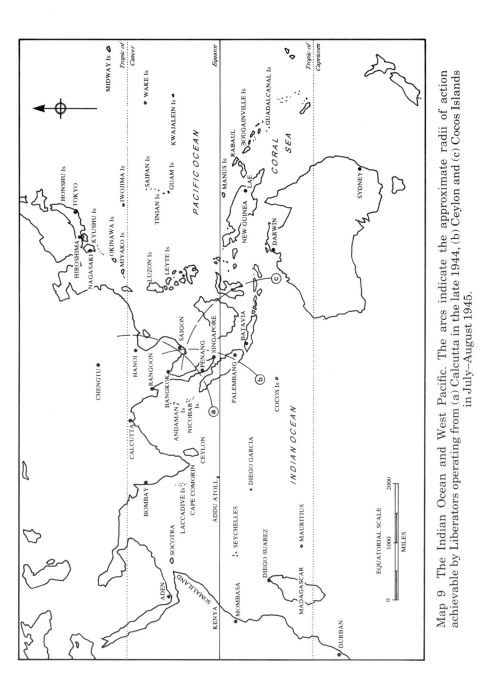

Map 9 The Indian Ocean and West Pacific. The arcs indicate the approximate radii of action achievable by Liberators operating from (a) Calcutta in the late 1944, (b) Ceylon and (c) Cocos Islands in July–August 1945.

German and Japanese U-boats operating in the Indian Ocean. Just as important it was a point of transshipment of strategic materials being carried between Germany and Japan. By mid-1944 the enemy were becoming increasingly worried about its security from Allied attack, but while attempts had been made by British submarines to mine its outer approaches it still seemed out of range of air attack. In early September, however, SEAC decided that Penang was such a worthwhile target that the attempt should be made to adapt some Liberators to the task.[17]

The choice fell upon 159 Squadron, based at Digri under command of one of the great unsung bomber COs of the war, Wing Commander James Blackburn.[18] As Eric Burchmore, the squadron engineer officer, remembers, Blackburn had been working hard to improve his aircraft's performance by removing such things as mid-position gun turrets and armour plating in order to save weight, and as a result the range/payload capacity had been raised to record levels. Even so Penang was 1,500 miles away, but Blackburn was a determined man. Burchmore writes:

> Calculations showed that with a full fuel load, including the bomb-bay overload tanks, 4 x 1000 lb mines could be carried, provided we had access to a 3,000 yard runway, and that the aircraft would withstand an all-up weight of 68,000 lbs (the normal maximum was 56,000). The operation would be risky from the start with a chance that the aircraft would not actually get off the ground.[19]

All the Squadron's 15 aircraft were prepared and moved to the American B-29 base at Kharagpur which possessed the necessary length of runway. One of the pilots recalls the CO saying that if he did not succeed in getting airborne each captain could decide for himself whether to have a go.[20] They all made it, though never with much to spare, and on 27/28 October Burchmore endured the longest 20 hours of his life before every one of them returned intact, their mission complete. Sixty mines had been delivered to the inner approaches to Penang harbour without enemy opposition – and to Burchmore's delight no aircraft needed afterwards more than a routine turn-round. They had all covered a distance equivalent to London to Moscow and back, one of the great bomber missions of the war, and had done exactly what the Navy wanted, placing the mines in 'precisely the positions ordered'.[21] The AOC later paid tribute:

> The very greatest credit must go to Wing Commander Blackburn, who by his personal example, enthusiasm and keenness demonstrated the effort that can be achieved by expert handling

of the aircraft, and so trained his crews that these magnificent results were achieved – not approached in any other theatre of war.[22]

Unfortunately a second attempt, mounted on 26 November, encountered dreadful weather and only three aircraft managed to locate their laying areas. Nevertheless the two operations had achieved the desired results. While no major ships were sunk by the mines, the Japanese lacked the means of clearing them, their use of the port was disrupted and most important of all the Germans decided to evacuate their base and withdraw to Batavia.[23] The U-boat threat in the Indian Ocean had gone.

So by this time had the Japanese surface threat. Ever since the attack on Ceylon in 1942 there had been fears that it might be repeated and at the end of 1943 the tasks of 222 and 225 Groups still included the defence of Ceylon and southern and eastern India against sea and air attack; hence two Beaufort torpedo bomber squadrons, one of Beaufighters for night air defence and four of Hurricanes were available, mostly based in Ceylon.[24] Then in early 1944 the Japanese began moving some of their major warships to Singapore. While the Admiralty – correctly as it turned out – thought they were probably making a tactical withdrawal from the Pacific theatre rather than planning an incursion into the Indian Ocean, the threat could not be ignored. Consequently, plans were laid for the assembly and despatch of air striking forces from Bengal including all the heavy bomber squadrons should the occasion arise, and bases in southern India and Ceylon were prepared and stocked for them.[25] Existing plans to re-equip the Hurricane squadrons with Spitfires were at the same time accelerated – and all this was happening just as the great land battles of Imphal and Kohima were about to commence. What effect might a major Japanese naval penetration towards India and Ceylon have had at that moment? Fortunately the enemy had no such intentions; intelligence that they were intent on using Singapore's facilities for repairs and training well away from the attentions of the US Navy and of Allied air power came as a distinct relief.[26]

The Americans were quick to see the advantages of keeping the enemy fleet in Singapore for a while, away from the action further east, so at their request Admiral Somerville launched a diversionary carrier strike against the naval base at Sabang on 19 April.[27] This and several subsequent attacks on Japanese bases were given extensive cover by the RAF's GR aircraft; for example, 50 sorties were flown in two days while the naval force was returning from a raid on Surabaya carried out on 17 May.[28] Such operations continued until the end of the year, by which time much of the Royal Navy's greatly expanded force in the Far East was being moved to the Pacific. Command of the Indian

Ocean and Bay of Bengal was at last firmly in Allied hands.

Strategic Air Operations

By European standards the Strategic Air Force at ACSEA's disposal in 1944 was tiny, though occasionally from June onwards it was augmented by about 100 B-29s of 20th US Bomber Command, based on several newly constructed airfields around Kharagpur, west of Calcutta. Though they were primarily intended for use against industrial targets in Japan from forward airfields in China, many of their 49 missions carried out between June 1944 and March 1945, when the B-29s were switched to the Pacific, were against long-range tactical targets in support of SEAC. One such attack, carried out on 10 August, involved 54 aircraft operating from China Bay against oil installations at Palembang. China Bay had been specially prepared with the 'friendly co-operation' of the British; the RAF went far beyond the bare essentials, virtually giving over the base to the Americans, and also set up an elaborate air-sea rescue force. It was in fact 'a glaring example of the extravagence of war', to quote the USAAF historian, for it achieved little and was not repeated, but it certainly exemplified the spirit of co-operation existing between the two air forces. Other B-29 missions were of more value, including attacks on Rangoon, Bangkok, Saigon and in particular the naval installations and commercial docks at Singapore which were bombed several times by forces of up to 100 aircraft.[29] Although Mountbatten did at one point ask for them to be placed under his command for a six-week period the Americans would not agree;[30] nevertheless the B-29 force – led for much of the time by General Curtis le May – in practice proved a valuable addition to ACSEA's striking power.

ACSEA's own Strategic Air Force consisted of the RAF's 231 Group, commanded by Air Commodore F J W Mellersh and comprising in January 1944 just four RAF squadrons, two still equipped with the faithful Wellington and two with Liberators, and also four USAAF squadrons of B-24s (Liberators) and one of Mitchells. So during the ensuing battles the total force numbered about 80 heavy and 50 medium bombers. Its size fluctuated as the year went on, with some of the American units being switched for a time to ferrying fuel over the Hump and 99 and 215 Squadrons converting from Wellingtons to Liberators, and by the end of the year the total force amounted to nine Liberator squadrons, all now under Mellersh's command. Of these four were American and five RAF (356 Squadron had just been formed), and it should be remembered that the RAF squadrons included a substantial number of men from the Royal Canadian Air Force. The problems of maintaining the aircraft should also be borne in mind; Eric

Burchmore points out that the fine laterite dust at Digri and Salbani made it very hard to service the more sophisticated equipment such as bombsights, gyromagnetic compasses and electronic items in general. He also mentions shortage of weapons, especially after the immense damage caused by the explosion of an ammunition ship in Bombay Harbour on 14 April 1944.[31]

By late 1944 the all-Liberator force was almost entirely geared to daylight operations; whereas hitherto the RAF squadrons had normally operated by night, it had always been difficult to pinpoint small targets at long range except in bright moonlight, and enemy air opposition had become so slight that it presented little danger. Only the long experienced 159 Squadron retained a night capability.[32] Maybe it was just as well that the enemy had few defences, for when Group Captain Leonard Cheshire spent two months in Eastern Air Command late in the year, he soon observed to Garrod that the heavy bomber squadrons were of lower standard than those of Bomber Command. Garrod was quick to point this out to Portal and request help from Harris at Bomber Command. A month later he could report that intensive training was under way and standards were definitely improving; he was particularly grateful to hear that 12 experienced Bomber Command crews were being sent to stiffen his squadrons.[33] The RAF bomber force in India, like so much else, had long been at the back of the queue; at last it was to receive at least some of the support it needed.

The essential task of the SAF in 1944 and 1945 may be simply stated: it was the interdiction of the enemy's entire transport system in South-East Asia in order to reduce his military power in Burma. In a sense this had always been the primary role of the longer range bombers, though they had been subjected to constant diversions and had in any case lacked the performance to cause serious disruption. Now they had better aircraft and support facilities coupled with growing experience, and faced a weakening enemy; interdiction, already a proven technique in Italy and about to be demonstrated to great effect in France, ought to be applicable too against the Japanese, even though the geography was so different.

To bring the materials of war to Burma from Japan itself, and from Manchuria where many of the industries were, entailed lines of communication extending over some 4,000 miles. During 1942 and 1943 the sea routes leading to South-East Asia and indeed round Malaya and Singapore to Burma had been virtually secure, as had the railways in Indo-China, Siam and Malaya, and in 1943 – using forced labour including many prisoners of war – the Japanese had built a rail link from Siam to Burma (Map 4). In Burma itself the ports and river routes had been subject to steadily increasing attack, but even so the

Japanese had succeeded in keeping them open. Now in 1944 all these communications were to be put under intense pressure. While the directive given to the SAF on 21 January still laid down that attacks on the enemy air force were to receive first priority this was not long followed in practice – such targets were better handled by the tactical air forces. For the strategic bombers the main objectives became ports and shipping, using mines as well as bombs, and rail communications – especially important junctions, workshops and bridges. Economic targets such as oil installations and factories were also included: the Japanese had so far been fortunate in Burma in that many of the supplies they needed could be locally produced.[34] It should be observed here that these were not in the strictest sense strategic targets – the genuine targets for strategic bombing lay in Japan and Manchuria. The so-called strategic bombers in India were really used in a long-range tactical role against a multitude of tiny targets; while of small significance individually, these were collectively of considerable importance in isolating the Japanese forces facing the Allies on the western perimeter from their main source of supply in the Japanese homeland.[35]

Of immediate value to the land battles of early 1944 were the constant attacks on the railways, which were particularly vulnerable at the main junctions, the many bridges, and along the long stretches where no alternative route existed, notably the Burma–Siam line.

Liberators regularly attacked major railway bridges, such as those on the 'railway of death'. (*AMWIS 294*)

Bangkok was a key target but being 1,100 miles away (the equivalent of a flight from the UK to Tunis) was until mid-1944 thought to be at the Liberator's limit of endurance. Then Wing Commander Blackburn's experiments with fuel consumption in 159 Squadron led to the payload being raised from 3,000 to 8,000 lbs, a remarkable improvement from which the whole SAF benefited.[36] The bridges came under steady attack, and while the Japanese were adept at repairing the smaller ones the constant disruption throughout Burma and further afield had a major effect on the supply of the Japanese armies. Some of the bigger bridges, such as the 1,650 ft one over the Sittang, proved impossible to repair in face of repeated attacks. As for the Burma – Siam route, to quote Clifford Kinvig:

> Once the line began to be raided regularly by the air forces, traffic came to a complete halt during the day and operated only at night. However in the early stages the main effect of the attacks was less the actual physical damage caused but rather the extent of the disorganisation produced.[37]

He goes on to say that the bombing was not particularly accurate and that it was the strafing of rolling stock and engines done by the Beaufighters that proved particularly effective. Even so, the Japanese raised the tonnage of supplies delivered along the railway from 70,000 in the first half of 1944 to 113,000 in the second. Yet as Kinvig concludes:

> In the end the immense investment in bombing the railway system paid off; at no stage did the strategic line, on which so many hopes were pinned, live up to the expectations of the planners.[38]

This – and indeed the entire assault on the railway system, which absorbed almost half the effort of the SAF during 1944 – was a continuing battle, one whose results were never absolute but which nevertheless played a central role in weakening the enemy's powers of resistance.

Entailing much less effort yet achieving very marked success was aerial minelaying, a concept which – perhaps surprisingly in the light of experience in north-west Europe – had had no place in the Allies' early strategic thinking. Previously done largely by the Americans this was taken over by 159 and 355 Squadrons in early 1944 and later became one of 159's specialities (as we have already seen in relation to Penang).[39] The mining of Rangoon early in 1943 had caused the Japanese to lose several ships and they stopped using the port other than for coastal vessels. This success led to the mining of smaller ports being used as alternatives, and then of ports in the Gulf of Siam, including Bangkok, and the evident effects of these operations on the enemy led in late 1944 to their extension even further afield. To quote the Narrators, 'the success of operations against ports, harbours and waterways, both by bombing and mining, must be judged not just by the number of sorties flown, or even the number of ships sunk, but by the absence of Japanese shipping from waters which had been mined and ports which had been bombed. The Japanese dared not risk their dwindling tonnage of shipping to the bombs or mines dropped by the Allied air forces'.[40] The effort required was modest: 327 aircraft despatched in the year November 1943 to October 1944 and laying 1,108 mines, for a loss of two.[41] It was one of the most cost-effective campaigns of the whole war – just as were Bomber Command's 'gardening' activities in European waters, also rarely given proper credit.

In the operations just described, and many others against ports, industrial and tactical targets, the losses were remarkably low – for the RAF, in 2,662 sorties between December 1943 and October 1944, 13 Liberators and five Wellingtons were lost, some of them not from enemy action but bad weather.[42] Nevertheless flying Liberators was certainly a hazardous business, and not least on take-off, as Terence O'Brien vividly describes:

> I never saw a fully loaded Liberator take off which did not brush the grass at the end of the strip ... there was a horrific fascination about the process ... its passage up the strip was more like that of a boat than an aircraft ... you would clench your fists, willing the thing clear of the ground, watching it thunder towards the reeds and then, miraculously every time despite its speed, its shape, its size and its weight, it would lumber into the air and miss disaster.[43]

And when things did go wrong, as with a 159 Squadron aircraft engaged on a radar monitoring mission on 31 January 1945, any crew members who fell into enemy hands were in deep trouble. On this occasion six survived the crash; all were tortured in the attempt to gain intelligence information, and the four NCOs among them were beheaded. One of them, Flight Sergeant SJ Woodbridge, was after the war awarded the George Cross; his citation is at Appendix F. An incident such as this provides another salutary reminder of what all aircrew who flew against the Japanese had to accept: to be shot down and captured would not mean what it normally meant in the European war.

Wing Commander Lucian Ercolani, who had flown a full tour of operations in Bomber Command, then joined 99 Squadron as a

Wellington flight commander and eventually succeeded Blackburn in command of 159 Squadron, echoes this. The thought of coming down among the Japanese was a constant anxiety, coupled with the fear of engine failure over the jungle or the Bay of Bengal, and the fright all too often occasioned when flying in monsoon conditions – especially by night.[44]

Special Duties Operations

Of all the missions flown in the Far East war few were more demanding than those of the special duties squadrons. Clandestine operations featured in every campaign of the Second World War, many of them under the auspices of the Special Operations Executive (SOE), and they depended heavily on dedicated air support by a wide range of aircraft whose tasks ranged from inserting and recovering agents to delivering arms and stores to insurgent forces. While the first full special duties squadron in the Far East was not formed until February 1944, a flight of Hudsons had been set up eight months previously, and the very first clandestine operation had actually taken place on 24 June 1942: prompted by the need for intelligence about Japanese movements, a Hudson belonging to the Air Landing School at Delhi parachuted two agents into northern Burma. The success of this operation led to three more in November 1942, when agents and stores were dropped, but shortage of aircraft and the relocation of the Air Landing School at Chaklala, 1,300 miles back from the forward base at Dum Dum, precluded larger scale activity. Early 1943 witnessed a successful drop near Bassein but poor visibility and serviceability problems thwarted a succession of attempts to make a delivery in the Toungoo area. At the same time, in an effort to achieve greater range than that of the Hudsons, 240 Squadron provided two Catalinas to take agents to Tavoy Island, southern Burma. The potential importance of such agents' work in intelligence gathering was now becoming recognised, but if their activities were to be built up and extended into areas outside Burma, especially in the first instance Siam, the RAF would need more and better aircraft and a dedicated organisation.[45]

No 1576 Flight was therefore established on 1 June 1943 and allotted six Hudsons, but thanks to the monsoon very few missions could even be attempted for several months; a key factor – one which affected all such operations – was the great strain that an unsuccessful sortie actually placed on the morale of the agents being dropped. Then, during the moon period of 11–19 October, no fewer than nine sorties into Burma were satisfactorily completed.[46] It remained clear, however, that aircraft of greater range were essential and in November the Air Ministry at last agreed to allocate three Liberators and nine

Catalinas. By February 1944 the Liberators had arrived and been modified for Far East conditions, and 1576 Flight became 357 Squadron, operating from Digri. The Catalinas, instead of being included in 357 Squadron as originally intended, were used to equip another new squadron, No 628, based at Redhills Lake near Madras, and the 240 Squadron crews who were already experienced in clandestine work were transferred to it. Yet not until May did the weather and sea conditions make its operations practicable, and in October, having flown a mere ten clandestine sorties as far as southern Burma and Bangkok, the squadron was disbanded. Given that submarines and patrol craft could undertake many of the coastal deliveries it was better for the RAF to be concentrating mainly on land-based operations.[47]

During 1944 these were the responsibility of 357 Squadron's handful of Liberators and Hudsons, the latter eventually being replaced by the more suitable Dakotas, and at the end of the year as the tasks built up a new Liberator squadron, No 358, was added. By now the operational base had been switched from Digri to Jessore, better placed for the receipt of agents and handling of stores,[48] and it was from here that support for the various agencies operating in Burma and elsewhere was provided for the last year of the war. These included Force 136, the Far East extension of SOE, whose tasks were subversion, sabotage and the preparation of resistance movements; the Inter-Service Liaison Department (ISLD), charged with collecting secret intelligence and carrying out counter-espionage; and the American Office of Strategic Services (OSS).[49] Terence O'Brien, who joined 357 Squadron in September 1944 and whose book *The Moonlight War* provides a superb insight into the whole business, describes the obsessive secrecy that surrounded everything, and particularly the activities of ISLD. There was nothing especially surprising about this – the same sort of thing had happened in Europe – but the refusal of the intelligence gatherers to have anything to do with the rapidly expanding Force 136 seemed to him both stupid and wasteful. Indeed on one occasion he was required to fly a Dakota all the way to Rangoon carrying a single 85 lb package for ISLD that could just as easily have been taken by another aircraft delivering to Force 136.[50]

357 Squadron had been making its mark for some time before O'Brien arrived. The Hudsons, their drops usually covered by nearby strategic bomber attacks, flew some 20 sorties to Burma in March, nearly all successful; unfortunately one aircraft was lost, whereupon the squadron medical officer, Flight Lieutenant George Graham, who had never before made a parachute jump, was dropped to try to aid the two injured survivors. One was beyond help but 15 days later, having avoided capture by the Japanese, the doctor and his companions reached an airfield in China with the other.[51] March also witnessed the

initial Liberator sorties, directed to Siam, but in April the hazards were again demonstrated when two aircraft made the first attempt to reach Indo-China, using Kunming as an advanced landing ground. One crashed in China, costing 13 RAF lives; the other made an incredible landing on the tiny airstrip at Fort Hertz. Incidents like these were unavoidable when inexperienced crews had to attempt one of the most difficult flights in the world – over the Hump from India to China.[52]

The squadron was not, however, to be deterred. Notwithstanding the onset of the monsoon, sorties to Burma continued – although all too often unsuccessful – and the Liberators began flying regularly over the Hump to ferry supplies for the advanced landing grounds near Kunming. From here, targets in Indo-China were within range, such as Hanoi and Langson (Map 2), and for the rest of the year two or three sorties were flown each month to deliver agents and supplies.[53] As O'Brien reminds us, the crews had more than just operational problems to contend with. Thanks to differences between the supporters of General de Gaulle and the officials of the Vichy regime, agents being sent to them often had to be kept separate, indeed ignorant of each other's existence. Then to make matters worse the Americans were opposed to any attempts to support the restoration of French authority in Indo-China; in their view assistance should be directed entirely towards the liberation forces led by Ho Chi Minh. Consequently crews staging through the American-controlled airfield at Kunming had to engage in elaborate deceptions to conceal the identity of their French passengers.[54] The official SOE historian refers to one of de Gaulle's representatives flying in a Hudson to Dien Bien Phu in November 1944 posing as a French Canadian member of the RAF and donning French uniform only when he landed.[55] Then as the scale of operations built up it often became impossible to use this route, and

we had to fly a thousand miles from India to do a drop when only a hundred miles from the DZ there were US airfields in China which, had we been able to use them, would have allowed us to quintuple the aid we gave the French forces.[56]

This brings to mind one particularly tragic incident. On 22 January 1945 11 Liberators of the recently formed 358 Squadron attempted to penetrate a massive frontal system in order to drop supplies in Indo-China; two succeeded and six brought back their loads, all – including the squadron CO – reporting ten-tenths cloud, severe icing and violent turbulence. The other three failed to return, the wrecks of two being later discovered in the Chin Hills. The third was never found. Sadly an American historian, Colonel Dunn, has recently tried to prove that all three were shot down by the USAAF and that the facts were ordered to be suppressed;[57] while this claim is of interest as a commentary on the Anglo-American disagreement over Indo-China, it runs counter to the location of the wrecks and the absence of any marks of gunfire. In any case, what chance would fighters have had in locating and destroying three Liberators at night in such weather? O'Brien is undoubtedly correct; as so often in the Far East war it was the weather itself that carried the blame.[58]

Dick Arscott, a pilot in 358 Squadron, reinforces this. Recalling his squadron's particularly high casualty rate, he considers the weather the greatest hazard; in earlier years operations had been restricted during the monsoon, but in 1944/45 they carried on regardless:

> Flying conditions were atrocious. Storm clouds developed more quickly than we could climb, so we were flying in the main through, around or underneath the clouds. Turbulence was always present. DZs could be as small as a cricket square, they could be anywhere, and some were very hazardous. Clouds covering hills no more than a mile away caused major problems of not only getting out of the valleys but getting into them in the first place.

Navigation was another problem, he says. There was supposed to be Loran coverage, but the navigators never found a signal fit to use and it was back to basics: drifts over the sea, astro when the sky could be seen, and inaccurate topographical maps. Fortunately he had the greatest confidence in the aircraft. Take-off at Jessore with a full load was never easy (several aircraft ran out of runway and crashed) but once airborne it would ride through the monsoon weather taking a terrible buffeting.[59] Arscott's view reflects that of many others who flew the Liberator in South-East Asia; it was a remarkably robust aircraft whose range and carrying capacity enabled it to carry out an immense variety of very demanding operations in some of the most difficult flying conditions in the world. Even so 357 and 358 Squadrons lost by the end of the war some 27 aircraft, only one of them due to enemy action.[60]

So by early 1945 the special duties Liberators of 357 and 358 Squadrons[61] were ranging far afield. In Indo-China there were some 50 DZs and 21 active W/T stations, but unfortunately the Japanese now clamped down on the French[62] and thereafter most of the longer sorties were directed to Siam and Malaya.[63] Many of their missions, however, together with those of the Dakotas which had replaced the Hudsons, went to Burma where – as we shall see later – the Force 136 agents whom they were delivering and supplying were providing invaluable support to the tactical aircraft of 221 and 224 Groups. As

Mountbatten says, many not only indicated targets but succeeded also in giving detailed reports of the results of attacks, while others assisted pilots who had been forced to bale out to return to the Allied lines.[64] Sir Keith Park summarises the achievement:

> From a handful of informants supplying skimpy information at great risk, the clandestine organisations grew by the end of the campaign into a powerful force capable of exerting a considerable influence on the course of the battle … between November 1944 and May 1945 over 1,350 sorties were flown in which 2,100 tons of stores and 1,000 liaison officers were dropped behind the enemy lines.[65]

Photographic Reconnaissance

1944 also witnessed striking advances in the realm of photographic reconnaissance. Thus far (p. 142), owing to the limitations of their aircraft, the radius of cover obtainable by 681 and 684 Squadrons had been restricted to 680 miles, rendering most of Siam – and more distant areas – out of reach. Moreover there had been a marked lack of co-ordination between the RAF and USAAF PR squadrons leading to considerable duplication of effort. To help remedy this situation all the Allied PR units were integrated within the Photographic Reconnaissance Force (PRF) on 1 February 1944 and placed under the command of Wing Commander (later Group Captain) S G Wise. Within his headquarters at Calcutta were located the necessary support facilities – a photographic reproduction laboratory, a negative library, photographic interpretation, and target map preparation. With the aircraft based nearby – the RAF initially at Dum Dum and then Alipore, and the USAAF (mainly Lightnings) at Barrackpore – a properly organised force was at last in prospect.[66]

One of its main tasks from now on was survey photography, intended to meet the long-felt need for accurate and up-to-date maps of Burma; another was to cover regularly the enemy airfields, thus making possible accurate aircraft counts and the preparation of target mosaics for the long-range fighters; a third was to monitor enemy communication routes and assess the damage being inflicted on them. By the end of May some 57% of Burma had been surveyed, yet understandably during the heavy ground fighting from March onwards it was the latter two tasks which took priority.[67] Alan Fox, who flew aboard Mitchells for two years as a photographer, describes some of the targets:

> perhaps the docks at Rangoon, or the airfield at Myitkyina, or – always a bitter moment this – the latest progress on the new Burma–Siam railway … airfields like Chieng Mai likewise struck

a slightly chilling note, with their rows of Japanese fighters drawn up in readiness on the tarmac. Sometimes as the aircraft moved with what seemed agonising slowness over the target, cameras whirring and clicking, one watched a few of them take off and start the long climb to intercept ... on occasion the return journey brought a twinge of guilt when it involved crossing the mountains on the India–Burma frontier. Down there were being fought some of the bitterest battles of the entire war ... while a few hours after landing at base I would be sitting in a Calcutta hotel with a rum and ginger at my elbow ... a certain decent humility was in order.[68]

Yet, as he goes on, airfield life could be gruelling. Of all his stations Pandaveswar was the worst. It lay in a furnace-like plain where temperatures up to 115°F made heat exhaustion or worse a constant threat for those working on aircraft, where every movement of wind carried sand with it and made life difficult not only for camera fitters but also for engine fitters, riggers, electricians and other skilled trades, where soya sausages were what bully beef had been to the infantry in the First World War, where the sudden onset of the monsoon set the floors of the tents awash, brought out the snakes, and caused the open latrine pits to overflow.[69] It is against conditions such as these that so many of the achievements recorded in this book – and not just those of the PR squadrons – need to be set.

Of the challenges facing the PRF in 1944 none was greater than to extend the radius of cover. Already on 15 December 1943 one of the first Mosquitos to join 684 Squadron had reached Bangkok, a sortie described by Wise as 'an outstanding effort, as no-one knew the extreme range of a Mosquito in this climate'.[70] In January 1944 a Mitchell got as far as Mergui – a 1,600-mile round trip – and on 27 March, after a period when lack of spares had caused servicing problems, a Mosquito covered 1,860 miles in photographing a large stretch of the Bangkok–Singapore railway. The following month another penetrated as far as Victoria Point and the Kra Isthmus in a 2,172 mile sortie – a massive extension of range – and in May the first coverage of the Nicobar Islands was achieved.[71]

For the next few months, however, operations were heavily curtailed by the monsoon, characterised – to quote Wise – 'by almost unbelievable banks of cloud up to 35,000 ft, stretching in unbroken layers for hundreds of miles in all directions with air currents and storms which made flying extremely dangerous.' The weather was not his only anxiety; experience had shown that, owing to poor communications, the PRF could not respond to requests from the RAF and Army tactical formations or pass information to them quickly enough, so in September plans were made to deploy squadron detachments forward alongside the operational headquarters, but this scheme did not work very well either. As Wise pointed out, poor W/T prevented close co-operation between different PR units, and landlines were no substitute. Telephone calls had to pass through civilian exchanges, it was often impossible to hear what was being said, and no improvement would be practicable until the war was over.[72] His experience was typical of the whole war in South-East Asia, where operations of every kind were bedevilled by inadequate communications.

Yet despite such tribulations the PRF continued its work and in August 684 Squadron extended its activities by sending a Mosquito detachment to China Bay from where it operated alongside the PR Liberators of 160 Squadron over the Andamans, Nicobars and northern Sumatra. These Liberators had longer range but had been suffering losses against Japanese fighters and ought only to be used where interception was unlikely; the Mosquitos on the other hand had the speed to avoid interception and by using drop tanks could still fly almost 2,300 miles. The challenge such sorties represented to their crews needs no stressing; to cover targets in Sumatra could entail an eight and three-quarter hour flight with the last 1,000 miles being across an ocean devoid of landmarks. Accurate navigation was essential, together with luck as regards the weather; few aircraft landed with more than 50 gallons of fuel remaining. Over the later part of 1944 these joint operations from Ceylon secured invaluable information about new Japanese airfields and progress on other ground installations.[73]

Meanwhile the many other activities of the PRF's RAF and USAAF squadrons continued, although in November 684 Squadron suffered a setback when all its 21 previously serviceable Mosquitos were temporarily grounded. A manufacturing fault had been discovered causing a splice in the leading edge to give way in the air.[74] By early 1945 all were back in service, however, and on 22 March a Mark XVI broke the long-distance record for a Mosquito with a flight of 2,493 miles which took it south of the Malayan frontier. The shorter range operations of 681 Squadron's Spitfires over Burma must not be forgotten; one of their most spectacular exploits was in November 1944 when two flew along the waterfront at Akyab at 50–200 ft without having a shot fired at them; excellent photographs were obtained.[75]

Throughout all these operations losses were light; between June and November 1944, for example, only five RAF and eight American aircraft were lost and only two might have been attributed to enemy action.[76] The main hindrances to the PRF were always the factors inseparable from flying in the tropics rather than the opposition of the enemy, which remained slighter than was usual in other theatres of war. Park paid them tribute, including alongside them the short range photography carried out by the tactical reconnaissance squadrons, and concluded:

> The work of PR has been of all the greater importance owing to the comparatively meagre intelligence available from ground sources: for air force purposes alone it provided an indispensable factor in the maintenance of Allied air superiority by providing speedy evidence of the location of enemy aircraft, while the work of the Strategic Air Force would have been unprofitable without the coverage of targets it furnished.[77]

11   Victory Beckons

Throughout 1944, as the fighting continued and the British and Americans were seizing the advantage, there had been much discussion about the longer term strategy to be pursued in South-East Asia in relation to the overall plans for the defeat of Japan. Then towards the end of the year there were major changes at command level, not least affecting the RAF, and much was being done to modernise the air forces and enable them to operate more effectively.

The Strategic Debate

The two Allies had always had different strategic aims, but when they had been mainly on the defensive and resources were limited, these had been of no great significance. The situation in 1944, however, brought them to the surface. At last the end of the war in Europe lay in prospect; indeed until September it seemed to many quite possible that Germany would be finished before the year was out. Minds were therefore turning to how best to use against Japan the far greater military power that would then be released. For the Americans the answer was comparatively straightforward: the effort should be concentrated on knocking out Japan itself as quickly as possible. For the British this seemed to take too little account of the post-war situation.

The fundamental question – not dissimilar to that being asked in Europe – can be simply stated: how far, if at all, should wartime operations be influenced by considerations of post-war policy which they might directly affect? In other words should the war strategy be directed solely to bring about the earliest possible end to hostilities, regardless of how it might affect the Allies' ability to handle further threats to peace after the war; or should attempts be made in the midst of war to gain post-war strategic advantages at the possible expense of immediate aims?[1] Churchill certainly had such considerations in mind, as for example when he minuted General Ismay on 23 June 1944:

The political importance of our making some effort to recover

217

British territory must not be underrated. Rangoon and Singapore are great names in the British eastern world, and it will be an ill-day for Britain if the war ends without our having made a stroke to regain these places and having let the whole Malay peninsula alone until it is eventually evacuated as the result of an American-dictated peace at Tokyo.[2]

At the same time he was conscious of the importance of being seen to assist the Americans in the main offensive against Japan itself. Reflecting later on the Quebec Conference of September 1944 he wrote:

For nearly three years we had persisted in the strategy of 'Germany First'. The time had now come for the liberation of Asia, and I was determined that we should play our full and equal part in it. What I feared most at this stage of the war was that the United States would say in after-years, 'We came to your help in Europe and you left us alone to finish off Japan'.[3]

But while such considerations were very much in mind during the debates of 1944 the German war refused to go away, and throughout the year virtually all Mountbatten's directives and plans remained conditional on what happened in Europe. Portal, ever the realist, had been right to remind him in January of the overriding priority of the war against Germany and to warn of further disappointments to come, adding 'it looks to me at the moment as if the role of the SEAC theatre may remain secondary'.[4] As long as that situation continued, Mountbatten would remain dependent on American resources – not least in air transport – to an extent that would preclude major operations which might seem to be furthering purely British interests.

Nevertheless Mountbatten and his staff – despite the strong opposition of Stilwell – decided in early 1944 to press yet again for the CULVERIN strategy (pp. 127, 154), their proposal being to penetrate the enemy perimeter in Sumatra and then work their way north via Malaya along the Asiatic coast, thus supporting the American and Australian thrusts from the central and south-west Pacific. This strategy was put forward in London and Washington by a group of Mountbatten's staff officers, known as the Axiom Mission. It received a mixed response in London. The Joint Planning Staff concluded that, provided Germany were defeated by October 1944, the resources required (including 39 RAF squadrons) could be available by March 1945; the Chiefs of Staff thought it would be better to contribute to the Pacific campaign by sending land and air units to operate with the Australians in their advance on the American flank towards the Philippines and Formosa; Churchill, strongly backed by the Foreign Office and War Cabinet, wanted the centre of gravity of Britain's Far

East operations to remain the Indian Ocean and supported Mountbatten's concept. This clear divergence of opinion between the Cabinet and the Chiefs was unresolved when the Axiom Mission went on to Washington, to be told that what the Americans wanted from Mountbatten in support of their Pacific strategy was the capture of Upper Burma in order to increase the capacity of the air supply route to China and expedite the laying of a pipeline. For this task they would in due course provide 400 more transport aircraft and three more air commandos. They were simply not interested, however, in CUL-VERIN, and when the Mission reported back to London in April Churchill accepted that his favoured operation was impracticable. Undaunted, however, in his quest for some kind of seaborne operation to make use of the forces Mountbatten already had available, he then proposed an attack on Simalur Island, just off the coast of Sumatra (Map 2), so that it could be developed as an air base to support later operations.[5] The Chiefs were far from thrilled.

For them there was still much to be said for preparing to send a task force to Australia; they were worried about the immense complexities of operating from the much troubled sub-continent of India, with its poor infrastructure, vast social problems and difficult climate, and Australia, despite its greater distance, seemed to offer a better prospect. So during May, June and July (coinciding with the launching of OVERLORD) a 'Middle Strategy' was devised and discussed with the Australians, New Zealanders and Americans. In addition to major naval and land forces this postulated a total air strength of 157 squadrons to be based on Australia by the end of 1945, including 78 RAF and 11 RAAF squadrons moved from Europe. Hardly surprisingly this came to nothing. While Australia and New Zealand were supportive, the Americans were far from enthusiastic – they saw no real point in the British trying to muscle in on the Pacific theatre, and given the likely speed of MacArthur's advance towards and through the Philippines any British contribution would almost certainly arrive much too late.[6]

Meanwhile Mountbatten was being left out on a limb, wondering what if any his long term role was to be and increasingly needing direction on what to do in the more immediate future. On the return of the Axiom Mission, however, he had little doubt that no further British resources would be sent to him until several months after the end of the war in Europe, and he decided to make his own plans for 1945 on that basis. So when a full-scale conference was called at last in London in August to consider Far East strategy Mountbatten had his plans ready. In essence there were three:

a. CHAMPION, soon renamed CAPITAL. This entailed advances by Stilwell to clear the mountains of northern Burma and by Slim into the central plain as far as Mandalay, all heavily dependent on air supply and therefore on extra American transport aircraft.

b. VANGUARD, soon re-named DRACULA. This entailed a combined airborne and seaborne assault on Rangoon, but would require support from outside the theatre. The airborne operation would involve a 480 mile fly-in by 900 transport aircraft and 650 gliders.[7]

c. CULVERIN. Churchill, still keen on Simalur or something like it, wanted this option considered. As he told the Chiefs on 6 July, the shame of Britain's disaster at Singapore could only be wiped out by its recapture. To that end an operation to take Simalur, followed by the tip of Sumatra, would lead to air domination of Singapore and Malaya.[8]

The initial reaction of the Chiefs, anxious about the implications of a long, arduous land campaign in the north, was to back DRACULA. If, as their Joint Planners pointed out, this took place by March 1945, central Burma could be cleared by mid-1945, a large-scale version of CULVERIN could be mounted immediately after the monsoon, and Malaya and Singapore could be recaptured by early 1946, before the expected end of the war against Japan. Inevitably there was much discussion about resources, the uncertainties of timing in relation to Europe, and the attitude of the Americans, but eventually it was agreed to give priority to DRACULA and to begin planning for the recapture of Malaya in readiness for the time when the necessary forces would become available. So on 18 August a telegram was sent to Washington seeking their views and on 1 September the Joint Chiefs endorsed DRACULA for March 1945 (subject to the European situation) while insisting that CAPITAL should go ahead in the meantime.[9] As SEAC was then told, London and Washington were agreed that the course of the war with Germany should allow forces to be released in October or November.[10] On the 16th Mountbatten was accordingly given his orders for both CAPITAL and DRACULA – but then, as so often in the past, the European priority reasserted itself. On 5 October, in the aftermath of the failure at Arnhem, the Chiefs of Staff telegraphed the Joint Staff Mission in Washington:

As a result of the worsening military situation our penetration into Germany is going to be resisted strongly and there is very hard fighting still in front of the Allied armies. We should be departing from first principles if we jeopardised the operation in Germany for the sake of DRACULA in March 1945 (by withdrawing troops for the campaign in Burma).[11]

So at the end of the day Mountbatten could do no more than revert to the only plan that seemed feasible with the forces he already possessed, namely CAPITAL coupled with an operation to clear the Arakan and capture Akyab, and his proposals to this effect were agreed by the Chiefs on 17 November.[12] It was the unforeseen pace of events that would eventually enable the longer term plans to be put back on track.

One other aspect of the strategic debate needs mention here. While the possibility of basing forces on Australia had been abandoned there remained much pressure for the British to contribute alongside the Americans in the direct assault on Japan. Plans were already afoot to provide a Royal Navy task force, and on 12 September, on their way to the Quebec Conference, Portal raised with Churchill the possibility of RAF participation from the Pacific in the bombing of Japan. Such a scheme had been first discussed in the Air Ministry in late 1943, and the forward thinking Sir Arthur Harris had made his views clear. Telling Portal of his concern about the shelving of proposals for a super bomber, he wrote:

> I regard with great apprehension the situation which would arise if we had defeated Germany and began to implement our promises with regard to the Japanese war. We ought to make a start so that we can contribute in the Far East and have a tenable position vis a vis the Americans afterwards.[13]

Now a year later, with 600 – 800 heavy bombers likely to be available fairly soon, it seemed appropriate to propose their use in the Far East. If half the aircraft were converted into tankers, as Portal suggested, in-flight refuelling would give the others a 1,500 mile radius of action, similar to that of the B-29s, thus enabling them to take part in the main bombing offensive against Japan that was just about to start. Churchill was keen on the idea, telling the House of Commons on 28 September that the United Kingdom would bear its part in the ever increasing air bombardment of the Japanese mainland, and on 27 October the CCS accepted the offer, subject to bases becoming available.[14] We shall return to this subject in Chapter 13.

Command Changes

By the end of 1944 Mountbatten not only had the directive he needed for 1945 but also three new Commanders-in-Chief. Admiral Somerville had been succeeded first by Admiral Sir Bruce Fraser and then (on Fraser's move to the Pacific) by Vice-Admiral Sir Arthur Power. General Giffard had been replaced by General Sir Oliver Leese. Then, last of Mountbatten's three originals to go, Sir Richard Peirse had been succeeded temporarily by Air Marshal Sir Guy Garrod.

Portal had written to Mountbatten in April, seeking his views about replacing Peirse and referring to continuing rumours about the affair with Lady Auchinleck[15] (p. 151), but Mountbatten made it clear he wanted Peirse to stay until the end of the year; while the 'triangle' was unsolved he saw little danger of matters coming to a head, and he wished the Navy and Army changes to be completed first. Making it clear that he had got on particularly well with Peirse as compared with the much older Somerville and Giffard, he told Portal:

> Peirse has never failed to give me unbiased and fearless advice and on the very few occasions when I felt I must override him in the light of arguments put forward by the Army he has taken my decisions cheerfully and loyally.[16]

At this precise moment Peirse was supporting Mountbatten over his problems with Giffard (p. 184); in a letter to Portal written with Mountbatten's blessing, Peirse pulled no punches in his criticism of the Army Commander, particularly his lack of understanding of the air and his opposition to new ideas.[17] We may wonder whether it was proper for Mountbatten to use his Air Commander in this way, but there can be little doubt about the confidence they had in each other.

Yet soon afterwards Portal was told by Dill in Washington about the opinion among the best USAAF young colonels, as reported by General Arnold, that all was not well with the RAF Command in Burma. According to them, the unaggressive leadership of Peirse and Baldwin was affecting the whole Command. Dill had met two of them – Cochran and Alison – and urged Portal to discuss the matter with Arnold.[18] Clearly there were anxieties in Washington, where the differences of opinion over No 1 Air Commando (pp. 173, 179) had been reported back. These doubts do not seem to have been shared by more senior Americans on the spot; indeed in September Stratemeyer, Peirse's deputy, urged Mountbatten to seek an extension for Peirse, who had been 'a wonderful chap to work for whose removal would break up a very fine Anglo-American family party'.[19] By now, however, the die was cast: Peirse's affair was becoming widely known and affecting both his work and his authority, and even when his designated successor was killed on the journey out Mountbatten felt unable to countenance an extension.[20] Peirse left for England on 28 November accompanied by Lady Auchinleck, aboard a transport aircraft whose flight plan had not been cleared; even their presence on it could only be deduced.[21] His RAF career was at an end, and he was quietly retired.[22]

Peirse has not had a good press. He presided over Bomber Command for one of its worst years, he then found himself in the middle of the Far East disasters and had the thankless task of trying to build up the RAF in India when it was at the back of the queue for everything. As a commander he was often regarded as somewhat remote and lacking the human touch. Then came the circumstances of his departure, when heart ruled head. But let none doubt the value of what he achieved. He fought interminable battles to win for his command the resources it needed for the Far East war; he led it through the multiplicity of operations we have so far described; and he contributed most ably to the higher direction of the campaign in South-East Asia. Group Captain Dennis David, who knew him out there, calls him a 'brilliant, kindly man'.[23] We have seen what Stratemeyer said about him; another American colleague, General Davidson of the 10th USAAF, later paid direct tribute for his 'patient and sympathetic handling of the problems of both services'.[24] Let Mountbatten, who knew better than anyone what Peirse had accomplished, have the final word. As he wrote on 30 November, while Peirse was still on his way home:

I can never be sufficiently grateful to you for the loyal support which you gave me from the day I arrived to the day you left. I wish everyone had given me the same degree of support.[25]

Portal had at first considered replacing Peirse by Air Chief Marshal Douglas, but by July his thoughts were turning to Air Chief Marshal Leigh-Mallory, currently the Air C-in-C for OVERLORD.[26] Mountbatten, who had worked with him at the time of the Dieppe Raid in 1942, was keen to have him; Eisenhower, consulted by Mountbatten, said his earlier doubts about Leigh-Mallory had gone; and Leigh-Mallory himself, who was approached by Mountbatten, jumped at the idea.[27] His appointment was agreed in September, but not everyone at SEAC was enamoured. Stratemeyer, who had first wanted Peirse to stay, later asked if Garrod could take over instead: 'We all love him and trust him; he's one of my great personal friends, and with him you'd continue to keep the happy family party'.

Mountbatten, reminding Stratemeyer of Leigh-Mallory's credentials, including all his latest experience and prestige, said the decision was firm. Reporting this exchange to Portal, he suspected Stratemeyer had been receiving unfavourable views about Leigh-Mallory; he would watch the situation closely.[28] There was to be no need, for Leigh-Mallory never arrived. His aircraft crashed in the French Alps on 14 November, its fate unknown until seven months later.[29]

Within days of his disappearance moves were afoot to find another successor for Peirse. Mountbatten's own preference was for Sir John Slessor, now commanding in Italy and recognised as one of the RAF's best brains. Slessor, though willing to go, told Portal he would prefer to become Air Member for Personnel, a move which coincided with Portal's own intentions,[30] and the name of Sir Keith Park now came into the reckoning. Park, currently C-in-C Middle East, had proved his

On Sir Richard Peirse's departure Air Marshal Sir Guy Garrod KCB OBE MC DFC, seen here at a forward airstrip, took over temporarily as Air C-in-C. (*AHB*)

great leadership qualities both in the Battle of Britain and in Malta, and on 26 November Portal compared the merits of the two officers in a minute to Sinclair. In his view Park would give three-quarters of his time to the Air Force and a quarter to higher strategy and politics; Slessor would give two-thirds to the latter and only one-third to the RAF. Park would be the more inspiring leader and would probably get on better with the Americans, with the government of India, and with Mountbatten – unless they differed on strategy, in which case there would be trouble. In essence, Portal wrote, Park had the better operational sense just as Slessor had the better political and strategic sense.[31] This was a perceptive and fair analysis, and since what the RAF in South-East Asia would need most over the coming months would be strong operational leadership the choice rightly fell upon Park.

Yet it took two months before the decision was announced[32] and not until 24 February 1945 did Park take over from Peirse's deputy, Garrod, who then left for Italy to relieve Slessor. It was Garrod, therefore, who directed most of the air planning for the great successes in Burma in early 1945. Mountbatten's parting tribute to him in a letter to Portal should be recorded:

In February 1945 Air Chief Marshal Sir Keith Park KCB OBE MC DFC, relieved Garrod. He is seen here (*right*) with his Deputy C-in-C (Air Vice-Marshal D Harcourt Smith CBE MVO) (*centre*) and SASO, AHQ Burma (Air Vice-Marshal G E Gibbs). (*AHB*)

Garrod has done exceptionally splendid work, both as Peirse's deputy and as Acting C-in-C for four months. Stratemeyer and Wedemeyer both asked to be allowed to recommend his appointment as Allied Air C-in-C after Leigh-Mallory's death.[33]

We are left to wonder why Garrod himself did not take over. As Stratemeyer wrote to General Eaker in Italy, commending to him his new Air C-in-C:

Sir Guy is a natural commander and leader ... he has won the respect and loyalty of *every American* and, I believe, of all the RAF over here. To my mind he is one of the finest officers we have in the Allied Air Forces ... Ira, he's a great guy.

Mountbatten went so far as to tell Garrod afterwards that of all the Cs-in-C with whom he had been associated (including Peirse, presumably) he would miss none as much; he wished he had taken more effective steps earlier on to ensure his being left permanently as Air C-in-C. He was still of this view in July 1945, even though 'his successor was playing up nobly'.[34]

So by late 1944 there were new single-service Cs-in-C and their arrival coincided with the move of the Army and Air Commanders and their operations staffs to Kandy so that they could work alongside Mountbatten in a proper joint Headquarters. There was also by this time an inter-Allied, inter-service Joint Planning Staff, whose members owed individual allegiance to their Cs-in-C and collective allegiance to him. The system worked well, in Mountbatten's view, proving its value for the rest of the war and over the subsequent early months of so-called peace;[35] Marshal of the Royal Air Force Sir Denis Spotswood, who was as a Group Captain his senior RAF planner, fully agrees.

The move to Kandy was not, however, without its disadvantages, both for the Army and the RAF. Most matters still necessitated close liaison and co-operation with the Government of India in Delhi, 1,500 miles away, and Peirse had originally felt that the AOA and his staff ought to remain there. The AOA himself (Air Vice-Marshal R V Goddard), however, considered this would be unworkable: he and the heads of the main administrative services had to be able to contribute to the policy-making in Kandy. Consequently a Headquarters, Base Area, South-East Asia (BAFSEA) was set up in Delhi under Air Marshal L N Hollinghurst; answering directly to the Air C-in-C, he and his staff from now on handled all the day to day matters arising from the RAF's presence in India. As Park says, this was neither a simple nor normal arrangement, but 'the separation of the Supreme Commander and the Headquarters of his Cs-in-C from the seat of the Government of India and from the duality of channels to the United Kingdom – either through the Government of India or direct – constituted an abnormal situation'. For anyone experienced in command staffwork the complexities are easy to imagine, yet the system was made to work. When AMSO (Air Chief Marshal Sir Christopher Courtney) visited in February 1945 and saw just how much negotiation was needed in Delhi in connection with the war he was left in no doubt about the value of BAFSEA;[36] Sir Denis Spotswood says that Hollinghurst virtually transformed the base area.[37]

Restructuring was also necessary in Stratemeyer's Eastern Air Command, where HQ 3TAF at Comilla no longer possessed a proper role. For one thing, 10th USAAF had become an independent formation in June, leaving AOC 3TAF (Air Marshal W A Coryton from August onwards) responsible only for 221 and 224 Groups. For another Slim was due to move his 14th Army HQ forward to Imphal where it would be alongside 221 Group, and his superior formation – a new Advanced HQ Allied Land Forces – would be co-located with EAC at Calcutta. As for 224 Group it would be continuing to work with XV Corps, also directed from Calcutta. So in December 3TAF was disbanded, leaving the RAF's two tactical groups answerable directly to EAC, thus paralleling the new Army structure. At the same time Coryton became Stratemeyer's deputy and also took command of a new administrative formation, RAF Bengal-Burma. Hitherto – and rather surprisingly – RAF administrative services in east Bengal had been provided by HQ 231 (Bomber) Group; now, with the area of responsibility extending eastwards, it was better to have a separate formation, one which would be capable of expansion as the armies and tactical air forces advanced into Burma.[38]

The essential structure was thus in place for the 1945 offensive, in which the two RAF tactical formations would operate on a mobile basis in the closest co-operation with their Army colleagues, and in accordance with principles of joint action laid down by the Supreme Commander.[39] 221 Group at Imphal was still under command of Air Vice-Marshal Vincent, who had led it with conspicuous success throughout the siege, had then had to cope with an enormous invasion of visitors (not all of them welcome) coming to see where the war had been, and in December had witnessed the knighting of four Generals for their part in the victory. Vincent wrote: 'the RAF, represented by 221 Group, got not even a Mention in Despatches'. There was something a little wrong here, as Slim was quick to point out to the Air

Mountbatten consults two of his field commanders: General Sir William Slim, GOC 14th Army (*right*) and Air Vice-Marshal S F Vincent CB DFC, AOC 221 Group. (*AHB*)

Air Commodore (later Air Vice-Marshal) the Earl of Bandon DSO, AOC 224 Group, sometimes irritated his superiors but was greatly admired by his men. (*AHB*)

Ministry, and Vincent later received the CB.[40] Writing of the debt owed by 14th Army to Vincent and his men, Slim made clear his views: 'I could not help thinking that sometimes the Army recognised their achievements more readily than some of the high Air Force headquarters'.[41] Vincent certainly felt the same (p. 302). As he wrote about Slim, whom he got to know better all the time: 'He was a grand fellow and one who fully appreciated and realised what the Group was doing for the Army'.[42]

A similar spirit of 'jointery' (to use the modern jargon) prevailed between 224 Group at Chittagong and General Christison's XV Corps. In July 1944 there arrived to take over from the respected but reserved Air Commodore Gray at 224 Group one of the RAF's most legendary characters, Air Commodore The Earl of Bandon, for ever known as 'The Abandoned Earl'. After distinguished service in Bomber Command he had been in India since November 1942 and worked for some time under Stratemeyer, who called him 'some guy – I can do business with him'. Mountbatten too was impressed not only by his spirit of leadership but also by evidence that he was invariably the most popular member of every mess. Unorthodox, extrovert, given to the most outrageous practical jokes, he might not always endear himself to some senior officers, but he would certainly inspire the confidence and affection of those under him and win the trust of the other Service commanders. General Christison quickly had any doubts dispelled; on asking what support in aircraft Paddy could give to the Army he was astounded and delighted to be told: 'The whole bloody lot if you want them'. It was not long before they were working happily together in a joint headquarters at Cox's Bazar.[43]

Such relationships were admirable; the successes of 1945 depended heavily on them, and we can understand the frustration of the operational commanders when some of the directives they received seemed over-detailed and restrictive of their decision-making. On the other hand, as the Narrators observe,

> owing to the very close association between the operational staffs of 221 and 224 Groups and their Army counterparts there was a tendency for the air commanders to enter into air support commitments which maintenance, supply and personnel reserves in the base areas did not always justify. The keenness of the RAF groups to ensure the fullest support for the ground forces was sometimes an embarrassment to Allied Air Headquarters, to whom the supply and equipment situation at times gave grave cause for anxiety.[44]

We shall turn to the support structure and some of its problems in a moment, but first we need to be aware of changes relating to the other critical air power role: air supply. Following the dissolution of Troop Carrier Command in June 1944 (p. 152) this had been the responsibility of 3TAF, but it was soon clear that the planning and control of the transport squadrons – which might soon have to carry out airborne operations as well – needed a separate HQ where the Army and Air authorities could work alongside each other. In October, therefore, a joint organisation was set up at Comilla comprising the Combined Air Transport Organisation (CATO) and the Combat Cargo Task Force (CCTF). The former took control of the whole military structure behind air supply and determined the priorities; the latter was an integrated US/British HQ under Brigadier General Evans, who answered directly to Stratemeyer for all the USAAF and RAF transport squadrons supporting 14th Army and XV Corps. Soon afterwards Air Commodore JDI Hardman took command of the RAF element, which in April 1945 became 232 Group.[45]

The land/air co-operation that ensued in planning and setting priorities certainly paid dividends over the coming months, though both Garrod and Park recognised that the 10th USAAF air supply system on the northern front was more efficient; the Americans gave theirs firmer backing, their communications links were better, and they were not short of personnel. Indeed Park later went so far as to say:

> Considering the complete dependence of the British Army on air supply and air reinforcement, it is remarkable how parsimonious its attitude was to meeting its responsibilities in providing MT, personnel and signal facilities required by the air supply organisation in Burma.[46]

This goes a bit far. There is always a balance to be struck in such matters, and rarely did anybody have enough of anything. Nor did the RAF always help its own cause. Hardman, for example, tells us of the organisational nightmare he encountered, whereby the RAF Dakotas came under three different authorities. Operationally they were controlled by the CCTF, yet like all other transport squadrons anywhere in the world they were administratively controlled by Transport Command in the United Kingdom, which exercised its authority through 229 Group in Delhi, a thousand miles away from HQ CCTF. Then to add to the confusion their administrative services were provided by RAF Bengal-Burma.[47] The implications of this can be imagined, and one wonders whether the Far East squadrons ought not to have been exempted from the Transport Command net until the war was over. But they were not, and we can merely echo the restrained sentiment of the Narrators: 'In view of the manifold complexities with which it was surrounded, the achievements of the air supply organisation during 1944/45 may well appear remarkable'.[48]

The State of the Force

Coincidental with all these command changes the strengthening and updating of the front line had also been under way, and by the end of 1944 some 68 operational squadrons were under RAF command, 42 of them in EAC. By March 1945, when the strength reached its peak, these figures came to 71 and 56 (Appendix C). In terms of aircraft, the RAF average operational strength in EAC in December was 627, rising in March to 772, and alongside them the USAAF had approximately equal numbers: 691 and 748.[49]

Turning to the shape of the RAF contribution to this Anglo-American air force in eastern India we find only two major changes. With air defence remaining firmly the responsibility of the Spitfire squadrons and the Liberator, Beaufighter and Dakota elements being expanded, it was only the advent of two new types of aircraft that represented significant advances. One of these, the Mosquito, was already making its mark in the PR role (p. 214/5) and in early 1944 the first few of the light bomber version flew operationally with 27 (Beaufighter) Squadron. Then the first of the Vengeance squadrons, No

By 1945 many more experienced pilots had arrived from Europe, including Squadron Leader J H 'Ginger' Lacey, of Battle of Britain fame, seen here with two other pilots of 17 (Spitfire) Squadron, March 1945. (*AHB*)

45, converted to the Mosquito, but soon after it became operational a fatal accident occurred to one of the aircraft and evidence was found of glue failure and faulty manufacture. Coryton, writing in December 1944, highlighted the real problem: the high humidity of the atmosphere for much of the year. In view of ACSEA's unhappy experience with wooden aircraft and fabric aircraft, he considered that unless suitable improvements could be made to overcome the effects of the climatic conditions, all aircraft employed in SEAC should be of metal construction.[50] Remedial measures were taken, the conversion of the four Vengeance squadrons was completed, and the Mosquitos – together with the Beaufighters – proved of immense value in hampering and destroying enemy movements during the 1945 campaign.[51] They continued in service in the Far East for a while afterwards, but the basic problem was never properly overcome.

The other new aircraft, too, had its problems but overall must be considered one of the RAF's great success stories from the Burma campaign. Up to late 1944 it was the Hurricanes that had borne the brunt of the RAF's ground-attack work in support of the Army, and right well had they done their job, not least during the battles of Imphal and Kohima as we have seen. The need for higher performance

The rains often made it tough going for the Mosquito, even on the ground.
(*AHB*)

aircraft was clear, however, and starting in mid-1944 nine Hurricane
squadrons were converted to the American P-47, called by the RAF the
Thunderbolt. With a maximum range (1,970 miles) almost double that
of the Hurricane, a maximum speed of 427 mph (over 100 mph faster),
a higher ceiling (36,500 ft), a much faster rate of climb (11½ minutes to

Many squadrons were re-equipped with the powerful Thunderbolt. (*AHB*)

20,000 ft), and more powerful armament (8 x 0.50″ guns and a 1,000 lb bomb load), the Thunderbolt was an immense improvement and a formidable weapon,[52] once worrying shortages of long-range tanks and specialist tools had been overcome.[53]

The then Squadron Leader Neil Cameron, who commanded 258 Squadron at the time, recalled converting to the Thunderbolt at Yelahanka in September 1944. Since the RAF never operated the aircraft other than in ACSEA, they were taught by Americans (RAF instructors took over later); the aircraft was single-seat so no dual practice was possible; and its weight, speed and power were something special. One Australian pilot who tried to dive with full throttle and see how fast it would actually go should have known better and Cameron had a difficult letter to write to his mother. He continues:

This was the first experience many of us had with the sound barrier, or Mach 1 as it came to be known. The word then was 'compressibility'. It meant the same thing, but aviators were just beginning to learn about the problem ahead of them.[54]

Eleven weeks after its first aircraft arrived, his squadron was trained in fighter-bomber operations and in action in 224 Group, where the Thunderbolt proved in his view an excellent ground-attack aircraft as well as a pure fighter and long-range bomber escort. While the light, very manoeuvrable Japanese fighters could easily turn inside the Spitfire or Hurricane, the new aircraft could dive away or use its extra speed to climb out of range.

Unusually for the RAF, which had not hitherto followed the German lead in their use of the Stuka, the Thunderbolt was often used as a dive-bomber. Warrant Officer Double, a pilot with 79 Squadron, describes the technique: 'initially we did high-level approach dive-bombing using instantaneous fuses, where we would 'roll' right over and dive vertically, using the gunsight to line up the target'.[55] 'Vertically' is something of an exaggeration; while it felt like that, says the former CO of 30 Squadron, it was in fact about 60°.[56] Double goes on to recall seeing several aircraft explode during the dive, and thought they had been hit by flak. Then pilots began complaining of a strong smell of 100 octane in the cockpit, and some of the fuel 'header' tanks were found to be split. As Cameron explains it, if an aircraft went into a steep dive the fuel would pour onto the very hot engine and explode. He concludes:

This episode shows how sloppy craftsmanship, thoughtless storage or bad fitting killed several valuable pilots before we discovered the root of the problem. These losses we could ill-afford.[57]

It might be mentioned here that the Thunderbolts could also – with great accuracy – drop napalm, the inflammable jelly-like petroleum product which, when detonated under pressure, could create a mini-fire-storm on the ground. The purpose, says Cameron, was to drive the Japanese out of their foxholes or suffocate them if they stayed inside. Whatever the later connotations attached to this weapon, Cameron felt it acceptable to use it against the Japanese at that time, 'having regard to the vicious manner in which our prisoners of war were being treated'.[58]

So much for the aircraft; what of their bases? Now that the great airfield expansion plan begun in 1942 was almost complete, there were by late 1944 some 45 all-weather airfields in Bengal and Assam in operational use by the RAF and the USAAF, together with many fair-weather strips (Map 6 shows the more important ones used by the RAF). Of the permanent ones, 17 were in and around Calcutta, 12 used by the long-range bombers and air defence fighters, and the rest by Le May's B-29s. Eight were east of the Ganges delta in a line stretching south from Agartala to Chittagong and Cox's Bazar; the more northerly were used by medium bombers and transport aircraft and the rest by the tactical aircraft of 224 Group. Another six, used mainly by 221 Group, were in the Imphal Plain and near Silchar. Finally in north-east Assam were 14 airfields (with four more under construction) used almost exclusively by the Americans to support the northern front and operate the Hump route.[59] A great many more military airfields and flying boat bases were spread across the length and breadth of India and Ceylon; as a measure of what was achieved in terms of construction and mainte- nance, Wing Commander Jefford has identified a total of 179 locations (some fair-weather only) where RAF squadrons were based at some stage of the war, and there were 61 more in Burma.[60]

Of the latter many would now have to be built or repaired as the armies advanced, and the planning for CAPITAL took much account of the need to construct forward airfields as quickly as possible for use by the tactical squadrons and the supply aircraft.[61] The actual building was the responsibility of the Royal Engineers, to whom enormous credit is due, though at least some of the air commanders wished the RAF could have had its own airfield constructors. Coryton was particularly concerned about this; while his tactical aircraft could operate reasonably well in monsoon conditions they required more all-weather strips and the Army was unwilling to allot them the necessary priority.[62] He had a point but the problem was really one of overall resources, and changing the organisation does not always help in such situations. Fortunately the main forthcoming battles were to be fought in the so-called dry season, when the fair-weather strips would normally be serviceable.

Another major requirement for the 1945 campaign was suitable communication and control arrangements. Much had been done to link the main headquarters and bases inside India itself with a proper landline network, and to provide them with their own local systems; the credit for this work must go to the Indian Air Formation Signals units without whose efforts the RAF could never have operated efficiently. Then in 1945 AFS units moved into Burma as the advance proceeded, their leading sections often being flown in to forward airfields.[63] Given, however, the distances involved, the very difficult terrain, the many climatic problems and the speed of the advance the air forces' communications there had to rely very largely on W/T. Hitherto there had been great difficulties in transporting the necessary radio equipment which had not – to put it mildly – been constructed for ease of movement in the local conditions, but during 1944 large quantities of a special vehicle designed to take all forms of communications equipment were built in Calcutta. By the end of the year a series of mobile signals units (MSUs) – some of them air transportable – were ready, backed up by a mobile signals servicing unit as well as by the base servicing unit. Unfortunately, the air transportable equipment being made in the UK failed to arrive (only that made locally was available), and never during the Burma campaign were there sufficient men or material to operate the signals services to full efficiency.[64] There were limits to what could be done by self-help, something on which the RAF in the Far East had to rely in large measure even at this late stage of the war.

It is against this background that two major changes in the operational control organisation should be seen. Coryton describes how the system developed in Europe for handling tactical air forces was examined in 3TAF and rejected, essentially owing to the factors of immense distance and bad communications. Whereas a group control centre (GCC) in Europe operated on a front of about 40 miles, 221 Group was responsible for a front 200 miles wide and its squadrons were spread 200 miles in depth. Moreover during 1944 air forces had had to operate for long periods in areas cut off by the enemy. Centralised control by a single GCC was therefore quite impracticable; there must be more than one filter/operations room in a group, and they must be transportable.[65] A flight sergeant who served with one of these describes how, after training at Sambre near Poona and then forming up at Silchar, they made their way during the 1945 campaign from Imphal to Toungoo, providing communications for control of aircraft movements, and intercommunication between wireless unit posts. Every four to six weeks they moved on, leapfrogging other similar units.[66] Reporting to them were the radars – known as AMES units; by the end of 1944 there were over 40 of these in 221 and 224 Groups, mostly operating in isolated, unpleasant and dangerous forward positions, and also mobile.

The other major change was the supersession of the AASCs, which had been located alongside corps headquarters (p. 191), by army support signals units (ASSUs), with visual control posts (VCPs) attached. This new system showed that the lessons taught by the RAF Component of Wingate's Special Force in conjunction with the Air Commando (p. 178) had been learnt. The VCP's tasks were to:

a.   assist aircraft to identify their targets, or to adjust them,
b.   cancel or delay operations if necessary,
c.   direct aircraft to secondary targets,
d.   direct aircraft from a cab rank, and
e.   co-ordinate and control heavy bomber operations.[67]

One post would be allocated to each brigade and comprise an army element together with an RAF controller (a junior GD officer) and signals personnel. Training was carried out at a special school set up at Ranchi, and it was soon found that the biggest problem was the provision of the right personnel, particularly the controllers. Nevertheless by December 1944 ten teams were operating and by May 1945 there were 34, two of them airborne in light L-5 aircraft. The VCPs certainly proved their value; as Park wrote:

Of the general success of the VCP system there can be no doubt, from both air and ground points of view. It contributed materially to that close and efficient cooperation of ground and air forces which was so marked a feature of the campaign of 1944-45.[68]

He went on to say, however, that it encouraged a questionable tactic, that of the cab rank. Popular as this was with the Army it was wasteful of flying effort, targets were not always to be found, and the weight of attack was usually small. Better in his view for the Army to provide airfields as close to the front line as possible. There was – and is – nothing unusual about this debate. Park was right to make the general point about the cost of cab ranks and standing patrols, but in the actual situation in Burma in 1945 the system was hard to fault.

Another facility whose importance needs no stressing was meteorological forecasting. An extensive plan involving the Indian Meteorological Department, the Indian Air Force and the RAF Meteorological Branch (all uniformed, serving in the RAFVR), had been drawn up in July 1942, but the resources needed were a long time coming; indeed two years later the RAF branch numbered only 24 officers and 70 airmen as against 47 and 220 in the plan. Nor did either the IAF section or the civilian department expand as hoped for. In mid-1944 it was being stated that aircrew lacked confidence in some of the forecast centres, and it was clear that the rapidly increasing requirements could not be met without drastic action. Consequently in

October it was agreed that, while I Met D would remain in charge of the observing stations, the British Meteorological Office would take responsibility for all forecasting for the RAF in India and for briefing of RAF aircrews. A Joint RAF-RN Meteorological Centre was set up at HQ ACSEA in Ceylon, and among other measures main forecasting centres were formed in December at HQ 221 and 224 Groups, replacing the RIAF sections. These came just in time, and 721 Forecast Centre stayed with HQ 221 Group throughout its forward advance; mobile wing forecast centres were also provided, acting independently owing to communication problems. By now real progress had been made towards overcoming one of the major difficulties in South-East Asia, namely forecasting the development and subsequent movement of thunderstorms, whose formation and behaviour could be critical for both operations and route flying.[69]

The emphasis on mobility was reflected too in the vast supply, servicing, repair and salvage organisation. By late 1944, as Park reminds us, there had been built up in Ceylon and India west of the Brahmaputra – an area almost as large as Europe – 'a large and efficient base maintenance organisation', including the base repair depots, the equipment depots and the aircraft storage units.[70] A suggestion had in fact been made in September by Mediterranean Allied Air Forces that the enormous spare capacity that now existed in the Middle East could be used to carry out the Far East's maintenance and repair work more efficiently, but this was firmly rejected. Those on the spot were satisfied that they could well meet the task; moreover all experience showed that maintenance backing should be as close as possible to the area of operations.[71] Whatever motives prompted the idea – preservation of local interests obviously among them – it made little sense, and certainly not for the period of offensive operations currently being planned. So India remained the base for all the fourth-line maintenance of aircraft, motor transport and marine craft, and for the supply of equipment, explosives, fuel and so on. Much of the work was done by local labour under British supervision, roughly in the ratio 5:1 – an unspectacular but essential task.

Ahead of them almost everything had to be mobile, and while some first-line servicing continued to be done in 1945 by squadron personnel most of it, together with second-line, was carried out by servicing echelons, each commanded by a wing engineering officer, part of a new wing organisation which was introduced for all squadrons flying single-engined and light twin-engined aircraft. The two or more squadrons in each wing were thus freed of responsibility for most of their maintenance (and also for their administration, it should be added) and enabled to concentrate on operations. The echelons were themselves mobile, they were usually up to strength and their personnel generally had experience of individual types of aircraft and

Nor should the RAF's elephants be forgotten. (*AHB*)

of field conditions. The system was an undoubted success and was later extended to other squadrons. Supporting the servicing echelons were the third-line units: the mobile repair and salvage units (RSUs) which stayed close to the squadrons, assisted with repairs and carried out all salvage; the forward repair depots (FRDs), more fully equipped and less mobile; and the repair and salvage sections (RSSs), semi-static units in the base area.[72]

The experience of an MT driver who served with 101 RSU typifies that of so many more men who helped keep the aircraft flying. He remembers the leaking basha huts; the primitive washing and toilet facilities; the monsoon when he was always wet; the baking heat when working in an aircraft; the ants, centipedes, snakes and other forms of wild life; the informal 'uniform' which so quickly replaced the official khaki drill. Yet with all the easy-going attitude, discipline was good and everybody worked with a will. He still treasures a copy of the message sent to his CO, Squadron Leader C W Lockhart, by Air Marshal Sir Hugh Saunders, AOC Burma, in October 1945:

I wish to record my appreciation of the very good work you and your unit have done whilst you have supported the Dakota squadrons in Burma. During this year you have already returned 232 Dakotas. This is equivalent to nearly ten squadrons. Without your help the airlift given to the 14th Army, to transportation of supplies and later to the evacuation of released prisoners of war would have been considerably curtailed.[73]

An understatement if ever there was one.

With the prospect of so many units of various kinds operating in different areas and constantly on the move their defence was of the utmost importance – not so much against air attack, which was unlikely on any scale, but against enemy ground forces. As Park explained, it became clear that

> advanced airfields, radar sites and other air force installations would not necessarily be guarded if their locations did not happen to fit into the tactical schemes adopted by the local Army formations, and that unless the air forces were to withdraw everything to a safe distance behind the front lines they would themselves have to provide the necessary defence force.[74]

This was a task for the RAF Regiment, which in late 1944 was not only heavily reinforced from the UK but extensively reorganised. Hitherto two-thirds of its strength had been deployed in the anti-aircraft role, but for 1945 the proportions were reversed, giving 20 field squadrons and 10 A/A.[75] Park stressed how invaluable they proved, pointing out that their defence of captured airfields protected the Army's lifeline as well as providing for air support and defence, and Vincent, who had nine field and five A/A squadrons in 221 Group, wrote:

> I consider it probable that the Group could not have occupied airstrips as far forward as we did, with consequently better close air support for the Army, had I not been confident that the RAF Regiment could have maintained the necessary security.[76]

Such were the main elements of the RAF that was about to be engaged in the 1945 campaign. In toto – including all those serving throughout the length and breadth of India and Ceylon – there were 93,000 RAF men and women in the theatre in September 1944 (10½ per cent of the RAF's total strength) and by May 1945 the figure would be up to almost 122,000 (13 per cent)[77] – considerably greater than the total strength of today's RAF. While the vast majority were men there were in India in December 1944 nine WAAF officers and 250 airwomen, and their numbers in India and Ceylon would be up to 1,300 by August 1945.[78]

This part of the story would be incomplete without some discussion of a problem that distinguished the war in South-East Asia from all the other RAF wartime campaigns. As the writer of the signals monograph put it, when summarising the many signals difficulties, 'another factor militating against the efficiency of communications was the fitness of

At Mountbatten's headquarters, in Kandy, much of the work was done by the Women's Services. Here are members of the WAAF who were employed on clerical duties, often highly confidential. (*AHB*)

personnel ... by far the biggest wastage was at the hands of tropical disease, especially in the first Arakan campaign'.[79] It was a similar tale right across the board, affecting all irrespective of status, colour of uniform, or location, and the RAF statistics on hospital admissions were revealing. Throughout the campaign, between 1941 and 1945, disease accounted for some 90 per cent of these, injuries a mere 10 per cent. The RAF medical historian outlines the challenge:

> The Medical Branch was faced with a tremendous problem in this theatre where large numbers of unseasoned airmen had to serve and operate in a country in which the variations of climate were extreme, where numerous serious diseases were endemic, and where civilian standards of hygiene and sanitation were sometimes exceedingly primitive.[80]

Then, to make the doctors' job more difficult, there was in the earlier days little co-operation between the Principal Medical Officer and other senior RAF staff officers: 'the general knowledge of and interest in preventive medicine was minimal in an area where it should have been maximal' and 'the medical branch were rarely consulted in war planning'. It was a long time before medical officers gained the right to be consulted, for example, about new building sites (many ranging from airfields to radar units were chosen regardless of their proximity to native villages and the consequent hygiene risks), and it took an uphill fight to persuade executives to insist on proper standards for latrines, ablutions, water supplies, food storage and preparation, and waste disposal. Nor was it easy to obtain commanders' active support for measures against the main diseases, especially malaria; not until July 1944 was the message driven home in a letter from Peirse to all units:

> During 1943 approximately 200,000 service days were lost in Air Command due to malaria, of which 18,000 were lost by aircrews … a very grave waste of manpower. In addition there is the incalculable loss due to interference with operations and training and due to the lowering morale and efficiency of those who have become chronic relapsing cases.[81]

He went on to remind all COs of their personal responsibility for the necessary preventive measures. Now at last the MOs began to receive the support they needed in relation to malaria discipline, and with the arrival of the first supplies of DDT in October the prospect for 1945 was far more promising.[82] Little progress was, however, being made in relation to dysentery, the second most widespread disease.

Improvements had been made too in the hospital service. By mid-1943 the RAF, largely dependent on the Army hospitals, was increasingly worried about what was happening to its aircrew and skilled tradesmen who became sick; in accordance with Army policy they were simply flown out to distant base hospitals and were often a long time away. To enable such men to be treated and returned to duty as quickly as possible a system of RAF mobile field hospitals was therefore instituted, linked to an RAF hospital in Calcutta. One MFH operated during the Imphal siege (p. 190 note 107) and by early 1945 no fewer than 13 were available.[83] Supporting them down the line were unit sick quarters, one at each wing HQ. Here, as with so many other parts of the RAF system, mobility was now the key, and overall the medical provision had been greatly improved.

Many are the men who remember with gratitude the ministrations of the doctors and the nurses, often in conditions very far from ideal. Less often thought of with pleasure are the dentists, but they were there too, as an armourer relates. Needing urgent treatment before flying from Imphal to the Aberdeen airstrip in March 1944 (p. 176) he located the dentist's caravan, was quickly fitted in and given an excellent filling. 'I shall always remember that squadron leader, one of the few and far between in those days, and he certainly knew his job'.[84] A simple tribute from one member of a vast team to another.

12 Burma Reconquered

We must turn now to the campaign that marked the culmination of almost three years of endeavour, leading in the remarkably short space of four months to the reconquest of most of Burma and the fall of Rangoon (Map 10). It was all made possible by the Anglo-American use of air supply on an unprecedented scale, and this in turn depended on the continuance of the air superiority that had been secured a year or so earlier.

Air Superiority

Few doubted that this could be achieved. Nevertheless the enemy had not been idle. Since 1942, having first improved the former British airfields and developed airfield groups round the strategic centres of Meiktila, Magwe, Toungoo and Rangoon, they had laid out a forward line of bases suitable for either offence or defence. Many more airstrips were prepared in different parts of Burma during 1943 and 1944, new back-up bases were constructed in Siam, and by mid-1944 Allied intelligence were convinced that the enemy air forces had become resigned to a defensive policy.[1] This was good from the point of view of the protection of Allied bases, but the threat to Slim's offensive remained clear, and not least when the Japanese began to develop multi-strip airfields at Toungoo and elsewhere. They would now be able to use two or more runways simultaneously and neutralisation would be more difficult.[2] They were also building many more aircraft shelters: by the end of 1944 there were 3,700, 1,000 constructed during that year.[3]

Airfields, however, are never much use without aircraft, as the British had learnt to their cost in Malaya, and although the Japanese would be able to move their aircraft around and conceal them they would never have anything like enough. They were not helped by the pressure of events elsewhere. In October 1944 General MacArthur launched his attack on the Philippines, whereupon the enemy switched a hundred of their aircraft from South-East Asia, and the outflow continued, made worse by losses due to attrition. Consequently the 525 operational aircraft which they had in South-East Asia in June

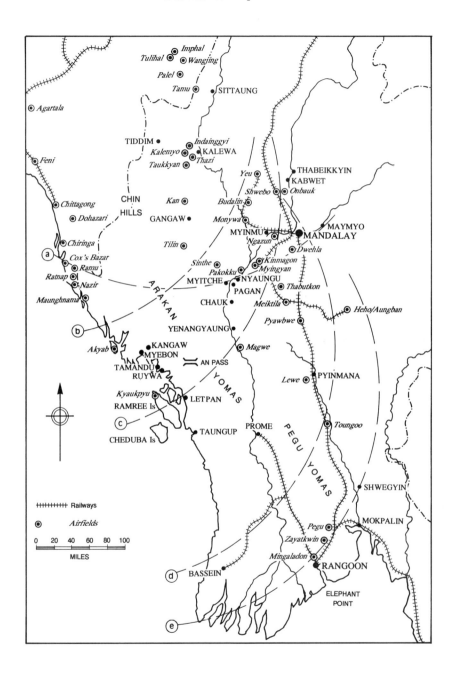

Map 10   The Burma Campaign 1945. The arcs indicate the 250 mile economic
radii of action of transport aircraft operating from (a) Tulihal, (b) Agartala,
(c) Chittagong, (d) Akyab and (e) Kyaukpyu.

(125 in Burma, the rest in Siam, Indo-China, Sumatra and Malaya) had reduced to 340 by December and 258 by January 1945. Of these 258, Allied intelligence placed 67 fighters (mainly Type 01 – Oscars), three bombers and 20 reconnaissance aircraft in Burma and 27 bombers and nine reconnaissance in Siam and Indo-China.[4] This was a total force of 126 front-line aircraft with which to confront EAC, whose strength by March 1945 had risen to over 1,500 (p. 230).

Yet even this small enemy force, almost hopelessly outnumbered, had its nuisance value and succeeded in diverting much effort which could more profitably have been used for offensive purposes. The fighter sweeps in late 1944 and early 1945, usually carried out by three to ten aircraft, would hit all sorts of targets, including some of the base airfields, and could be particularly effective against recently established forward strips beyond the radar warning net. Occasionally too they got through to the Dakotas: in November, for example, five were shot down while dropping supplies along the Tiddim road and on 12 January four more were destroyed near Onbauk.[5] Their Dinah reconnaissance aircraft also appeared from time to time, four being shot down by Spitfires in September and October,[6] and on 25 December three Lily bombers penetrated to Calcutta, giving 89 Squadron's Beaufighters two kills.[7] The scale of such incursions might be small, but significant defensive effort was needed to guard against them.

Allied air effort was also directed against the enemy airfields and two raids on those at Rangoon on 18 October and 20 October were timed to coincide with MacArthur's Philippine landings. Considerable numbers of enemy aircraft were destroyed or damaged in the air and on the ground, and the attacking force included RAF Beaufighters, Mosquitos and Thunderbolts together with USAAF P-47s (Thunderbolts) and P-38s. Similar sweeps continued in November, but with the enemy hard to find and increasingly disinclined to 'mix it', most of the Allied aircraft were switched to more productive roles. Several successful long-range missions were, however, carried out in early 1945 against airfields in Siam by Mustangs of the USAAF Air Commandos.[8]

Summing up the consequences of all these operations for the enemy, Park records that between June 1944 and the beginning of May 1945 some 165 of their aircraft were destroyed on the ground or in the air, with 47 probables and 152 damaged, against a total effort of 1,845 sorties.[9] While EAC's losses were far greater – during the six months November 1944 to April 1945 they totalled 492 (196 RAF and 296 American)[10] – these must be set against the far greater number of aircraft deployed and the scale and extent of their operations.

Typical of the Spitfire squadrons which did so much to win this battle for air superiority was 273 Squadron, which we met briefly in

Ceylon (p. 101). Having converted from Hurricanes to Spitfires, it arrived at Chittagong in May 1944 at the start of the monsoon; as Wing Commander Piper, then one of the squadron pilots, recalls, they were plagued with mosquitos, everything ran with water, and prickly heat became endemic – not least amongst the pilots, who had to wear full flying kit while maintaining immediate readiness. He remembers nothing to recommend Chittagong. Cox's Bazar, where they went in August, was better, being near the sea, but six aircraft still had to be kept at immediate readiness to cope with the occasional raid which might arrive unannounced. They were also tasked with ground attack operations, on one of which a foursome including Piper destroyed four river boats, believing them to be Japanese, only to be told on their return that four Indian RASC boats had just been sunk by Oscars. 'For Oscars read Spitfires' it soon became clear, though the boats were well beyond the agreed bomb-line. In December they moved south again to Maunghnama and in late January to the very short 800 yd strip that had just been captured at Kyaukpyu, on Ramree Island. Here, able for the first time to carry bombs, they devoted even more of their time to close support of the ground troops fighting on the mainland, and were delighted when Paddy Bandon, their AOC, having removed his air rank badges, flew operational sorties with them as a flying officer. The only senior member of the Group staff ever to visit them, Piper says, he usually arrived in his Harvard, wearing the shortest of shorts despite an order that all personnel should wear trousers at all times. They all loved him.[11] This was leadership – whatever one may say about the risks of his being shot down.

An MT driver with 7273 Servicing Echelon, which supported 273 Squadron throughout, echoes Piper's comments about their AOC. He also describes the 'family spirit' that pervaded the squadron and the admiration the ground personnel held for the pilots (who included Canadians, Australians and New Zealanders), not least since the men knew what could happen should they fail to return. The losses hit the airmen hard: between 31 May 1944 and 7 June 1945 11 pilots were killed in action.[12] As for the tradesmen themselves, Piper's concise words say it all: 'The superb ground crews: I never worried about my aircraft. I wish I had got to know them better'.

Air Supply

Air superiority was not the only requirement if the transport aircraft were to do their job. To support what was hoped to be a fairly rapid advance they would themselves have to operate from bases that were within range, and most important of all there must be enough of them – considerably more than in the past. Yet as Slim later wrote, a constant anxiety in all his plans was the amount of airlift he could rely on getting.[13] At such a late stage in the war this may seem surprising, and during the planning stage for CAPITAL in autumn 1944 it seemed as though there would be sufficient. Leaving aside the USAAF squadrons committed to the Hump and to the support of NCAC, it was expected that by January 1945 the CCTF (p. 229) would comprise the four long-serving RAF squadrons (100 aircraft), two very welcome squadrons of the RCAF (Nos 435 and 436 − 50 aircraft), and eight newly arrived American squadrons, together with two Air Commando units (about 230 aircraft). This size of force operating from bases in East Bengal and around Imphal should have been capable of delivering the 861 tons that would be required daily by 14th Army and XV Corps during the peak period from March to May 1945.[14]

By November, however, there was a new anxiety, for a major Japanese offensive in southern China was threatening not only to destroy many of Chiang Kai Shek's forces but also to take out one of the Americans' main groups of airfields at Kweilin and Liuchow (Map 2). General Wedemeyer, who after serving as Mountbatten's Chief of Staff became the Generalissimo's American Chief of Staff on 31 October (Stilwell having been recalled), was thus quickly under pressure and on 20 November asked Mountbatten to release two USAAF combat cargo squadrons for use in China. Ten days later, with the backing of the United States Chiefs of Staff, he urged the withdrawal of two Chinese divisions from NCAC, a move for which yet more air transport would be needed. The threat, as he saw it, now extended to the essential supply terminal area around Kunming, and he feared the Chinese Central Government itself might collapse.[15] Mountbatten and the British Chiefs were thoroughly alarmed, and on 2 December the latter told the Americans of their deep concern over Wedemeyer being given what amounted to a blank cheque on all American air forces in South-East Asia, since it placed Mountbatten in constant danger of having the transport aircraft for CAPITAL withdrawn.[16]

To meet the immediate situation Mountbatten felt obliged to release three squadrons to Wedemeyer[17] and partly to replace them by two RAF squadrons (Nos 117 and 194) which had been temporarily moved back to India for rehabilitation and to provide training for airborne operations. Slim, whose advance into Burma was gaining pace, as we shall shortly see, writes of his shock at being awakened at dawn on 10 December by the roar of large numbers of aircraft taking off near his headquarters at Imphal. Asking what was going on he was told that three of the USAAF Dakota squadrons allocated to his maintenance were on their way to China, and the 14th Army supplies loaded into the earlier flights had been dumped on the Imphal strip. We can understand his consternation and the implications this surprising news had for his operations and the complex support organisation. While the lost tonnage was eventually restored, Slim later estimated that his campaign plans were delayed by two or three weeks, a serious blow considering how much had to be done in the short campaigning season before the monsoon would break.[18]

The position could easily have been worse, for as Mountbatten reported to the Chiefs on 13 December, Wedemeyer was now looking for yet another two squadrons. The conflict of priorities continued for several more weeks, and Mountbatten felt compelled to spell out the stakes to the Chiefs of Staff on 1 January:

The advance of the Army into Burma depends absolutely on air supply, because the land lines of communication are inadequate ... a halt may be forced on 14th Army unless the three [American] squadrons are released or replaced from outside the theatre by 1 March.[19]

A few days later Leese entered the fray, warning that unless the extra transport aircraft were forthcoming the Army might have to withdraw behind the Chindwin for the monsoon, and on the 18th Mountbatten was so concerned about the effect on 14th Army's operations that he instructed Garrod to prepare to convert one of the Liberator squadrons for supply dropping. Garrod was far from keen: Liberators were not suited to this role and could help the Army much better as heavy bombers. Other airmen thought the dangers were being exaggerated; Stratemeyer suggested to Garrod on the 19th that the real bottleneck was the Army's inability to get the supplies to the airheads, not the CCTF's capacity to deliver them.[20] Whatever the rights and wrongs of this argument – and Stratemeyer had a point – the American Chiefs eventually relented, and on 1 February Wedemeyer returned two of his squadrons.

Two extra RAF squadrons were now also on their way, No 267 from Italy and No 238, recently formed in the UK with the intention of going to Australia to support the Navy's Pacific Fleet.[21] Both these squadrons were operating by March and in May they were joined by two more – the re-formed 96 Squadron, and the re-equipped 215 Squadron, which had hitherto flown Liberators. To improve matters further, the RAF squadron establishments were raised from 25 to 30 aircraft apiece on 1 March, so that by May 1945 the RAF's close support transport force in South-East Asia – only six months previously limited to some 100 aircraft – was 240 strong, 300 if one includes the invaluable RCAF squadrons.[22]

This very marked RAF expansion was just as well. For one thing, even by January the Army was needing far more supplies than the 861 tons per day originally estimated (in that month the daily delivery was 1,031; in February 1,575), and it was decided to increase the sustained

rate for RAF Dakotas from 100 to 125 hours per month, the intensive
rate to 185 hours, and the maximum rate to 250 hours; moreover EAC
was authorised to exceed the sustained rate to any extent necessary.[23]
As a result the squadrons averaged 3,500 hours per month, 500 more
than the sustained rate, from then on and as Hardman states Nos 194
and 436 (RCAF) Squadrons each flew over 4,800 hours in one
particular month – an 'all-time record' he claims.[24]

Then in March it became clear that the Americans were determined
to devote all their resources in South-East Asia to supporting a
counter-offensive in southern China; with the reconquest of central
Burma about to be achieved, what happened thereafter to the south
and south-east would be none of their concern. Thus linked with
Chinese pressure for immediate withdrawal of the American and
Chinese forces in the NCAC came a renewed threat to the USAAF
transport squadrons contributing to the support of 14th Army,
engaged at this moment in the critical battles around Meiktila (p. 263).
'The loss of the aircraft', wrote Slim, 'would have been fatal to my
operations'.[25]

So once again Mountbatten had to do battle. While reluctantly
accepting the withdrawal of some of the land forces, he told the Chiefs
of Staff of the extreme pressure under which all his transport aircraft
were operating and that he regarded them as a single force, all to be
used by him as the military situation demanded. He therefore
requested their firm and early assurance that all these aircraft would
be retained in support of his operations.[26] London had no doubt about
what was at stake, and Churchill gave the Chiefs his backing in a
message to Marshall. Pointing out the importance always attached by
the Americans to the Burma campaign in the interests of aiding China,
he pleaded for its successful conclusion not to be put at risk:

> I feel entitled to appeal to General Marshall's sense of what is fair
> and right between us, in which I have the highest confidence, that
> he will do all in his power to let Mountbatten have the
> comparatively small additional support which his air force now
> requires to enable the decisive battle raging in Burma to be
> won.[27]

His intervention paid off. On 3 April the Americans undertook not to
remove their air resources from Burma before the fall of Rangoon, or
1 June, whichever date was earlier, though they would not agree to
Mountbatten retaining all the transport aircraft for a further two
months as he wanted. In the end, therefore, there were just enough,
but one feels that those conducting the land campaign ought to have

been spared all the anxiety.

To get the best results from the aircraft that were available it was necessary to base them as far forward as possible. Hitherto all the Army's operational areas in northern Burma had been within the 250-mile economic range of Dakotas operating from the main bases at Comilla, Agartala and Imphal (Map 10). Once the battle moved south of Mandalay, however, there would be increasing range/payload penalties, and although several squadrons could operate from Chittagong this would provide only limited benefit. The only answer, as Slim puts it, was to bring the air supply bases nearer. 'The islands of Akyab, Cheduba and Ramree, all in Japanese hands off the Arakan coast, would, if taken quickly, provide excellent airfields within the necessary 250-mile radius of most of Burma south of Mandalay'.[28] Moreover such bases could be directly reached and supplied by sea. Here, then, was one of the main aims given to Christison's XV Corps, Bandon's 224 Group and their Naval colleagues in the third Arakan campaign in early 1945: to seize the sites for airfields needed to support Slim's offensive towards Rangoon. In the event Akyab was occupied in early January and Kyaukpyu, on Ramree Island, a few weeks later. There followed intensive work – under the urgent and frequent representations of Air Command, says Park[29] – to construct the airfields and installations, and on 20 March the first of the four squadrons to operate from Akyab (62, 194, 267 and 436) moved in. The first of Kyaukpyu's squadrons (31, 117 and again 436) arrived on 15 April.[30] This was a fine achievement and as we shall see the timings coincided almost perfectly with the speed of 14th Army's advance – though in the event Ramree came into use too late to make a major contribution.

It is impossible to overstate the critical importance of these air supply operations. The daily tonnage delivered – most of it air-landed – rose to a peak of 1,800 tons in April 1945, more than double the original estimate but still less than was being asked for, and in total between 2 January and 21 May, by which time Rangoon had fallen and the monsoon begun, 14th Army (and 221 Group moving with it) received 210,000 tons (XV Corps, which could be largely supplied in other ways, received 7,500). Compared with this only 5,500 tons were delivered by road, though a further 38,700 tons were carried by the invaluable Inland Water Transport (IWT) service which had been improvised by the Army with the assistance of the Royal Navy down the Chindwin and Irrawaddy.[31] The figures speak for themselves and should be coupled with the air evacuation of no less than 130,000 casualties.[32] Truly the victory of 1945 would have been utterly impossible without the superb Anglo-American air supply operation, yet at the time – incredibly – many who should have known about it did not. Air Chief Marshal Courtney, AMSO, who visited India in February, reported back to Portal:

> I do not know whether the major part being played by the allied air forces in this theatre is generally appreciated. I certainly did not realise it before my visit (he had been on the Air Council since 1940!) and, judging by the official communiqués broadcast by the BBC, there must be others who do not realise it either. The facts are that the 14th Army is almost entirely maintained by the CCTF and that 221 Group is providing practically all the artillery support.

Portal's comment on this is revealing:

> I have heard the same thing from other people recently. However, I do not want to do anything to disturb inter-Service relations and I think we can afford to be generous. I believe RAF morale is excellent.[33]

Here was an opportunity missed. It is hard to imagine that Slim and his 14th Army would have taken exception to a spot of well-judged RAF PR, whatever might have been said in Whitehall.

There might even have been scope for a little publicity about a most unusual Sunderland operation in support of the IWT service. It was carried out between 8 February and 9 March by the aged aircraft of 230 Squadron, tasked to convey heavy marine engines from Bombay via Bally (Calcutta) to an alighting area on the Chindwin near Kalewa. The report compiled by Squadron Leader A W Deller, the detachment commander, describes his first attempt to cross the intervening mountains: having 'persuaded' his Sunderland to 10,700 ft he faced a solid wall of cloud concealing the peaks, and amid much turbulence and able only just to maintain safe flying speed he had to turn back. His second attempt two days later just made it, and the alighting, unloading and take-off were safely accomplished. Over the next weeks, despite considerable difficulties over briefings, communications, lack of dinghies at Bally, and engine servicing, seven more invaluable sorties were completed, four by the same aircraft.[34]

So the Sunderlands too made their contribution to supplying Slim's Army. Nor must we ignore the light aircraft, most previously provided by the Americans but in 1945 supplemented by several flights of RAF Sentinels (L-5s), 100 of which had been acquired by the British. One of the pilots remembers 'volunteering' in England as one of 30 ex-EFTS instructors for an unspecified and unusual job, whereupon they all ended up at Imphal. Each was allotted an L-5 and flights were attached to the various Corps. He himself became the personal pilot of General

Messervy, commanding IV Corps, and he and his colleagues – lacking formally defined roles – simply turned their hands to whatever the Army wanted them to do.[35] First and foremost was the evacuation of casualties from tiny landing strips to the forward airfields where Dakotas could take them back to the base hospitals, but communications work, supply delivery, leaflet dropping, deception operations, even emergency rescue were all part of the routine. As another light aircraft pilot recalls, 'we flew in conditions when the birds walked, with no navigational aids, and from strips merely bulldozed out of the jungle, surrounded by tall trees'. Their only protection .38s and Ghurka knives, they often had no idea where the enemy was, and they lived in 'utterly appalling' conditions – yet he never knew such comradeship. How the ground crew kept the aircraft flying he will never know.[36]

A similar comment comes from then Warrant Officer Peart, who flew Tiger Moth air ambulances during the siege of Imphal and continued to fly a variety of aircraft – Ansons, L-5s, Expediters[37] – as a member of 224 Group Communications Squadron until mid-1945. He too turned his hand to everything, including ferrying VIPs such as Slim and Williams, both of whom he remembers with affection. One regular and very important task was the delivery to the multitude of units of *SEAC News*, the newspaper edited by the distinguished journalist Frank Owen, which did so much to maintain the morale of the fighting men of all three Services.[38]

Air superiority – indeed virtual air supremacy – and air supply were thus the keys to victory. We must now see how that victory was actually won.

The Preliminary Advance

As we saw in Chapter 9 the great battle of Imphal was over by the end of June 1944 and on past experience, the monsoon well under way, one might have expected a pause in the active campaigning. This time, however, with the enemy defeated and disorganised, it was essential to allow them no respite. 14th Army would therefore pursue the Japanese through the jungle-covered mountains to the south and east in the hope that when the monsoon ended they would have reached the Chindwin and be ready to take the battle into central Burma in early 1945.

The initial operations during July were devoted to clearing the enemy from the hills overlooking the Imphal plain; then came the first major advance to the south-east, leading on 4 August to the capture of Tamu. Despite the indescribable state of confusion found in and around the town it was an invaluable gain, not least when two RAF squadrons were moved up to the reconditioned airstrip in October.

Vincent's aircraft, with the Hurricanes bearing the brunt of the close support operations, had already done much to assist the land offensive, and they continued to support the two advances that now developed, one eastward towards Sittaung and one southward along the Kabaw Valley (known as Death Valley because of a reputation for malaria and typhus) towards the important enemy base area around Kalemyo. Sittaung, on the Chindwin, was reached on 4 September, but the very difficult terrain of the Kabaw Valley, amid appalling weather, took longer to negotiate; Kalemyo was eventually taken on 14 November, and the important Chindwin port of Kalewa to the east on 2 December.[39] It had taken 11 Division four months to cover the 100 plus miles from Tamu to Kalewa, and in face of constant opposition they had depended for their food and ammunition entirely on the transport squadrons, operating under conditions of almost unbelievable difficulty. Group Captain Donaldson, who led the two RAF squadrons involved at this time (Nos 117 and 194), reminds us that for the first time they were supporting an army on the offensive:

> The Army were having to penetrate mountainous, jungle-covered terrain which had from time immemorial formed an almost impenetrable barrier. Virtually all supplies had to be dropped. DZs were continually being moved and were often difficult to find. The approaches to many were hazardous. Distances from supply bases were increasing. And overall, the monsoon was at its height. Nevertheless in the ensuing months the squadrons increased their hours … a great tribute not only to our aircrews but to all our ground personnel who seldom allowed our aircraft availability to fall below 90%.[40]

Donaldson's squadrons had also been contributing to the support of a second southward advance from Imphal, along the even more difficult route to Tiddim and thence to Kalemyo. Here 5 Division too had to be entirely supplied by air-drop and provided with constant air support, again largely furnished by Hurricanes. This proved particularly important in October, when the soldiers encountered a well equipped Japanese force holding strong defensive positions at Tiddim itself. A seven-day battle ensued; since the limited artillery force had to rely on scarce air-dropped ammunition the Army had to depend very largely on air support and the RAF operated at high intensity against bunkers, gun positions and strongpoints.[41] Slim's tribute to the work of 221 Group at this time should be recalled:

> What the regular air supply and support for 5 Division meant in skill and strain to the aircrews only those who have flown among those shrouded hills can judge. Yet throughout the whole of this

monsoon the fighters of Vincent's 221 Group flew over our troops every single day. I do not think such devotion has ever been surpassed in any air force, and I doubt if it has been equalled.[42]

For the enemy such operations had a different meaning. On 14 October a Japanese soldier wrote in his diary: 'We are bombed and machine-gunned so much that the men seem to be absolute wrecks both physically and mentally. We all pray that some of our own aircraft – even one or two – could be sent up'.[43]

So by December 14th Army was where Slim wanted it to be, up to the Chindwin and indeed across it in places. The monsoon was over, enabling extensive airfield construction work to proceed around Kalemyo. One enemy airfield, Taukkyan, was in fact captured intact, and several new airstrips were quickly built for Dakotas, fighter bombers and light aircraft.[44] Then on 3 January Vincent flew in; it was time for the joint Army/221 Group Headquarters to move up from Imphal.[45] Many more RAF units were making their way forward too, as one of their men remembers:

The road from Palel to Tamu (and onwards) was just a track being bulldozed by the Royal Engineers. We began to see the results of the battle – groups of five or six dead Japanese every ten miles or so. The horror of war was coming closer – most of us seemed to draw into ourselves. Our side-arms were checked and ready for use. Guards were posted at every meal stop. Water bottles had been filled with heavily chlorinated water and we were rapidly acquiring an oriental pallor from the yellow dye in the Mepacrine tablets which with salt tablets we took daily as a protection against malaria and dehydration. And so we arrived at our first operational site near Kalemyo, where we set up our ops/filter unit.[46]

The scene was thus set for Operation CAPITAL, the offensive into central Burma in the attempt to destroy the main Japanese Army and so clear the way to Rangoon, but essential for its success was the seizure of the coastal bases and airfields in the Arakan. This would be the task of Christison's XV Corps, Bandon's 224 Group and Force W, the substantial naval force that had recently been built up in the Bay of Bengal and was commanded by Admiral B C S Martin.[47]

The Third Arakan Campaign

It was on 8 November that Mountbatten ordered Operations ROMULUS and TALON – the conquest of north Arakan and the capture of Akyab. Serious campaigning had been impossible during the monsoon, but now detailed plans were drawn up for two main southward thrusts, one to clear the Mayu peninsula, the other down the main river valleys to reach the coast at Myebon, and for a seaborne assault on Akyab (Maps 7 and 10). The offensive began on 12 December, the region which had seen such bitter fighting a year before was quickly taken and by the end of the month the coastal area as far as Foul Point, only six miles from Akyab, was in British hands. The inland attack too was going well.[48]

In support of these operations Bandon's Group now included six squadrons of Thunderbolts, four based well forward at Ratnap and Nazir, three RIAF Hurricane squadrons, a wing of three Beaufighter squadrons recently re-deployed to Chiringa, and two Spitfire squadrons – together with the four USAAF Mitchell squadrons at Feni and the Lightning squadron, still at Chittagong.[49] Not all this effort was devoted to the direct support of XV Corps; the Beaufighters in particular continued to spend most of their time on the longer-range interdiction of enemy lines of communication. Nevertheless it was a formidable force, most of which – in the virtual absence of the enemy air force – could be used to assist the Army. In addition Bandon could request help from Mellersh's heavy bombers, as he did for example on 21 December when 69 RAF and USAAF Liberators dropped 236 tons on military dumps at Taungup, opposite Ramree Island – the heaviest attack so far against a single target in South-East Asia.[50]

To direct their operations Bandon's squadrons depended on accurate information from many sources, such as photographic reconnaissance, Y Service listening posts, VCPs operating alongside the Army, radar and observer units. Much of this work entailed great risks, none more so than those run by such radar parties as that led by Warrant Officer Nevill. Having piloted Beaufighters in the UK he found himself in India in 1944 preparing to parachute behind enemy lines with a party of some 20 volunteers, mainly radar operators, accompanied by a platoon of Gurkhas for protection. Their first mission began on 14 December, when they were dropped with all their equipment by three Dakotas about 40 miles east of Akyab. The site planned for them was ideal – probably thanks to the work of Force 136 – and they were quickly able to start using their miniature radar to observe the surrounding area, to pinpoint enemy taking-off and landing areas, and to report their positions by W/T to Cox's Bazar. We can imagine their delight when ten days later they watched six Thunderbolts hit targets which they had reported. They were there three weeks before being collected by the Army on 4 January. Such work – and Nevill and his men undertook two further operations near Mandalay and Rangoon in March and May – deserves our tribute.[51]

That Nevill's party was relieved so soon was partly thanks to the unexpectedly rapid fall of Akyab. The attack had originally been planned for 20 January, but on 30 December the Joint Force Commanders advanced the date to the 3rd. It was to be the first amphibious assault mounted by the British in the Far East war, led by 3 Commando Brigade, followed up by 25 Division, and supported by naval bombardment and 220 aircraft of 224 Group.[52] Then on 2 January, the Commanders suspecting that the Japanese strength had been greatly reduced, Bandon sent his SASO, Group Captain Dennis David (a former Battle of Britain pilot), to take a look. Flying his L-5 as low as 50 ft he reported that he could see no sign of the enemy, whereupon Bandon and Christison both flew in and landed, to be warmly welcomed by the locals and told that the enemy had gone.[53] The bombardment was called off and the landing took place unopposed. So the Allies had quickly come into possession of a very valuable port, a fairly good main airfield and seven satellite strips. Both port and airfield were in much need of repair, yet the first Spitfires of 67 Squadron arrived on the 5th and by the 8th the whole squadron was operating 'under difficulties'. It was just as well, for the next day six Oscars tried to attack ships in the harbour; five were shot down.[54]

By now, also strongly supported by 224 Group and largely supplied by air drops, the Army was advancing steadily down the Kaladan Valley, and on 13 January the amphibious force which had been allowed easy passage at Akyab carried out an opposed landing at Myebon, well supported by Thunderbolts, Hurricanes and Mitchells. Myebon was relatively lightly held – like Akyab and Ramree Island it was not regarded as of great importance by the Japanese, who were concentrating their efforts around Kangaw and Taungup in order to cover the two main routes across the Arakan Yomas and thus protect the rear of their forces in the Irrawaddy valley. The significance to the Allies of the airfields escaped them.[55]

Even so the Japanese were not to give up Ramree without a fight. The attack on this 40-mile-long island was mounted by 26 Division, which landed at the northern end near Kyaukpyu on 21 January supported by heavy naval bombardment, the dropping of 360 tons of bombs by 86 Liberators (54 RAF), air strikes by Thunderbolts and Mitchells, and the top cover of the fighters.[56] The nearby airfield was soon captured, but there was steady resistance as the Army fought its way south and not until 17 February was the whole island cleared. Meanwhile Cheduba had been taken without a fight on 26 January. The concentration of naval forces for these operations, which included the battleship *Queen Elizabeth*, offered an attractive target to the Japanese air forces, and while the Spitfire and Thunderbolt patrols usually drove them off, two ships were damaged – one seriously – when eight Oscars got through at dusk on 12 February in conditions of very poor visibility.[57] This was an enemy who never gave up.

There followed two months' work to bring the main airfield at Kyaukpyu up to proper standard – a task in which 2967 Field Squadron, RAF Regiment, gave invaluable assistance[58] – and while the Spitfires managed to operate from there throughout (p. 245), it was late April before Dakotas could use it as a base (p. 249) and four Thunderbolt squadrons could move up. Neil Cameron, who led 258 Squadron in from Ratnap, remembers the 'very rough' living conditions amid a strange mixture of jungle, scrub, rocks, cliffs and sea. Ramree could have been made into a tolerable resort under modern conditions, but in 1945 it was just a mosquito-ridden patch with a long steel-planking airfield from which the Thunderbolt squadrons could operate over most of southern Burma.[59]

The landing on Ramree had virtually coincided with another landing by 3 Commando and 25 Division, this time in an attempt to cut off the Japanese forces retreating south along the lower Kaladan valley. The objective was the heavily defended area at Kangaw, on the main (so-called) north-south coast road and covering the approaches to the An Pass into central Burma. The attack went in on 22 January, starting what Bandon called 'the vital battle of the Arakan campaign'.[60] While the initial landings, backed by Mitchells, Thunderbolts and Hurricanes, went well, the Army was soon held up by two strongly fortified hill features. There ensued a bitter fight lasting several weeks, involving 12,000 British troops and costing the Commandos in particular heavy casualties; on the enemy side 2,000 dead were counted,[61] and their total losses must have been far greater in a battle Mountbatten considered comparable in ferocity with the Admin Box and Kohima.[62] It was Japanese artillery, well sited and with plentiful supplies of ammunition, that constituted the main problem; the beach-head was being constantly shelled and unless these positions could be captured the landing was doomed to failure. Bandon, who initially had to support the Ramree battle at the same time, describes the tactics used to give the ground forces the help they needed:

The hills were heavily wooded and it was difficult to know exactly where the defensive positions were. The general principle was to use napalm, land mines and heavy bombs to blast away the jungle to reveal the positions which could afterwards be bombed by fighter bombers ... B-25s attacked the top of each feature first, followed immediately by Thunderbolts who bombed and strafed the edges of the feature so that enemy troops who might run down the hillside could be caught in the open. The next day four Liberator squadrons attacked the feature – preceded three minutes before by Hurricanes which marked the centre of each target area. The heavy bombing was a beautiful piece of work.

Thunderbolts followed up the Liberators, attacking the reverse slopes and areas not covered by the heavy bombers. A smoke screen was laid and as the ground attack was due to start 24 Thunderbolts made dummy attacks.[63]

This was close support of high quality requiring careful planning, co-ordination and control, and calling for great skill and courage on the part of the crews; during the most intensive week's fighting, leading up to the capture of Kangaw itself on 30 January, some 900 sorties were flown by the fighter bombers, and the area received over 750 tons of bombs and 17,000 gallons of napalm, delivered by the Thunderbolts.[64]

Despite all these efforts the Japanese still succeeded in withdrawing the bulk of their forces and with Slim's main offensive building up in central Burma it was necessary to try to prevent the enemy moving reinforcements across the passes from the Arakan. Consequently another amphibious assault was planned at Ruywa, intended to lead to the capture of An and the closure of the An Pass. This landing was preceded by a 10-day naval and air bombardment of Tamandu, just to the north, starting on 5 February, and the attack was launched on 15 February, supported by Hurricanes, Spitfires and Thunderbolts, and assisted by the first airborne VCP (p. 236).[65] There ensued a long fight, lasting well into April, before An itself was taken: Christison had to cope most of the time without air supply, all of which was needed from early March for 14th Army, and many of the enemy succeeded in crossing the pass to the Irrawaddy.[66]

Meanwhile yet another combined landing had taken place, this time on 12/13 March at Letpan, and by the end of the month XV Corps was nearing Taungup in the hope of cutting the main road across the Arakan Yomas leading to Prome, though Taungup itself was not occupied until 29 April. During March and April, therefore, when the closure of the An Pass track and the Taungup-Prome road really mattered, the task devolved upon 224 Group, for whom these routes became the principal objective. Both were kept under daily attack, partly with the object of cratering the surface or causing landslides,[67] and the Prome road was eventually 'maintained in its now permanent state of unserviceability'.[68]

Much of this work was undertaken by the Beaufighters from Chiringa, now much more powerfully armed than hitherto with eight 3'' rockets.[69] According to Bandon it was they that first discovered the An Pass track, and their attacks on the two routes – sometimes by night as well as by day – caused the enemy enormous problems.[70] Such low-level operations had their dangers – not least when in November 1944 two 27 Squadron aircraft briefed to attack road transport on the Taungup Pass were shot down not by the enemy but by Lightnings of the USAAF.[71] The Beaufighters were not, of course, confined to this role. Their task, as always, was to seek out and destroy the enemy wherever he moved, be it by road, rail or water, and in 1945 they penetrated as far as Siam, including on one occasion a 1,300 mile round trip to Tavoy, and frequently attacked shipping both in the Gulf of Martaban and in the waterways west of Rangoon. At the same time they were frequently employed in close support of the XV Corps operations we have just described[72] – truly ubiquitous aircraft.

The Thunderbolt too proved to have many uses. Neil Cameron's squadron, No 258, for example, attacked just about every kind of target: troop positions and observation posts, gun batteries, barracks, ammunition and supply dumps, airfields and airstrips, railways, bridges, ferries. Based at Ratnap in 224 Group, they had the range to carry out attacks in the Irrawaddy Valley and return to the Arakan to refuel. Alternatively if landing strips and fuel were available they could spend the day there before recovering to base.[73] This illustrates an important point: many of Bandon's squadrons were available not only to support XV Corps in the Arakan but also to assist 221 Group and 14th Army in central Burma.

Another role needs stressing also, long-range bomber escort. David Dick, one of the pilots, speaks of most of 30 Squadron's effort in late 1944 being devoted to long-range operations over southern Burma, either escorting heavy bombers or carrying out fighter sweeps.[74] On 3 and 4 November, for example, 30 and 135 Squadrons contributed to an Allied force of 125 Thunderbolts and Lightnings which escorted 49 B-29s and 29 Liberators (mostly RAF) in a successful series of attacks on railway yards and airfields at Rangoon; all the escorts had been concentrated at Cox's Bazar – where they presented what could have been an attractive target to the enemy – for the 850-mile round trip.[75] Long-range bomber operations continued, albeit usually on a smaller scale, during 1945, and the Thunderbolts were regularly called upon.

By April the three Force Commanders in the Arakan were turning their attention to what was expected to be the climax of their endeavours, the amphibious assault on Rangoon; at the same time, however, they were very conscious of the increasing pace of Slim's advance in central Burma, an advance to which their own operations, particularly those of 224 Group, were making a major contribution. It is to the great campaign fought by 14th Army and their airmen colleagues that we must now address ourselves.

Operation CAPITAL

The planning for CAPITAL had been under way since September 1944 (pp. 219-220), its aim the reconquest of Burma as far south as Mandalay (Map 10). At first it was assumed that the enemy would resist strongly in the plain around Shwebo, where his main forces could be attacked by 14th Army from the west and by NCAC (now commanded by General Sultan) from the north. By mid-December, however, it was becoming clear to Slim – partly thanks to air reconnaissance – that the enemy was not prepared to fight a major battle so far north. Since Slim's real object was the destruction of the Japanese Army he therefore had to recast his plans, devising what Louis Allen calls his 'master stroke'[76] – a major southward thrust, taking the advantage of surprise, to seize the important enemy headquarters, supply base and communications centre at Meiktila, 80 miles south of Mandalay. Thus the enemy confronting his other forces to the north as they advanced towards Mandalay would suddenly find their supply routes and their lines of retreat cut and be compelled to fight the critical battle on ground of his choosing.[77]

Slim gave his commanders their orders on 18 December. Messervy's IV Corps was to work its way south from Kalemyo along a narrow, tortuous road through the Myittha valley to Gangaw and thence south-east to Pakokku, where it would force a crossing across the Irrawaddy and seize Meiktila. This advance would depend totally on air supply (with the construction of new airstrips a top priority) and also on an elaborate deception plan designed to mislead the enemy about its scale and purpose. Stopford's XXXIII Corps was to advance south-east from Kalewa to take Monywa (thus opening up the Chindwin as a supply route), Yeu, Shwebo and the adjacent airfields, from where, in conjunction with the NCAC advance, Mandalay would be captured.[78] Supporting them – in addition to the CCTF – would be Vincent's 221 Group, its staff closely involved in all the planning and shortly due to move forward to the new joint Headquarters at Indainggyi, close to Kalemyo.

Vincent could call on 18 squadrons, eight of them still flying the faithful Hurricane (two in the fighter reconnaissance role, the rest in close support). For short-range work at low level in conditions of air superiority they remained invaluable. For longer range operations he had three Thunderbolt squadrons and three of Beaufighters and Mosquitos, and four Spitfire squadrons provided his air defence. In addition he could call on 224 Group, as we have seen, and on medium and heavy bomber support from the SAF. His tasks can be summarised:

a. to maintain air superiority and protect the transport aircraft,
b. to give direct support to the Army,
c. to destroy enemy defences ahead of the ground forces, and
d. to disrupt enemy communications and destroy his installations, supplies and headquarters.[79]

For such operations the squadrons would need bases as close as possible to the advancing ground forces, and it was not long before the shorter range aircraft, the Hurricanes and Spitfires, were able to start moving forward from their existing airfields in the Imphal plain. The new base area around Kalemyo received three squadrons in mid-December and these were able to assist the early stages of both Corps' offensives.

In the case of IV Corps, as Slim reminds us, the whole success of the coming battle depended on the secrecy of its advance:

> A single Japanese reconnaissance plane, investigating too closely a cloud of dirt, might sight a line of tanks moving slowly towards Pakokku and realise what that meant ... throughout daylight Vincent's fighters patrolled over the route and as far as I know no Japanese scout ever penetrated his screen without being shot down for his daring.[80]

Unfortunately one major obstacle lay across the route, for at Gangaw the enemy had developed an extensive system of gun emplacements into a strong defence line. To deploy too many troops against it might arouse Japanese suspicions, so on 10 January an 'earthquake' operation was laid on by 221 Group. It lasted 90 minutes, beginning with concentrated bombing by the four Mitchell squadrons of the USAAF 12th Bombardment Group; then came low-level strikes by 146 Squadron's Thunderbolts and 34 and 113 Squadrons' Hurribombers, with 42 Squadron's Hurricanes on call by the VCP. As the final strike went in the infantry followed up into the enemy positions. IV Corps' subsequent message summarises the result: 'Thank you for your most excellent earthquake. Thanks to your effort whole position captured with only loss of two own infantry wounded'.[81] As far as Slim was concerned, Gangaw had been taken by the air force.[82]

So by mid-January IV Corps was able to resume its covert advance towards Pakokku and by the end of the month was within striking distance of the Irrawaddy. In addition to those near Kalemyo, airstrips had been opened at Kan and Tilin, and the former enemy strip at Sinthe was about to be brought into use, both by Hurricanes and Spitfires and by the Dakotas. A 31 Squadron pilot remembers the intensity of their operations. He did four trips a day into Sinthe. Some were by night; on one occasion the controller called: 'Bandits in circuit. You are 48th to land; circuit without lights at Angels 9.1' – whereupon the 49th asked 'is that above sea level or ground level?'[83]

Meanwhile XXXIII Corps, having crossed the Chindwin at Kalewa and further north, had been moving rapidly towards the more open country north of Mandalay and by mid-January several valuable airfields – Yeu, Onbauk, Shwebo and Budalin – were in British hands.

The enemy had tried hard to render the runways unusable by cratering them, digging trenches and placing booby traps, but the taxi-tracks could usually be used by fighters, and it rarely took more than a few days before the engineers had runways ready for the transport aircraft. So as 19 Division closed up to the Irrawaddy north of Mandalay in late January – and established two bridgeheads north-east of Shwebo – the Dakotas were able to air-land their supplies and the fighters provide short-range support. Lack of airfields and supply problems, however, made it impracticable to bring up the Thunderbolts, Beaufighters and Mosquitos at this stage, and they continued to operate from Imphal.[84]

XXXIII Corps was also advancing parallel to the Chindwin towards the Irrawaddy south-west of Mandalay and by the 18th was approaching the strongly held town of Monywa. Here as elsewhere in the advance to the Irrawaddy it was becoming increasingly clear that air power – leading the advance – was causing the utmost confusion to the enemy by literally blasting them out of their prepared ground positions.[85] After some 400 fighter bomber sorties against Japanese defences outside the town on 18 and 19 January, a 90-minute attack was directed at the enemy rifle butts on the 20th; Mosquitos of 45 and 82 Squadrons, now at last in action, led the way with 500lb bombs, followed by 20 Squadron's Hurricanes with rockets and finally 146 Squadron's Thunderbolts with bombs – all observed not only by the VCP but by the troops waiting to move in. The strikes, especially those with rockets, were delivered with great accuracy; the troops' morale was strongly boosted; and while heavy fighting was necessary to clear the town the enemy's powers of resistance had been much weakened. General Gracey summed up in a signal to Vincent: 'All ranks 20 Division thank you for magnificent support resulting in speedy capture of Monywa and Myinmu'.[86]

By the end of January, therefore, 14th Army had closed up to the Irrawaddy for almost all the stretch between Myitche and Thabeikkyin – a well defended enemy bridgehead on the west bank at Kabwet having been cleared after highly effective Thunderbolt, Hurricane and Spitfire strikes on the 28th.[87] There was now a short pause for redeployment, to enable the supply to catch up and to plan for the next phases, and on 9 February Slim and Vincent moved their joint HQ forward from Indainggyi to Monywa, where it would be well placed for the coming battles. In addition to his RAF squadrons Vincent now had operational control of the four USAAF Mitchell squadrons, while it had been agreed that the four Thunderbolt and Mustang squadrons of 1 and 2 Air Commandos, recently sent by General Arnold and based in the Arakan, should be allotted to support IV Corps, from whom they would receive their orders direct and not through 221 Group.[88] This may seem a surprising arrangement, bearing in mind the experience with the original Air Commando (pp. 173, 179), but in practice it worked.

The scene was thus set for Slim to complete the deception he had planned. He had to keep the enemy convinced for as long as possible that Mandalay was his main objective and that his force near Pakokku was relatively small and not a major threat. On 10 February, therefore, he ordered 19 Division to open the offensive towards Mandalay.[89] This division had secured its two bridgeheads east of Shwebo a month earlier and been under heavy attack ever since, but strongly supported by the fighter squadrons based only a few miles to the west it had held on. Slim had visited the bridgeheads and found the men loud in their praise of Vincent's airmen, some flying five or six sorties a day, helping to locate and silence Japanese artillery and shooting up tanks.[90] Now it was time to break out and over the next few weeks 19 Division steadily forced its way south towards the city.

Meanwhile on 12 February, to reinforce the message, 20 Division fought its way across the Irrawaddy west of Mandalay near Myinmu. Here too the attempt to establish and hold the bridgehead was bitterly contested and needed every bit of help 221 Group could provide. One particular incident earned high praise. On the 19th two of 20 Squadron's Hurricanes which were on patrol waiting for a target from the VCP had been told to keep an eye open for tanks, and Flight Lieutenant Farquharson spotted a suspicious looking heap of green leaves. He and his No 2, Flight Lieutenant Ballard, fired their cannon at the branches which were blown away to reveal a tank. Others were then found and the whole of 20 Squadron was called up. In a series of 29 sorties, 10 with RP and 19 with 40 mm ammunition, 13 tanks were completely destroyed. This was a serious blow to the enemy, whose resources in armour were now very limited, and an immense boon to the hard-pressed Gurkhas. As 20 Division signalled: 'Nippon Hardware Corporation has gone bust. Nice work 20 Squadron. Tanks, repeat Tanks a lot!'.[91]

A few days later, on the 24th, a third assault was launched across the Irrawaddy, this time by 2 Division at Ngazun, closer to Mandalay; this too quickly developed into a hard battle, strongly supported by the airmen, and not until about 5 March were 2 and 20 Divisions ready to launch their break-outs.

Meanwhile much had been happening in the IV Corps sector further south. Early on 14 February 7 Division set out on what Kirby calls 'the longest opposed river crossing attempted in any theatre in the Second World War'.[92] The position chosen was just north of Nyaungu, where the Irrawaddy was 2,000 yards wide, and in the attempt to mislead the enemy as to its extent and location Mosquitos and Beaufighters had undertaken a deception operation (CLOAK) entailing the delivery of all sorts of special devices.[93] The assault itself met fierce initial resistance but by the end of the day, under an air and artillery curtain of fire, three battalions were across and a subsidiary landing a few miles to the south near the ancient ruins of Pagan had also been accomplished. The bridgehead was rapidly reinforced and within three days 17 Division was able to start moving into it and then onwards towards Meiktila. It had been accepted that in an advance of the speed required it would be impossible to hold the ground to the rear, and 17 Division pressed on in the knowledge that it must depend totally on air supply – air-dropped until such time as an airstrip was captured. This happened on the 26th, when Thabutkon was seized.[94] The craters and slit trenches obstructing the 5,000 ft runway were quickly filled in and next day – under the watchful eyes of patrolling Spitfires and Thunderbolts – 53 USAAF Dakota sorties arrived from Palel, bringing in part of a reinforcing brigade. The remainder arrived over the next few days at this highly exposed and dangerous airstrip where, but for the work of the RAF Regiment in dealing with Japanese snipers and infiltrators, operations might quickly have become impossible.[95] In all 665 USAAF and RAF sorties arrived in five days, an outstanding achievement, with many aircrews averaging 12 hours' flying time per day.[96]

Speed was now of the essence. While Meiktila was held only by a 'scratch garrison'[97] it was essential to capture it before the enemy could reinforce it and on the 28th, to try to ensure that the enemy air forces based near Rangoon could not intervene, the SAF sent 39 Liberators to Mingaladon to try to saturate the airfield.[98] The following morning, strongly supported by 221 Group, 17 Division launched its attack and by 4 March after bitter fighting the town was in its hands, together with the vital main airfield two and a half miles to the east. This and a strip to the north were immediately brought into use. Thabutkon was abandoned and 17 Division, still relying entirely on air supply, consolidated its positions to await the inevitable counter-attack.[99] It was at precisely this moment that Mountbatten (p. 248) was having to fight to keep his American transport aircraft.

By early March, therefore, Slim was ready for the critical battles. Meiktila was his and to the north XXXIII Corps was poised to strike at Mandalay. February had been a good month, and not least in inter-Service co-operation. Vincent's squadrons had flown 7,826 sorties, half of them in bombing attacks on enemy defences, a quarter in protecting the unarmed transport aircraft, the rest in operations behind the enemy lines.[100] SAF operations in support of the land forces had also reached their zenith, no less than two-thirds of the Liberator sorties being directed against battlefield targets;[101] there had been major contributions too from 224 Group and the Air Commandos, not to mention the PR squadrons. Let Slim paint the picture:

The Allied air forces ranged all over Burma as far south as Rangoon, on a plan designed almost entirely to help 14th Army. Enemy fighter squadrons were driven farther and farther back, his communications harried all round the clock, his movement by day made perilous and by night delayed. Our attacks were preceded by devastating 'earthquake' bombardments; our bridgeheads as we clung to them screened from fire by the air. Never, I believe, was air co-operation closer, quicker or more effective; never was it more gratefully appreciated than by 14th Army and its commander.[102]

General Leese too had no doubts. Reporting on the battle at Mountbatten's conference on 23 February he stressed that close tactical air support had to a very great degree made good the deficiency in artillery which under present conditions it was so difficult to get forward and keep supplied.[103] Vincent, whose squadrons were to raise their effort to 8,745 sorties in March, reminds us of what was entailed:

Almost every aeroplane exceeded the maximum degree (of operational intensity laid down by the Air Ministry) for *six consecutive months* – a wonderful effort of the pilots and the groundcrews and also of the aircraft depots back in India which kept us supplied with remarkably little waiting.[104]

March was to provide their greatest test, as 14th Army's six divisions sought to destroy the enemy's Burma Area Army. This too was six divisions strong and while they were already heavily depleted and almost entirely lacked air support one thing was certain: they would fight to the death. The evidence was soon forthcoming. By 9 March 19 Division, advancing from the north, had reached Mandalay Hill, on the outskirts of the Burmese capital, but still needed four days of bitter fighting to capture it. Ahead lay Fort Dufferin, a one-mile-square urban enclosure surrounded by a moat and a 23 ft high brick wall, 12 ft wide at the top and 30 ft thick at the base. While the city had been heavily bombed, not least by the SAF on 13 January, the walls of the fort remained undamaged, and when the Mitchells tried to breach it on 15 March with 2,000 lb bombs dropped from 6,000 feet they failed to hit it. The three Thunderbolt squadrons of 910 Wing at Wangjing tried next with 500 lb bombs, some of the aircraft using a forward strip at Thazi for refuelling. On the 16th, flying at low level, they attempted unsuccessfully to breach the walls from the inside; next day, ably directed from above by their commander, Group Captain Bernard Chacksfield, they switched the direction of attack so that the bombs hit the outside of the fort, and a number of partial gaps were made.[105] The night assault that followed met strong resistance, however, and had to be abandoned. Then on the 20th, after intensive artillery bombardment and further air attacks, several Burmese appeared and reported that the few remaining Japanese had departed;

they had had enough and were needed elsewhere. The battle of Mandalay was over. The next day Vincent flew Slim as his passenger in an L-5, landed on the racecourse, and joined him for a triumphal entry into the city.[106]

Elsewhere too there was heavy fighting. 2 and 20 Divisions had begun to advance east from their bridgeheads towards Mandalay on 5 March and by the 15th had cleared much of the territory immediately to the south of the city. Over the same period 7 Division, needing to open up land communications with 17 Division at Meiktila as soon as possible, was unable to break clear of its bridgehead at Nyaungu and then came under heavy attack from the south. Not until the end of March could the forces in Meitkila be relieved, although 20 Division had made contact from the north a week earlier.

7 Division in Meiktila had therefore to depend on air supply and reinforcement for a whole month, and for much of that time was subject to the fiercest of attacks by an enemy determined to reopen his main escape route from Mandalay. For some 10 days the defenders consolidated their hold on the town and mounted a series of raids to the south, east and north in order to keep the Japanese at arm's length for as long as possible; then on 15 March, just as 9 Brigade (of 5 Division) was about to be flown in as reinforcement, the enemy launched their attack on the airfield, recognising its critical importance for the survival of the garrison. Nevertheless, despite the enemy getting close enough to fire at the aircraft, only one of the 54 that touched down that day was hit. The same night, however, the Japanese managed to dig themselves in beside the runway and not until the afternoon of the 16th were they cleared sufficiently to allow another 28 Dakotas to land, one being destroyed. The 17th was better, with 60 landing, at which time 9 Brigade was able to take over the airfield's defence. The enemy now redoubled his efforts – a parked aircraft was set on fire that night – and from then until the end of the siege on 1 April heavy enemy fire meant that supplies usually had to be dropped rather than air-landed.[107] Brian Stanbridge of 31 Squadron recalls taking supplies to Meiktila and evacuating casualties:

> The strip was taken over every night by the Japanese and retaken every morning by our troops. It was under constant mortar fire which caused the loss of several aircraft while unloading. Our turn-rounds were the quickest ever. We could never be sure who was in control of the landing field so each morning we would look carefully at the troops on the side of the strip during the landing run, and if they had slant eyes would overshoot and return to base.[108]

At times, during the height of the battle, the only aircraft flying into Meiktila were the seven L-5s of 'C' Flight, 194 Squadron, which put up what Vincent calls an outstanding performance to bring out casualties.[109] John Dunbar piloted one of them and in turn pays tribute to the incredible bravery of the men on the ground, including a medical officer of the RAF Regiment who worked under fire throughout the battle:

> On one of the last nights before relief arrived he was the only officer left alive and he personally led the morning bayonet attack to clear the strip so that I could land with his desperately needed consignment of blood plasma. I cannot recall his name and to the best of my knowledge his heroism was never recorded or recognised – it was that sort of war.[110]

Park and Vincent too paid tribute to the men of the Regiment, who were charged with the defence of the actual airstrip and several times had to recover it in the morning after the Japanese had infiltrated overnight. There was a price to pay: two officers, including the CO, Wing Commander C M Lander, and 12 other ranks killed. Nor was it just the men of the Regiment who proved themselves grand fighters, Vincent reminds us; so did the servicing commandos, the radar personnel, the men of Air Formation Signals.[111] Nobody who was at Meiktila was out of the firing line.

They were fortunate in one key respect: it was 221 Group whose aircraft controlled the skies and ensured that the Dakotas could pass unmolested. Moreover there was air support whenever needed – even though the Air Commandos had been withdrawn on 12 March and switched largely to the longer range attacks on enemy airfields. Nevertheless, with the four Thunderbolt squadrons of 905 Wing (based in the Arakan in 224 Group) under his operational control throughout, Vincent had considerable striking power which was used to good effect as the Japanese were gradually dislodged.[112] As Slim says: 'in spite of the fiercest resistance, our infantry, supported where possible by tanks, and almost always by fighter bombers placing their loads within a hundred yards of our troops, gradually forced back the enemy from the airfield'.[113] At the same time 908 (Mosquito) Wing was contributing by repeated attacks on the enemy rail and road communications, supply dumps and oil pipelines, though in late March it was decided to limit this offensive to road movements so as not to prejudice the Army's subsequent operations.[114]

So by the end of March the enemy, having suffered enormous losses, had given up hope of recapturing Meiktila. Slim had won the victory he wanted and, to quote Kirby, 'Burma Area Army had virtually ceased to exist as a fighting force'.[115]

Objective Rangoon

Rapid though the advance had been it had not really been fast enough, for little more than a month remained before the arrival of the monsoon would put a brake on operations. Somehow, if 14th Army was not to be left stuck in central Burma, still heavily dependent on air supply, Rangoon with all its port facilities had to be taken by the beginning of May. Moreover, once Rangoon was in British hands it should be possible to exploit the Burma victory by moving on quickly towards Malaya and Singapore.

Such matters had already been considered by Leese, Slim and Stratemeyer on 19 March, and on the 22nd they asked Mountbatten to consider mounting a direct amphibious assault on Rangoon. The thought that 14th Army might end up having to fight a heavy battle around Rangoon in the monsoon rain filled Slim with foreboding, and since there now appeared to be enough sea, land and air forces available – even without reinforcements from Europe – a modified version of Operation DRACULA seemed sensible as an insurance. The planning machine was quickly set in motion and on 2 April Mountbatten and his Cs-in-C decided the operation would be feasible in the first week of May. It would be carried out from the Arakan using the naval forces based there and reinforced from Ceylon; 26 Division would make the assault, with another division in reserve if necessary; and 224 Group would provide the air cover and close support for the landings. Carrier-borne aircraft would protect the task force.[116]

There was much to be done in the remaining month, and immediately two major air constraints were apparent (Map 10). First there would have to be an airborne assault on the Japanese artillery overlooking the entrance to the Rangoon River at Elephant Point; the necessary parachute battalion was available from 44th Indian Airborne Division, but the transport aircraft were not and the Chiefs of Staff could not meet in time Mountbatten's request for the loan of two fully-trained squadrons from Europe. The naval and air advice was firm: unless the defences were neutralised the enemy would be able to prevent all convoy and minesweeping operations, but Park could not guarantee that bombing alone would suffice to deal with them, and heavy naval bombardment was precluded by the shallow water. Now totally persuaded of the critical importance of DRACULA (14th Army was still heavily engaged 300 miles north of Rangoon) Mountbatten overrode Leese's objections and decided on 10 April that the two USAAF air commando troop carrier squadrons must be immediately withdrawn from supply operations in order to train for the airborne attack.[117]

The second constraint related to close air support, essential to help deal with the heavy opposition the invasion force could expect. The longer range aircraft would be able to reach the area from Ramree, where work to complete a 2,000 yard all-weather runway was being speeded up, but Ramree was 250 miles away, too far for the Spitfires and Hurricanes, and its capacity would be limited. Park made it clear that if Toungoo were not taken in time he would have to advise against DRACULA from the air point of view, though Stratemeyer thought that by what he called 'some extravagant use of air power' it should be possible to provide the minimum support required.[118] Mountbatten, however, was persuaded, ordering that 14th Army's advance be speeded up in order to seize the airfields near Pyinmana and Toungoo.[119] Every risk should be taken, including that of very heavy casualties – for there would be a risk of even greater casualties to the DRACULA force if it received inadequate air support.[120] Toungoo, the more important centre, possessed two all-weather airfields only 160 miles from Rangoon, so when General Mansergh, commanding 5 Division near Meiktila, was given his orders on 7 April, he was told to be there by the 25th. This would allow just a week to make the airfields serviceable and move in the squadrons before D-Day on 2 May. It was the 11th before his drive south could begin; Slim describes his feelings as he watched vehicle after vehicle pass, loaded with Indian soldiers grasping their weapons, and on their faces the same look as their commander, alert and eager.

> A dull roar above me made me look up. That noise, three years ago, would have sent us all diving for cover. Now I was the only one to raise my head and see our fighters streaking south across the sky. We took them for granted, yet it was they who made possible this swift move of soft vehicles, almost nose to tail, down one road.[121]

221 Group, as Slim knew, was doing its utmost to keep pace with his advance. Already the Spitfires and Hurricanes of 906 Wing had moved forward to Dwehla, south of Mandalay, and very soon those of 909 Wing would be in the same area, providing the air defence and close support needed by IV Corps. To the west 907 Wing's Spitfires and Hurricanes were at Sinthe, supporting XXXIII Corps, and before the end of April the longer range Thunderbolts and Mosquitos of 910 and 908 Wings would be at Myingyan and Kinmagon, NW of Meiktila. Vincent himself would soon have his headquarters alongside Slim at Meiktila, and ahead of him would be the mobile advanced group control centre, controlling the three short-range wings.[122]

Up to about 12 April their operations were geared to the continuing heavy battles being fought by IV and XXXIII Corps in the attempt to break through the Japanese defences along a line running roughly between Chauk, on the Irrawaddy, and Pyawbwe, south of Meiktila.

Then, as the resistance crumbled, there were two main thrusts, the stronger one by IV Corps along the main road/rail route towards Toungoo and Pegu, and the other by XXXIII Corps along the Irrawaddy towards Prome. The latter encountered the stronger resistance, particularly around the Yenangyaung oilfields, but on 19 April the airfield at Magwe was taken – of great importance to the RAF both symbolically and practically – and 907 Wing was operating there from the 29th. Not until 3 May, however, did the Corps reach Prome; its advance had been limited by the constraints of air supply, and steadily deteriorating weather had slowed its progress and made air operations more difficult.[123] Significantly 221 Group was able to mount only 5,161 sorties altogether in April, compared with the 8,745 of the previous month.[124]

IV Corps, on the other hand, was able to move more rapidly. 5 Division reached Pyinmana on the 19th and next day occupied the airfield at Lewe, whereupon the engineers moved in. On the 21st the American gliders arrived with bulldozers and other equipment from Meiktila, which had already been developed and stocked up as IV Corps' supply base, and crash-landed nearby. Then eight Oscars put in one of their rare appearances, destroying five of the gliders; had they arrived a few minutes later they would have found the first supply aircraft coming in to land.[125] Meanwhile 5 Division was pressing forward and on the 22nd was in Toungoo – three days ahead of schedule. The town and nearby airfields were virtually undefended; the enemy had appreciated the threat too late and thanks to the efforts of Force 136, supported for so long by the special duties squadrons, many of the reinforcements they tried to send were ambushed by the Karen guerrillas in the Shan Hills to the north-east. The fighter aircraft too had played their part, not least by attacking and disrupting enemy headquarters wherever they could be found, though on the 22nd one of their strikes went astray when a British column already several miles south of Toungoo was shot up. Given the pace of the advance the occasional mistake was inevitable.[126]

Although the runways at Toungoo's two airfields, Main and Tennant, were in poor condition they were quickly made fit for use – again after the arrival of glider-borne equipment – and on the 24th some 56 CCTF aircraft were able to land supplies,[127] notwithstanding another attempt by the Oscars to intervene. As at Lewe the enemy sustained losses when intercepted by Spitfires but still caused considerable damage and casualties on the ground. On the 29th 12 Oscars made their last strike against 14th Army in the Burma war, with little success,[128] and by then the two Spitfire and Hurricane wings (906 and 909) were moving into Toungoo, together with detachments of Thunderbolts from 910 Wing. The air support so urgently needed for DRACULA was in place, just in time.

A Beaufighter operating from a forward airstrip near Mandalay, April 1945.
(*AHB*)

For 14th Army it was not sufficient to reach Toungoo, and during the last days of April they raced on in hope of beating DRACULA to Rangoon. With great support from the Hurricanes, Mosquitos and Beaufighters in attacks on enemy road and river transport, they managed to cut the enemy's only escape route NE of Pegu on the 30th, and next day, with Pegu in their hands, they stood only 50 miles from the city. Then suddenly the weather took over, with torrential rain not only halting the advance but also flooding the airfields at Toungoo. Tennant quickly became unusable and while Main was just able to cope with the transport aircraft and one fighter squadron, all the other aircraft that had been brought in had to be flown back north as soon as conditions permitted.[129] Fortunately it did not really matter.

Despite 14th Army's disappointment at not quite reaching its ultimate goal, its 250-mile dash southwards from near Meiktila had taken only three weeks and – uniquely for an advance of this distance at such speed – had depended totally on air supply. Some of this had come from squadrons newly based at Akyab, but their capacity was limited and the main effort still came from bases further north, where the squadrons had to operate at increasingly uneconomical range. Whenever possible the supplies were air-landed, as we have seen, at newly captured airstrips, but many units could only be supplied by air-drop. Flight Lieutenant Dix, a navigator who had come with 267 Squadron from Italy, writes:

In some sectors the Army was advancing so rapidly that the actual front-line position could only be guessed. We would be briefed to fly as far south as we thought safe along the road and railway towards Rangoon and drop our load to any allied army unit we could identify. We would see a small group of tents or jeeps at the side of the road, and wait in a small circuit for them to identify themselves if we had any doubts whether they were ours or theirs. We would drop some of the load, then fly south to find more campsites. It was obvious that this kind of free roaming drop could not have been carried out if the Japanese had had any heavy guns to fire at us with.[130]

One might add that the whole air supply operation would have been impossible without air superiority, and even with it, as Park observes:

Had the enemy used his fighters effectively instead of frittering away their effort on infrequent low-level attacks against forward troops, he would have been able to do great execution among our supply aircraft, thus seriously impeding the advance.[131]

That the Japanese did not do this betrays a remarkable failure at command level to appreciate the critical importance of air supply to 14th Army – though they may have been deterred by fear of suffering unacceptable losses themselves against the escorting fighters.

In recognising the significance of air supply we must remember that the greater part of the work was still being done by the Americans, who in March delivered 75 per cent of the 88,500 ton total and in April were responsible for 70 per cent of 80,000 tons. Nor must we forget the value of casualty evacuation; nearly 14,000 men were brought out in March and 13,000 in April, mostly by the RAF.[132] There was another task too, a new one. On 28 April, forces approaching Pegu heard that some 400 Allied prisoners of war being taken to Moulmein had been abandoned nearby by their captors; sadly, before they could be located, they had been mistaken by aircraft for Japanese (they were wearing khaki, of course, not the green now worn by all British troops) and strafed, several being killed or wounded.[133] This was a tragic accident, but the RAF quickly did what it could to make amends by flying the survivors out to India. There would be many more such missions of mercy.

Meanwhile DRACULA was about to commence. The three force commanders, Martin, Christison and Bandon, had started their detailed planning on Ramree Island on 9 April. The main landings, they decided, would take place on both banks of the Rangoon River, some 20 miles downstream from Rangoon, on 2 May, preceded by the parachute drop of a Gurkha battalion near Elephant Point the previous day. The naval assault force, including carriers with two squadrons of Fleet Air Arm Hellcats and two of Seafires, would assemble at Kyaukpyu and Akyab and sail on 27 April.[134] The land-based air support on which Bandon could call would amount to 38 squadrons, comprising eight Liberator and four Mitchell, six USAAF P-38, P-47 and P-51, and 20 RAF Beaufighter, Mosquito, Thunderbolt, Hurricane and Spitfire squadrons. One of the latter, No 273, would fly into the beachhead as soon as possible after the landings.[135]

Up to 1 May all proceeded according to plan. Before dawn a VCP was dropped west of Elephant Point to mark the DZ and set up a Eureka beacon, and 700 Gurkhas followed half an hour later, delivered from 38 Air Commando Dakotas, escorted by P-51s. Unfortunately the paratroopers suffered casualties later on from bombs dropped by one of the Liberators carrying out a preliminary attack on the Japanese positions; nothing daunted they went on to annihilate the garrison. The way was thus clear for the convoys to approach the river that night and launch the landing craft for the journey upstream. At 0500 hours on the 2nd, following up some 300 sorties against them on the previous day, the two assault areas again came under heavy air attack, and at 0700 the troops began to go ashore.[136]

Very soon their suspicions were confirmed. There was no opposition; the enemy had stolen away. During the night there had been a report that aircraft flying over Rangoon the previous afternoon had seen painted on the roof of Rangoon gaol the words 'JAPS GONE, RAF HERE, EXTRACT DIGIT'. The wording was a clear sign to anyone familiar with RAF slang that this was a genuine message from the

On 1 May 1945 signs are seen painted on the roof of Rangoon gaol – the words EXTRACT DIGIT are out of sight on this photograph. (*AMWIS 308*)

British prisoners known to be held there, but the DRACULA commanders decided it did not justify an immediate change of plan. The absence of resistance on the 2nd, however, tended to confirm it, and some of the troops were re-embarked in order to move upstream more quickly. Then at 15.15 Wing Commander A E Saunders, CO of 110 Squadron, decided to land his Mosquito at what appeared to be a completely deserted Mingaladon. He soon found he was right, but having damaged his aircraft on the much cratered runway was unable to take off again. He and his navigator proceeded to the gaol, where they found the Senior British Officer, Wing Commander L V Hudson RAAF,[137] and 1,400 prisoners of war happy to confirm the enemy's departure. The two of them then went on to the docks, commandeered a sampan and sailed downstream to meet the invading forces.[138] Slim records that 14th Army was rather pleased at this performance: 'If we could not get to Rangoon first ourselves, the next best thing was for someone from 221 Group, which we regarded in all comradeship as part of the 14th Army, to do it'.[139]

There was a sad postscript to what otherwise was a great day. Wing Commander Nicolson, previously OC 27 Squadron (p. 140) and now in charge of flying training at Eastern Air Command, wanted to see for himself what Liberator operations were like and persuaded 355 Squadron to fly him on a mission against Japanese gun positions in Burma. Over the Bay of Bengal an engine caught fire and the aircraft went in; just two men survived to tell the tale, but no trace of Nicolson or the others was ever found.[140] Thus perished the only pilot to be awarded the Victoria Cross in the Battle of Britain.

By strange coincidence it is Nicolson's CO of 1940 who next features in our story. It was Group Captain John Grandy, now commanding one of the two RAF Dakota wings, No 341, who flew over Rangoon on 4 May, dropped a package of Allied flags and then landed safely at Mingaladon, the first CCTF pilot to do so.[141] The author of *Wings of the Phoenix* tells us that

he was astonished and delighted to find an RAAF officer (Wing Commander Hudson), somewhat irregularly dressed in a loincloth, already there as Officer Commanding RAF Mingaladon, and in charge of Burmese gangs who were filling holes and clearing up debris. Dozens of airmen – many of whom had been in solitary confinement for six months, and almost all of whom had suffered cruelty and humiliation at Japanese hands – had walked from Rangoon gaol, but none asked to return to freedom in Grandy's Dakota. They said they had a more important job to do where they were, preparing the airfield. In the end three who had been longest in enemy hands, and were therefore the weakest, were ordered and helped by the others into the Dakota.[142]

The next day General Montgomery took the German capitulation on Luneburg Heath and on the 7th Germany surrendered unconditionally. The European war was over. What now for the hundreds of thousands of soldiers, sailors and airmen still confronting the Japanese in the Far East?

13　Finishing the Job

The news of VE Day was received with mixed feelings. 273 Squadron, whose Spitfires had just flown into Mingaladon, quite naturally did not celebrate quite as enthusiastically as people did in the United Kingdom. Those at home seemed unaware that the Japanese war was not yet over; there was scant press coverage; the men felt bitter and forgotten.[1] Up country the thoughts of 79 Squadron were even worse. In April they had taken their Thunderbolts forward from their 'happy' base at Wangjing to Myingyan, in central Burma; they had then briefly moved on to Toungoo but on 6 May, thanks to the weather, were back at Myingyan. It was a terrible place, says Jack Reid, ridden with malarial mosquitos and flies, afflicted by sandstorms, surrounded by battle devastation, and short of the most basic needs, even drinking water. His sentiments are understandable: 'It was whilst we were here that VE Day was announced and you never saw such a fed-up, miserable bunch'.[2]

Keith Park's words were more properly measured: the occasion was celebrated sincerely but without a 'high spirit of enthusiasm'.[3] Nevertheless he and the other Commanders-in-Chief were convinced that the reinforcements long promised by London on the defeat of Germany would now be forthcoming, thus enabling them not only to clear the rest of Burma but also to achieve their great strategic objective, the liberation of Malaya and Singapore.[4] At last, they believed, theirs would be the priority for resources. They might have known better.

Restructuring

No sooner was Germany beaten than it became clear that the political truce in the UK was over; the coalition government ended on 23 May and the parties began to play for political advantage in readiness for a General Election on 5 July. Not the least important factor was the Service vote, and two measures announced by the caretaker government took little account of the continuing war in the Far East. First a scheme to start releasing the longer-serving 'hostilities only' personnel led to the return home of some of the more senior and

275

experienced personnel and caused increasing shortages in certain 'difficult' trades, and then on 6 June the Secretary of State for War announced that the Army's overseas tour was to be reduced from three years eight months to three years four months. This caused consternation in SEAC because of both its effect on future operations and the difficulties of implementing it owing to shortage of transportation. Park immediately sought to forestall any similar sudden announcement relating to the RAF, whose tour length for single men was four years, but felt obliged to recommend a reduction to three and a half years by 1 December.[5] So from now on there were anxieties about the efficiency of the force as more and more experienced men departed, and about the morale of many who were still there, who feared that they would find themselves at the end of the job queues when they eventually did get home and felt themselves the victims of unfulfilled promises.[6] Moreover the longer the war continued the worse it would get.

At the same time the long-held hopes of an increase in squadron strength and re-equipment with more modern, better armed aircraft were dashed. Whereas a target of 116 squadrons had originally been set this was cut to 87 on account of the world-wide shortages of shipping and manpower that were now apparent, and also because of a decision to give priority to an RAF contribution to the air assault on Japan[7] – of which more later. So Lancasters, for example, needed to re-equip the Liberator squadrons, could not be available until mid-1946 at the earliest.[8] Essentially, therefore, ACSEA would have to carry on for some time with the forces already in the theatre.

Significantly too, it would have to cope without the Americans. With the fall of Rangoon and the removal of the Japanese threat to the China supply lines it was time for the USAAF to disengage from Burma and concentrate its efforts in China itself. This transfer was not unexpected (p. 248) and was in some ways a blessing in disguise, for it would not have been easy to deploy large American as well as British air forces in southern Burma. Better now for them to go their separate ways, with 10th Air Force resting and refitting before moving to China and the RAF concentrating on the drive towards Singapore. So on 1 June General Stratemeyer, who had since December 1943 combined command of the American Air Forces in India with that of Eastern Air Command, withdrew his units from ACSEA. Park marked the occasion with an Order of the Day which concluded:

Without the support of the American Air Forces in Burma we could not have defeated the Japanese Army as rapidly and as decisively in 1945. All British Forces, both land and air, are deeply grateful for the whole-hearted support and complete harmony that existed between the American and British Air

Force units in this Theatre. I am exceedingly proud to have had these American Air Force units in my command.[9]

As for Stratemeyer himself – to quote Mountbatten – he had provided 'an outstanding example of how an Allied Air Commander should conduct himself',[10] an observation which certainly reflected the views of the senior RAF officers with whom he had worked.

The American departure marked the end of Eastern Air Command, in whose place was now created an entirely RAF command structure designed to handle the remaining tasks in Burma and the offensive operations being planned to the south and east. Coryton and many of the RAF staff from EAC moved to Rangoon as HQ RAF Burma, leaving the recently created 228 Group in Calcutta to administer the units remaining in north-east India. The Liberator squadrons, formerly part of the Strategic Air Force, continued as 231 Group but now under command of a South African, Major General J T Durrant; 232 Group, under Air Vice-Marshal Hardman, took over the RAF supply squadrons on the demise of the CCTF; the PR squadrons from the disbanded Allied Photographic Reconnaissance Force became 347 Wing; and plans went ahead for their eventual deployment to the Rangoon area, intended as the main base for future operations.[11] Here, notwithstanding the monsoon conditions, three main airfields – Mingaladon, Zayatkwin and Pegu – were being rapidly furnished with 6,000 ft all-weather runways and it was hoped that all the heavier aircraft would be operating from there by 1 October.[12]

Meanwhile the roles of the tactical groups had to be readjusted. Bandon's 224 Group began to withdraw from the Arakan to south India at the end of May in order to re-equip and prepare for the invasion of Malaya, while 221 Group – based from May onwards at Mingaladon – took over the entire responsibility for Army support operations in Burma. It now worked with 12th Army, newly formed from some of the units of 14th Army and commanded by General Stopford (14th Army itself, like 224 Group, was designated for Malaya). While there was to be no real respite for 221 Group, the arrival of the monsoon did lead to a lull in operations and enabled some of its squadrons to be rested and re-equipped. As a result the Group by the end of June was very largely a Thunderbolt, Mosquito and Spitfire force.[13] It also had a new AOC, Air Vice-Marshal C A Bouchier. On 21 May his predecessor, Vincent, had been the delighted recipient of a captured 105mm gun, presented to 221 Group by Slim as a token of 14th Army's appreciation of its never-failing air support, and Vincent's own leadership, not least during the Battle of Imphal and the recent race through Burma, had been greatly admired by his own men and by his Army colleagues.[14] He ranks high amongst the RAF's wartime operational commanders.

Burma: the Final Phase

Despite the rapid advance through Burma and the capture of Rangoon there remained much to do, for the large Japanese forces that had been cut off would doubtless try to make their escape to the east in order to fight another day. While the British were by early May holding two corridors, one along the Irrawaddy valley and the other along the railway route between Pegu, Toungoo and Meiktila, there remained an estimated 18,000 of the enemy in the hilly Pegu Yomas in between, and a further 30,000 in the mountains to the east of the Sittang and holding the river crossings in the south (Map 10). IV Corps' main objectives, therefore, were to prevent the Japanese breaking out from the Pegu Yomas and annihilate them, to harass their forces retreating from the north, and to destroy those guarding the escape route between Mokpalin and Shwegyin. It was in this area that the heaviest fighting took place, marked particularly by a British attempt in May to seize a crossing over the Sittang and a Japanese counter-attack west of the river in early July which led to the Battle of the Sittang Bend. Then on 20 July began the attempted enemy break-out from the Pegu Yomas south of Toungoo.[15]

The intense fighting during these last three months was marked yet again by the highest level of co-operation between the RAF and the soldiers on the ground, and all at a time when airfields were being repaired and developed, squadrons were being reorganised and redeployed, and some of the worst monsoon conditions of the whole war were often threatening to make operations next to impossible. The Toungoo airfields, ideally located, were thus usable only by two squadrons of Spitfires; the other Spitfires, together with the Beaufighters and Hurricanes, operated mainly from Mingaladon, and for most of the time the four Thunderbolt and two Mosquito squadrons had to be based well north at Meiktila and Kinmagon respectively.[16] They had, however, one great advantage: the last of the Japanese air forces had departed. Their estimated strength of 255 aircraft in South-East Asia, including 184 fighters, was largely deployed in Sumatra; only 32 fighters and 18 other aircraft were even based in Siam.[17] So it was in conditions of total air supremacy that the RAF's 56 squadrons could now operate (Appendix C).

Park had no doubt about what his men should do. Signalling his senior staff on 25 May he referred to the 50,000 Japanese still in Burma:

These yellow vermin [sic] are escaping in large numbers eastwards into Siam and southwards towards Malaya and we shall consequently have to fight them again when they are refreshed and re-equipped. It seems to me better to kill them now while in reduced circumstances.

While appreciating the weather limitations, he urged what he called a new technique on the lines of a submarine hunt:

> I strongly recommend the introduction of a Jap killing competition between squadrons and wings. The whole area occupied by the Japanese could be divided into sections for regular air reconnaissance with small striking forces standing by at call. Unless we increase our present low operational effort, we shall allow many Japs to escape the bag as well as allow the aircrews to become stale through inactivity.[18]

These were bloodthirsty but understandable sentiments – this for him was no time to show mercy – and Coryton, having spoken to Vincent, promised to do everything possible to prevent the enemy escaping. On the other hand, he went on more realistically, such operations were severely hampered by bad weather, the dearth of all-weather airstrips and the extreme difficulty of locating the Japanese in thick jungle.[19]

What happened in practice can be illustrated by the operations of a typical week, 24–30 June, when owing to thunderstorms with frequent heavy and widespread rains 94 of the 232 tactical sorties had to be aborted. Much of the Thunderbolt and Mosquito effort was devoted to enemy troops, stores and transport in the enemy base area between Mokpalin and Moulmein, but other targets attacked at Army request ranged as far north as Heho, where enemy forces were still holding out east of Meiktila. A further 106 sorties were despatched against communications targets (only seven unsuccessful), some of them by Spitfires carrying out standing patrols over the Sittang and destroying many rivercraft, and others by Mosquitos attacking rail and river communications and fuel dumps. Also joining in the action were Liberators, which not only bombed an important stores area but on the 24th dropped 80 x 1,000 lb bombs on the railway bridge at Kanchanaburi, breaking several spans of the main bridge and also cutting the by-pass. There were also 56 special duties missions (11 unsuccessful) by Liberators, Dakotas and Lysanders; many of these were into Burma in order to supply Force 136, whose guerrillas were not only inflicting heavy losses on the enemy themselves but also directing some of the air strikes.[20]

The final battle reached its climax in July, when most of 221 Group's operations were concentrated on close support during the hard-fought battle of the Sittang Bend. Never did the men of the VCPs have a harder testing time than this, as for example when Flight Lieutenant J T Taylor, trapped with 600 Gurkhas for five days, directed up to 17 aircraft at one time on to targets only 250 yards away.[21] Then the 18,000 Japanese trapped in the Pegu Yomas – ill-equipped, under-nourished, disease-ridden, yet preferring death to surrender – attempted their break-out. Every aircraft was turned on them, directed by four VCPs working alongside the Army headquarters, and their bombing and strafing accounted for at least 2,000, probably many more, of the 10,000 enemy who died. Of the 3,045 sorties flown by 221 Group in the RAF's last full month of active operations in the Second World War, all but 429 were successful despite the weather, and 92% were in direct support of the ground forces. Stopford paid them tribute: 'On all sides I hear nothing but praise for the keenness and determination of pilots to get through. You have all played a great part in 12th Army's first big operation'.[22] The RAF had come a long way since 1941 in Malaya.

It had come a long way too in the sphere of air supply, which in July 1945 was once again a cardinal factor in assuring triumph for the Allied ground forces. By now the American squadrons had departed and the seven RAF and two RCAF Dakota squadrons of 232 Group (some 270 aircraft) were undertaking the entire task. It remained substantial. Admittedly the port of Rangoon was quickly reopened in May but such was the build-up of forces in the immediate area, together with the demands of reconstruction, that it was impracticable for the land forces operating further north to switch to ground supply. Consequently throughout May, June and July most of them remained dependent on air supply delivered through such airfields as Magwe, Myingyan, Meiktila and Toungoo Main. Akyab had come into its own as a transport base, operating three squadrons; two more were at Kyaukpyu, though the hastily built runways were often flooded and in need of repair; the others flew from Chittagong and Tulihal. The pressure was intense: up to 10 June, the last day on which American squadrons were available, the daily load that could be delivered was 1,474 tons; thereafter it was 880. While the planning tried to take account of this reduction, many difficulties arose in practice and to meet the Army's needs the squadrons had to operate at high intensity.[23]

Of all their problems the greatest remained the weather. May, when the monsoon broke, was bad enough; June and July were dreadful. Flight Lieutenant Dix, a Canadian, was at Akyab with 267 Squadron: he never saw a Japanese aircraft; for him the enemy was the weather, with torrential and continuous rain at base for weeks on end. Tents and possessions were perpetually wet or damp; the temperature even at night was 90°, with humidity almost 100 per cent; mosquitos and other insects threatened to eat one alive. Then came the flying. He would take off in heavy rain, enter cloud at 300 ft, climb amid heavy turbulence to 10,000 ft to clear the mountains, let down still in cloud until breaking out over the central plain, pinpoint his position visually, and find his destination. On the return journey the same hazards applied, necessitating a gradual let-down over the sea until breaking cloud at 300 ft and duly landing on a sometimes flooded runway.[24]

Simon Eden, a navigator with 62 Squadron, described to his father, Anthony Eden, the Foreign Secretary, a particularly bad but far from untypical air-drop sortie in May:

> We flew along towering banks of cloud trying to find a gap. Those clouds, with savage up and down currents of air, meant destruction to any Dakota that tried to force its way through. Gently we nosed our way along till we saw a gap. We tried it, we got through the first barrier, and on to the next. This time the gaps were not so obliging. We descended to try our luck underneath. The mist and rain enveloped us in a blinding shroud; we flew by instruments and instinct, peering out through the windscreen wipers, trying inadequately to deal with the torrential water that hammered its ceaseless tattoo on the aircraft. The currents of air caused the plane to bump, pitch, and jolt; it was blown we could only guess where. The normal air navigation, as used over Europe, is useless over the hills and valleys of Asia. In squalls like these you guess and keep your fingers crossed. The time came when we judged ourselves over the Irrawaddy and its fertile valley. Slowly we went down, we must find the river to check up our position on the map. Eyes were really strained this time. The pilot opened up the throttle time and time again as the shadow of a hill crept below our wings, dangerous, sombre and forbidding. Then again we would go down and once we saw a green hill top half a mile off our port wing, and the summit was above us. We were in a valley. God alone knew what valley. We never stayed to find out; we went up again to try later. This game continued for ten minutes that seemed like an eternity. Then the weather cleared and the Irrawaddy lay before us, glimmering in the sun, a friendly symbol of safety.[25]

Yet despite such conditions many aircrews regularly flew three, and occasionally four, sorties on the same day.[26] Dix remembers 6 June, when he delivered a load of fuel in drums to Kinmagon and then another to Toungoo; here about 30 Dakotas were in the circuit waiting to land on a temporary airstrip under direction from a hastily erected control tower which had no radar and only limited-range portable radio equipment. His third mission was to Magwe with 6,500 lbs of tinned milk, and on the way home he joined in a search for a Dakota reported missing over the Arakan.

Losses were inseparable from this sort of flying, and June was a disastrous month with no fewer than 12 Dakotas paying the price.[27] On the 25th Dix joined in another search for one of them over jungle-clad mountains, mostly cloud covered, but they found nothing. This time it was Eden's aircraft that had disappeared (on the 23rd); the burnt-out wreck and the remains of the crew were eventually found by a Gurkha patrol a month later.[28]

The weather continued to be the main handicap during July when supply-dropping once again formed a major part of the Dakotas' activities and six more aircraft were lost. Only by air drop was it possible to supply the troops engaged in the close and bitter fighting as the Japanese tried to break out from the Pegu Yomas; as Park points out, many of the DZs were only 100 yards from the enemy and some of the containers overshot the mark and fell into their hands. It spoke well for the aircrews – harassed by ground fire – that more did not, for the Japanese were in dire straits and desperate to get hold of the supplies they contained.[29] Such was their enthusiasm to lend a hand that crews even brought the occasional 100lb bomb which they pushed out while crossing the enemy positions.[30] Like the strike squadrons, the Dakota squadrons played a key role in this last great battle.

Objective Singapore

While the action continued in Burma the planners in Kandy had been hard at it, for with the capture of Rangoon the way seemed open for a fairly rapid advance in the direction of Singapore, always seen as Britain's prime military objective in the South-East Asian war. As far back as August 1944 it had been agreed in London that Mountbatten should prepare plans to recapture Malaya and Singapore, and thus open up communications with the south-west Pacific.[31] So in October he told the COS that as a first step he proposed to land in March 1945, ie. before the monsoon, either in the Tavoy/Mergui area or at Hastings Harbour and Victoria Point (Map 4), his object being to establish a naval and air base from which to mount an attack on Malaya later in the year.[32] The Chiefs were not enthusiastic, fearing such an attack could endanger the operations in Burma, and at SEAC neither Leese nor Garrod was keen on Hastings Harbour; Garrod doubted if proper air cover could be provided and thought airfields might take too long to construct.[33]

By now the increasing divergence of British and American interests in South-East Asia was becoming clear and not until 3 January 1945 was Mountbatten given his new directive by the CCS. This indicated that while his first objective was the liberation of Burma his second was to recapture Malaya and reopen the Straits of Malacca – a task he must be prepared to undertake without American participation.[34] Suitably forewarned, his planners produced their future strategy paper on 6 February. It assumed that, even if metropolitan Japan were to be defeated fairly soon, the considerable enemy forces remaining in South-East Asia would be well supplied and might hold out rather than surrender, so SEAC must be prepared for major operations to secure the main bases and break up the chief centres of resistance. Since Singapore was clearly the key it must be the next major objective and it was essential to act quickly, which meant launching the offensive before the end of the year. On the air side Japanese opposition would probably be small, low quality, and a rapidly wasting asset; the RAF on the other hand had a large force available but would need to be able to operate from airfields near Rangoon and also – most important – from a forward air base. After considering various options the study came out in favour of Phuket Island, south of the Kra Isthmus, for the advanced base (Map 2); 610 miles from Rangoon it would be within ferry range for all the aircraft, and it was only 400 miles from Malacca. It could be seized in October, followed by a landing in Malaya in January 1946.[35]

The concept of operations was circulated a fortnight later and already the timescale had been brought forward so that Phuket would be taken in June, followed by a four-division attack on Malaya in the Port Swettenham/Port Dickson area in October (Map 1). The plan was approved by Mountbatten and his commanders on 23 February, with 1 June as the target date for the landing on Phuket, and the COS agreed it on 2 March.[36] Detailed planning for the Phuket attack (Operation ROGER) was already under way. Despite reports that the Japanese garrison consisted of only one battalion, the Army proposed to use two divisions, one for the initial assault on the island and an adjacent bridgehead on the mainland, and the other to consolidate. This scale of attack would necessitate a substantial amphibious force, and until an airfield was secured air cover would have to be provided from carriers. Park, who was very keen to secure the advanced air base and feared the operation might be called off if it became too large, thought the military requirements excessive; indeed it almost seemed as though there would scarcely be room on the island for everybody. Mountbatten and Power felt the same way but the Army insisted. The RAF plans for the development of the base were finalised on 22 March. It was to be fully operational, with three all-weather runways, by D+100, and the air forces, commanded by Air Commodore W A D Brook, would include four Spitfire squadrons, three Mosquito and two Liberator.[37]

It was at precisely this moment that the commanders in Burma asked Mountbatten to resurrect DRACULA, the amphibious assault on Rangoon (p. 267), and it immediately became clear that this could only be done by switching the forces being earmarked for ROGER. The COS, too, told Mountbatten that ROGER should not start until it was clear that the fall of Rangoon was imminent, and despite the reluctance of his planning staff to see ROGER seriously delayed Mountbatten decided on 3 April to postpone it by six to nine weeks.[38]

The consequences for the invasion of Malaya and recapture of Singapore were obvious, and minds quickly turned to the possibility of making up lost time by going to Malaya direct. The resultant planning paper of 28 April stressed the increasing pace of events, the urgency of taking action and the further reduced enemy air threat; it went on to point out the value of surprise and the economy of effort. On the other hand the 1,080 mile distance between Rangoon and Port Swettenham would preclude land-based air assistance by all but the strategic bombers, and until airfields were captured fighter cover and ground support would have to be provided entirely by carrier-based aircraft. In the absence of an intermediate naval and air base there would be considerable risks, but the only alternative was to delay the whole strategy and if extra carrier resources could be provided the risks were acceptable.[39]

Park, understandably, was not happy. So concerned was he about the air risks that he even suggested an armed reconnaissance by a commando brigade against Phuket in the hope it would prove possible to seize control quickly. Mountbatten too would have preferred a stepping stone, but was prepared to go ahead without one provided the COS promised him adequate carrier-borne air strength. The decision was made on 3 May; while Park declared himself reluctant to cancel all planning for ROGER, the other Cs-in-C wanted all effort now to be concentrated on ZIPPER (the Malayan invasion). So on the 8th Mountbatten ordered the planning for ZIPPER and the subsequent capture of Singapore (MAILFIST) to proceed. D-Day was to be set for late August. A week later the COS told him they could not release the four light fleet carriers he wanted from the Pacific Fleet; they would, however, give him another assault escort carrier, making nine in all, and two general purpose escort carriers to ferry RAF Spitfires. With these he had to be content.[40]

So Park had to accept the inevitable. With the abandonment of the Phuket operation, he wrote, 'there vanished a stepping stone to Singapore which the British air forces could well have utilised to great advantage'.[41] There was, on the other hand, another base – albeit more distant – now available to him. It lay 1,040 miles SSW of Singapore in the Cocos Islands (Map 9). Despite the presence there of a cable station, guarded by an army platoon, the Japanese had never tried to occupy them and in July 1944 the COS decided to investigate the building of a staging post between Ceylon and Australia for aircraft that might need to be moved between SEAC and the south-west Pacific. The SEAC planners, realising that such a base could also be valuable for PR and bombing operations, were enthusiastic, but although the project was quickly approved it was not until early 1945 that the necessary resources could be provided.[42] The main party, under RAF command and ultimately numbering some 6,500 men (including army and construction workers), began to arrive on 20 March; a month later Spitfires of 136 Squadron, sent to provide air defence, were airborne; and on 28 May the first Liberators landed on the newly built 2,000 yard airstrip, laid with PSP.[43] Work to complete the airfield continued for two more months, but it was usable from June onwards and set to become, in Park's words, 'a most valuable offensive air base'.[44]

The initial staff study for ZIPPER appeared on 15 May, confirming the intention to attack with four divisions in the area between Port Swettenham and Port Dickson. The enemy opposition was expected to be one battalion on D-Day, rising to 1½ divisions by D+31; naval opposition would be negligible; their air strength would be a small proportion of the 150/175 operational aircraft spread through Siam, Indo-China, Sumatra and Malaya. By now the three Force Commanders had been appointed, Bandon representing the RAF, and when they met on 30 May to decide the date for D-Day the Army had to insist for manpower reasons on the later of the two possible dates dictated by the tide conditions, namely 9 September.[45]

The plan was complete by 25 June. As Park summarises it from the air point of view, the Liberator squadrons from Rangoon and Cocos would carry out large-scale preliminary operations against enemy radars, railway communications, airfields and shipping, and continue

A Liberator takes off from the recently laid PSP airstrip on the Cocos Islands in August 1945. (*AHB*)

these during the assault phase. On D-Day itself 180 carrier-based Hellcats, Wildcats and Seafires were to provide air cover and attack the enemy's communications and troop concentrations, continuing until about D+6, when three Spitfire squadrons (together with Sentinels and Austers for casualty evacuation) would fly from their carriers into the first captured airstrip, Kelanang. It was hoped to have a second airfield, Port Swettenham, open by D+12 and a third, Kuala Lumpur, by D+20, thus enabling eight Thunderbolt squadrons, five Mosquito squadrons and some Dakotas to make the 1,000 mile flight from Rangoon. Meanwhile Bandon and his 224 Group advanced headquarters would have arrived on D-Day itself, closely followed by essential ground staff, including some 2,500 members of the RAF Regiment to capture and hold the airfields and to protect radar sites. By D+23 there would be some 19 tactical squadrons based on the three airfields ready to support the drive on Singapore, with two squadrons of Dakotas available for air supply, six more on call for airborne assault operations, a Sunderland squadron on air sea rescue duties, and two Beaufighter squadrons for use in the later stages of the advance.[46]

Before we leave the planning it is worth considering briefly the enemy assessment of British intentions. In their view during May, landings were likely in August on Phuket or northern Sumatra, with the object of securing the air bases necessary for subsequent operations; then in November or December Malaya would be attacked in the Alor Star/Penang area, the immediate object the northern airfields. Only when these were in use would landings be attempted near Port Dickson. While the Japanese certainly reinforced Malaya and Singapore during June and July their dispositions in September would have been not only behind schedule but also inappropriate to the type and direction of attack being planned. Nevertheless they were planning to use all their aircraft – training and transport as well as front-line – in suicide attacks on Allied shipping and then fight on without an air force. Up to 2,000 pilots were ready to volunteer for this role, more than enough for the 800 or so aircraft available in the entire Southern Area. Many of these, however, were still in Java in September, and the number that could actually have been concentrated within reach of the invasion area in the critical opening phase – and in face of surprise British attacks on their airfields – would almost certainly have been small. Even so some would have got through and on the evidence of the successes of Kamikaze pilots in the Pacific theatre might well have inflicted serious damage on both ships and airfields.[47] This should not, however, have proved critical.

Preparatory Operations

There was much to be done in the air to help prepare the way for ZIPPER, with the PR aircraft, the GR squadrons, the long-range bombers and the SD units all having their parts to play. Their contributions in 1944 were described in Chapter 10, and much of their work in early 1945 was linked to the Burma battles covered in Chapter 12. By mid-1945, however, their tasks were changing and no longer were they operating with the Americans alongside them.

Of the two PR squadrons comprising 347 Wing, 681 now moved its Spitfires forward to Mingaladon, from where it could support 12th Army, but 684's Mosquitos had to remain based at Alipore. Their greatest problem, apart from the omnipresent bad weather, was that of extending their area of cover; even when one of them had broken the long-distance record on 22 March 1945 with a flight of 2,493 miles along the Bangkok-Singapore railway it was able to penetrate only just beyond the Malayan frontier. Consequently the early photographic reconnaissance of Malaya, including the planned invasion area, had to be carried out by FAA aircraft operating from carriers.[48] In July, however, a 684 Squadron detachment of four Mosquitos began to operate from Cocos over Sumatra and Malaya and by the end of the month 60 per cent of the PR cover needed for ZIPPER had been obtained. At the same time another detachment was operating from China Bay, Ceylon, over the Andaman and Nicobar Islands.[49]

Ceylon, although a long way from the main scenes of action, remained an important base. While the submarine threat which had hitherto been 222 Group's chief raison d'être was effectively past by the end of 1944, slight risks remained and with the Indian Ocean routes critical for SEAC's supply the Catalinas and Liberators continued their routine patrolling until the end of the European war in May 1945. At the same time, however, there was other work to do. Partly because of the constant disruption of their railways, the Japanese forces spread throughout Burma, Siam and Malaya, as well as those in Sumatra and Java, were increasingly dependent for their supplies on great numbers of ships, mainly small coasters, and during the Burma battles of early 1945 these were subject to constant naval and air attack. Much of the air contribution was provided off the Arakan coast and south-east of Rangoon by the Beaufighters, Mosquitos and Spitfires of 224 Group, but from February onwards 222 Group joined in, using the Liberators of 203 and 354 Squadrons, operating from Kankesanterai and Cuttack (Map 6). Their wide-ranging objectives included ships and ports in the Andaman Sea and Sumatra, and on 26 March six Liberators co-operated with RN destroyers in sinking an enemy convoy trying to reach the Andaman Islands. Another important joint operation took place on 15/16 May, when the Japanese were again trying to reach the

Andamans, this time so as to evacuate their troops. While this was mainly a naval action, with carrier-borne Avengers taking part, the Liberators' sighting of the heavy cruiser *Haguro* was a key factor leading to the ship's destruction off Penang.[50] Co-operation between air, surface and submarine forces was paying off in many ways as the Japanese sought to re-deploy their dwindling forces and keep them supplied, and when Liberators began to operate from Cocos in July the noose was further tightened.

Aerial mining too had its part to play in the anti-shipping offensive. Some of this was done by the American B-29s, which had the range to reach as far as Singapore, but after their departure at the end of March the task devolved entirely on the Liberators of 159 and 160 Squadrons, based respectively at Digri and Minneriya. The former was to operate north of Penang, and up to 10 July, when the last mines were laid near Bangkok, targets were addressed along the whole length of the Tenasserim coast and in the Gulf of Siam. The latter was to cover the areas further south: a flight engineer remembers that most of the armament, all the oxygen equipment, all the armour plate, even the chemical toilet were removed from the aircraft in order to enable them to cover targets such as Jumbhorn and Singora in Siam, Penang and Port Dickson in Malaya, and eventually Singapore.[51] It was on 26/27 March that eight of 160 Squadron's Liberators made the 3,460 mile round trip from Ceylon, the first RAF aircraft to reach the city since February 1942. All returned safely, five having laid in the target area; they reported no opposition and many ships in harbour. Two months later, on 23/24 May, 160 Squadron carried out its last mission to Singapore; this time no large ships were visible, and the life seemed to have gone out of it.[52] The last tanker to reach Japan had in fact left in March; Singapore, for so long beyond reach of the Allies and the centre of enemy power in South-East Asia and the East Indies, was now effectively cut off from the Japanese homeland. No longer could Japan draw on the oil and the many other raw materials for which she had gone to war in 1941.

Without doubt the primary reason for this was the ever increasing pressure imposed on her maritime power by the Americans in the Pacific campaign. Nevertheless by 1944 and 1945 her southern ports and sea communications were under sustained Allied attack, with the air forces of the British, the Americans and the Australians making their contributions alongside the navies. It is impossible to assess the precise contribution of each element in the Allied offensive; while aerial mining by the USAAF and RAF in South-East Asia, for example, accounted for seven ships over 500 tons between September 1944 and May 1945, its main effect must be seen in terms of the progressive denial to the Japanese of many of their vital seaways and anchorages.[53] As one might expect, it was the cumulative effect of a

Liberators attack the enemy tanker *Toho Maru* on 1 June 1945. (*Lucian Ercolani*)

host of different measures that led to the breakdown of the sea transportation system so essential to the enemy war effort.

At the end of May minelaying was stopped in the Straits of Malacca and at Singapore, so as not to create problems for ZIPPER, and thereafter the mining and many of the shipping strike operations took place in the South China Sea. A notable one began when a Sunderland of 230 Squadron, flying an armed reconnaissance mission from its new base near Rangoon, spotted the 10,000 ton tanker *Toho Maru* heading north under escort in the Gulf of Siam. Enemy ships of such size were rare indeed by this point in the war, and on 15 June a force of Liberators was despatched on the 2,500 mile round mission. Appalling weather forced some of them back, and the first three to attack, belonging to 99 Squadron, were all damaged by AA fire and failed to hit the target. The second three, from 356 Squadron, also went in at low level and although damaged achieved one hit. The third trio, led by Wing Commander Ercolani of 159 Squadron, secured several hits and left the tanker burning from stem to stern.[54] They had put paid to the last enemy supply ship of any size to be sunk off South-East Asia – a fitting climax to the efforts of the RAF's strategic bombers over the years.

There was of course still much else for them to do. Up to May most of their effort had been linked to the Burma campaign but now, while still compelled to operate from airfields in India until new ones were ready at Rangoon, they had to try to penetrate further afield. Among their targets were the Andaman Islands, whose harbour installations at Port Blair were heavily bombed on 17 May, and the railway line leading south towards Singapore. Most of their objectives entailed round flights of at least 2,000 miles, compared with the 1,200 miles of Bomber Command's Berlin raids, and one of the longest, 2,400 miles, was made by seven aircraft to the rail junction of Surasdhani on 6 June. By mid-July they were penetrating as far as the harbour at Singora and railway bridges just north of the Malayan border.[55] Mountbatten and Park were now regretting the lack of a large force of heavy bombers in order to conduct a continuous and widespread offensive against Japanese communications in preparation for ZIPPER; hard as their Liberator squadrons were worked during these final months there were too few of them, and their effectiveness was limited by range and by weather.[56]

They had another important task also. As we saw in Chapter 10, 357 (SD) Squadron had long been at work supporting the clandestine activities of Force 136, and by May 1945 was equipped with Lysanders[57] and L-5s for short-range operations as well as with Dakotas and Liberators. Operating alongside it from Jessore was 358 Squadron, entirely Liberator equipped, and they continued to devote most of their attention to Burma and Siam, where by August some 30 W/T stations were operational, each the centre of a widespread resistance network that was ready to go into action with the Siamese army against the Japanese. The build-up would have been impossible without the SD squadrons – including the Catalina flight of 240 Squadron which carried out some remarkable coastal deliveries and was 'as always, forthcoming and willing to take risks', according to Sir Andrew Gilchrist who worked there with SOE.[58]

Malaya, on the other hand, was almost impossible to reach from India during the monsoon, and if clandestine forces were to be built up there in readiness for ZIPPER they would have to be largely supported from elsewhere. Ever since the fall of Malaya guerrilla groups, mainly Chinese, had been operating in the interior, some of them assisted by British officers who had stayed behind. However, as one of them, Colonel Spencer Chapman, described, until 1945 the only means of contact with the outside world was by submarine and for most of the time the parties were totally out of touch. Nevertheless the intelligence picture was gradually being built up and after several Force 136 groups had been dropped in blind, contacts were established with the guerrillas. By May, the Liberators having carried out a number of hazardous missions to deliver liaison officers, radios and other supplies, it had been decided to arm and train some 3,500 men ready to harass the Japanese during the ZIPPER landings. To provide them with the wherewithal in little more than three months would make enormous demands on the limited airlift available, and most of the job would have to be done from Ceylon.[59]

Consequently in May 160 Squadron was converted from minelaying to special duties, the re-formed 8 Squadron, also equipped with Liberators, came to join them at Minneriya, and so did part of 357 Squadron. According to Chapman, they carried out 249 sorties to Malaya during June and July, 69 per cent of them successful. A flight engineer with 160 Squadron remembers the secrecy surrounding their operations; moreover, since Ceylon was not an 'operational theatre' they were not even issued with appropriate flying rations for their 18 – 24 hour missions. The overloaded aircraft would need a two-mile take-off run, they had no external aids so navigation was by dead reckoning and astro, there were no weather forecasts. Eventually, shortly before sunset, the DZ would – hopefully – be located in a clearing in some jungle-clad valley and the drops made. There was always the risk of interception (the crews had undergone jungle survival training just in case) but incredibly the worst never happened. Then came the long flight home and the arrival back at base with tanks fast running dry.[60] Our flight engineer concludes:

We would taxi into dispersal and tell the ground crews how things had gone. We who were aircrew should never forget those over-worked, under-paid, seldom mentioned and under-appreciated men who made it possible to do what we did.[61]

By late July the efforts of the Minneriya Liberators began to be supplemented by those of 99 and 356 Squadrons based at Cocos at slightly shorter range, and over the next two months (mostly after the official end of hostilities) a further 756 sorties were carried out, 80% successful. These little known operations earned high praise from Chapman and many others in Malaya. Chapman records Mountbatten telling him that only one Japanese battalion was in the invasion area when ZIPPER went in; their main forces were far to the north, their route would have taken them where the guerrillas were waiting for them, and not many would have got through.[62] The Liberators had done a remarkable job.

Target Japan

As we reflect on the tasks confronting the limited force of largely ageing long-range bombers in preparing the way for ZIPPER, it is hard not to sympathise with Mountbatten and Park, for it was becoming clear that Whitehall was much more interested in enabling the RAF to contribute to the direct assault on Japan. The Air Ministry had begun to make plans for this politically driven operation in October 1944 and in November the energetic and enthusiastic Air Marshal Sir Hugh Lloyd, who had made his name in the air defence of Malta and later commanded the Mediterranean Coastal Air Force, was appointed Force Commander Designate.[63] From then until April 1945 when they moved to Bushey Park, he and his staff were located at Headquarters Bomber Command, where Sir Arthur Harris and his colleagues gave them all the help they needed with 'thoroughness, efficiency and above all willingness'.[64]

Lloyd's was a daunting prospect. He had to accept that his preparations for TIGER FORCE, as his project came to be known, would receive priority only when the German war was over, and in November 1944 that still seemed a long way ahead. Then there was the question of bases and aircraft range; to operate from northern Luzon in the Philippines (Map 9), which seemed the only realistic possibility at that time, would entail 2,000 mile round flights even to southern Japan, and 3,500 miles as far as Tokyo; the range/payload limitations for the Lancaster or its successor, the Lincoln, would be severe, although Portal hoped 3,000 mile flights with 6,000 lb loads would be achievable.[65] Admittedly investigations and trials of in-flight refuelling had been under way for some time but it was becoming clear that this offered no realistic solution in relation to the technology of the day. Leaving that critical aspect aside for a moment there were a host of other problems inseparable from the fact that TIGER FORCE would be a small Bomber Command based on an island in the Pacific 14,000 miles by sea from its home base and would have to take everything with it. At least, however, Lloyd could expect the Americans to provide and construct the airfields, as the Air Ministry assured him in January 1945.

His hopes on that point were quickly dashed in February, when General Kuter, USAAF Assistant Chief of Staff, Logistic Planning, told Portal that the Americans could not even meet all their own constructional needs; British plans would therefore have to include all development 'from tide water to aircraft'. For Lloyd, on his way to Washington for detailed discussions, the implications were highly disturbing, and while he found the USAAF staff generally helpful and co-operative there was no escaping the fact that the RAF would have to build and support its Luzon base almost entirely on its own. As he told Portal on his return, the expert examination now necessary might show that the difficulties were too great and the cost prohibitive.

The ball was now passed to the Principal Administrative Officers (PAOs) Committee, who reported on 16 April on the practicalities of building a base for 20 heavy bomber squadrons in the Cagayan Valley of north Luzon. Their detailed study identified a host of problems, not least that during the construction period 71,500 RAF and 34,500 Army personnel would be needed, and it showed that not until February 1946 could the first airfield be ready for use. The whole project was, in their view, impracticable. Nevertheless when the COS discussed it on the 19th, neither Portal nor the First Sea Lord, Admiral Cunningham, was prepared to concede defeat for TIGER FORCE: the Pacific Fleet was already committed alongside the Americans[66] and they felt it essential – as the Prime Minister was insisting – that the bombers also should make their contribution to the final assault.[67]

Meanwhile events were moving on. On 1 April American forces had landed on Okinawa, in the Ryu Kyu Islands much closer to Japan; they hoped to complete its capture within a month whereupon they could develop it for air bases, and they would follow up by capturing another island, Miyako, to the south, which they would offer to the RAF. Not only was Miyako some 450 miles closer to Japan than Luzon, thus bringing the major targets within good range/payload distance, but the island would be much cheaper and easier to develop. Lloyd, back in Washington in mid-April, took no persuading, but the key problem remained: how could Britain provide the necessary logistic effort? The Army had made no provision for it; there remained many planned RAF and Army commitments in Europe and South-East Asia; continuing attempts to persuade the Canadians to provide engineer support alongside their promised operational squadrons were getting nowhere; and there was a serious shortage of shipping. At the end of the month 'the future of TIGER FORCE did not look very promising' writes Lloyd, and the planners in London believed there was now a straight choice between that and ZIPPER. Then on 5 May the Americans cancelled the assault on Miyako.

Yet only a few days later Portal heard from General Marshall that it might after all be possible to accommodate TIGER FORCE on Okinawa itself, and when Lloyd returned to Washington once again at the end of May he found the Americans increasingly enthusiastic. While General Eaker explained to him that the RAF deployment would have to be restricted initially to two squadrons unless firm undertakings were given about the scale of logistic support that would be provided, Lloyd succeeded in bringing back to London an American proposal for 10 squadrons (220 aircraft, including some Mosquitos) to be based in Okinawa under their control; 10 more might follow later. The COS accepted this on 4 June, and a week later Churchill signalled his strong support to Marshall. The PAOs meanwhile compiled a far more promising report than that relating to Luzon (15,000 RAF operational personnel would be needed, together with 7,500 constructors and 12,390 Army); this was quickly agreed and a decision made to sail the first convoy, even though the Americans had not yet notified its destination. Conveying 3,000 construction personnel, plus equipment and vehicles, SHIELD FORCE left Liverpool for Panama and the Pacific in late June, its departure a clear statement to the Americans of Britain's intent.

Nevertheless, after Lloyd had inspected the personnel at West Kirby he noted that few had been overseas before; while there would be no doubt of their efficiency once in the theatre there was a lack of enthusiasm for visiting new places or gaining new experiences. 'All war interest had been lost with the end of the German war. The Japanese war was too remote for them'. Nor was there much enthusiasm at SEAC. Admittedly ACSEA had been advised of the project the previous October, but only in May 1945 was it really taken seriously and its implications recognised. Then on 2 June Park heard from the Air Ministry that his build-up for ZIPPER was to be delayed in favour of TIGER FORCE, and he and Mountbatten voiced strong protest, reminding the COS of their past disappointments at SEAC always taking second place and pointing out the consequences for their forthcoming offensive to re-take Singapore. The Chiefs' response did nothing to mollify them, merely observing that direct British participation in the attack on Japan had long been agreed policy and must inevitably have a degree of priority.[68]

It was time for Lloyd and his planning team to view the operating area, and in July they visited Guam, Okinawa and Manila. Everywhere they were warmly received: the Americans agreed the arrangements to receive the first two convoys, SHIELD and VACUUM; on Okinawa, where everything would be developed on a 'super austerity' basis, the British construction troops would work within the overall American plan and under their orders (a very different situation from that envisaged for Luzon); many of the supplies and materials required both for construction and for operations would be provided by the Americans; and a staging post would be established at Clark Field, north of Manila. On the 19th the team were back in Washington conferring with General Spaatz, recently appointed Commanding General of the Strategic Air Forces in the Pacific. It had already been decided that 5 Group, commanded by Air Vice-Marshal Hugh Constantine, would be the first formation to deploy; they would be based on Okinawa alongside their old comrades from the European war, the 8th US Air Force, and would operate directly under Strategic Headquarters, and Spaatz now requested RAF representation on his staff. He went on to ask if two Tallboy squadrons could be operational by 15 October; the USAAF would have no similar squadrons ready before 1946,[69] and before the invasion of Kyushu on 1 November he wanted to take out several major bridges between Tokyo and Shimonoseki as well as the Kammon tunnel linking Honshu and Kyushu.[70] 'We accepted the request', writes Lloyd.

Immediately it was 'all systems go'. The two Lancaster squadrons which had used the 12,000 lb bomb so successfully against the _Tirpitz_ and other precision targets in the European war, Nos 9 and 617, were selected, their preparation started, and the necessary ships chartered for late August. By then SHIELD FORCE would have reached Okinawa with VACUUM not far behind, and Lloyd and his HQ staff would have joined them. Already Air Vice-Marshals Satterly and Sharp, Lloyd's SASO and AOA, had discussed with SEAC such matters as staging facilities for the bombers and transport aircraft,[71] and the establishment of an aircraft reserve at Cawnpore. TIGER FORCE – at least its first two squadrons – was at the beginning of August firmly 'on'.

Surrender

Among those helping to plan TIGER FORCE in Washington was a former CO of 617 Squadron, Group Captain Cheshire, now serving in the British Joint Staff Mission and well placed to understand the likely cost in human life and suffering that the forthcoming assault on Japan would entail. On 17 July he was told that the Americans had detonated an 'atomic bomb' at Alamogordo the previous day, that unless the Japanese were persuaded to surrender this would be used against them, and that he was to be the official British observer.[72] Within days he was on Tinian Island, from where a B-29 took off to drop the first atomic bomb on Hiroshima on 6 August. Three days later Cheshire witnessed the explosion of the second one at Nagasaki and on the 10th the Japanese government announced their decision to surrender. Cheshire never doubted that it was right to use the bomb. Certainly victory would eventually have been gained without it, but only after further destruction and loss of life that would have exceeded by far that caused at Hiroshima and Nagasaki. Nor were such implications confined to Japan. Throughout the Far East, wherever there was fighting, wherever prisoners-of-war and internees were held and often dying in inhuman conditions, wherever there were local populations trying to survive the rigours of occupation, the continuance of the war would have served only to compound the suffering.

Certainly this was true in South-East Asia. Mountbatten had been told about the bomb in Potsdam on 24 July but such was the secrecy surrounding it that nobody else at SEAC was informed before the first one was dropped. He was, however, allowed to signal that the Japanese might capitulate any time after mid-August, and to order contingency plans to be prepared.[73] By the time the Japanese government formally accepted the demand for unconditional surrender on the 14th Mountbatten had received his orders from London. Foremost among his tasks was the seizure of Singapore and the key areas of Malaya; others included the completion of the Burma reoccupation and the rapid despatch of forces to Siam, Indo-China, Hong Kong, Java and

Sumatra. The rounding up of the Japanese and the restoration of law and order were prime objectives, but very much in the minds of Mountbatten and his commanders was the recovery of the many prisoners-of-war and internees, 100,000 or more of whom were known to be spread about the theatre, most of them in dire straits.[74] There would be much for the RAF to do.

Initially, however, there was great uncertainty. How long would the news of the surrender take to reach the many enemy units, particularly the more isolated ones? Would they all obey the order? When would the primary surrender ceremony take place in Tokyo? MacArthur, the Supreme Allied Commander, was insistent that only after this were other surrenders to take place and re-occupations of enemy-held territories to commence. In the event the formal surrender document was not signed until 2 September,[75] and keen though Mountbatten was to get a move on he had to accept the frustrating delay. On 7 August he had actually set the 28th as the target date for the seaborne reoccupation of Singapore, but on the 22nd he had to tell his staff that it seemed they were acting 'rather precipitately' and might, quoting MacArthur, 'get us all into trouble'.[76]

The situation was particularly tricky in Burma, where the Army was still engaging large numbers of Japanese. Despite orders having been issued on 15 August for the suspension of all Allied land, air and sea operations in South-East Asia some of the enemy continued to resist and on the 20th Mosquitos of 110 Squadron were called in to bomb Japanese troops attacking a Force 136 unit near Shwegyin. This, the last RAF air operation of the Second World War, was by remarkable coincidence carried out by the same squadron that had undertaken the first one on 4 September 1939, when its Blenheims attacked the German battleship *Admiral Scheer* off Wilhelmshaven.[77]

On 20 August another Mosquito, this time of 684 Squadron operating from Cocos, flew ACSEA's longest PR mission, covering 2,600 miles in a flight over north Malaya. Such missions were of special importance in preparing for the reoccupations: the targets reached extended from Penang to Surabaya, in Java, and they encountered more opposition than at any other time – at Palembang in particular AA fire was intense. The shorter range PR aircraft sometimes received a different response, as when a 681 Squadron Spitfire pilot was wildly cheered by prisoners-of-war held in one of the camps near Kanchanaburi.[78]

The urgency of getting help to the prisoners was certainly a major consideration when Japanese representatives signed an agreement in Rangoon on the 27th to assist and obey the British commanders, and Mountbatten decided to accept the risks of starting the long planned operations for the Recovery of Allied Prisoners-of-War (RAPWI). Over the next four days, in Operation BIRDCAGE, Thunderbolts and

An air drop of supplies for British prisoners to Changi airfield, August 1945.
(Slightly damaged photo from Sir Lewis Hodges' private collection)

Liberators dropped 18 million leaflets over 58 towns and 55 camps
extending from Singapore to Saigon and from Bangkok to Sumatra. At
the same time aircraft from India, Burma, Ceylon and Cocos
commenced Operation MASTIFF, the dropping of food, medicine and
radios to all the camps that could be found; medical teams too were
parachuted in.[79] There followed the operations to bring out the
prisoners and internees; by the end of October 71,000 had been
evacuated from South-East Asia, mostly by sea but including 3,000 by
air, and there were more to come, particularly from Java.[80] Many of
the air evacuees went by Sunderland to Ceylon; a 205 Squadron pilot
remembers how light were his passengers, many of whom had to be
carried aboard at Seletar; every available space had been hastily fitted
out with bunks for the 11-12 hour flight to Ceylon. He had reached the
Far East just too late for the war itself but in time to witness its
aftermath; what he saw haunts him still.[81] He is not alone; our 273
Squadron MT driver also remembers the near skeletons he saw on
stretchers at Seletar, some of whom he felt could never survive. He,
like so many more, can never forgive.[82]

The RAF's part in the reoccupation of the vast territories overrun by

A mission of mercy: on 3 September 1945 prisoners-of-war released in Siam
are flown from Bangkok to Mingaladon. (*AHB*)

the Japanese falls strictly outside the scope of this history and is well
covered in the first four chapters of Sir David Lee's *Eastward*. Suffice it
to summarise the initial course of events. On 2 September, the day of
the Tokyo surrender, Penang was occupied and the first Spitfire and
Mosquito squadrons to return to Malaya flew in. Three days later they
went on to Singapore, which had just been surrendered, and landed at
Tengah and Seletar. On the 9th the ZIPPER force, including 224
Group's Advanced Headquarters, went ashore as planned between
Port Swettenham and Port Dickson; it was fortunate they were
unopposed, for the beaches turned out to be poor and landing
conditions became chaotic, but the RAF had Spitfires at Kelanang by
nightfall.[83] Then on the 12th Mountbatten and his senior commanders
held the formal surrender ceremony in Singapore.

Meanwhile the RAF transport force had flown Army advanced
parties into Bangkok on the 3rd and into Saigon on the 7th, and as the
build-up in Siam and Indo-China continued resident squadrons of
Spitfires and Mosquitos were deployed. Hong Kong had been
reoccupied by the Navy on the 1st; on the 4th the SHIELD convoy,
originally destined for Okinawa and TIGER FORCE, arrived to help
disarm the Japanese, maintain order and restore public services;[84] and
Spitfires arrived a week later. Finally there was the series of
operations to regain the Dutch East Indies, which began with a naval

Peace at last: Sir Keith Park waits with General Slim and Admiral Power for the formal surrender ceremony at the City Hall, Singapore, 12 September 1945. (*AHB*)

landing near Batavia on 15 September and developed into a long, difficult campaign lasting well into 1946.[85]

The RAF had another responsibility, one which has usually received scant regard: its role in the occupation of Japan itself. Among the tasks given to Mountbatten on 13 August was to provide two brigade groups for the British Commonwealth Occupation Force,[86] and while the inclusion of an RAF element was not specified some RAF personnel went in with the advance party. Then in 1946 an Air Element (BCAIR) was constituted under Air Vice-Marshal Bouchier and Nos 11 and 17 Squadrons, flying Spitfires, were based first at Iwakuni and then at Miho until the force was withdrawn in March 1948. Altogether some 2,000 RAF men served with it, assisting among other things in supervising the repatriation of Japanese troops and the destruction of vast qualities of military equipment, as well as simply 'showing the flag'.[87]

Nor has much attention been given to the work of a small but dedicated group of airmen who had a totally different job. Of the many aircrew recorded as 'missing' at the end of the war, some were recovered from prison camps and the fate of others was explained through interrogation of prisoners, but at the end of 1945 300 aircraft, with 1,000 airmen, remained unaccounted for in Burma. In February 1946, building on the experience of the Missing Research Enquiry Service in Europe, five search teams were formed, each of three men, to work in Burma, the Imphal area, Siam and Indo-China. As well as the obvious hazards they had to cope with bandits, wartime destruction and political restrictions, yet eventually by mid-1947 200 reports were complete with only 50 outstanding. They also turned to Malaya but with little success, for the lapse of five years had destroyed most of the evidence. It was now clear that further investigations would be a waste of time; the teams had done all that was humanly possible:

> With complete disregard of personal discomfort, the teams for long periods lived under the most abominable conditions, during monsoon periods were wet for days on end, trekked through thick jungle and swamp, over mountain and valley completely cut off from white civilisation.[88]

It is thanks to them that many airmen who would otherwise simply be recorded as 'missing' have known graves. Yet when the visitor stands at Kranji, that evocative memorial on Singapore Island overlooking the Johore Strait, he still finds the names of 2,990 airmen of the British Commonwealth who died in the war in South-East Asia and have no known grave.[89] 2,464 of these came from the United Kingdom, out of a total of 4,858 RAF casualties recorded in 1946 as killed and missing in the war against Japan.[90]

Of the remaining 526 named at Kranji 197 came from Canada, 208 from Australia, 61 from New Zealand, five from South Africa, 49 from India and Pakistan, and six from Malaya. They and their fellow countrymen were just as much part of the Forgotten Air Force as their RAF comrades-in-arms.

14 Reflections

Many themes run through our story. First and quite simply the RAF in the Far East was – like the other Services – always at the back of the queue for everything. Brooke-Popham and Pulford knew it only too well in 1941; Peirse was constantly frustrated by it; even Park, who was hoping for better things in 1945, fared little better. For most of the time this was understandable. The United Kingdom was itself a war zone; the protection of the homeland had to come before all else. Before December 1941 the defence of territories several thousands of miles away against an attack that might never materialise was bound to be of lesser importance, and afterwards there could still be little to spare. This one accepts.

It is harder, however, to accept the ignorance. Churchill, for all his great qualities and achievements, made judgements about the defensibility of Singapore that were quite unjustified – as he himself later admitted. That is not to say that he was prepared to write it off, as conspiracy theorists have suggested,[1] in order to drag the USA into the war; he was only too well aware of its value to the United Kingdom's position in the world. He did not, however, know the area, and this was brought out again later on as he set up SEAC and urged on Mountbatten a variety of schemes for amphibious operations designed to expedite the recapture of Singapore.[2] Then came his determination to be seen by the Americans to contribute to the final assault on Japan itself; it was one thing to despatch a large part of the Fleet to the Pacific but quite another to attempt to send a large portion of Bomber Command as well. For all his vision he found it difficult to recognise the military realities of fighting a major war in tropical conditions so far from home.

It was important, therefore, that the Chiefs of Staff and their subordinates should be properly informed and able to keep him in order, and on the air side there was ample exchange of signals and letters between Portal and his staff and the air commanders on the spot. Yet few of the senior men in the Air Ministry had served in the Far East, and hardly ever did anyone in a key post go out to see things for himself. Brooke-Popham felt totally forgotten; Peirse received just one top-level visit, when Ludlow-Hewitt, the IG, came out in 1942; and when Courtney, AMSO, appeared in 1945 he told Portal afterwards, 'I believe that I am the first Member of Council to visit India, either in peace or war', adding Mountbatten's pointed comment that three members of the Army Council had recently been there.[3] In his diary Mountbatten wrote about Courtney's visit: 'despite the work involved, everyone is delighted that Whitehall is at last taking an interest in South-East Asia',[4] 'at last' being the telling phrase. One recognises that the air journey took a long time, and a worthwhile visit could entail a lengthy absence from London, yet it was not thought impossible to call back Mountbatten fairly often for consultations. And if the most senior officers could not get away from the Air Ministry they could surely have sent their deputies. Yet as late as the end of 1944, when ACSEA operations were looming increasingly large, Air Commodore Cross – recently appointed Director of Operations (Tactical) with responsibilities including South-East Asia – was refused permission to make a visit, even though he had never been there. It would take too long, he was told.[5] Yet he was allowed a trip to the Mediterranean, a theatre where he had himself recently served.

One other observation must be made. Vincent records how he recommended a number of immediate decorations in May 1945 to signify 221 Group's vital part in the victory. All but two – CBEs for his two air commodores – were returned by Park. 'The group captains commanding wings, several squadron leaders and senior NCOs were ignored. I was disgusted'.[6] Vincent felt strongly about this, not least since the Army seemed to handle these things so much better, and both Slim and Mountbatten felt that the RAF was parsimonious. Almost certainly the fault lay in the Air Ministry, not with Park or his predecessors, and it merely serves to reinforce the judgement that ACSEA was in too many respects 'out of sight, out of mind'.

It is against this sense of isolation, of being on nobody's priority list, of not even having its efforts properly appreciated, that the RAF's achievements in South-East Asia must be set. The strong air force of 1945, covering all the roles of air power, was built up from almost nothing after the early disasters; Garrod, who contributed so much himself, was speaking from the heart at the farewell lunch given him by Mountbatten in February 1945 when he reflected on 'the most difficult circumstances imaginable' under which he had seen SEAC grow up, and on the example now being set in how an Allied inter-Service campaign could be conducted.[7] Andrew Gilchrist, the Foreign Office official who was in South-East Asia throughout and worked with Force 136, acknowledged not just the RAF but Mountbatten's whole team:

When I think of the handicaps under which Mountbatten laboured – repeated hold-ups in promised man-power, supplies and shipping, fantastic political entanglements due to American policy in China – I am amazed that so much was done. It was not Mountbatten's fault that opportunities were repeatedly missed and well-planned operations repeatedly cancelled.[8]

Not least of the difficulties, as we have seen, arose from the conflict of priorities between the British and Americans, the former seeing Burma as the stepping stone for the reconquest of Malaya, Singapore and the East Indies, and the latter concerned with it only as the means of securing the route to China. The USAAF, therefore, had long-term objectives quite different from those of the RAF, yet they were operating from the same base areas and for much of the time their tasks were similar. It was a situation quite different from any other theatre where the two air forces worked together, and with the Americans putting much emphasis on independent transport and B-29 operations it could have caused great problems. Yet as the USAAF historians write:

Given the differences of priorities, it is a tribute to the British and American commanders within SEAC and EAC that integration worked so well. Despite many differences of opinion, patience and understanding at the top set a pattern for all elements of the command.[9]

Air transport and supply made it all possible, much of it provided by the Americans. (*Wings of the Phoenix*)

While this account has concentrated on the RAF's work it must be remembered that the greater part of ACSEA's air supply and strategic bomber operations was carried out by the Americans, and that their close support aircraft also made major contributions. The war in South-East Asia deserves an honoured place in the long and continuing story of co-operation between our two air forces.

What they achieved in relation to the land fighting in the later stages of the war is suitably summarised by Mountbatten:

> Air operations – striking at the enemy's airfields; at his supply centres; at his ports and shipping; at his rail and road communications; at his forward concentrations, and also at his front-line positions – formed the background and the unceasing accompaniment to the land fighting. Land advances depended for their success on air protection from enemy interference. In most cases, the air forces provided the spearhead of the attack; during the operations they fought the enemy in the air and harried him on the ground; and after the battle they continued to attack his communications and bases, and to weaken his fighting organisation.[10]

Their other great achievement, made possible by air superiority, is well stated by Hardman:

> The whole campaign has been a striking illustration of a fact new in warfare – namely that air power can be used to transport, supply and support ground troops entirely independently of ground channels. This has been South-East Asia's contribution to the art of war.[11]

Park set it in context, observing that 'air supply in Burma made history which outdistanced in merit and achievement the more publicised air supply operations of the war in Europe such as that of Arnhem or the food-dropping to the Dutch in Holland'. Important and commendable though these were, 'they bore no comparison to the enormous and sustained efforts of transport crews who faced the hazards of monsoon weather'.[12] As a wing commander wrote from personal experience with 194 Squadron in 1944: 'a defenceless Dakota flying at night through storms and darkness to bring succour to our troops behind the enemy lines in Burma seemed, at any rate to me, to be one of the most daring and magnificent enterprises of the air war in any theatre'.[13]

Yet when all is said and done we must remember, as the airmen themselves knew, that 'the final glory was with the soldier'.[14] It was the men on the ground, far more numerous than the airmen, who engaged the enemy in close combat, endured the greater hardship, suffered the vast majority of the casualties. Perhaps, however, we are wrong to distinguish the airmen and the soldiers in this way, for in reality they were a close-knit team, each often able to witness what the others were doing and frequently able to help them do it. There had not been much evidence of teamwork in Malaya, but by 1944 and particularly 1945 they had brought their acts together to an extent unsurpassed in any other theatre of the Second World War. Neil Cameron, commanding 258 Squadron, was one who recognised the importance of knowing what it was like on the ground and deliberately spent time with the forward troops, being shelled, mortared and sniped in the process.[15] Denis Spotswood was another, taking time away from his high-level planning desk in Kandy to fly with the 10th Air Force, to share experiences and ideas with Paddy Bandon, to visit Imphal at the height of the siege, and – one of the most uncomfortable experiences of his life – to spend ten days with the Gurkhas in the jungle along the Tiddim road. He needed to experience the conditions for himself, to be sure that the top brass were not asking people to do the impossible.[16] It was in ways such as this that the team was welded. Nor must we forget the third element of the team, the sailors. Dennis David remembers from the final Arakan campaign the tremendous rapport that existed between all three services: put simply 'we trusted each other'.[17]

Trust and comradeship were crucial too within the RAF, and if ever squadron spirit was important it was in the Far East war. Many men, aircrew and groundcrew alike, write in glowing terms about 'their squadron' and the way everyone pulled together. Mr Horsman, a fitter with 79 (Thunderbolt) Squadron in 1944/1945, says 'the time spent on 79, in spite of all the privations and the fact that none of us knew if we would ever see home again, was the happiest of my 4½ years in the RAF. The spirit and comradeship were second to none'.[18] According to Mr Gwinnell of 273 (Spitfire) Squadron, who describes the close bonds between the pilots and groundcrews, any flight problem involved everyone from the CO down. The feeling of 'belonging' – that quality that unites a family – was most evident; 'the very real concern that each had for the other was something I had never experienced – it has in fact never left those of us who survived'.[19] In a lighter vein Mr Hutchings of 194 (Dakota) Squadron recalls two aircraft stopping over at Chittagong. His pilot, who had just been promoted, arrived at his hut with a plentiful supply of beer, announcing that he would rather celebrate with friendly faces from his own squadron than with strangers in the officers' mess. In due course a military policeman appeared, asked for the CO and was pointed towards the squadron leader enjoying himself with the rest of the lads, whereupon he quietly departed.[20] Inevitably there were traditionalists who disapproved of what they considered over-familiarity between the ranks, but the nearer one got to the front line the less appropriate did the formalities seem.

Squadron spirit was just as important in the Liberator squadrons, recalls Lucian Ercolani, who is convinced that he got more aircraft in the air through squadron servicing than he would have done under a centralised system.[21] Park certainly had no doubts about the need for squadrons to be self-contained and for the ground organisation to be mobile and flexible, pointing out that during the advance in 1945 squadrons had often become separated from their servicing echelons for days on end and had depended on their own ground crews for everything.[22] It was in situations like this that the wide-ranging skills and personal qualities possessed by the senior tradesmen who had been trained at establishments like Halton came into their own; many of Trenchard's 'brats' served in the Far East, and whether it was in the desperate situation of Malaya, in the jungles of Burma or in the often isolated bases spread throughout India, Ceylon and the remoter outposts they gave ample return on the investment made in them. Simon Eden, whose letters to his father we have already quoted, paid them and all their 'mates' a poignant tribute:

> It is these boys behind the scenes that the public forget; they have no glamour, these oil-stained mechanics. They fight with the spanner, not with sword, gun or pistol. Yet they can win or lose their battles with consequences as disastrous as an army that loses in the field. Working, toiling, fighting in the heat of the tropics are men who come from all roads of life; some married, some single, rich and poor, all mixed together and miles from home. There are few things to keep these men amused, yet they laugh because they must. If they cease to be amused they cease to live.[23]

His words will be echoed by all who flew in the Far East; all aircrew to whom I have spoken have urged the importance of giving proper credit to the men who made their operations possible.

Leadership, as always, was crucial. It fell short at times in Malaya, and even later not all the squadron commanders were up to the job. As time went on, however, men who had learned their trades against the Luftwaffe came out and the great majority proved well capable of leading from the front. It was certainly not easy. They had to work from bases whose living and working conditions frequently tested to the limits the men's skill, physical endurance and morale; they operated with minimal navigation aids in weather that generally knew no parallel in the other theatres of war; they flew distances which at times far surpassed those experienced elsewhere. Then, never to be forgotten, they were up against an utterly determined foe whose pilots believed that the RAF were cowards, and that they themselves were invincible; certainly the enemy would fight to the death.[24] RAF crews knew the fate that could await them if they crashed or were shot down and survived. They might be lucky enough to be quickly rescued, they might perish in the jungle or just conceivably they might evade. Wing Commander Nottage of 177 Squadron was one who did escape, the captain of the only Beaufighter crew shot down over enemy territory to do so; having crash-landed near Moulmein on 26 April 1945 he hacked out a small landing strip with local help, got word back, and was flown out by a Sentinel.[25] Otherwise they faced either torture and death or incarceration in some ghastly prison camp. No wonder there was the occasional case of LMF (lack of moral fibre) but these were rare; Cameron records only two while he was commanding 258 Squadron. His own reputation at the time he left is worth recounting as typical of many others:

> The Squadron loses a CO whose whole thought was for 258. He has led it in two operational seasons, first in Hurricanes and then in Thunderbolts, to the rank of a really first-class squadron. He commands the greatest respect and loyalty from the AC2 upwards which has been reflected in the work of all personnel. As

The groundcrew were all-important. These men belonged to 607 Squadron, which flew its Spitfires at Imphal in 1944 and moved forward to Rangoon, close behind the Army, in 1945. (*Norman Franks*)

a leader on Ops the pilots wish for none better. It is with great regret that we lose a great skipper and a good friend.[26]

Mention of prisoners prompts a final reminder of those airmen who, alongside their far more numerous Army colleagues, had spent much of their war as 'guests of the Emperor'. In 1945 many were in Japan, many more in the East Indies, and some in Singapore, Siam and Burma. Let the stories of Sam Crocker and Johnnie Johnstone stand for them all. Crocker, an electrical fitter, reached Sumatra from Egypt with the 84 Squadron ground party on 14 February 1942, and was quickly on his way to Oosthaven and Java where he joined up with the Blenheims at Kalidjati. Unable to get away from Tjilatjap he duly found himself incarcerated in the Batavia gaol, where he quickly became accustomed to the tenko regime, the unexpected beatings, the poor food, the insanitary conditions, the onset of tropical disease, and the hard labour on a nearby airfield. Yet, if these were 'pretty intolerable conditions' there was far worse to come. In April 1943 he underwent a nightmare journey by 'troopship' to Ambon; as he now writes 'we did not know that out of our party of one thousand fit men (half of them RAF) only one third would survive to the end of their captivity, and of this third many would be too broken in health and spirit ever to live a normal life again'. Their task in this 'hell on earth' was to construct an airfield and by the time he and his remaining comrades returned to Java a year later the Japanese had turned them into old men. From then on he was somewhat more fortunate, though several months' work still lay ahead building underground hide-outs for the Japanese off the Bukit Timah Road in Singapore.[27]

Johnstone, a pilot with 60 Squadron, was shot down in his Blenheim after attacking the Japanese invasion fleet off Siam on 9 December 1941, and he and his crew were duly handed over by the police to the Japanese and brutally interrogated. A spell of inhuman treatment in a Saigon gaol followed, after which they were moved to the main prison camp at Changi. Then he and 60 other RAF men were detailed for one of the parties building the Siam-Burma railway, all of whose hardships he endured. Late in 1943 he was withdrawn to Kanchanaburi, by which time he had contracted almost every disease possible and nearly died. Thanks to slightly better conditions and his own determination he pulled through, and from now on there was the encouragement of hearing and seeing the Allied bombers at work. Then in July 1945 the prisoners were made to dig an enormous trench and became convinced that this was to be their own mass grave; none doubted that they were saved by the sudden surrender prompted by the use of the atomic bomb. There followed the arrival of a parachute team, the dropping of supplies, and in September air evacuation to Rangoon. He had been a prisoner of the Japanese longer than almost anyone else and survived the worst of the excesses they could inflict.[28]

It is no wonder that Mountbatten, having become aware of the many Japanese atrocities in Burma and then met many of the survivors of the labour camps, could never as long as he lived bring himself wholly to forgive the Japanese for their behaviour towards their prisoners.[29] True, their code of military conduct was entirely different from that of the Allies, and also from those of Germany and Italy, but it was inexcusable to mete out the sort of treatment they did to men who had done nothing to deserve it. Moreover it was treatment whose effects are felt to this day by many who survived and are still with us. While we remember in this book the achievements of the forgotten air force – and of their many comrades-in-arms – let us keep in mind those who died at enemy hands and those whose later lives have been blighted by what happened to them. Indeed some survivors, even today, still feel strongly not just about their treatment by the enemy but also about the uncomprehending behaviour of many British civilians and servicemen when they returned home; they had done their best with the aircraft and equipment given to them, writes one, and were not guilty of any conduct which would justify the accusations of cowardice sometimes levelled at them.[30] Hopefully we of a later generation are better able to understand.

So at the end of the day what was achieved? In military terms, after a series of appalling British disasters, the Japanese Army and Air Force suffered a major defeat, and victory was won thanks to a remarkable alliance between the ground forces and well-applied air power. There had been little glory in the early years, when the airmen had lacked the wherewithal for the job they were given and had rarely used to best advantage what little they had. Later, however, they provided a classic demonstration of what air power could do when dedicated to joint operations with the Army and the Navy, and the record of what the RAF achieved in the only major tropical campaign in its history is one of which it can be rightly proud. Air supply – one of the most valuable applications of air power in the post-war era – finds its genesis more in South-East Asia than in any other theatre of the Second World War.

In wider terms, however, was it all worth while? The cost was huge, and ultimately it was the American drive across the Pacific towards Japan itself, culminating in their use of the atomic bomb, that delivered the victory. Yet it was inconceivable that the United Kingdom should leave the Japanese war entirely to the Americans and while it proved impossible to hold the line in South-East Asia the further loss of India would have been catastrophic. So in part the great battle was for India, which in any case provided the majority of the land forces and a small but growing part of the air forces, of whom

Baldwin wrote: 'when victory is won India will owe a great debt of gratitude to her flying sons of the IAF'.[31] The battle was also for Burma itself, where the Japanese had no right to be, but in addition it was intended to lead the way back to what it was hoped would again become the centre of British power and influence in the Far East: Singapore.

In the event British power was restored, but only briefly; soon both India and Burma were independent, and by the 1970s Singapore and Malaysia also. Yet at least – unlike the Dutch in Indonesia and the French and later the Americans in Indo-China – Britain was able to leave Asia with some dignity.[32] In this process the RAF played its part, not only in India and Burma but after the war in Malaya and in the Borneo Confrontation, and if we compare the political and economic situation in this very important part of the world today with what obtains so widely elsewhere the efforts of the Forgotten Air Force, together with those of the Forgotten Army and the Forgotten Navy, deserve their share of the credit.

Appendix A

RAF STRENGTH IN SINGAPORE AND MALAYA: 7 DECEMBER 1941

Aircraft	Unit	Location	Serviceable	u/s	Totals
Vildebeest	36 Squadron	Gong Kedah/			
		Seletar	15	3	
Vildebeest	100 Squadron	Seletar	16	2	36
Hudson	1 Squadron RAAF	Kota Bharu	8	6	
Hudson	8 Squadron RAAF	Kuantan	8	5	
Hudson	MU		2	2	31
Catalina	205 Squadron	Seletar	3	2	5
Blenheim I	27 Squadron	Sungei Patani	8	4	
Blenheim I	60 Squadron	Kuantan	9	4	
Blenheim I	62 Squadron	Alor Star	12	1	
Blenheim I	MU			5	43
Blenheim IV	34 Squadron	Alor Star	21	2	
Blenheim IV	MU			1	24
Buffalo	243 Squadron	Kallang/Kota			
		Bharu	11	12	
Buffalo	453 Squadron	Sembawang	19	5	
Buffalo	488 Squadron	Kallang	14	3	
Buffalo	21 Squadron RAAF	Sungei Patani	23		
Buffalo	MU		12	27	126
			—	—	—
			181	84	265

These figures are based on AHQ Far East signal Q497 dated 9 December 1941 to Air Ministry, quoted in Narrative 1, Appendix IV. They differ from those contained in Appendix J of Brooke-Popham's Despatch, which seems to have been based on unit establishment, and gives the usually quoted totals of 158 front-line and 88 reserve. Shores and Cull, op. cit. pp. 57 – 58, show the figures as 163 and 88. Given their omission of the 14 serviceable aircraft held in the MU our totals agree, but they do not state their sources and there are differences of detail – not surprising when one considers the constant changes of location and serviceability states. Richards and Saunders, Vol 2, refer to 233 serviceable aircraft – too high a figure.

Appendix B

On 9th December, 1941, all available aircraft from the Royal Air Force Station, Butterworth, Malaya, were ordered to make a daylight attack on the advanced operational base of the Japanese Air Force at Singora, Thailand. From this base the enemy fighter squadrons were supporting the landing operations.

The aircraft detailed for the sortie were on the point of taking off when the enemy made a combined dive-bombing and low level machine-gun attack on the airfield. All our aircraft were destroyed or damaged with the exception of the Blenheim piloted by Squadron Leader Scarf. This aircraft had become airborne a few seconds before the attack started.

Squadron Leader Scarf circled the airfield and witnessed the disaster. It would have been reasonable had he abandoned the projected operation which was intended to be a formation sortie. He decided, however, to press on to Singora in his single aircraft. Although he knew that this individual action could not inflict much material damage on the enemy, he, nevertheless, appreciated the moral effect which it would have on the remainder of the squadron, who were helplessly watching their aircraft burning on the ground.

Squadron Leader Scarf completed his attack successfully. The opposition over the target was severe and included attacks by a considerable number of enemy fighters. In the course of these encounters, Squadron Leader Scarf was mortally wounded.

The enemy continued to engage him in a running fight, which lasted until he had regained the Malayan border. Squadron Leader Scarf fought a brilliant evasive action in a valiant attempt to return to his base. Although he displayed the utmost gallantry and determination, he was, owing to his wounds, unable to accomplish this. He made a successful forced-landing at Alor Star without causing any injury to his crew. He was received into hospital as soon as possible, but died shortly after admission.

Squadron Leader Scarf displayed supreme heroism in the face of tremendous odds and his splendid example of self-sacrifice will long be remembered.

(Supplement to the *London Gazette*, 21 June 1946)

Appendix C

RAF STRENGTH BY FRONT LINE SQUADRONS IN INDIA COMMAND / ACSEA 1942–45

BENGAL/EAC	JUL 1942	JAN 1943	JUL 1943	JAN 1944	JUL 1944	DEC 1944	MAR 1945	JUL 1945
Heavy Bomber		1 Liberator	1 Liberator	2 Liberator	3 Liberator	5 Liberator	5 Liberator	4 Liberator
Medium Bomber	1 Wellington	1 Wellington	2 Wellington	2 Wellington	2 Wellington 1 Warwick (ASR)	1 Warwick (ASR)	1 Warwick (ASR)	
Light Bomber	2 Blenheim	2 Blenheim 2 Bisley	1 Blenheim 2 Bisley	4 Vengeance	2 Vengeance	1 Mosquito	4 Mosquito	7 Mosquito
Day Fighter	6 Hurricane 1 Mohawk	9 Hurricane 2 Mohawk	8 Hurricane 1 Mohawk	5 Spitfire 12 Hurricane	7 Spitfire 2 Hurricane	7 Spitfire	6 Spitfire	14 Spitfire
Night Fighter			1 Beaufighter	1 Beaufighter	1 Beaufighter	1 Beaufighter	1 Beaufighter	
Twin-engined Fighter			1 Beaufighter	2 Beaufighter	1 Beaufighter	3 Beaufighter	4 Beaufighter	1 Beaufighter
Fighter Bomber				2 Hurricane 1 Mohawk	5 Hurricane	7 Thunderbolt 7 Hurricane	9 Thunderbolt	11 Thunderbolt
Fighter-Recce			1 Hurricane	2 Hurricane	3 Hurricane	2 Hurricane	13 Hurricane	5 Hurricane
Air Observation Post					1 Auster	1 Auster	1 Auster	1 Auster
General Recce	2 Hudson	2 Hudson						
Special Duties					1 Hudson/ Liberator 1 Catalina	1 Hudson/ Liberator	1 Liberator/ Dakota/ Lysander 1 Liberator	1 Liberator/ Dakota/ Lysander 1 Liberator
Photo Recce	1 Hurricane/ Mitchell	1 Hurricane/ Mitchell/ Spitfire	1 Hurricane/ 1 Mitchell/ Spitfire	1 Spitfire 1 Mosquito/ Mitchell	1 Spitfire 1 Mosquito/ Mitchell	1 Spitfire 1 Mosquito/ Mitchell	1 Spitfire 1 Mosquito	1 Spitfire 1 Mosquito
Transport	1 DC 2/3	1 Dakota 1 Hudson	1 Dakota	1 Dakota	4 Dakota	4 Dakota	8 Dakota	9 Dakota

222/225 GROUPS

Fighter	3 Hurricane 1 Fulmar	3 Hurricane	4 Hurricane	4 Hurricane	2 Spitfire 1 Hurricane 1 Thunderbolt	3 Spitfire 2 Hurricane 4 Thunderbolt	3 Spitfire	2 Spitfire
Night Fighter				1 Beaufighter	1 Beaufighter	1 Beaufighter		
Twin-engined Fighter					2 Beaufighter	3 Beaufighter 2 Mosquito	2 Beaufighter	2 Beaufighter
Light Bomber	1 Blenheim							
General Recce (land)		1 Hudson 1 Wellington	1 Hudson 1 Liberator	1 Wellington 2 Liberator	1 Wellington 3 Liberator	1 Wellington 3 Liberator	4 Liberator	3 Liberator
General Recce (FB)	4 Catalina	5 Catalina	6 Catalina	6 Catalina	6 Catalina 1 Sunderland	6 Catalina 1 Sunderland	5 Catalina 1 Sunderland	3 Sunderland
Torpedo Bomber	1 Beaufort	1 Beaufort	2 Beaufort	2 Beaufort	1 Beaufort 1 Beaufighter			
Total	24	33	34	52	56	68	71	66

Notes
1. This table covers RAF squadrons and squadrons of other Air Forces which were under RAF command. It does not include units of the United States Army Air Force.
2. The figures are derived from the appendices to the AHB Narrative and, for 1945, SD161 (Location of RAF Units). Owing to the frequent movements and re-equipment of squadrons it is difficult to produce absolutely precise figures for any one point in time, and a slight element of approximation has been necessary.
3. The figures for 222/225 Groups exclude squadrons under AHQs East Africa and Aden, although their operations were increasingly co-ordinated by AOC 222 Group.
4. The figures for the Catalina squadrons in 222 Group include one Dutch squadron and one Royal Canadian Air Force.
5. The figures for March 1945 include six Hurricane squadrons of the Royal Indian Air Force, and two Dakota squadrons of the RCAF. By July the RIAF contribution had risen to five Spitfire and three Hurricane squadrons.

Appendix D

AIR COMMAND SOUTH-EAST ASIA 1944–45

Air Command South-East Asia
(New Delhi, later Kandy)
Air C-in-C: ACM Sir Richard Peirse (16.11.43)
AM Sir Guy Garrod (16.11.44.)
ACM Sir Keith Park (25.2.45)

Eastern Air Command
(New Delhi, later Calcutta; disbanded 1.6.45)
Air Commander: Maj Gen George E Stratemeyer USAAF (16.12.43)

Base Air Forces South-East Asia
(New Delhi; formed 6.11.44)
AM Commanding: AM L N Hollinghurst (6.11.44)

Asst Air Commander: AVM T M Williams (16.11.43)
AVM A Gray (19.7.44)
AM W A Coryton (14.12.44)

228 Group
(Barrackpore; formed 27.2.45)
AOC: Air Cdre H V F Battle (27.2.45)

Strategic Air Force
(Calcutta; disbanded 1.6.45)
Air Commander: Maj Gen Howard C Davidson USAAF (16.12.43)
Air Cdre F J W Mellersh (20.6.44)

3rd Tactical Air Force
(Comilla; disbanded 4.12.44)
Air Commander: AM Sir John Baldwin (16.11.43)
AM W A Coryton (15.8.44)

231 Group
(Calcutta)
AOC: Air Cdre F J W Mellersh (7.1.44)
Maj Gen J T Durrant SAAF (15.6. 45)

221 Group
(Imphal, later Indainggyi, Monywa, Meiktila, Rangoon)
AOC: Air Cdre (later AVM) S F Vincent (17.2.44)
AVM C A Bouchier (15.6.45)
Air Cdre A M Wray (14.7.45)

224 Group
(Chittagong, later Cox's Bazar)
AOC: Air Cdre A Gray
Air Cdre (later AVM) The Earl of Bandon (19.7.44)

225 Group
(Bangalore)
AOC: Air Cdre P H Mackworth
AVM N L Desoer (16.8.44)
AVM H N Thornton (4.5.45)

226 Group
(Palam)
AOC: Air Cdre L M Iles
Air Cdre W L Freebody (1.2.45)

227 Group
(Bombay, later Agra)
AOC: Air Cdre F J Vincent

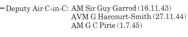

Deputy Air C-in-C: AM Sir Guy Garrod (16.11.43)
AVM G Harcourt-Smith (27.11.44)
AM G C Pirie (1.7.45)

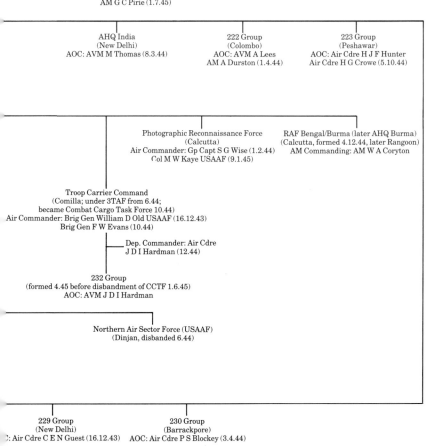

AHQ India
(New Delhi)
AOC: AVM M Thomas (8.3.44)

222 Group
(Colombo)
AOC: AVM A Lees
AM A Durston (1.4.44)

223 Group
(Peshawar)
AOC: Air Cdre H J F Hunter
Air Cdre H G Crowe (5.10.44)

Photographic Reconnaissance Force
(Calcutta)
Air Commander: Gp Capt S G Wise (1.2.44)
Col M W Kaye USAAF (9.1.45)

RAF Bengal/Burma (later AHQ Burma)
(Calcutta, formed 4.12.44, later Rangoon)
AM Commanding: AM W A Coryton

Troop Carrier Command
(Comilla; under 3TAF from 6.44;
became Combat Cargo Task Force 10.44)
Air Commander: Brig Gen William D Old USAAF (16.12.43)
Brig Gen F W Evans (10.44)

Dep. Commander: Air Cdre
J D I Hardman (12.44)

232 Group
(formed 4.45 before disbandment of CCTF 1.6.45)
AOC: AVM J D I Hardman

Northern Air Sector Force (USAAF)
(Dinjan, disbanded 6.44)

229 Group
(New Delhi)
C: Air Cdre C E N Guest (16.12.43)

230 Group
(Barrackpore)
AOC: Air Cdre P S Blockey (3.4.44)

Appendix E

INDIA COMMAND 1942–43

Air Headquarters India
(New Delhi)
AOC in C: ACM Sir Richard Peirse (6.3.42)

Deputy AOC in C: AM Sir John Baldwin (9.10.42)
AM Sir Guy Garrod (27.4.43)

Air Headquarters Bengal
(Barrackpore)
AOC: AVM D F Stevenson (20.4.42)
AVM T M Williams (1.1.43)

Headquarters 222 Group
(Colombo)
AOC: AVM J H D'Albiac (13.3.42)
AVM A Lees (1.12.42)

Headquarters 221 Group
(Asansol)
AOC: Air Cdre H J F Hunter (20.4.42)
Air Cdre H V Rowley (1.5.43)

Headquarters 223 Group
(Peshawar)
AOC: Air Cdre P H Mackworth (5.5.42)
Air Cdre A Gray (2.8.42)
Air Cdre H J F Hunter (1.5.43)

Headquarters 224 Group
(Calcutta, later Chittagong)
AOC: Air Cdre G E Wilson (24.8.42)
Air Cdre A Gray (2.1.43)

Headquarters 225 Group
(Bangalore)
AOC: Air Cdre P H Mackworth (2.6.42)

Headquarters 226 Group
(Karachi, later Palam)
AOC: Air Cdre L M Iles (9.5.42)

Headquarters 227 Group
(Lahore, later Bombay)
AOC: Air Cdre F J Vincent (24.8.42)

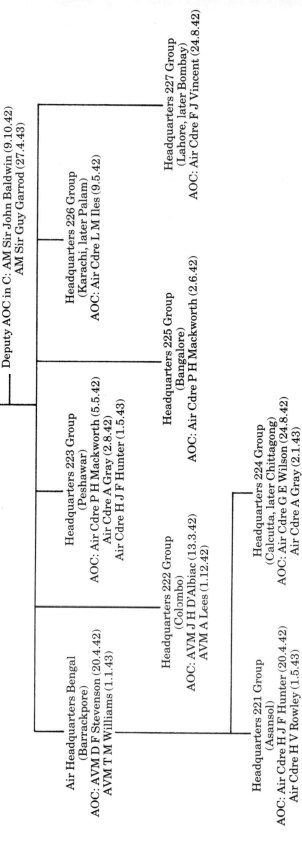

Appendix F

Flight Sergeant Woodbridge was a wireless operator in the crew of a Liberator aircraft which crashed in the jungle in Burma whilst engaged in an operation against the Japanese on the 31st January 1945. Together with five other members of the crew he was captured by the Japanese. All six were subjected to torture at the hands of their captors in an endeavour to obtain information which would have been of use to the Japanese Intelligence Service. Eventually the four non-commissioned officers were separated and conveyed by motor transport to a forest, where they were put to death by beheading. Three officers and three non-commissioned officers of the Imperial Japanese Army were subsequently brought to trial by a Military Court charged with the torture and murder of the four airmen; they were all found guilty. Three were hanged and three sentenced to terms of rigorous imprisonment. At the trial it was revealed that the Japanese concentrated their efforts on Flight Sergeant Woodbridge, the wireless operator, in an endeavour to obtain technical information regarding wireless equipment, secret codes, wavelengths, etc. A Japanese technical officer was detailed to make the interrogation and the services of two interpreters were engaged, but in spite of repeated torture, including kicking, beating with belts and with a sword, Flight Sergeant Woodbridge steadfastly refused to reveal any information whatever. The final interrogation took place actually at the place of execution, when it was obvious to the unfortunate prisoner that he was to be put to death; even so he maintained his courageous attitude to the end, merely remarking that if the Japanese were going to kill him they should do it quickly. After all efforts to make him speak, including further torture, were found to be fruitless this gallant non-commissioned officer was beheaded on the 7th February 1945. Flight Sergeant Woodbridge behaved throughout with supreme courage. His fortitude, loyalty to his country and his complete disregard for his own safety, even unto death, constitute one of the highest examples of valour in the annals of the Royal Air Force.

(Supplement to the *London Gazette*, 28 September 1948)

Bibliography

1. Commanders' Despatches and Reports

Air Chief Marshal Sir Robert Brooke-Popham: *London Gazette*, 20 January 1948, No. 38183

Air Vice-Marshal P C Maltby: *London Gazette*, 20 February 1948, No. 38216

Air Vice-Marshal D F Stevenson: *London Gazette*, 11 March 1948, No. 38229

Vice-Admiral The Earl Mountbatten of Burma: Report to the Combined Chiefs of Staff, HMSO 1951

Air Chief Marshal Sir Richard Peirse: *London Gazette*, 13 March 1951, No 39173

Air Chief Marshal Sir Keith Park (June 44–May 45), *London Gazette*, 6 April 1951, No 39196

——, (May–September 45), *London Gazette*, 13 April 1951, No 39202

Air Vice-Marshal F J W Mellersh, PRO: AIR 23/1935–6

Group Captain S G Wise, PRO: AIR 23/1940, 1988

Air Vice-Marshal W A Coryton, PRO: AIR 23/4682

Air Vice-Marshal S F Vincent, PRO: AIR 23/1938–9

Air Vice-Marshal the Earl of Bandon, PRO: AIR 23/1937

Air Marshal Sir Hugh Lloyd, PRO: AIR 23/2753-4

2. Commanders' Personal Papers

Marshal of the Royal Air Force Lord Portal: Christ Church, Oxford

Air Chief Marshal Sir Robert Brooke-Popham: Liddell Hart Centre for Military Archives, King's College, London

Air Chief Marshal Sir Edgar Ludlow-Hewitt: Air Historical Branch (RAF)

Air Chief Marshal Sir Richard Peirse, RAF Museum, Hendon

Air Chief Marshal Sir Guy Garrod, Imperial War Museum

3. Air Historical Branch Narratives, Monographs and other documents, now available in the Public Record Office

Narrative, *The Campaign in the Far East*, Vols 1–6. These volumes were compiled in the late 1940s by Squadron Leaders E J Cutler and R J Lockwood and Mr D Craik from the mass of primary records then held in AHB and now lodged in the PRO. The Narratives themselves are also in the PRO at AIR 41/35, 63, 36, 64. In view of the in-depth study the authors were able to undertake I have considered it proper to quote them directly on occasion, identifying them simply as the Narrators. In the end notes the six volumes are referred to as Narrative 1, 2, 3, 4, 5 and 6.

Narrative, *The RAF in Maritime War*, Vol VII, Part III, Indian Ocean Operations, November 1943–August 1945: AIR 41/75–78.

Monographs
AP 1116, Signals Vol 5, 1952, AHB(RAF)
AP 1134, Meteorology, 1954, AHB(RAF)
AP 3227, Signals, Vols 1, 2, 1958, AHB(RAF)
AP 3235, Air Support, 1955, AHB(RAF)
AP 3236, Works, 1956, PRO: AIR/10/5559
AP 3397, Maintenance, 1954, PRO: AIR/10/5552

4. Official Histories

The War Against Japan. Vol I, S Woodburn Kirby, HMSO 1957
Vol II, S Woodburn Kirby, HMSO 1958
Vol III, S Woodburn Kirby, HMSO 1961
Vol IV, S Woodburn Kirby, HMSO 1965
Vol V, S Woodburn Kirby, HMSO 1969
SOE In the Far East, S. Cruickshank, OUP 1983
The RAF Medical Services, Vol III, S C Rexford-Welch, HMSO 1958
The War at Sea 1939–1945, Vol I, S W Roskill, HMSO 1954
Vol II, S W Roskill, HMSO 1956
Vol III, Part 2, S W Roskill, HMSO 1961
British Foreign Policy in the Second World War, Vol II, L Woodward, HMSO 1971
Grand Strategy, Vol III, Part II, J R M Butler, HMSO 1964
Vol IV, M Howard, HMSO 1972
Vol V, J Ehrman, HMSO 1956
Vol VI, J Ehrman, HMSO 1956

5. Other Official Publications

Air Ministry Weekly Intelligence Summaries (AMWIS), PRO: AIR/22/69–83, 373

Air Force Lists
Wings of the Phoenix – The Official History of the Air War in Burma, HMSO ,1949
Air Transport Operations on the Burma Front, published by the Air Staff, HQ ACSEA 1944
US Strategic Bombing Survey Report: Air Operations in China, Burma, India – World War II, AHB(RAF)
IAF over Burma, published by Inter-Services Public Relations Directorate, GHQ, New Delhi 1944, AHB(RAF)
Japanese Record of Air Operations, PRO: AIR 23/8455

6. Published Books

Alderson, Squadron Leader Gordon, *History of RAF Kai Tak* 1972
Allen, Louis, *Singapore 1941–1942*, Davis Poynter 1977
Allen, Louis, *Burma, The Longest War 1941–45*, Dent 1984
Appleyard, Squadron Leader Keith, *Short History of Tengah*, 1967
Barnett, Corelli, *Engage the Enemy More Closely*, Hodder & Stoughton 1991
Bidwell, Shelford, *The Chindit War*, Hodder & Stoughton 1979
Boyle, Andrew, *Trenchard*, Collins 1962
Brookes, Flight Lieutenant A J, *History of 100 Squadron*
Burton, Fred H, *Mission to Burma* (177 Sqn), Blackburns of Bolton 1991
Cameron, Marshal of the RAF Lord, *In the Midst of Things*, Hodder & Stoughton 1986
Card, Frank, *Whensoever: 50 years of the RAF Mountain Rescue Service*, Ernest Press 1993
Chapman, F Spencer, *The Jungle Is Neutral*, Chatto & Windus 1950
Churchill, Winston S, *The Gathering Storm*, Cassell 1948
——, *Their Finest Hour*, Cassell 1949
——, *The Hinge of Fate*, Cassell 1951
——, *Closing the Ring*, Cassell 1952
——, *Triumph and Tragedy*, Cassell 1954
Craven, W F and Cate, J L, *The Army Air Forces in World War Two*, (Vols I, IV, V), Office of Air Force History, Washington, new imprint 1983
Cross, Air Chief Marshal Sir Kenneth, *Straight and Level*, Grub Street 1993
Dean, Sir Maurice, *The RAF and Two World Wars*, Cassell 1979
Dunlop, E E, *The War Diaries of Weary Dunlop*, Penguin 1986
Elphick, Peter and Smith, Michael, *Odd Man Out: the Story of the Singapore Traitor*, Hodder & Stoughton 1993
Escott, Squadron Leader Beryl, *Women in Air Force Blue*, Patrick Stephens 1989

Fergusson, Bernard, *Beyond the Chindwin*, Fontana 1945 (first published)

Ford, Daniel, *Flying Tigers*, Smithsonian Institution Press 1991

Fox, Alan, *Autobiography – A Very Late Development*, Industrial Relations Research Unit, University of Warwick 1990

Franks, Norman, *First in the Indian Skies* (31 Sqn), Life Publications 1981

——, *The Air Battle of Imphal*, William Kimber 1985

Gilbert, Martin, *Finest Hour*, C & T Publications 1983

——, *Road to Victory*, C & T Publications 1986

Gillison, Douglas, *Royal Australian Air Force 1939–42*, Australian War Memorial 1962

Gilchrist, Sir Andrew, *Bangkok Top Secret*, Hutchinson 1970

Grant, Major General Ian Lyall, *Burma: The Turning Point*, Zampi Press, Chichester 1993

Gwynne-Timothy, John R W, *Burma Liberators – the RAF in SEAC*, Vols. I and II, Next Level Press, Toronto 1991

Harris, Marshal of the RAF Sir Arthur, *Bomber Offensive*, Collins 1947

Hinsley, F H and Stripp, Alan, *Code Breakers – the Inside Story of Bletchley Park*, OUP 1993

Hyde, H Montgomery, *British Air Policy between the Wars 1918–1939*, Heinemann 1976

Innes, David J, *Beaufighters over Burma* (27 Sqn), Blandford Press 1985

Jefford, Wing Commander C G, *RAF Squadrons*, Airlife 1988

Kelly, Terence, *Hurricanes over the Jungle*, William Kimber 1977

——, *Battle for Palembang*, Robert Hale 1985

Kinvig, Major General Clifford, *River Kwai Railway: the Story of the Burma–Siam Railroad*, Brassey's 1992

Lee, Air Chief Marshal Sir David, *Eastward – the RAF in the Far East 1945–1972*, HMSO 1984

——, *And We Thought the War Was Over*, Harmsworth Publishing 1991

Lucas, Laddie, *Wings of War*, Hutchinson 1983

——, *Out of the Blue*, Hutchinson 1985

Middlebrook, Martin and Mahoney, Patrick, *Battleship*

Morrison, Ian, *Malayan Postcript*, Faber & Faber 1942

O'Brien, Terence. *The Moonlight War*, Collins 1987

——, *Out of the Blue – a Pilot with the Chindits*, Arrow Books 1988

——, *Chasing after Danger*, Collins 1990

Orange, Vincent, *Sir Keith Park*, Methuen 1984

Parry J F (ed), *Burma Volunteer Air Force 1940–42*, privately published 1988

Pearcey, Arthur, *Dakota at War*, Ian Allen 1982

Percival, Lieutenant General A E, *The War in Malaya*, Eyre & Spottiswoode 1949

Rhodes-James, Richard, *Chindit*, Murray 1980

324   *Bibliography*

Rhodes-James, Sir Robert, *Anthony Eden*, George Weidenfeld & Nicolson 1986

Richards, Denis and Saunders, Hilary, *The Royal Air Force 1939–1945*, Vol 2, *The Fight Avails*, HMSO 1975

Richards, Denis, *Portal of Hungerford*, Heinemann 1977

Rusbridger, James and Nave, Eric, *Betrayal at Pearl Harbour*, Summit Books 1991

Saunders, Hilary, *The Royal Air Force 1939–1945,* Vol 3, *The Fight is Won*, HMSO 1975

Seth-Smith, Michael, *The Abandoned Earl*, an unpublished biography, held in AHB (RAF)

Shores, Christopher and Cull, Brian, *Bloody Shambles*, Vols 1 and 2, Grub Street 1992 and 1993

Shorrick, Squadron Leader Neville, *Lion in the Sky*, Federal Publications, Singapore 1968

Slessor, Marshal of the RAF Sir John, *The Central Blue*, Cassell 1956

Slim, Field Marshal Lord, *Defeat into Victory*, Cassell 1956

Stripp, A A M, *Codebreaker in the Far East*, Cass 1989

Swinson, Arthur, *Kohima*, Cassell 1966

Terraine, John, *The Right of the Line*, Hodder & Stoughton 1985

Thetford, Owen, *Aircraft of the RAF since 1918*, 8th Edition, Putnam 1988

Thomas, J Helsdon, *Wings over Burma* (67 Sqn), Merlin Books 1984 (republished 1991)

Tomlinson, Michael, *The Most Dangerous Moment – The Japanese Assault on Ceylon, 1942*, Mayflower 1979

Tsuji, Colonel Masanobu, *Singapore: the Japanese Version*, St Martin's Press, New York 1960

Turnbull, Patrick, *Battle of the Box*, Ian Allan 1979

Vincent, Air Vice-Marshal S F, *Flying Fever*, Jarrolds 1972

Warner, Philip, *The Lonely Soldier*, Buchan & Enright 1981

Williams, Douglas, *194 Squadron – The Friendly Firm*, Merlin Books 1987

Winton, John, *The Forgotten Fleet*, Michael Joseph 1969

Ziegler, Philip, *Mountbatten*, Guild Publishing 1985

Ziegler, Philip (ed.), *Personal Diary of Admiral the Lord Louis Mountbatten*, Collins 1988

Notes

1 Towards the Rising Sun

1 Air Historical Branch Narrative, *The Campaigns in the Far East*, Vol 1. p. 2.
2 Ibid.
3 Kirby, *The War Against Japan*, Vol I. p. 6.
4 Hyde, *British Air Policy between the Wars 1918–1939*, p. 155.
5 Ibid.
6 Kirby, op. cit. p. 6.
7 Trenchard Papers, cited Boyle, p. 552; Hyde, op. cit. p. 156.
8 Narrative 1, p. 3.
9 Slessor, *The Central Blue*, p. 75.
10 Hyde, op. cit. p. 157.
11 Allen, *Singapore 1941–1942*, p. 40.
12 Narrative 1, p. 6.
13 Kirby, op. cit. p. 11.
14 Narrative 1, p. 7.
15 Narrative 1, p. 9.
16 Terraine, *The Right of the Line*, pp. 29–30, quoting an article by Dr David J Wrench, *RUSI Journal*, March 1980.
17 Kirby, op. cit. p. 13.
18 Percival, *The War in Malaya*, p. 43.
19 Kirby, op. cit. p. 14.
20 Despatch of Sir Robert Brooke-Popham, para. 52.
21 Allen, op. cit. p. 41.
22 AP3236, p. 435.
23 Kirby, op. cit. p. 16.
24 Percival, op. cit. p. 17.
25 It was Tedder also who recommended that a civilian (Mr C P Vlieland) be appointed Secretary of Defence 'to provide a counterpoise to the excessive weight of the Army command in defence counsels'. Allen. op. cit. p. 233.
26 Percival, op. cit. p. 17.
27 Narrative 1, p. 16.
28 Kirby, op. cit. p. 14.
29 Narrative 1, p. 19.
30 Ibid, p. 16.
31 Ibid, p. 20.
32 Slessor, op. cit. p. 207.
33 Air Ministry Monthly Intelligence Summaries.
34 AP 3236, p. 436.
35 AP 3397, pp. 359–60.
36 Narrative 1, p. 20.
37 Ibid, p. 19.
38 Kirby, op. cit. p. 21.
39 Ibid.

2 The Years of Neglect

1 Brooke-Popham Despatch, para. 46.
2 Churchill, *The Gathering Storm*, p. 371.
3 Brooke-Popham Despatch, para 13.
4 Allen, op. cit. pp. 220, 234.
5 Kirby, op. cit. p. 24.
6 Ibid, p. 26.
7 Narrative 1, p. 25.
8 Kirby, op. cit. p. 27.
9 The ODC was an inter-Service Committee of the War Cabinet, chaired by the Under-Secretary of State for the Colonies, and including the Directors of Plans of the three Services. The RAF Director was Air Cdre Slessor.
10 Narrative 1, p. 26.
11 Ibid, p. 27.
12 Kirby, op. cit. p. 30.
13 Narrative 1, p. 28.
14 Kirby, op. cit. p. 33.
15 AMWIS 46, 18 July 1940.
16 Narrative 1, p. 29.
17 Ibid.
18 Churchill, *Their Finest Hour*, p. 385.
19 Ibid, p. 592.
20 AMWIS 57, 58, 59; 3, 10 and 16 October 1940.
21 Kirby, op. cit. p. 48.
22 Allen, op. cit. p. 48.
23 Narrative 1, p. 30.
24 Ibid, p. 31.
25 Ibid, p. 32.
26 Churchill, op. cit. p. 623.
27 Kirby, op. cit. p. 55.
28 Narrative 1, p. 33.
29 Kirby, op. cit. p. 54.
30 Rusbridger and Nave, *Betrayal at Pearl Harbour*, pp. 98–106 contain a full discussion of this incident and its implications. See also Rusbridger's article in *Encounter*, May 1985. Earlier accounts suggesting that the *Automedon* was sunk by a submarine can be discounted.
31 Kirby, op. cit. p. 50.
32 Ibid, p. 51.
33 Allen, op. cit. p. 54.
34 Ian Morrison, *Malayan Postscript*, p. 12.
35 Percival, *The War in Malaya*, p. 30.
36 Plt Off E M Cox arrived at Kallang in May 1941, having served at Ford, in 11 Group. A man of wide experience who had served in the First World War, he wrote a memorandum in April 1942, a copy of which was passed to the Inspector General (p. 123): Ludlow-Hewitt Papers, Folder 14.
37 Sqn Ldr Allanson, who was detached for signals duties at AHQ in December 1940, remembers encoding a signal for Brooke-Popham in which he spelt out to Whitehall exactly what was needed if Singapore was to be able to repel attack. Allanson remains convinced that Brooke-Popham did everything he could.
38 Brooke-Popham Despatch, Appendix A.
39 Ibid, para. 7.
40 Narrative 1, p. 39.
41 Percival, op. cit. p. 31.
42 Narrative 1, p. 48.
43 Percival, op. cit. p. 31.
44 Cox Memorandum, op. cit. p. 15.
45 Narrative 1, p. 39.
46 Gillison, *RAAF Official History*, Vol I, p. 163.
47 Recollections of Mr A J Fowden.

48 Recollections of Mr L W Chapman.
49 Recollections of Flt Lt P Reynolds.
50 Recollections of Mr E Hayes.
51 Brooke-Popham Despatch, para. 46. See also Brooke-Popham's correspondence with General Ismay and Sir Arthur Street, PUS, (Folders V 1 and V 2 of his personal papers) which provides valuable understanding of his views at this time.
52 Narrative 1, p. 49.
53 Kirby, op. cit. p. 50.
54 Narrative 1, p. 50.
55 Cox Memorandum, op. cit. p. 5.
56 Narrative 1, p. 50.
57 AMWIS 23, 9 February 1940.
58 AMWIS 39, 30 May 1940.
59 AMWIS 52, 29 August 1940.
60 AMWIS 59, 16 October 1940.
61 AMWIS 75, 5 February 1941.
62 AMWIS 77, 19 February 1941.
63 Gilbert, *Finest Hour*, p. 1046.
64 The Japanese system of numbering each type of aircraft used the last one or two digits of the year of issue. Since 1940 equated with the Japanese year 2600, aircraft brought into service in 1940 were simply designated Type 0, which Allied jargon converted to Zero. Strictly the term Zero applied to the navy version; the slightly different army version eventually became known by its Allied code name Oscar. Kirby, op. cit. Vol II, App. 23.
65 AMWIS 81, 19 March 1941.
66 AMWIS 85, 16 April 1941.
67 AMWIS 107, 17 September 1941.
68 Cox Memorandum, op. cit. p. 8. Cox adds that the information *was* disseminated in Burma and India.
69 Narrative 1, p. 63.
70 AMWIS 122, 31 December 1941.
71 AMWIS 84, 9 April 1941.
72 AMWIS 100, 30 July 1941. For an outline of the organisation of the Japanese air forces see Kirby. op. cit. Appendix 5.
73 Thetford, *Aircraft of the Royal Air Force since 1918*, pp. 546/7.
74 Narrative 1, p. 43. See Shores and Cull, *Bloody Shambles*, Vol I pp. 33–8, 42–6 for full particulars of the formation of the Buffalo squadrons. Vols I and II provide a very detailed account of all the air operations, Japanese as well as Allied, up to April 1942.
75 Brooke-Popham Despatch, Appendix L.
76 Recollections of Mr H A Cullingworth.
77 Narrative 1, p. 44.
78 Gillison, op. cit. p. 170.
79 Narrative 1, p. 44.
80 Ibid, p. 45.
81 Recollections of Mr F W Lewis.
82 Cullingworth recollections.
83 Recollections of Mr C G Hutchings.
84 Lewis recollections.
85 Morrison, op. cit. p. 11.
86 Brooke-Popham Papers, Folder V 4.
87 Morrison, op. cit. p. 11.
88 Gillison, op. cit. p. 170.
89 Narrative 1, p. 44.
90 The British term 'radio direction finding' (RDF) was superseded by the American term 'radar' in 1942. To avoid confusion 'radar' will be used throughout this book.
91 Links through Malaya depended on open telephone lines shared with the Army and the civil administration; on one occasion the C-in-C was cut off when his three minutes were up – Richards and Saunders, *The Fight Avails*, p. 8.
92 Recollections of then Sqn Ldr T C Carter, OC Radio Installation and Maintenance Unit, who also sent me a copy of the report on the RDF organisation in the Far East

1941/2 which he wrote later in 1942.
93 Carter states that 250 MRU could plot a Blenheim flying at 10,000 feet at a range of 100 miles.
94 AP 3227, pp. 249–251.
95 Recollections of Mr J Hall.
96 Narrative 1, p. 41. Shores and Cull, op. cit. p. 32.
97 Thetford, op. cit. I have used his spelling of Vildebeest.
98 Recollections of Mr R Mager.
99 Brookes, *History of 100 Squadron*.
100 Narrative 1, p. 42.
101 Reynolds recollections. Mr P N Negretti, another observer with 62 Squadron, makes similar observations.
102 Brooke-Popham Despatch, para. 86.
103 For details of the MVAF see Shores and Cull, op. cit. Vol I. pp. 26–27.
104 Percival, op. cit. p. 105.
105 Woodward, *British Foreign Policy in the Second World War*, Vol II, p. 32.
106 Dean, *The RAF and Two World Wars*, p. 245. Sir Maurice Dean, an Air Ministry civil servant, was working with the Air Staff at this time.
107 Quoted in Allen, op. cit. p. 17.
108 Narrative 1. p. 40.
109 AP 3236, pp. 438–40, and Appendix 17, which states the position at each RAF unit in December 1941. See also Maltby Despatch, App A.
110 Despatch of AVM P C Maltby, paras. 17–25.
111 Richards and Saunders. op. cit. p. 8; only 17% of the anti-aircraft guns authorised ever reached Malaya.
112 Narrative 1, p. 40.
113 AP 3397, pp. 361–7.
114 Shorrick, *Lion in the Sky*, p. 60. AP 3236, pp. 684–88, also provides considerable detail about Seletar – its power supply and wiring, its fuel installations, the problems of air conditioning etc.
115 Gillison, op. cit. p. 164.
116 Shorrick, op. cit. p. 60.
117 Chapman recollections.
118 Recollections of Mr F Wooldridge.
119 Cullingworth recollections.
120 Carter recollections.
121 Narrative 1, pp. 37–8; Brooke-Popham Despatch, paras. 42–5.
122 Kirby, op. cit. pp. 61, 66, 70, 75, 80.
123 Narrative 1, p. 39. The flare-path layout needed for night flying was based on an article in the RAF magazine TEE EMM.
124 Maltby Despatch, paras. 32–41. Moorings for 20 Catalinas were prepared. Runway extensions for B-17s were started; only Gong Kedah was completed. Preparations were made to receive Dutch Glenn Martin bombers at Sembawang and Buffaloes at Kallang.
125 Allen, op. cit. p. 52, referring to General Percival's letter of 7 January 1942 to Professor J R M Butler, lodged in the Percival Papers.
126 Kirby, op. cit. p. 77.
127 Narrative 1, p. 57.
128 Ibid, p. 58.
129 Brooke-Popham Despatch, para. 95.

3   The Paper Fortress

1 Narrative 2, p. 1.
2 Ibid, p. 2.
3 Allen, op. cit. pp. 99–100. This contains a full discussion of the questions surrounding MATADOR.
4 Narrative 2, pp. 4–5.
5 Allen, op. cit. p. 107. See also Shores and Cull, op. cit. pp. 76–7.

6 To relieve the congestion the seven Vildebeests were transferred to Gong Kedah (two of those despatched from Seletar had had to return).

7 Narrative 2, pp. 6–7; much of the subsequent detail is drawn from this volume.

8 Maltby Despatch, op. cit. para. 671.

9 Percival, op. cit. p. 110.

10 The United States Fleet was attacked at 0800 hours local time on 7 December, equating to 0200 hours on 8 December in Malaya. Thus the Kota Bharu landing started 45 minutes before the air raid on Pearl Harbour.

11 Gillison, op. cit. gives a detailed account of 1 Squadron's operations, pp. 210–18. This and subsequent air actions are all described by Shores and Cull.

12 Reynolds also says that on approaching Patani they were attacked by Zeros and turned away rather than press home their attack.

13 The aircraft had been attacked by six Zeros and so badly damaged that it barely managed to get back.

14 Maltby Despatch, op. cit. para 673.

15 Morrison, op. cit. p. 92.

16 Allen, op. cit. p. 244.

17 Carter recollections. Mr J Hall also recalls this night. He was on the duty watch at Changi when they plotted an estimated 20 aircraft without IFF and were told by the Filter Room they could not possibly be labelled Japanese aircraft since war had not been declared.

18 Mr A J Fowden remembers the clear, moonlit Sunday night; the blackout at Seletar was announced at 0200, and the bomb explosions two hours later preceded the air raid warning by several minutes.

19 Narrative 2, pp. 7–8. The Order of the Day and Portal's signal are quoted in full.

20 This account relies, except where otherwise indicated, on Narrative 2, pp. 16–21.

21 Maltby Despatch, op. cit. para. 183; this comments that later events indicated a leakage of information to the Japanese. See also Note 23.

22 It did not help when 21 Squadron's Buffaloes were announced operationally unfit owing to lack of gun-firing solenoids (Narrative 2, p. 25). New ones were flown from Kallang the next morning.

23 Heenan, an officer in a Punjab regiment, had arrived in Malaya in late 1940, spent three months at Seletar in 1941 learning about intelligence, and in June moved to Alor Star as a liaison officer with the RAF. His story is told by Peter Elphick and Michael Smith in *Odd Man Out*; they describe how he came to pass information to the Japanese, was arrested on 10 December, tried and later shot in Singapore. They suggest that the timing of the raid on Alor Star was determined by information sent by Heenan, and that the success of the overall Japanese air campaign owed much to his work on their behalf, but their evidence is almost entirely circumstantial. There is little doubt that he was a traitor; whether his activities had much effect in relation to all the other intelligence sources used by the Japanese is a very different matter.

24 This account again relies largely on Narrative 2, pp. 25–27.

25 Reynolds recollections. Sergeant Calder is still alive, living in New Zealand.

26 Roskill, *The War At Sea*, Vol I, p. 563.

27 Narrative 2, p. 34.

28 Middlebrook and Mahoney, *Battleship*, p. 109.

29 Brooke-Popham Despatch, para. 106.

30 Maltby Despatch, para. 212.

31 Allen, op. cit. p. 142.

32 Narrative 2, pp. 37–38.

33 Ibid. Japanese records do not confirm the air sighting. According to Richards and Saunders (op. cit. p. 26) these aircraft mistook Force Z for two Japanese warships.

34 Shores and Cull, op. cit. pp. 100–104. Cox, op. cit. p. 19, calls it 'a disgraceful affair'.

35 Narrative 2, pp. 27–32.

36 Ibid, p. 41.

37 Middlebrook and Mahoney, op. cit. provides an excellent account; the timings given there differ slightly from those quoted in the Narrative but the variations are not significant.

38 Roskill, op. cit. p. 565.

39 Maltby Despatch, para. 217.

40 Barnett, *Engage the Enemy More Closely*, p. 414.
41 Narrative 2, p. 43.
42 Middlebrook and Mahoney, op. cit. p. 257; Shores and Cull, op. cit. p. 125.
43 Middlebrook and Mahoney, op. cit. p. 297. In practice it would have been very difficult to provide as many as six aircraft at one time.
44 Slessor, op. cit. p. 277.
45 Harris, *Bomber Offensive*. p. 275.
46 Hayes recollections.
47 Recollections of Mr J Linnell.
48 Narrative 2, p. 59.
49 Ibid, p. 31.
50 Ibid, p. 34.
51 Maltby Despatch, paras. 222, 223. Gillison, op. cit. p. 249. McCauley was OC Sembawang; he eventually became Chief of Air Staff, RAAF.
52 Allen, op. cit. pp. 195–96; Shores and Cull, op. cit. pp. 155–156.
53 Recollections of then Flt Sgt D Wilcox, W Op/AG
54 Recollections of Dr A N H Peach.
55 Narrative 2, p. 57.
56 Linnell recollections.
57 AMWIS 136 dated 8 April 1942.
58 Tsuji, *Singapore, the Japanese Version*, p. 130. Colonel Tsuji was at the time Chief of the Operations and Planning Staff, 25th Japanese Army, Malaya.
59 Narrative 2, pp. 49–60 contains a full account of these operations.
60 Ibid, Appendix V.
61 Ibid, pp. 61–62.
62 Percival, op. cit. p. 147.
63 Tsuji, op. cit. p. 146.
64 Narrative 2, pp. 80–86, from which this section of the account is largely drawn.
65 Shores and Cull, op. cit. p. 303.
66 Recollections of Mr D Turner. See also Terence O'Brien, *Chasing after Danger*, pp. 167–188, where he describes his flight out from St Eval and the awful state of Tengah when he arrived.
67 Recollections of Sqn Ldr J A Stephen, Mr L W Chapman.
68 Narrative 2, p. 109.
69 Gillison, op. cit. p. 267. Bowden went on to say 'anything that is not powerful, modern and immediate is futile'.
70 Narrative 2, p. 74.
71 Ibid, pp. 91, 92, 100.
72 Shores and Cull, op. cit. Chapters 8 and 9 cover the air.defence of Singapore in great detail.
73 Recollections of Mr S Fielding.
74 AMWIS 126, 28 January.
75 Recollections of Mr W R Washington, a ground tradesman.
76 Narrative 2, Appendices VII, IX. These were total strength, not just air defence.
77 Sqn Ldr Carter is specific about the date, pointing out that Mersing was not closed down in mid-January as stated in Richards and Saunders, op. cit. p. 35.
78 Ibid, pp. 103–104.
79 Recollections of Mr L W Chapman.
80 Narrative 2, Appendices VII, IX. The Order of Battle for 18 January lists 25 Vildebeests, 11 Hudsons, 8 Blenheims, 3 Catalinas and 24 Buffaloes.
81 Percival, op. cit. p. 188.
82 Ibid, p. 199.
83 Mr C Hardman, who arrived with the Gibraltar reinforcements, recalls the struggle to take off, when the Pratt and Whitney engines had to be pushed beyond their two minute limit in auto-rich.
84 Richards and Saunders, op. cit. pp. 32–33.
85 Narrative 2, pp. 88–94 covers these operations in some detail.
86 Ibid, p. 95.
87 Ibid, p. 111.
88 Kirby, op. cit. pp. 241, 388.

89 Minute from Sinclair to Churchill, 20 December 1941: AHB (RAF).
90 Kirby, op. cit. 263–265.
91 Maltby Despatch (Appendix D of draft, copy in AHB).
92 Ibid, para. 293.
93 Stephen recollections.
94 Narrative 2, p. 117.
95 Portal minute to Churchill, 17 February 1942, Portal Papers M23.
96 Maltby Despatch, paras. 346–354.
97 Tsuji, op. cit. p. 198.
98 Kirby, op. cit. p. 331. Narrative 2, p. 114. These differ about the size of the escort. The fleet had left Saigon on 22 January and was carrying the 18th Division.
99 Narrative 2, p. 116, note 2.
100 Kirby, op. cit. p. 332.
101 Recollections of Sqn Ldr R Allanson, a 36 Squadron pilot who survived.
102 Brookes, op. cit.
103 Narrative 2, p. 115.
104 Shores and Cull, op. cit. Vol II. p. 39 – part of a very full account of the disaster. See also O'Brien, op. cit. pp. 192–207; O'Brien piloted one of 62 Squadron's Hudsons.
105 Narrative 2, p. 116.
106 Brookes, op. cit. Appleyard's history of Tengah also records this incident and describes the difficulties in preparing the Hurricanes for the operation.
107 Richard Allanson, who wanted to help me in the hope of according a suitable epitaph to those who lost their lives while 'doing their damndest' in those utterly outdated aircraft.
108 Hayes recollections. He and his comrades were paraded on arrival before a Guards Lieutenant Colonel and berated for their slovenly appearance.
109 Fielding recollections.
110 Wilcox recollections.
111 Lewis recollections.
112 Kelly, *Hurricane over the Jungle*, p. 65.
113 Narrative 2, p. 120.
114 Ibid, p. 119.
115 Kirby, op. cit. pp. 353–354.
116 Narrative 2, pp. 128–129. Gillison, op. cit. p. 349 refers to the bitter reaction of the ground troops, but quotes Wavell's belief that the decision to withdraw the air forces was inevitable – one of the lessons of Crete.
117 Gilbert, *Road to Victory*, p. 52; in an exchange of minutes on 28/29 January Portal had told Churchill the bombers were being withdrawn for their own protection and would continue to operate against Japanese airfields in Malaya.
118 Churchill, *The Hinge of Fate*, pp. 85–86. He had indeed been closely following events; in a minute to Portal on 27 January (Portal Papers M8a) he asked for a clear account of each of the 51 Hurricanes: 'is it born, is it alive, is it wounded or is it dead?'
119 Maltby Despatch (draft, held in AHB).
120 Kirby, op. cit. p. 338. Among those who left at the same time was the SASO, Air Cdre W E Staton, who carried the AHQ documents which were later used as the basis of the AHB Narrative (op cit. p. 132).
121 Narrative 2, p. 130.
122 Morrison, op. cit. p. 178.
123 Narrative 2, pp. 131–132. See also Shores and Cull, op. cit. p. 385, where the Army Air Force losses are given as 331. 46 more were lost through bad weather, according to the Narrative; the Naval Air Force suffered the rest.
124 At least one modern author says the Japanese found neatly parked British aircraft on the runways at Tengah; in fact the only aircraft left were wrecks.
125 Carter recollections.
126 Hall recollections.
127 Recollections of Mr R Barkus.
128 Chapman recollections.
129 Stephen recollections.
130 Narrative 2, p. 133.
131 Percival, op. cit. p. 287.
132 Gillison, op. cit. p. 351.

133 Allanson remembers all too well that there were 'quite a few' dead-beat officers at that time and believes they had been sent out to keep them where they could do least harm.

134 Though Gillison, op. cit. p. 327, tells us that Pulford actually intended on one occasion to fly with one of 205 Squadron's Catalinas in an attack on Gong Kedah.

135 Wilcox recollections. See also Shores and Cull, op. cit. Appendix II – a critical report written by Wg Cdr F N Wright, OC 8 Squadron, RAAF.

136 Portal Papers, PM Minute 23, 17 February 42.

137 Morrison, op. cit. p. 95.

138 Richards and Saunders, op. cit. p. 5.

139 Morrison, op. cit. p. 190.

4   The Chain of Disaster

1 Alderson, *History of RAF Kai Tak*, p. 13.

2 Kirby, op. cit. p. 18.

3 Ibid, p. 34.

4 Maltby Despatch, op. cit. para 50.

5 Brooke-Popham says there were four Vildebeests but the other sources say three.

6 Kirby, op. cit. p. 115.

7 Alderson, op. cit. pp. 32–33.

8 Kirby, op. cit. p. 147.

9 Ibid, p. 116.

10 Brooke-Popham Despatch, para 16.

11 Maltby Despatch, para 61.

12 Narrative 2, p. 71.

13 Ibid.

14 Ibid, p. 65.

15 Ibid, pp. 74–76.

16 Maltby Despatch, para. 400.

17 Narrative 2, p. 138. Shores and Cull, op. cit. Vol II pp. 45–57.

18 Maltby Despatch, paras 397–398.

19 Narrative 2, p. 138.

20 Maltby Despatch, para 413.

21 Kelly, *Battle for Palembang*, pp. 29–31, quoting Air Cdre Vincent in *History of 226 Group*.

22 Gillison, op. cit. p. 385.

23 Narrative 2, p. 121.

24 Cullingworth and Fowden recollections.

25 Gillison, op. cit. p. 387: Maltby Despatch, paras. 421–423.

26 Kirby, op. cit. p. 357.

27 Maltby Despatch, para 428. The 84 Squadron history (held in AHB) reminds us that these sorties, entailing refuelling stops at Medan, required 13 flying hours in order to drop 4 x 250lb bombs. See also O'Brien, op. cit. p. 206, who takes Maltby to task for relying too much on 84 Squadron's report and implying that only the morale of the Blenheim crews from the Middle East was high.

28 Narrative 2, p. 128; the series of moves between Java, Sumatra and Singapore is too complex to explain in this brief account.

29 Ibid, p. 129; Kelly, op. cit. pp. 29–32.

30 Narrative 2, pp. 161–162; Kelly, op. cit. pp. 34–42 gives a detailed description of these attacks based on his own recollections; there are differences on points of detail. See also Shores and Cull, op. cit. Vol II. pp. 63–66.

31 Gillison, op. cit. p. 389.

32 Kelly, op. cit. pp. 48–50.

33 Aircraftman D Linsley's launch was bombed; he was marooned but eventually got to Sumatra and Padang, from where he was evacuated by the Royal Navy. Just one example of many.

34 Narrative 2, p. 144. See Shores and Cull, op. cit. Vol II pp. 89–126, for a detailed account of the Palembang air battles.

35 Narrative 2, pp. 140–142.
36 Ibid, p. 143; Kelly (op. cit. pp. 82–132) gives an excellent description of the battle for P1, including a personal recollection from Maguire (later Air Marshal Sir Harold Maguire). This includes the story of his encountering a Japanese captain, when each challenged the other to surrender. Maltby (paras 455–462) also describes the battle.
37 Narrative 2, p. 144. Shores and Cull (p. 107) refer to 20 Hudsons; some of these were flown to Java on the 14th.
38 Kelly, op. cit. pp. 133–134.
39 Narrative 2, p. 144.
40 Maltby Despatch, paras. 465–467. Gillison also records the attack on the Zeros, but Kelly disputes this.
41 Narrative 2, p. 145. Maltby Despatch, para 478.
42 Kelly, op. cit. Epilogue.
43 File 'Singapore Operations' – AHB (RAF).
44 Kirby, op. cit. p. 351.
45 Meeting of the Pacific War Council 17 February 1942: quoted in Gilbert, op. cit. p. 62.
46 Wavell to Churchill, 16 February 1942; quoted in Churchill, *The Hinge of Fate*, p. 124.
47 Ibid, p. 127.
48 Kirby, op. cit. p. 432.
49 File 'South West Pacific C-in-C' – AHB (RAF); Narrative 2, p. 147; Maltby Despatch, para 512.
50 Churchill, op. cit. p. 129.
51 Maltby Despatch, paras 356, 499.
52 Ibid, para 358.
53 Narrative 2, p. 148.
54 Maltby Despatch, para. 489.
55 Barkus, Fowden, Wilcox, and Washington recollections.
56 Narrative 2, p. 149; Maltby Despatch, paras. 496, 497. Thirty nine crated Hurricanes had been erected in Batavia in early February; 17 went to Sumatra, 12 to the Dutch (they were never used), 10 to the RAF in Java.
57 Narrative 2, p. 150.
58 So named after its Australian commander, Brigadier A S Blackburn VC.
59 Gillison, op. cit. p. 438.
60 Maltby Despatch, para. 533. Shores and Cull, op. cit. Vol II. pp. 242–246.
61 Maltby Despatch, para. 535.
62 This whole incident, including the court of inquiry, is described in some detail in Maltby's Despatch paras 537–542. See also Shores and Cull, op. cit. Vol. II. pp. 295–302.
63 Kelly, *Hurricane over the Jungle*, p. 184.
64 Portal Papers, PM Minute 23b, 24 February 1942.
65 Kirby, op. cit. p. 444.
66 Narrative 2, pp. 155–156. This points out that 10 Dutch Kittyhawks and Buffaloes were also engaged in the operations on 1 March.
67 File 'Java' – AHB (RAF). Maltby actually referred to '232 Squadron', but 232 had been merged into 242 Squadron, not the other way round.
68 Maltby Despatch, para. 695; this report (para 569) also summarises the operations of the Fighter Wing in Sumatra and Java, during which about 40 enemy aircraft were shot down and heavy casualties inflicted on ground troops. About 60 Hurricanes were lost, mostly on the ground.
69 205 Squadron Log of Events, compiled by Mr C Hardman; see also Mr Keon-Cohen's account of the final moves of 205 Squadron (copy in 205 Squadron folder, AHB).
70 Narrative 2, pp. 155–156.
71 According to Stephen they were lucky – a Japanese cruiser passed them only a mile away in the Sunda Straits.
72 Wilcox, Washington and Reynolds recollections. See also O'Brien, op. cit. pp. 239–240.
73 Barkus recollections. Mr F W Lewis agrees about the appalling living conditions and the dysentery, but recalls no improper behaviour by the staff.
74 Maltby (para 574) refers to the difficulty of evacuating tradesmen whom the Dutch civil population thought of as military personnel; while the Dutch military authorities

334 *Notes (pages 78–86)*

realised they would be better used elsewhere the civilians often saw them as deserters.
75 Narrative 2, p. 158. A detailed account of this escape appears in the Log of the Scorpion (the name given to the boat), copy in AHB's 84 Squadron folder.
76 Maltby Despatch, paras 576–587: Narrative 2, pp. 158–159.
77 Ibid, paras. 588–596, 610–613.
78 Ibid, para. 601–603.
79 Dunlop, *The Diaries of Weary Dunlop*, p.4.
80 Maltby Despatch, paras. 607–609.
81 Fowden recollections; account by Plt Off Keble-White, 84 Squadron folder (AHB).
82 Command 6832, *Strength and Casualties of the Armed Forces and Auxiliary Forces of the UK, 1939–1945*, published June 1946. In referring to these figures it must be remembered that the 5,000 or so captured in Java included men of the RAAF and RNZAF.
83 Account by Plt Off L F McNally RAAF, 84 Squadron folder.
84 Dean, op. cit. p. 249.
85 Maltby Despatch (draft). Strangely this tribute does not appear in the published version.

5 India under Threat

1 Churchill, op. cit. p. 176. Gilbert, op. cit. p. 48.
2 Gilbert, op. cit. p. 49; J R M Butler, *Grand Strategy*, Vol III, part II, p. 417.
3 Defence Committee (Operations) 42, 6th Meeting.
4 Narrative 2, pp. 165–167.
5 Allen, *Burma: The Longest War*, p. 8.
6 Narrative 2, p. 168.
7 Despatch of AVM Stevenson, para. 10.
8 Slim, *Defeat into Victory*, p. 6.
9 Narrative 2, p. 168.
10 Kirby, *The War against Japan*, Vol II, pp. 14, 21.
11 Narrative 2, p. 171.
12 Slim, op. cit. p. 5.
13 The BVAF had been formed in 1940; Sqn Ldr M P C Corkery became its Chief Flying Instructor and stayed with it until its aircraft were flown out from Magwe to India in March 1942. The surviving pilots became the nucleus of the 221 Group Communications Flight, and after the war some of them played leading roles in the formation of the Burma National Air Force. The story of the BVAF is recounted in a history compiled by J F Parry, one of the pilots, in 1988, and loaned to me by another, J G Booth.
14 Narrative 2, pp. 171–175. A full and racy account of the AVG is contained in Daniel Ford's *Flying Tigers*. See also Craven and Cate, *The Army Air Forces in World War Two*, Vol I, pp. 484–488.
15 AVM D F Stevenson, DSO MC had been D of Ops (Home) from January 1938, and AOC 2 Group from February 1941. He was informed of his appointment to command the Air Forces in Burma on 12 December, Portal referring to him as a 'thoroughly up-to-date officer of proved ability'. (Portal Papers, PM Minute dated 11 December 1941).
16 Stevenson Despatch, para. 3.
17 AOC's Appreciation of the Air Situation: Stevenson Despatch (Appendix D to draft – held in AHB).
18 Peirse Papers, Folder 23.
19 Stevenson Despatch, paras. 29–31.
20 Narrative 2, p. 183.
21 Stevenson Despatch, para. 40.
22 Kirby, op. cit. p. 21.
23 Narrative 2, p. 183.
24 Gp Capt A S Mann, then a 28 Squadron pilot, records that 1 and 28 Squadrons had been sent their Lysanders after army co-operation squadrons in the UK and Middle East had been re-equipped with more modern aircraft. He recalls their extreme vulnerability to air opposition and ground fire.
25 Narrative 2, p. 186.

26 Stevenson Despatch paras, 54–60. Slim, op. cit. p. 13, compares the fighters in similar terms. The designation 'Army 97' simply indicated the aircraft's vintage, ie 1937 (cf p. 27, note 64).
27 Narrative 2, p. 182. Stevenson Despatch, para. 63. Shores and Cull, op. cit. pp. 241–251.
28 Stevenson Despatch, para. 89.
29 Narrative 2, pp. 190–191.
30 Gp Capt Mann describes the invaluable work done by two recce pilots of 28 Squadron who converted to the Hurricane and formed 'Recce Flight Mingaladon'.
31 Kirby, op. cit. p. 73.
32 Stevenson Despatch, paras. 90–91.
33 Kirby, op. cit. p. 67.
34 Stevenson Despatch, para 112, Narrative 2. p. 191.
35 Stevenson Despatch, para 73. Narrative 2. p. 192. On pages 221–222 the Narrators compare Allied and Japanese losses; altogether during the whole campaign the AVG claimed 179 enemy aircraft destroyed, the RAF 54. The AVG lost 19 Tomahawks shot down, the RAF 28 Buffaloes and Hurricanes. Given the difficulties of interpreting the Japanese records, the Narrators judge these claims fair. See, however, Shores & Cull, op. cit. Vol II, p. 284, which suggests they were generous.
36 Stevenson Despatch, para. 78; recollections of Mr R Chappell, an RAF policeman serving with 517 AMES.
37 Stevenson Despatch, paras. 79–84.
38 Gillison, op. cit. p. 405.
39 Kirby, op. cit. p. 85.
40 Slim, op. cit. p. 15.
41 Narrative 2, p. 193.
42 USSBS Report, *Air Operations in China, Burma, India – World War II*, p. 11.
43 Kirby, op. cit. p. 100.
44 Stevenson Despatch, paras. 120–127.
45 Mr L Ransom, *Where there's a Wheel* – private manuscript, copy in Imperial War Museum.
46 Stevenson Despatch, paras. 128–141. Narrative 2. p. 194.
47 Slim, op. cit. p. 9.
48 Mr H T Hathaway, who had reached Burma in January and carried out airfield defence and anti-aircraft duties at Zayatkwin, a satellite of Mingaladon, was moved to Akyab where he and others were formed into No 1 Ground Defence Unit and remained for several more weeks.
49 Burwing comprised 17 Squadron (Hurricanes), 45 Squadron (Blenheims), part of 28 Squadron (Lysanders) and a weak AVG squadron.
50 Akwing comprised 67 Squadron (Hurricanes), a GR flight and a small communications detachment.
51 Stevenson Despatch, paras. 178–179.
52 Shores and Cull, op. cit. Vol II, p. 347.
53 Narrative 2, p. 197. Shores and Cull, op. cit. Vol II, pp. 349–352.
54 Narrative 2, p. 213; this summarises a Japanese account of their air operations in Burma.
55 Ibid, pp. 197–203; this gives a detailed account of the attacks and summarises the report of the CO, Gp Capt H Seton Broughall.
56 Stevenson Despatch, para. 200.
57 Slim, op. cit. p. 42.
58 Ibid, p. 27.
59 Narrative 2, p. 203. This states that, though premature, the movement was in fact carried out under complete control.
60 These probably belonged to 517 AMES, the radar unit, whose men were also moved into China. where they remained until early 1943. Chappell recollections.
61 Mr L Ransom, op. cit. This is a particularly fascinating account.
62 Narrative 2, p. 203.
63 Kirby, op. cit. pp. 150–151; this offers a useful comparison between the Japanese air campaigns in Malaya and Burma.
64 Narrative 2, p. 204.

65 Slim, op. cit. p. 43.
66 Kirby, op. cit. p. 161.
67 Narrative 2, p. 204.
68 Kirby, op. cit. p. 206.
69 Recollections of Sqn Ldr J F P Archbold. See Lucas, *Wings of War*, pp. 198–202, for an excellent description of the first 215 Squadron operation – so-called – on 1 May, written by Ralph Fellows, an air observer.
70 Narrative 2, pp. 208–209.
71 Slim, op. cit. p. 50.
72 Narrative 2, p. 210.
73 Kirby, op cit. p. 213.
74 Narrative 2, p. 211.
75 Allen, op. cit. pp. 87–88.
76 Kirby, op. cit. p. 214.
77 Kirby, op. cit. p. 105.
78 Tomlinson, *The Most Dangerous Moment*, p. 23. Tomlinson's book provides a detailed account of this whole episode.
79 Narrative 3, p. 24.
80 Roskill, op. cit. Vol II p. 24.
81 Kirby, op. cit. pp. 106–108.
82 AP 3236, p. 448. China Bay was opened in September 1939; it was a grass airfield and by December 1941 many of its permanent buildings were complete.
83 Mr L W Chapman, who arrived at Koggala in early March 1942, remembers how everything had to be improvised: paraffin lanterns were used for the flarepath, Catalinas could only be refuelled when beached, using five gallon drums, and everything had to be used to destruction.
84 Narrative 3, p. 9.
85 Recollections of Wg Cdr A G Conway, provided by Mr R Jackson. 258 Squadron's new CO was Sqn Ldr P C Fletcher, now ACM Sir Peter Fletcher. Some of its men had escaped from Java, having served with the same squadron there and in Singapore and Sumatra.
86 War Office Telegram WX 4875 7/3/42 – AHB.
87 Narrative 3, pp. 22–24. The Fulmar was a two-seat carrier-borne fighter with similar fire power to the Hurricane but lacking its performance. It had been derived from the prototypes of the Fairey Battle.
88 Tomlinson, op. cit. p. 65.
89 Portal Papers, PM Minute 23d, 27 February 1942.
90 Carter recollections. According to AP 1116, p. 63, the Colombo radar was in fact working; its failure to detect was caused by troublesome permanent echoes, by gaps in the vertical polar diagram, and by an inefficient watch-keeping roster.
91 Roskill, op. cit. p. 23.
92 War Office Telegram WX 4870 7/3/42 – AHB; Kirby, op. cit. p. 109.
93 Roskill, op. cit. pp. 25–26; Kirby, op. cit. pp. 116–118.
94 The Japanese were unaware of the existence of this island base, situated at the southern tip of the Maldive Islands. Addu Atoll was developed after the war by the RAF as a staging post, known as Gan.
95 Tomlinson, op. cit. describes the maltreatment accorded them by their captors, both immediately and later in Japan, and records that Birchall was awarded the OBE for his courageous work on behalf of his men while a prisoner-of-war. He later rose to high rank in the Royal Canadian Air Force.
96 Tomlinson, op. cit. p. 22.
97 Narrative 3, p. 27.
98 Tomlinson, op. cit. pp. 99–102.
99 Narrative 3, p. 28. Tomlinson, op. cit. p. 111; Shores and Cull, op. cit. Vol II. pp. 395–404.
100 Narrative 3, p. 27. One of the wireless operators had sent a message which read as though his aircraft was under attack, whereas in fact he was re-transmitting a signal picked up from another Catalina.
101 Portal Papers, PM Minute 15, 15 April 1942.
102 Narrative 3, pp. 30–31; Shores and Cull, op. cit. Vol II. pp. 412–423.
103 Narrative 3, p. 32.

104 Ibid, p. 31. Tomlinson. op. cit. pp. 143–146. Churchill, op. cit. p. 159.
105 Roskill, op. cit. p. 28.
106 Butler, op. cit. p. 486.

6 Priorities and Preparations

1 Note by CAS, Portal Papers, Box C File 1, E2.
2 Gilbert, op. cit. p. 25.
3 Richards, *Portal of Hungerford*, p. 248.
4 Butler, op. cit. pp. 471–474.
5 Kirby, op. cit. pp. 113–114; Narrative 3, p. 76.
6 Richards, op. cit. p. 305.
7 Minute from Sinclair to Prime Minister, 10 December 1941: AHB (RAF).
8 Craven & Cate, op. cit. p. 371.
9 Portal Papers, PM Minutes 13, 13a, 31 January 1942; in a letter to General Auchinleck on 25 November 1941 Portal had described Peirse as 'very steady and sound'. (Box C, Folder 4.)
10 Ibid, Peirse to CAS, 5 May 1942 (Box C, Folder 4).
11 Peirse Papers, Folder 25, E1.
12 Peirse Papers, Folder 25, E13. See also Narrative 3, pp. 15–16.
13 Narrative 3, pp. 2–7.
14 AIR 23/2704, The Modernisation of the Air Forces in India, p. 4.
15 Narrative 2, p. 8; AP3397, op. cit. pp. 371–373.
16 Kirby, op. cit. p. 112.
17 Narrative 3, p. 14.
18 AP 3397, p. 378.
19 Churchill, op. cit. p. 176.
20 Kirby, op. cit. pp. 187–189, and Appendix 24.
21 By November 1943, 34 all-weather and 11 fair-weather strips had been handed over to the USAAF. Craven and Cate, op. cit. Vol 4, p. 444 lists these airfields and describes the many construction problems.
22 Narrative 3, pp. 43–45; AP3397, pp. 377–378; Kirby, pp. 112–113, 191, 301.
23 Kirby, op. cit. p. 382.
24 AP3397, p. 382.
25 Ibid, pp. 378–380.
26 AP3277, Vol II, pp. 256–264.
27 Carter recollections.
28 Narrative 2, p. 49. AP3277, Vol II, p. 257. AP 1116 contains, at Appendix 8, an extract from a letter written by an RAF officer in charge of a road convoy delivering VHF equipment to a sector operations room in southern India in October 1943. He describes a nightmare journey along appalling waterlogged roads in vehicles which constantly broke down – conditions which were all too typical.
29 *Wings of the Phoenix*, Chapter 2.
30 Narrative 3, p. 37.
31 Portal Papers, PM Minute 25.
32 Ibid, Minute 25b.
33 Butler, op. cit. p. 528.
34 Gilbert, op. cit. p. 91.
35 Ibid, p. 29: Butler, op. cit. p. 528.
36 Portal Papers, PM Minutes 17, 17b, 18 and 24 April 1941.
37 Butler, op. cit. pp. 487–488.
38 Narrative 3, p. 39.
39 Ibid, p. 40.
40 Ibid, p. 48.
41 Recollections of Mr E R Henman, who draws attention to Peter C Smith's comprehensive book *Vengeance*.
42 Narrative 3, App. 2.
43 *Wings of the Phoenix*, Ch. 2.
44 Narrative 3, p. 40.

45 Ibid, p. 39.
46 Ibid, pp. 38–41.
47 Allen, op. cit. p. 96, quoting from the Irwin papers.
48 Recollections of Mr C Hutchings.
49 Narrative 3, pp. 41–43.
50 Ibid, App. 11; Narrative 4, App. 15. AP3397, p. 553 quotes higher figures, eg. December 1943: 1,807 aircraft in flying units, including 1,014 operational.
51 Ibid, App. 2.
52 Ibid, pp. 49–51.
53 Ibid, pp. 36–37.
54 Ibid, p. 37.
55 AHQ signal 19 April 1942; AM signal 25 April 1942, Portal Papers, Box C, Folder 4.
56 Letter 24 May 1942, Portal Papers, Box C, Folder 4.
57 Ludlow-Hewitt Papers, IG Diary File – 1942 Tour, Paper 23, 10 July 1942.
58 Ibid, Paper 25, 9 July 1942.
59 Peirse Papers, Folder 25, E7.
60 Portal Papers, Box C, Folder 5, E11b.
61 Ibid, Box D, Folder 5, E28.
62 Narrative 3, p. 37.
63 Air Force Lists.
64 AIR 22/311: Personnel Statistics 3 September 1939 – 1 September 1945.

7 Hopes Deferred

1 Kirby, op. cit. p. 235.
2 Gilbert, op. cit. p. 105.
3 Ibid, pp. 121–122.
4 Kirby, op. cit. p. 236.
5 Gilbert, op. cit. p. 123.
6 Kirby, op. cit. p. 249.
7 Stilwell had been appointed Chief of Staff to Chiang Kai-shek in February 1942 and had also taken command of all United States Army forces in the China-Burma-India (CBI) theatre of operations.
8 Kirby, op. cit. Chapter 17 covers these policy discussions in detail.
9 Ibid, p. 364.
10 Gilbert, op. cit. p. 355.
11 Kirby, op. cit. pp. 368–369.
12 Gilbert, op. cit. p. 392.
13 Kirby, op. cit. pp. 419–422; Gilbert, op. cit. pp. 478–479.
14 Thomas, *Wings over Burma*, Chapter 9.
15 Conway recollections; Narrative 3, p. 64.
16 Narrative 3, p. 66.
17 Ibid, pp. 105–106; *Wings of the Phoenix*, p. 24.
18 Japanese Record of Air Operations, Chapter III. This document was compiled after the war, partly from memory, by a staff officer of 5 Air Division. A copy was obtained in Tokyo in 1946 by AVM Bouchier.
19 Narrative 3, p. 150.
20 Ibid, pp. 64–65.
21 Ibid, pp. 106–107.
22 Conway recollections.
23 Thomas, op. cit. p. 65.
24 Narrative 3, pp. 108–111.
25 Thomas, op. cit. p. 66.
26 Narrative 3, p. 112.
27 Slim, op. cit. p. 134. O'Brien (op. cit. p. 282), who met Williams in Java, speaks of the confidence he inspired – unlike all the other senior officers he met at that time, apart from Staton.
28 Narrative 3, p. 112.
29 Allen, op. cit. p. 92.
30 Kirby, op. cit. p. 249.

31 Ibid, p. 251.
32 Narrative 3, p. 80.
33 Ibid, p. 82.
34 Ibid, pp. 85–86; note by Sqn Ldr (later Gp Capt) A S Mann, OC 28 Squadron.
35 Kirby, op. cit. p. 336.
36 Narrative 3, pp. 83–85.
37 Slim, op. cit. p. 159.
38 Kirby, op. cit. p. 355.
39 AP 3235, p. 125.
40 Narrative 3, p. 87.
41 In conversation with a Burmese officer, Wingate misheard the word 'lion, 'chinte', as 'chindit' and adopted the term for his force.
42 Kirby, op. cit. p. 244.
43 Allen, op. cit. p. 120.
44 Narrative 3, p. 89.
45 Kirby, op. cit. App. 25, p. 499.
46 Allen, op. cit. p. 123. Sir Robert Thompson later played a key role in the Malayan Emergency.
47 Narrative 3, p. 90.
48 Kirby, pp. 309–310.
49 Narrative 3, p. 98, and 5, p. 6.
50 Ibid, pp. 93–96.
51 Ibid, p. 100.
52 Ibid, p. 97.
53 Wingate Report, quoted in Narrative 3, p. 97.
54 Slim, op. cit. p. 163.
55 Churchill, *Closing the Ring*, p. 577.
56 Fergusson, *Beyond the Chindwin*, p. 240.
57 Allen, op. cit. p. 148.
58 Narrative 3, p. 101.
59 Ibid, p. 98.
60 Kirby, op. cit. p. 329.
61 Narrative 3, pp. 61–62.
62 Ibid, App. 13, para 6 (interim history of Japanese Army Air Force in Burma).
63 Ibid, pp. 68, 69, 73. Kirby, op. cit. pp. 258–259.
64 Ibid, pp. 115–118, 141–142.
65 *Wings of the Phoenix*, p. 34.
66 Ludlow-Hewitt Papers, E14.
67 Narrative 3, p. 137.
68 AHQ Intelligence Report, Beaufighters over Burma, provided by Gp Capt P H Baldwin, who commanded 177 Squadron at the time.
69 Reproduced via the excellent account of 27 Squadron's work in Burma by Innes, *Beaufighters over Burma*, pp. 86–87.
70 Burton, *Mission to Burma*, p. 41. This is a most useful account of 177 Squadron's work in Burma, written by a Beaufighter observer.
71 AMWIS 199, 26 June 1943.
72 Fox, *A Very Late Development*, p. 116.
73 Narrative 3, pp. 122, 144.
74 Recollections of Flt Lt N Hunt, a Hudson navigator.
75 Narrative 3, p. 58. Kirby, op. cit. pp. 126–127.
76 Kirby, op. cit. pp. 133–144 describes the Madagascar campaign.
77 Narrative 3, pp. 70–71.
78 Ibid, p. 124.
79 Japanese Record, op. cit. Part I.
80 Narrative 3, p. 145.
81 Recollections of Mr A Lowe.
82 Narrative 3, App. 9.
83 *Wings of the Phoenix*, p. 40.
84 Narrative 3, pp. 60–61; Kirby. op. cit. pp. 240–241.
85 *Air Transport Operations on the Burma Front*, p. 8.

86 Narrative 3, pp. 56–57.
87 *Air Transport Operations on the Burma Front*, pp. 3–6.
88 Narrative 3, p. 140. One of 31 Squadron's pilots at this time was Flt Lt David Lord, who later won a posthumous VC over Arnhem.
89 Narrative 3, App. 8.

8   Towards the Offensive

1 Narrative 4, p. 1. Wavell's powers did not extend to the Navy and RAF in Ceylon.
2 Ibid, p. 2.
3 Kirby, op. cit. pp. 370–371.
4 Gilbert, op. cit. p. 408.
5 Kirby, op. cit. p. 388.
6 Portal Papers, Box D Folder 5, E7, 17 June 1943. Tedder was Air C-in-C in the Mediterranean; Douglas, previously AOC-in-C Fighter and Coastal Commands, was now AOC-in-C Middle East; Coningham was AOC Desert Air Force.
7 Howard, *Grand Strategy*, Vol IV, p. 578.
8 Gilbert, op. cit. p. 470.
9 Ziegler, *Mountbatten*, p. 237. Peirse Papers, Folder 29 (letter to Portal dated 9 June 1943).
10 Narrative 4, p. 3.
11 Ibid, pp. 4–6.
12 Craven and Cate, op. cit. Vol IV. p. 451.
13 Portal Papers, PM Minute 49.
14 Ehrman, *Grand Strategy*, Vol V, pp. 140–143 discusses Stilwell's position in detail.
15 USSBS Survey, p. 21.
16 Craven and Cate, op. cit. Vol. IV, p. 453.
17 Narrative 4, pp. 7–10. One of Stratemeyer's main reasons was his separate responsibility for the training and maintenance of Chennault's 14th AF in China. See Craven and Cate, op.cit. Vol IV, pp. 454–457 for the American account of this debate.
18 Mountbatten's Report to the Combined Chiefs of Staff, para 38.
19 Narrative 4, pp. 10–11.
20 Ziegler, op. cit. p. 249.
21 Portal Papers, File 12, Correspondence with Supreme Commander SE Asia, E1.
22 Ziegler, op. cit. p. 249.
23 Portal Papers, Box C, Folder 7, E1, 16 September 1943.
24 Ziegler, op. cit. p. 237.
25 Portal Papers, Box C, Folder 7, E2.
26 Ibid, E3, 26 January 1944.
27 Narrative 4, p. 15.
28 Slim, op. cit. p. 212.
29 Narrative 4, pp. 15–16.
30 Stratemeyer's report on operations, quoted in Peirse Despatch, para. 6.
31 Narrative 4, p. 16.
32 Portal Papers, File 12, E2, 2a.
33 Ziegler, op. cit. pp. 278–279. Ziegler also describes the atmosphere of the HQ at Kandy – the luxury, the overstaffing, the absence of economy, but goes on to say that Mountbattens do not come on the cheap. 'Kandy was an efficient HQ, but it was also an expertly contrived entertainment'.
34 Narrative 4, p. 14.
35 Ehrman, op. cit. p. 132.
36 Ibid, pp. 134–135.
37 Slim, op. cit. p. 214.
38 Ehrman, op. cit. p. 148. Kirby, Vol. III, pp. 13–14.
39 Ehrman, op. cit. pp. 186–190. Kirby, op. cit. pp. 54–66.
40 Kirby, op. cit. Vol. III. p. 66.
41 Stratemeyer's General Order, quoted in Narrative 4, p. 26.
42 Narrative 4, Appendices 5, 7.
43 Peirse Despatch, para 13.

44 Ibid, para. 151.
45 Conway recollections.
46 The section became No 1 Airborne Salvage Squadron on 23 March 1944, its main job being the emergency repair of Dakotas which had forced landed in Burma. It also carried back damaged Spitfires. AP 3397, p. 395.
47 Slim, op. cit. p. 225.
48 Recollections of Squadron Leader R Mitchell.
49 Quoted in Peirse Despatch, para 194, from which much of the detail is taken.
50 The work of WEC, the Far East out-station of GCCS at Bletchley Park, is described by Mr A A M Stripp, who worked there as an Army Lieutenant in 1943–1945, in *Code Breakers*, pp. 288–299, and in his earlier book *Codebreakers in the Far East*. WEC operated alongside a large American signals intelligence unit, and a number of small Army and RAF intercept units were deployed forward in support. Of particular use to them were enemy signals about the ferrying of replacement aircraft and – later on – about their withdrawal. Japanese reports of RAF and American air attacks were also invaluable, since they could be compared with the Allied reports and assessments. Such was the success of the American and British sigint units, of which WEC was an important part, that by later 1944 the enemy's entire Order of Battle had been worked out.
51 See Mellersh Despatch, para. 22, for a description of the air-sea rescue organisation.
52 Craven and Cate, op. cit. Vol IV. p. 510.
53 Note by AI 3(d), Air Ministry, 25 May 1944 (held in AHB). Though written in May, the assessment is generally appropriate to the situation at the beginning of the year.
54 AMWIS 186, 27 March 1943.
55 Narrative 4, p. 30. The Japanese estimated that the Allies had 1,000 aircraft in India at the end of 1943, and that this would increase to 1,500 by summer 1944 – Kirby, op. cit. p.77.
56 Even so Japanese aircraft production continued to increase until it peaked in September 1944. Narrative 4, pp. 30–31.
57 Narrative 4, p. 31. Kirby, op. cit. p. 43.
58 Narrative 4, pp. 32–33.
59 Ibid, p. 43.
60 Dean, op. cit. p. 250.
61 Peirse Despatch, para. 18.
62 Japanese Record of Air Operations, Pt. II.
63 Ibid.
64 Narrative 4, pp. 34–36.
65 Japanese Record, Pt. II.
66 Kirby, op. cit. p. 121.
67 Mountbatten Report, para. 63.
68 Ziegler, op. cit. p. 254, quoting Mountbatten's personal diary.
69 Narrative 4, p. 39.
70 Ibid, p. 40. Kirby, op. cit. p. 122.
71 Peirse Despatch, para 18.
72 Narrative 4, pp. 40–41. Kirby, op. cit. p. 122. Richards and Saunders, Vol 3. pp. 312–313, describe this day's action and the contribution of OC 136 Squadron, Wg Cdr A N Constantine, another who had learnt his trade during the Battle of Britain, when he flew night fighters.
73 *Wings of the Phoenix*, p. 47.
74 USSBS Report, p. 12.
75 Narrative 4, p. 72.
76 Ibid.
77 Peirse Papers, Folder 25, E1.
78 Ludlow-Hewitt Papers, E34.
79 Peirse Despatch, p. 13 of draft, held in AHB.
80 Narrative 4, pp. 71–78: this contains a detailed account of the counter-air operations.
81 USSBS Report, p. 15.
82 Narrative 4, App. 13.
83 Narrative 4, App. 20.
84 Narrative 4, p. 91.

9   The Battle Joined

1 Kirby, op. cit. p. 118. Mountbatten Report, pp. 31–36.
2 Mountbatten, op. cit. para. 63.
3 Allen, op. cit. p. 173. Narrative 4, p. 49.
4 Kirby, op. cit. p. 77.
5 Mountbatten Report, para. 64.
6 Narrative 4, pp. 46–47.
7 Kirby, op. cit. p. 123.
8 Turnbull, *Battle of the Box*, p. 40. This is a detailed account of the second Arakan campaign.
9 Mountbatten Report, paras. 39–41.
10 Turnbull, op. cit. p. 45.
11 Narrative 4, p. 49.
12 Slim, op. cit. p. 240.
13 Mountbatten Report, para. 79.
14 Allen, op. cit. p. 178. Allen speaks of 65 Japanese aircraft being destroyed, clearly an error, though as Kirby points out (op cit. p. 143), many of the damaged aircraft, which lacked self-sealing tanks, may have failed to return to base. The contemporary ACSEA report (*Air Transport Operations on the Burma Front*) gives the scores as 8 destroyed, 3 probables, 53 damaged, for the loss of 4 Spitfires.
15 Kirby, op. cit. p. 127.
16 Slim, op. cit. p. 236.
17 Saunders, *The Fight is Won*, pp. 315–316 contains a description of 62 Squadron's operations.
18 Turnbull, op. cit. p. 55. Slim, op. cit. p. 236.
19 ACSEA Report, op. cit. p. 13.
20 Williams, *194 Squadron – The Friendly Firm*, pp. 25–27.
21 Allen, op. cit. p. 178.
22 Narrative 4, p. 51, and 5, pp. 12–15..
23 Ibid, pp. 51–52. Mountbatten Report, para. 78.
24 Narrative 4, p. 55.
25 Ibid; Turnbull, op. cit. p. 55.
26 Narrative 4, pp. 56–58.
27 Ibid, pp. 58–59.
28 Slim, op. cit. p. 234.
29 Narrative 4, p. 60.
30 Ibid, pp. 61–62.
31 Slim, op. cit. p. 179.
32 Kirby, op. cit. p. 148.
33 Narrative 4, pp. 66–67.
34 Turnbull, op. cit. p. 80.
35 Slim, op. cit. p. 246.
36 Mountbatten, op. cit. para. 92.
37 Allen, op. cit. p. 177.
38 Turnbull, op. cit. p. 54. He points the contrast with the French failure in their drops ten years later under almost exactly similar conditions at Dien Bien Phu.
39 Kirby, op. cit. pp. 170–171. Narrative 4, pp. 138–139.
40 Bidwell, *The Chindit War*, p. 64. Craven and Cate, op. cit. Vol IV, pp. 503–504.
41 Narrative 4, pp. 135–137.
42 Ibid.
43 Bidwell, op. cit. p. 65.
44 Narrative 4, pp. 140–141. The airstrips were named after the main thoroughfares of New York, London and Calcutta.
45 Slim, op. cit. pp. 260–262. Narrative 4, pp. 145–146.
46 Narrative 4, pp. 146–150.
47 Bidwell, op. cit. pp. 104–105. See also O'Brien, *Out of the Blue*, pp. 56–57; O'Brien, one of the RAF pilots who marched with Wingate's columns, is particularly critical of the failure to make proper use of air reconnaissance.
48 ACSEA Report, op. cit. p. 17.
49 Quoted in Peirse Despatch, para. 36. Williams, op. cit. p. 32.

50 Narrative 4, p. 153.

51 Rhodes-James, *Chindit*, p. 63. O'Brien. op. cit. pp. 64–70 describes his arrival by glider.

52 Narrative 4, p. 157.

53 Bidwell, op. cit. p. 108. At the same time Bidwell rightly criticises Wingate's refusal to use paratroops in the initial stages.

54 Narrative 4, p. 155.

55 Flown in at the same time were two Servicing Parties, one to service Spitfires at Broadway, the other Hurricanes at Aberdeen. These were similar to the Servicing Commandos used in NW Europe. Recollections of Mr T Stocks.

56 Ibid, p. 79. Vincent, *Flying Fever*, p. 151. Allen, op. cit. p. 352.

57 Narrative 4, p. 165.

58 Williams, op. cit. p. 39. Bidwell, op. cit. p. 137.

59 Allen, op. cit. pp. 346–348. Slim, op. cit. p. 269. Williams, op. cit. p. 38.

60 This is not the place to assess Wingate's qualities; these are well considered by Kirby, Bidwell and others.

61 Narrative 4, pp. 165–169, and 5, pp. 15–21.

62 Bidwell, op. cit. p. 219. Deryck Groocock observes that it was not quite such a painless operation as Bidwell implies; three Dakotas were in fact lost and a good many more damaged.

63 Ibid, pp. 169, 217.

64 Narrative 4, pp. 173–176 discusses the technicalities.

65 Ibid, pp. 177–185 covers this subject at length.

66 Bidwell, op. cit. p. 123.

67 Rhodes-James, op. cit. p. 33.

68 Ibid, p. 81.

69 Peirse Despatch, para. 43. On one occasion an RAF officer dropped hand grenades from an L1 – shades of the First World War!

70 Narrative 4, p. 177.

71 Peirse Despatch, para. 42.

72 Narrative 4, p. 186. Saunders, op. cit. p. 332.

73 Narrative 4, pp. 169–171.

74 Rhodes-James, op. cit. pp. 128–129.

75 Ibid, p. 140.

76 Narrative 4, p. 194.

77 O'Brien, op. cit. gives a vivid account of his experiences, describing how the strain and privation were taking their toll.

78 Rhodes-James, op. cit. p. 159. Jennings stayed by the lake afterwards, looking after another 450 sick men and trying to organise their evacuation by water. He eventually flew out on 27 July – 'by any standards a remarkable effort' for which he received the MC (p.177).

79 Narrative 4, pp. 200–202. Coryton Despatch. pp. 4–5.

80 Narrative 4, p. 189.

81 Mountbatten, op. cit. para 94. Slim, op. cit. p. 291.

82 See, for example, Allen, op. cit. pp. 193–194; *Wings of the Phoenix*, pp. 70–71.

83 Quoted from *Battles Long Ago*, an excellent personal memoir lent me by Mr R S Ridgway, a navigator with 194 Squadron.

84 Narrative 4, p. 94.

85 Ibid. pp. 98–99. Kirby, op. cit. p. 245.

86 Allen, op. cit. p. 196. Grant, in *Burma: The Turning Point*, describes the Tiddim Road battles in detail.

87 Ibid, pp. 242–243. Peirse referred to this in a letter to Portal on 13 May, saying that he fully backed Mountbatten vis a vis Giffard. Peirse Papers, Folder 25.

88 Kirby, op. cit. pp. 197–200; Mountbatten's Report places the meeting with Slim and Baldwin on the 13th.

89 Ziegler, op. cit. p. 272.

90 *Wings of the Phoenix*, p. 74.

91 Narrative 4, pp. 101–103.

92 Portal Papers, PM Minute 24b, 3 and 4 April 1944.

93 Narrative 4, pp. 103–106.

94 Kirby, op. cit. p. 324.

95 Peirse Despatch, para. 67.
96 Kirby, op. cit. p. 327. Narrative 4, p. 108.
97 Narrative 5, p. 25. Accounts differ on the precise numbers.
98 Allen, op. cit. pp. 235–238.
99 Swinson, *Kohima*, pp. 90, 91, 140. He records (p. 175) that every tin of rations dropped by the RAF contained cigarettes; after three weeks GHQ sent a bill for these, to be told that only when the Japanese paid for the proportion they had received would 5 Brigade consider paying for theirs.
100 Williams, op. cit. p. 41.
101 Narrative 4, pp. 108–114.
102 Vincent, op.cit. p. 150.
103 Recollections of W/O G E Jones – IWM 86/84/1.
104 Narrative 4, pp. 115–117.
105 Recollections of Mr B Dennis.
106 Vincent, op. cit. p. 155.
107 An RAF mobile field hospital, staffed during the siege entirely by male nurses, coped with all the sick cases, and most men were returned direct to their units, their specialist skills being urgently required.
108 Narrative 4, pp. 118–119.
109 Ibid, p. 122.
110 Slim, op. cit. p. 303.
111 *Wings of the Phoenix*, pp. 85–86.
112 Kirby, op. cit. pp. 307–308.
113 Ibid, p. 304.
114 Quoted in Swinson, op. cit. p. 95.
115 Recollections of Mr F Higgins, whose detailed account of the organisation and work of the AASC provides a valuable source of reference.
116 Slim, op. cit. p. 311.
117 Narrative 4, pp. 124–126, 128.
118 Franks, *The Air Battle of Imphal*, pp. 90, 99, 191, 198, 200. Vincent Despatch, p. 2, and App. H, which quotes the enemy losses as 32 destroyed and 24 probables.
119 Narrative 4, p. 129.
120 Swinson, op. cit. p. 242.
121 Slim, op. cit. p. 368.
122 Quoted in Kirby, op. cit. p. 374.
123 Grant, op. cit. p. 224.
124 Narrative 4, Appendices 9, 13.

10 The Long Arm of Air Power

1 Kirby, op. cit. p. 376.
2 Narrative, *RAF in Maritime War*, Vol. VII, Pt. III, pp. 43–46 and Fig. 6.
3 Narrative 4, p. 259.
4 Ibid, pp. 259–260.
5 Peirse Despatch, para 106.
6 Narrative 4, p. 261.
7 Maritime War Narrative, pp. 30–31.
8 Ibid, p. 55. The board of inquiry considered the decision not to send cover was justified.
9 Ibid, p. 54.
10 Ibid, p. 129 C.D. AMWIS 268, 21 October 1944.
11 Ibid, Introduction.
12 Roskill, op. cit. Vol III, Pt. 1, p. 220.
13 Maritime War Narrative, pp. 111–118. On its passage south through the Atlantic U852 had torpedoed SS *Peleus* and murdered her crew; its captain would stop at nothing.
14 Ibid, pp. 66–70. A detailed account of this operation has been drafted by Arthur Banks for inclusion in his forthcoming book on air operations in the Indian Ocean; this draws heavily on the recollections of Sqn Ldr (later AVM) J N Stacey, who directed activities from Mauritius.

15 Peirse Papers, Box 3/29.
16 Roskill, op. cit. p. 205.
17 Maritime War Narrative, pp. 207–209.
18 Blackburn had earned two DFCs with 70 Squadron in North Africa and the DSO commanding 148 Squadron in supply dropping operations over the Balkans. He received another DSO and the American DFC in India.
19 Recollections of Air Cdre E Burchmore.
20 Recollections of Mr D C Elliott.
21 Despatch of ACM Sir Keith Park, para 117.
22 Despatch of AVM F J W Mellersh, para 17.
23 Maritime War Narrative, pp. 210–214.
24 Ibid, pp. 16–17.
25 Peirse Despatch, para 125.
26 Kirby, op. cit. p. 379.
27 Ibid, p. 381.
28 Narrative 4, p. 264.
29 Craven and Cate, op. cit. Vol V, pp. 20–168.
30 AIR 23/2271, E12, a message to the COS dated 11 September 1944 requesting their use for DRACULA (p. 220).
31 Burchmore recollections.
32 Narrative 4, pp. 232, 236–237.
33 Portal Papers File 12, Correspondence with C-in-C ACSEA, E2, 2a, 3 and 26 December 1944.
34 Narrative 4, p. 264.
35 Ibid, p. 229.
36 *Wings of the Phoenix*, p. 110.
37 Kinvig, *River Kwai Railway*, pp. 175–177.
38 Ibid, p. 183.
39 Maritime War Narrative, p. 162.
40 Narrative 4, p. 242.
41 Ibid, p. 240.
42 Ibid, p. 241.
43 O'Brien, *The Moonlight War*, pp. 101–102.
44 Discussion with the author.
45 Narrative 3, pp. 62, 69, 119.
46 Ibid, pp. 121, 142.
47 Ibid, pp. 247, 251.
48 Ibid, p. 252.
49 Kirby, op. cit. Vol IV, p. 30.
50 O'Brien, op. cit. pp. 17–19, 76.
51 This incident is fully described by Frank Card in his history of the RAF Mountain Rescue Service. Graham, who subsequently helped Wg Cdr (later Gp Capt) Tony Smyth form the Aircrew Mountain Centre in Kashmir, was awarded the DSO.
52 Narrative 4, pp. 248–249.
53 Ibid, pp. 250–251.
54 O'Brien, op. cit. p. 13.
55 Cruickshank, *SOE in the Far East*, p. 129.
56 O'Brien, op. cit. p. 107; Gp Capt R H Arscott, then a pilot with 358 Squadron, makes precisely the same point.
57 Article in the *Glasgow Herald*, October 1986.
58 O'Brien, op. cit. pp. 107–108.
59 Arscott recollections.
60 Cruickshank, op. cit. p. 33.
61 Both COs would reach high rank in the post-war RAF. Wg Cdr Bob Hodges (357 Squadron), already distinguished for his work in SD operations in Europe, became ACM, Wg Cdr Peter Farr (358 Squadron) AVM.
62 Cruickshank, op. cit. p. 130.
63 Many of the operations in support of Force 136 in Malaya during 1945 were flown by Liberators of 160 Squadron, based in Ceylon (Chapter 13).
64 Mountbatten Report, para. 291.
65 Park Despatch, para 123.

346 *Notes (pages 214–228)*

66 Narrative 4, pp. 254–255.
67 Ibid.
68 Fox, *A Very Late Development*, p. 115.
69 Ibid, p. 122.
70 Wise, 1st Despatch on PRF Operations, para 3.
71 Narrative 4, pp. 254–255.
72 Wise, 2nd Despatch, paras 2, 6, 11.
73 Maritime War Narrative, pp. 187–190.
74 Wise, 2nd Despatch, para 6. See also p. 231.
75 Park Despatch, para 131.
76 Wise, 2nd Despatch, para 12.
77 Park Despatch, para 132.

11 Victory Beckons

1 Narrative 4, p. 280.
2 Gilbert, op. cit. p. 834.
3 Churchill, *Triumph and Tragedy*, pp. 129–130.
4 Portal Papers, Correspondence with Supreme Commander SE Asia, E2a, 25 January 44.
5 Ehrman, op. cit. Vol V. pp. 434–461 – a full coverage of this strategic debate.
6 Ibid, pp. 461–485.
7 Park Despatch, para 12.
8 Gilbert, op. cit. p. 845.
9 Ehrman, op.cit. pp. 486–503.
10 AIR 23/2271, E21 (SAC (44) 8th Meeting (0)).
11 Gilbert, op. cit. p. 983; AIR 23/2273, E5.
12 Ehrman, op. cit. Vol. VI. pp. 168–169.
13 Portal Papers, Box C, Folder 2, E6, 29 October 43.
14 Ehrman, op. cit. Vol. V, pp. 503, 523; Vol. VI, p. 233; LLoyd Despatch, p. 4.
15 Portal Papers, Box C, Folder 7, E5, 19 April 44.
16 Ibid, E6, 16 May 44.
17 Peirse Papers, Folder 23, E17a, 13 May 44.
18 Portal Papers, Box C, Folder 7, E7.
19 Ibid, E13, 19 October 44.
20 Ziegler, op. cit. p. 237.
21 Portal Papers, Box C, Folder 7, E9, 12 December 44.
22 The circumstances of his affair with Lady Auchinleck are discussed in Philip Warner's *The Lonely Soldier*, pp. 263–264.
23 Conversation with the author.
24 Peirse Papers, Box 3, E 31, 24 May 45.
25 Ibid, 30 November 44. On Peirse's death in 1970 Mountbatten wrote in similar terms to his widow, the former Lady Auchinleck.
26 Ziegler, op. cit. p. 286.
27 Portal Papers, Box D, Folder 4, E12, 16 August 44.
28 Ibid, Box C, Folder 7, E13, 19 October 44..
29 See the author's account of Leigh-Mallory's accident, published in Lucas, *Out of the Blue*, pp. 269–270.
30 Portal Papers, Box D, Folder 6, letters dated 18 and 19 November 1944.
31 Ibid, Box D, Folder 5, E 19, 26 November 44.
32 Orange, *Sir Keith Park*, pp. 199–200.
33 Portal Papers, File 12, E8, 6 March 45.
34 Letters reproduced in Garrod Papers: IWM 87/49/1.
35 Mountbatten Report, p. 78.
36 Park Despatch, paras 147–156. Mountbatten Report, p. 86.
37 Conversation with the author.
38 Park Despatch, paras 157–161.
39 Kirby, op. cit. Vol. IV. App. 3.
40 Vincent, op. cit. pp. 160–162.
41 Slim, op. cit. p. 405.

42 Vincent, op. cit. p. 166.
43 Seth-Smith, *The Abandoned Earl*, pp. 113–116.
44 Narrative 4, p. 314.
45 Ibid, p. 306; Mountbatten Report, p. 86.
46 Park Despatch, p. 36 of draft; this comment was excised from the published version. See Saunders, op. cit. pp. 348–349 for discussion of some of the ground organisation problems.
47 Hardman Despatch, pp. 55–56.
48 Narrative 4, p. 308.
49 Ibid, App. 33. 34.
50 Coryton Despatch, App. K.
51 Vincent Despatch, p. 4.
52 Thetford, op. cit. pp. 460–461. Mr P G Bates, a pilot with 5 Squadron, states that the 1000lb bombs which the Thunderbolt could lift were too heavy to load manually, so only 2 x 500lb bombs were carried.
53 Coryton Despatch, App. J.
54 Cameron, *In the Midst of Things*, p. 80.
55 Recollections of Mr J Double.
56 Recollections of Sqn Ldr R Skinner.
57 Cameron, op. cit. p. 84.
58 Ibid, p. 83.
59 Kirby, op. cit. pp. 37–38.
60 Jefford, *RAF Squadrons*, App. 11, Maps 44–46.
61 Kirby, op. cit. pp. 103–104.
62 Coryton Despatch, para. 21.
63 AP 3327, Vol 2, pp. 272–275 describes this work in some detail.
64 Ibid, pp. 268–270.
65 Coryton Despatch, App. E.
66 Recollections of Mr J Midgley.
67 AP 3235, pp. 134, 135. AP 3327, Vol. 2, p. 271 details their equipment.
68 Park Despatch, para. 78.
69 AP 1134, pp. 367–391, provides a full account of this subject, and pp. 358–366 cover East Africa and the western Indian Ocean.
70 Park Despatch, para 172.
71 AP 3397, pp. 388–390.
72 Ibid, pp. 391–395. Narrative 4, p. 308.
73 Recollections of Mr H W McOwan.
74' Park Despatch, para. 183.
75 Ibid, Coryton Despatch, App. G.
76 Vincent Despatch, p. 6.
77 AIR 22/311, Personnel Statistics, 3 September 1939 – 1 September 1945.
78 Escott, *Women in Air Force Blue*, App. K. See also pp. 209–210 for a brief description of the types of work they did.
79 AP 3237, Vol. II, p. 277.
80 Rexford-Welch, *The RAF Medical Services*, Vol. III, p. 570 et seq.
81 Ibid, p. 654.
82 Vincent Despatch, App. O records the formation of a mobile hygiene and malaria control section, September 1944.
83 Rexford-Welch, op. cit. pp. 103, 704, 709.
84 Recollections of Mr T Stocks.

12 Burma Reconquered

1 AMWIS 260, 26 August 1944.
2 AMWIS 271, 11 November 1944.
3 AMWIS 284, 10 February 1945.
4 Narrative 4, pp. 214, 317, 361. App. 30 gives the Japanese Order of Battle for January 1945, including Sumatra, Java, Borneo and Malaya.
5 Park Despatch, para. 39.
6 Narrative 4, p. 216.

7 Bandon Despatch, p. 11.
8 Ibid, p. 10. Park Despatch, para. 40. Two of these special units now existed, though Craven and Cate (op. cit. Vol V, p. 208) admit that Washington had over-estimated the need for this type of unit in Burma.
9 Park Despatch, para. 35.
10 Narrative 4, App. 37.
11 Recollections of Wg Cdr G R Piper; copies supplied by Mr J Dixon and Mr L Gwinnell.
12 Recollections of Mr L Gwinnell, who sent much invaluable material about 273 Squadron.
13 Slim, op. cit. p. 382.
14 Kirby, op. cit. Vol IV, pp. 105–106, App. 11.
15 AIR 23/2276, E 32.
16 Kirby, op. cit. p. 129.
17 Mountbatten Report, p. 104.
18 Slim, op. cit. pp. 395–396.
19 AIR 23/2278, E 76.
20 AIR 23/2279, E 32, 89, 110, 121; AIR 23/2280, E 13, 14, 35; Mountbatten Report, p. 114.
21 Another Dakota squadron, No 243 (which we earlier saw flying Buffaloes), went directly to Australia in early 1945 and was soon operating routes to the Navy's forward bases at Manus island (Map 9) and in the Philippines. 238 Squadron joined it in June. Narrative 6 records their activities.
22 Kirby, op. cit. p. 207; App. 15. AIR 23/2280, E 53.
23 Ibid, p. 204. Sustained rates were defined as those maintainable indefinitely, intensive rates applied to a period of about a month, maximum rates to ten days.
24 Hardman Despatch, p. 12.
25 Slim, op. cit. p. 444. Allen, op. cit. p. 400.
26 Signal from Mountbatten to COS 19 March: AIR 23/2282, E 19.
27 Ehrman, Vol. V, p. 196. Kirby, op. cit. pp. 315–320. AIR 23/2283, E 70.
28 Slim, op. cit. p. 383.
29 Park Despatch, para. 60; see also p. 30 of draft.
30 Kirby, op. cit. p. 410.
31 Ibid, p. 409, App. 22, 23, which contain a detailed account of the supply operations.
32 Hardman Despatch, p. 28. This figure relates to Dec 44–Aug 45.
33 AIR 8/1280.
34 Report on the Chindwin Operation by 230 Squadron, copy provided by Mr D L Holloway, who flew as an air gunner on one of the sorties.
35 Recollections of Mr J D Dunbar.
36 Recollections of Mr D J Johnson.
37 These were twin-engined light communications aircraft supplied to the RAF by the Americans – Thetford, op. cit. p. 610.
38 Recollections of Mr C Peart, who specially recalls the dangerous landing strips in the jungle, the warmth of the welcome he received, and the gratitude of the casualties he flew out.
39 Narrative 4, p. 221. Kirby, op. cit. pp. 149–154.
40 Pearcy, *Dakota at War*, p. 62.
41 Narrative 4, p. 223. Kirby. op. cit. p. 50.
42 Slim, op., cit. p. 358.
43 AMWIS 287, 3 March 1945.
44 Kirby, op. cit. pp. 156–157.
45 Vincent, op. cit. p. 165.
46 Midgley recollections.
47 Winton, *The Forgotten Fleet*, p. 177. Chapter 17 describes the Royal Navy's role in the third Arakan campaign.
48 Kirby, op. cit. pp. 136–141.
49 Bandon Despatch, App. C. Narrative 4, pp. 315–316.
50 AMWIS 280, 13 January 1945.
51 Extracted from a detailed and fascinating account provided by Mr P Nevill, AFM, whose biggest anxiety was that the noise of the generators might alert the enemy to their presence.

52 Kirby, op. cit. p. 141. See AIR 23/2274 for the detailed plan for the direct assault on Akyab (JPS 58).
53 Seth-Smith, op. cit. p. 112.
54 Narrative 4, p. 320.
55 Kirby, op. cit. pp. 215–216.
56 AMWIS 284, 10 February 1945.
57 Narrative 4, pp. 325–326. Kirby, op. cit. pp. 219–220.
58 Bandon Despatch, App. N.
59 Cameron, op. cit. p. 82.
60 Seth-Smith, op. cit. p. 126.
61 Narrative 4, p. 324.
62 Mountbatten Report, p. 113.
63 Bandon Despatch, App. D. p. 6.
64 Ibid. AMWIS 285, 17 February 1945.
65 Bandon Despatch App. E. describes the use of the airborne VCPs in the operations at Ruywa and Letpan.
66 Narrative 4, pp. 326–327. Kirby. op. cit. pp. 342–349.
67 Kirby, op. cit. p. 407.
68 AMWIS 297, 12 May 1945.
69 Innes, op. cit. p. 105.
70 Bandon Despatch, p. 8.
71 Innes, op. cit. p. 106.
72 Bandon Despatch, pp. 7–8.
73 Cameron, op. cit. p. 81.
74 30 Squadron records, researched by AVM D Dick.
75 For a full account of this operation – code-named ERUPTION – see Narrative 4, pp. 329–335.
76 Allen, op. cit. p. 394.
77 Slim, op. cit. p. 393. Kirby, op. cit. pp. 163–165.
78 Kirby, op. cit. p. 168. IV Corps' deception plan is at App. 20.
79 Narrative 4, pp. 355–356.
80 Slim, op. cit. p. 404.
81 Narrative 4, pp. 359–360.
82 Slim, op. cit. p. 406.
83 Recollections of Mr N Macrae.
84 Narrative 4, pp. 356–357. For details of the land operations see Kirby, op. cit. pp. 171–189.
85 Ibid, p. 361.
86 Ibid, pp. 362–363. Myinmu, on the Irrawaddy, was captured at about the same time.
87 Kirby, op. cit. p. 186.
88 Kirby, op. cit. pp. 182, 253, 254.
89 Ibid, pp. 258–259.
90 Slim, op. cit. p. 416.
91 Narrative 4, p. 366. *Wings of the Phoenix*, pp. 125–126.
92 Kirby, op. cit. p. 264.
93 Narrative 4, pp. 366–367.
94 Kirby, op. cit. p. 268.
95 Narrative 4, pp. 371–372.
96 Hardman Despatch, p. 4.
97 Allen, op. cit. p. 439.
98 Narrative 4, p. 372.
99 Kirby, op. cit. pp. 270–271.
100 Narrative 4, p. 370.
101 Park Despatch, para 85.
102 Slim, op. cit. p. 411.
103 SAC (45) 7 Mtg(O): AIR 23/2281, E41
104 Vincent, op. cit. p. 174.
105 Kirby, op. cit. p. 299. Narrative 4, p. 375. *Wings of the Phoenix*, p. 127. Recollections of Mr J Reid, who flew Thunderbolts with 79 Squadron.
106 Vincent, *Flying Fever*, p. 174. Three weeks earlier, when Slim wanted to fly to

Thabukton to watch the assault on Meiktila, the RAF had refused to accept the risk – it would take anyone else but not him. So he hitched a lift with the Americans and – unlike Wingate – got away with it (Slim, op. cit. p. 446). Fate nearly caught up with Slim, however, on 1 May when an RAF Dakota taking him to look at Rangoon was damaged by LAA and had to turn back (Ibid, p. 493).

107 Kirby, op. cit. p. 307.
108 Recollections of AVM Sir Brian Stanbridge, quoted in Franks, *First in the Indian Skies*, p. 134. *Wings of the Phoenix* (pp. 129–130) reminds us of the work of the nursing orderlies who flew in the Dakotas and records the award of the Military Medal, unusual in the RAF, to one of them, LAC Ian Fiddes.
109 Vincent Despatch, App. O.
110 Recollections of Mr J Dunbar.
111 Park Despatch, para. 185. Vincent, *Flying Fever*, p. 176. One Army witness, Colonel Alasdair Tuck, thought too much was asked of the RAF Regiment and speaks of morale being at rock bottom – Allen, op. cit. p. 449.
112 Narrative 4, pp. 373–374.
113 Slim, op. cit. p. 455.
114 Kirby, op. cit. p. 312.
115 Ibid, p. 313.
116 Ibid, pp. 327–328. Mountbatten Report, p. 145. SAC(45) 10th Mtg (O) – AIR 23/2283, E69.
117 Mountbatten Report, p. 146.
118 AIR 23/2283, E103, 113, 114.
119 Kirby, op. cit. p. 329.
120 Mountbatten Report, p. 146.
121 Slim, op. cit. p. 497.
122 Kirby, op. cit. p. 366. Park Despatch, App. XI.
123 Kirby, op. cit. pp. 370–377.
124 Narrative 4, p. 386. The main reduction was in the number of close support sorties, which fell from 4,270 in March to 2,008 in April and partly reflected the different type of fighting on the ground.
125 Hardman Despatch, pp. 5–6.
126 Kirby, op. cit. p. 386. Slim, op. cit. p. 500.
127 Hardman Despatch, p. 6.
128 Narrative 4, p. 384.
129 Kirby, pp. 388–393.
130 Recollections of Flt Lt H J Dix.
131 Park Despatch, para. 39.
132 Narrative 4, App. 36.
133 Slim, op. cit. p. 502.
134 Narrative 4, p. 336.
135 224 Group Operation Order 4/45, reproduced as App F to Bandon Despatch.
136 Narrative 4, pp. 338–340.
137 Narrative 4, p. 387. Hudson had been shot down over the Irrawaddy while commanding 82 Squadron.
138 Kirby, op. cit. pp. 395–396. Allen, op. cit. p. 480.
139 Slim, op. cit. p. 507.
140 Innes, op. cit. p. 110.
141 Hardman Despatch, p. 8. Gp Capt Grandy had commanded 249 Squadron in the Battle of Britain. He is now Marshal of the RAF Sir John Grandy.
142 *Wings of the Phoenix*, p. 136.

13 Finishing the Job

1 Memoirs of Wg Cdr G R Piper.
2 Recollections of Mr J Reid.
3 Park Despatch, May–September 1945, para. 537.
4 Ibid, para. 4.
5 Ibid, paras. 523–536. Kirby Vol V pp. 83–92, where the whole subject and its wider

implications are discussed.

6 AIR 24/1339, which contains an Air Staff briefing note for Mountbatten dated 21 July 1945.

7 Park Despatch, para. 505. Narrative 4, para. 397, speaks of 47 operational squadrons having been scheduled to reach ACSEA from Europe three months after VE Day.

8 AIR 24/1339, exchange of letters with Air Ministry, 9 and 21 July 1945.

9 Park Despatch, para. 55.

10 Mountbatten Report, p. 211.

11 Kirby, op. cit. pp. 32–33.

12 Park Despatch, paras. 46, 47.

13 Narrative 4, pp. 401–402.

14 Ibid, p. 403.

15 Kirby, op. cit. pp. 11–25, 36–47.

16 Narrative 4, p. 407.

17 Ibid, p. 408.

18 AIR 23/2285, E8.

19 Ibid, E10.

20 AMWIS 307, 21 July 1945, pp. 1–2.

21 *Wings of the Phoenix*, pp. 139–140.

22 Park Despatch, paras. 152, 153.

23 Ibid, paras. 187/220. Hardman Despatch, p. 9.

24 Recollections of Flt Lt J Dix.

25 Letter from Simon Eden to his father, reproduced from the biography of Anthony Eden pp. 299–300 with permission of the author, Sir Robert Rhodes-James.

26 Gp Capt D Croucher, then a navigator with 62 Squadron, recalls that they operated on alternate days.

27 Hardman Despatch, p. 10.

28 Rhodes-James, op. cit. pp. 300–302, records the messages sent to Anthony Eden by Park and Mountbatten.

29 Park Despatch, para 221.

30 Recollections of Sir Denis Spotswood.

31 AIR 23/2270, E43, E44.

32 AIR 23/2275, E2, 29 October 1944. For the staff appreciations see AIR 23/2274, E1, E2.

33 AIR 23/2276, SAC (44) 22nd Meeting (O), 28 November 1944.

34 AIR 23/2280, E75. Ehrman. op. cit. Vol VI, pp. 185–188.

35 AIR 23/2280, E85 (JPS 88).

36 AIR 23/2281, E23 (JPS 115), E41 (SAC (45) 7 Mtg (0), E57.

37 Park Despatch, paras. 11, 12. See Narrative 4, pp. 399–400 for the full order of battle for ROGER.

38 AIR 23/2282, E34, 35, 57, 58, 61.

39 AIR 23/2284, E26: JPS 140 – *Means of Expediting Capture of Singapore.*

40 Ibid, E37, 56, 66, 71.

41 Park Despatch, para. 15.

42 Kirby, op. cit. pp. 60–62.

43 Drawn from an article by Wg Cdr D Martin on the development of the Cocos Islands, published in *Flight*, 17 February 1949. Mr S Overend was a crewman aboard one of the air sea rescue launches; they arrived three months before the main party.

44 Park Despatch, para 32.

45 Kirby, op. cit. pp. 63–65.

46 Park Despatch, paras. 365–375; see Kirby, op. cit. App. 4 for the outline order of battle.

47 Park Despatch, paras. 451–468. Kirby, op. cit. pp. 91–92. See Maritime Narrative pp. 429–434 for a discussion of Kamikaze attacks.

48 Mountbatten Report, p. 174. Maritime Narrative, pp. 405–408.

49 Park Despatch, paras. 451–468.

50 These operations are described in detail in the Maritime Narrative, pp. 417–424, 503–518. See also Park Despatch, paras 259–266, and Winton, op. cit. pp. 219–231.

51 Recollections of Mr F W Cooper.

52 Maritime Narrative, pp. 241–286.

53 Ibid, pp. 293, 302.

54 Ibid, pp. 519–520. Park Despatch, paras. 172–181.

55 Park Despatch, paras. 167–171. AMWIS 310, 311.

56 Mountbatten Report, p. 180.

57 In his Despatch, paras. 297–301, Park pays special tribute to 357 Squadron's Lysander Flight for their support of Force 136 behind enemy lines in Burma, when they infiltrated personnel, conveyed operational stores, and evacuated casualties often in foul weather, using very small strips and very close to Japanese patrols.

58 Gilchrist, *Bangkok Top Secret*, p. 194.

59 Chapman, *The Jungle is Neutral*, pp. 358, 366, 411–413.

60 Sqn Ldr G Smith, who piloted a 357 Squadron Liberator, lost an engine on one such mission and flew back for 9½ hours on three.

61 Cooper recollections.

62 Chapman, op. cit. pp. 413, 422.

63 Later Air Chief Marshal Sir Hugh Lloyd, C-in-C Bomber Command.

64 Lloyd Despatch, p. 6. Except where otherwise indicated the rest of this account is based on his Despatch.

65 Letter from Portal to Kuter, 1 February 1945 (correspondence between Professor Kenneth P Werrell, Radford University, and the author).

66 The work of the Pacific Fleet is described in John Winton's *The Forgotten Fleet*.

67 Preparations were also afoot at this time for a Mosquito squadron, No 618, to use the Highball anti-shipping spinning bomb (a derivative of 617 Squadron's 'bouncing bomb') on carrier-borne operations with the Pacific Fleet. The squadron was based at Narramine, New South Wales, in early 1945 but never became operational.

68 AIR 8/1278: signals dated 14 October 1944, 1 June 1945, 6 June 1945, 13 June 1945.

69 According to Werrell, B-29s modified to carry the RAF's two big bombs, Tallboy and Grand Slam, would have been ready by September/October.

70 Craven and Cate, op. cit. Vol V, calls this the most important single transportation target in Japan, but only mentions a plan to close it by using boats loaded with explosives. Strangely, the USAAF official history makes no reference whatsoever to the intended RAF participation in the Okinawa-based bombing offensive – despite the existence of ample documentation in the US archives.

71 Park Despatch, paras. 64–66. AIR 24/1339 – meeting of 2 July 1945 between Park and Sharp.

72 'A Reflection' by Group Captain Lord Cheshire VC, pp. 135–138, published in *The Means of Victory*, Charterhouse Publications 1992.

73 Mountbatten Report, op. cit. p. 182.

74 Ibid, p. 183. Kirby, op. cit. pp. 228–229.

75 Kirby, op. cit. p. 230.

76 AIR 24/1339: notes of AIR C-in-C's meetings 7 and 22 August 1945.

77 Narrative 4, p. 416.

78 Park Despatch, paras. 304, 317, 319.

79 Narrative 4, pp. 418–419. Lee, *Eastward*, pp. 4–5.

80 Kirby, op. cit. pp. 247–249.

81 Recollections of Mr J R Taylor.

82 Gwinnell recollections.

83 Kirby, op. cit. pp. 268–269.

84 The second Okinawa-bound convoy, VACUUM, had been diverted to Singapore.

85 In addition to his account of these operations in *Eastward*, Sir David Lee has also written an entertaining book sbout the Java story: *And we thought the war was over*.

86 Kirby, op. cit. p. 229.

87 Information supplied by Mr C Smyth, Secretary BCAIR Japan Association. See also *Plan for a British Commonwealth Force to participate in the Occupation of Japan*, published by Joint COS in Australia, 15 May 1946 (copy in AHB).

88 AIR 24/1758: *Air Command Far East Monthly Intelligence Summary*, January 1948.

89 Commonwealth War Graves Commission Memorial Register 16.

90 Command 6832: *Strength and Casualties of the Armed Forces and Auxiliary Services of the UK 1939–1945*, published June 1946.

14 Reflections

1 Rusbridger and Nave, op. cit. p. 154, accuse him of not sharing with the Americans Britain's knowledge of the FECB and GCCS work against the Japanese naval codes in 1941. Had he done so, they claim, Pearl Harbour would never have occurred, and Singapore would have been saved.
2 Allen, op.cit. pp. 631–632.
3 AIR 8/1280: AMSO Report to CAS dated 15 March 1945.
4 Mountbatten Diary, p. 191.
5 Cross, *Straight and Level*, p. 296. Admittedly Air Vice-Marshal Williams, Cross's superior, had recently returned from India and knew the local picture.
6 Vincent, op. cit. p. 179.
7 Mountbatten Diary, pp. 189–190.
8 Gilchrist, op. cit. p. 100.
9 Craven and Cate, op. cit. Vol V. p. 205.
10 Mountbatten Report, p. 31.
11 Hardman Despatch, Foreword.
12 Park Despatch, para. 221.
13 The words of Wing Commander Russell, of 177 Wing, quoted in Mr R S Ridgway's personal memoir, p. 126.
14 *Wings of the Phoenix*, p. 51.
15 Cameron, op. cit. p. 90: quoted from 258 Sqn ORB.
16 Conversations with the author.
17 Conversation with the author.
18 Material supplied by Mr J Reid, 79 Squadron.
19 Gwinnell recollections. Sadly his squadron (No 273) was never allotted an official badge and therefore – despite the pleas of its squadron association – goes unrecognised in such places as St Clement Danes. I am pleased to be able to record in this book its distinguished work in the Far East war.
20 Recollections of Mr C Hutchings.
21 Conversation with the author.
22 Park Despatch, paras. 561–566.
23 Rhodes-James, op. cit. pp. 299–230.
24 Group Captain David – conversation with the author.
25 *Wings of the Phoenix*, p. 141.
26 Cameron, op. cit. p. 89: quoted from 258 Sqn ORB.
27 Taken from a full and fascinating account of his wartime experiences loaned to me by Mr S Crocker. Some reports suggest that the tunnels were being built as extermination chambers for the prisoners-of-war if the Allies landed in Singapore.
28 Taken from *Johnnie*, a tribute by the 30 Squadron Association, loaned by AVM Dick. Johnstone later commanded 30 Squadron in the Berlin Airlift and retired as a Wing Commander. He died in 1991.
29 Ziegler, op. cit. p. 274.
30 Recollections of Mr W F Holder, who flew with 205 Squadron before being taken prisoner in Java.
31 Quoted in *IAF over Burma*.
32 Allen, op. cit. p. 633.

Chronology

June 1921	British government decides to build a naval base at Singapore.
December 1921	Seletar chosen as site for first RAF airfield.
October 1927	Departure of Far East Flight from Plymouth.
February 1928	Far East Flight reaches Singapore.
January 1929	205 Squadron formed at Seletar.
September 1931	Japan seizes Manchuria.
December 1933	RAF HQ set up in Singapore.
December 1934	Japan denounces Washington Naval Treaty.
October 1936	Air Commodore A W Tedder appointed AOC Far East.
July 1938	General Dobbie reassesses the main threat to Singapore as coming from the north.
August 1938	Air Vice-Marshal J T Babington appointed AOC Far East.
September 1939	*Outbreak of war in Europe.*

1940

March	Far East request for major increase in air strength turned down in London.
June	*Italy enters the war; France surrenders.*
July	General Tojo appointed Minister of War in Tokyo.
August	COS propose target figure of 336 aircraft for Far East.
August/ September	*Battle of Britain at its height.*
September	Japan invades northern Indo-China and signs Tripartite Pact with Germany and Italy.
October	Far East Command requests 582 aircraft. COS recommend formation of unified command.
November	Air Chief Marshal Sir Robert Brooke-Popham appointed C-in-C. Anglo-Dutch conversations in Singapore.

1941

March	Vichy government allows Japan to use military facilities in southern Indo-China. First Buffalo squadrons formed in Singapore.
April	Japan signs Neutrality Pact with USSR.
	Air Vice-Marshal Pulford appointed AOC Far East.
	Air Ministry declines to send Hurricanes to the Far East.
	221 Group forms in Burma.
22 June	*Germany attacks USSR.*
24 July	Japan occupies southern Indo-China.
20 August	Brooke-Popham warns COS of deplorable weakness of Allied defences.
1 September	American Volunteer Group arrives in Rangoon.
16 October	General Tojo becomes Prime Minister of Japan.
22 November	Brooke-Popham considers war virtually certain.
1 December	No 2 Degree of Readiness ordered.
2 December	Force Z arrives at Singapore.
6 December	Japanese invasion fleet sighted; No 1 Degree of Readiness ordered.
8 December	Enemy landings at Singora, Patani and Kota Bharu. Northern airfields attacked. First bombing of Singapore.
10 December	*Prince of Wales* and *Repulse* sunk.
12 December	Japanese Army breaks through at Jitra.
14 December	Japanese Army breaks through at Gurun.
15 December	Defence of Burma transferred to India from Far East Command.
16 December	Japanese invade Borneo.
16/17 December	Penang evacuated.
23/25 December	Heavy air raids on Rangoon.
25 December	Hong Kong surrenders.
27 December	Lieutenant General Pownall replaces Air Chief Marshal Brooke-Popham as C-in-C Far East.

1942

1 January	Air Vice-Marshal Stevenson becomes AOC Burma.
2 January	Army withdraws from Kampar.
3 January	First reinforcement convoy reaches Singapore.
5 January	Battle of the Slim River.
11 January	Kuala Lumpur evacuated.

12 January	First daylight air raid on Singapore.
13 January	Second convoy reaches Singapore, with 51 Hurricanes.
14 January	Army crosses into north Johore.
15 January	ABDACOM forms under General Wavell.
18 January	225 (Bomber) Group forms at Palembang.
22 January	Third convoy arrives in Singapore.
22–24 January	Bomber squadrons re-deploy from Singapore to Sumatra.
23–29 January	Heavy daylight raids on Rangoon.
24 January	Fourth convoy arrives in Singapore.
26 January	Japanese landings at Endau.
27–30 January	Arrival of Hurricanes in Singapore from HMS *Indomitable*.
29 January	Fifth convoy arrives in Singapore.
30 January	Japanese occupy Moulmein.
31 January	All troops withdrawn to Singapore Island from Johore.
3/4 February	Heavy air raids on Singapore docks.
5 February	Last convoy arrives in Singapore.
9/10 February	232 Squadron fights its last operations from Kallang and is withdrawn.
11 February	Air Vice-Marshal Maltby becomes AOC RAF Far East.
12 February	*German battleships* Scharnhorst *and* Gneisenau *make their Channel Dash*.
13 February	Air Vice-Marshal Pulford leaves Singapore.
14 February	Japanese paratroop landings at Palembang.
15 February	Singapore surrenders. RAF attacks Japanese convoy and barges near Palembang.
16 February	Sumatra evacuated.
23 February	Battle of Sittang River.
24/25 February	Heavy air battles over Rangoon.
27/28 February	Battle of the Java Sea.
1 March	Japanese landings in Java.
2 March	Air Marshal Peirse succeeds Air Vice-Marshal Playfair as AOC-in-C India.
8 March	Hostilities cease in Java. Fall of Rangoon. Burwing formed at Magwe.
12 March	221 Group re-formed at Calcutta.
21/22 March	Japanese air attacks on Magwe.
1 April	224 Group formed in Calcutta.
5/9 April	Japanese air attacks on Ceylon.

18 April	First USAAF raid on Tokyo, led by Colonel Doolittle.
19 April	Formation of AHQ Bengal.
29 April	Japanese capture Lashio, cutting the Burma Road.
1 May	Japanese occupy Mandalay.
4–8 May	Battle of the Coral Sea.
5 May	British land in Madagascar.
6 May	Japanese capture Corregidor, Philippine Islands.
8 May	Japanese occupy Akyab.
3–6 June	Japanese Navy defeated in Battle of Midway.
21 June	*Rommel captures Tobruk.*
1–4 July	*8th Army at El Alamein.*
7 August	American landings at Guadalcanal, Solomon Islands.
19 August	*Dieppe Raid.*
23 October	*Battle of El Alamein begins.*
26 October	Japanese Air Force opens offensive against RAF airfields in Bengal.
8 November	*Start of TORCH, the invasion of North Africa.*
17 December	Start of first Arakan campaign.
20–28 December	Calcutta bombed by JAF.

1943

15/16 January	Calcutta bombed by JAF.
24 January	*Casablanca Conference ends with call for unconditional surrender of Germany, Italy and Japan.*
31 January	*Russians announce their victory at Stalingrad.*
7 February	Americans complete recapture of Guadalcanal.
13 February	First Chindit expedition launched.
7 March	Japanese counter-attack in Arakan.
12 May	*German and Italian forces surrender at Tunis.*
16/17 May	*Bomber Command attacks the Ruhr Dams.*
23 June	General Auchinleck succeeds Field Marshal Wavell as C-in-C India.
9/10 July	*Start of HUSKY, the invasion of Sicily.*
24 July– *3 August*	*Bomber Command destroys much of Hamburg.*
20 August	General Stratemeyer takes command of US air forces in India.
24 August	Quebec Conference ends with decision to form South-East Asia Command under Mountbatten.
8 September	*Italy surrenders.*
9 September	*Allied forces land at Salerno.*

16 September	Allied forces capture Lae, New Guinea.
13 October	General Arnold approves plan to use B-29s, based near Calcutta, to bomb Japan.
1 November	American forces land on Bougainville, Solomon Islands.
6 November	*Russians recapture Kiev.*
16 November	Air Chief Marshal Sir Richard Peirse becomes C-in-C ACSEA.
November	XV Corps launches its advance in the Arakan.
5 December	JAF bomb Calcutta.
15 December	American forces land in New Britain.
16 December	British and US air formations in South-East Asia integrated in ACSEA; EAC established under Major General Stratemeyer.
31 December	Newly-arrived Spitfires score their first major success against JAF.

1944

22 January	*Allied landing at Anzio, Italy.*
1–8 February	American forces begin recapture of Marshall Islands with attack on Kwajalein.
4 February	Japanese launch offensive in Arakan.
10 February	Japanese surround 7 Division at Sinzweya, starting the two-week Battle of the Box.
11 February	German oil tanker *Charlotte Schliemann* sunk east of Mauritius.
20 February	*USAAF begins 'Big Week', a series of major bombing attacks on Germany.*
5 March	Wingate's Chindits launched into northern Burma.
8 March	Japanese commence advance on Imphal.
19 March	5 Division starts its airlift from Arakan to Imphal.
24 March	General Wingate killed in air crash.
29 March	Imphal encircled.
30/31 March	*Nuremberg attacked by Bomber Command.*
2 April	First USAAF B-29 lands in India.
4 April	Climax of 3 TAF's counter-air campaign against JAF in Burma.
5 April	Kohima encircled.
April	HQ SEAC transfers from Delhi to Kandy.
17 April	Japanese begin new offensive in China.
20 April	Kohima garrison relieved.

17 May	Stilwell's forces capture Myitkyina airfield.
4–5 June	*Rome occupied.*
6 June	*D-Day landings in Normandy.*
12 June	*First V1 bombs launched against England.*
15 June– 9 July	American forces capture Saipan, Mariana Islands.
15/16 June	First B-29 attack against Japan, from forward base at Chengtu.
22 June	Battles of Kohima and Imphal end with reopening of land communications.
20 July	*Failure of Von Stauffenberg's attempt to kill Hitler.*
21 July–10 August	American forces capture Guam, Mariana Islands.
31 July	*Americans capture Avranches, as the break-out from Normandy begins.*
15 August	*Allied landings in southern France.*
20 August	*Falaise pocket closed; US forces reach River Seine.*
25 August	*Germans surrender Paris.*
8 September	*First V2 attack on London.*
17 September	*Start of attempt to force Rhine crossings at Arnhem.*
18 October	Stilwell recalled to Washington.
20 October	Americans land on Leyte, Philippine Islands.
27 October	159 Squadron lays mines at Penang.
28 October	First B-29 operations from Marianas.
1 November	Air Marshal Coryton succeeds Air Marshal Baldwin as Commander 3 TAF.
24 November	First B-29 operations from Marianas against Japan.
27 November	Air Marshal Garrod takes over from Air Chief Marshal Peirse as Acting C-in-C ACSEA.
2 December	IV Corps captures Kalewa, on the River Chindwin.
12 December	XV Corps begins to advance in the Arakan.
16 December	*Germans launch Ardennes offensive.*
26 December	Leyte captured.

1945

1 January	*Operation BODENPLATTE launched by Luftwaffe.*
3 January	Akyab occupied.
9 January	American forces land on Luzon, Philippine Islands.

10 January	221 Group carries out 'earthquake' operation at Gangaw.
17 January	*Russians capture Warsaw.*
21 January	British land on Ramree Island.
22 January	Amphibious assault at Kangaw, Arakan.
28 January	First convoy on Burma Road reaches Chinese frontier.
2 February	*Start of Yalta Conference.*
4 February	American forces enter Manila.
10 February	Slim opens offensive towards Mandalay.
13 February	*Russians capture Budapest.*
13/14 February	*Dresden bombed by RAF and USAAF.*
14 February	7 Division forces crossing of River Irrawaddy, near Nyaungu.
15 February	Amphibious assault at Ruywa, Arakan.
19 February	American forces land on Iwojima.
25 February	Air Chief Marshal Park succeeds Air Marshal Garrod as C-in-C ACSEA.
1/4 March	Capture of Meiktila.
7 March	*American forces cross Rhine at Remagen.*
9/10 March	Major night incendiary attack on Tokyo – 84,000 killed. Major attacks on this and other Japanese cities follow, continuing until the end of the war.
9/20 March	Capture of Mandalay.
15/31 March	Battle to hold Meiktila.
23/24 March	*Montgomery crosses the Rhine at Wesel.*
26 March	Capture of Iwojima completed.
1 April	American forces land on Okinawa.
12 April	*Death of President Roosevelt.*
13 April	*Russians capture Vienna.*
16 April	*Russians launch offensive across River Oder.*
22 April	IV Corps reaches Toungoo.
26 April	*American and Soviet forces meet at Torgau.*
29 April	*Hitler commits suicide.*
1 May	Airborne landing at Elephant Point.
3 May	Rangoon reoccupied.
4 May	*Admiral Dönitz surrenders German forces in NW Germany.*
7 May	*German forces surrender unconditionally at Rheims.*
8 May	Mountbatten orders plans to be prepared for direct assault on Malaya.
23 May	*Caretaker government formed by Churchill.*
25 May	Japanese suicide attacks start on Allied warships.

28 May	First Liberators land at Cocos Islands.
1 June	All USAAF units transferred from EAC.
4 June	COS accept American proposal for 10 RAF bomber squadrons to be based in Okinawa.
15 June	Liberators sink tanker *Toho Maru*.
22 June	Resistance on Okinawa ceases.
16 July	First atomic bomb is detonated at Alamogordo.
16 July	US Army Strategic Air Forces in Pacific set up under General Spaatz, controlling 20th AF (Marianas) and 8th AF (Okinawa).
20 July	Japanese in Pegu Yomas start attempt to escape.
26 July	*Labour victory in British General Election announced.*
6 August	Atomic bomb dropped on Hiroshima.
8 August	USSR declares war on Japan.
9 August	Atomic bomb dropped on Nagasaki.
10 August	Japanese offer to surrender.
14 August	Japanese accept Allied surrender terms.
2 September	Japanese sign unconditional surrender aboard USS *Missouri*.
9 September	ZIPPER landings in Malaya.
12 September	Surrender ceremony in Singapore.

Glossary

1. Abbreviations

AA	Anti-aircraft
AASC	Army Air Support Control
ABDACOM	American, British, Dutch and Australian Command
ACF	Air Commando Force, USAAF
ACSEA	Air Command South-East Asia
AFS	Air Formation Signals
AFTU	Air Fighting Training Unit
AHQ	Air Headquarters
AI	Airborne Interception
AMES	Air Ministry Experimental Station (the euphemism for a radar station)
AMSO	Air Member for Supply and Organisation
AOC-in-C	Air Officer Commanding-in-Chief
AOA	Air Officer Administration
AOC	Air Officer Commanding
AOP	Air Observation Post
ASSU	Army Support Signals Unit
ASV	Air to Surface Vessel (radar)
AVG	American Volunteer Group
BAFSEA	Base Air Forces South-East Asia
BCAIR	British Commonwealth Occupation Force (Air)
CAS	Chief of Air Staff
CATO	Combined Air Transport Organisation
CBI	China/Burma/India Theatre of Operations (American)
CCS	Combined Chiefs of Staff (British and American)
CCTF	Combat Cargo Task Force
CID	Committee of Imperial Defence
COL	Chain Overseas Low (radar)
COS	Chiefs of Staff (British)
DCAS	Deputy Chief of Air Staff
DZ	Dropping Zone

EAC	Eastern Air Command
EFTS	Elementary Flying Training School
FAA	Fleet Air Arm
FECB	Far East Combined (Intelligence) Bureau
FTS	Flying Training School
GCC	Group Control Centre
GCCS	Government Code and Cypher School (Bletchley Park)
GCI	Ground Controlled Interception (radar)
GHQ	General Headquarters
GOC	General Officer Commanding
GR	General Reconnaissance
HF	High Frequency (radio-telephony)
IFF	Identification Friend or Foe
IOGROPS	Indian Ocean General Reconnaissance Operations
ISLD	Inter-Service Liaison Department (intelligence)
IWT	Inland Water Transport
LRP(G)	Long-Range Penetration (Group)
MFH	Mobile Field Hospital
MRU	Mobile Reporting Unit
MT	Motor Transport
MU	Maintenance Unit
MVAF	Malayan Volunteer Air Force
NCAC	Northern Combat Area Command (American)
ODC	Overseas Defence Committee
OSS	Office of Strategic Services (American intelligence)
OTU	Operational Training Unit
PAOs	Principal Administrative Officers
PR	Public Relations
PR (U)	Photographic Reconnaissance (Unit)
PRF	Photographic Reconnaissance Force
PSP	Pierced Steel Planking
RAAF	Royal Australian Air Force
RASC	Royal Army Service Corps
RCAF	Royal Canadian Air Force
RDF	Radio Direction Finding (later known as radar)
RIAF	Royal Indian Air Force (IAF until 1 April 1943)
RIMU	Radio Installation and Maintenance Unit
RNAS	Royal Naval Air Service
RP	Rocket Projectile
RSU	Repair and Salvage Unit
SAF	Strategic Air Force
SASO	Senior Air Staff Officer
SD	Special Duties

SEAC	South-East Asia Command
SOE	Special Operations Executive
TCC	Troop Carrier Command
3 TAF	Third Tactical Air Force
TO SSF	Type O Single-seat Fighter (Zero)
USAAF	United States Army Air Force
VCAS	Vice Chief of the Air Staff
VCP	Visual Control Post
VHF R/T	Very High Frequency Radio-Telephony
WEC	Wireless Experimental Centre (New Delhi)
WOU	Wireless Observer Unit
Y Service	The system that monitored enemy RT transmissions

2. *Code Words*

ANAKIM	An amphibious operation designed to capture Rangoon in 1943
BIRDCAGE	The dropping of leaflets to the prisoner-of-war camps, August 1945
BUCCANEER	An operation to recapture the Andaman Islands, proposed for 1944
CAPITAL	The Allied land offensive in north and central Burma, 1945 (initially CHAMPION)
CLOAK	The deception operation to cover the Irrawaddy crossing, February 1945
CULVERIN	An amphibious assault on Sumatra and Java, proposed for 1944
DRACULA	The combined airborne and seaborne assault on Rangoon, 1945 (initially VANGUARD)
HA-GO	The Japanese offensive in the Arakan, February 1944
MAILFIST	The plan to recapture Singapore, late 1945
MASTIFF	The delivery of supplies to the prisoner-of-war camps, August/September 1945
MATADOR	The plan to anticipate a Japanese attack on Malaya in 1941 by an advance into Siam
ROGER	An assault on Phuket Island, proposed for summer 1945
ROMULUS	The offensive in north Arakan, late 1944/early 1945
SHIELD	The first support convoy for TIGER FORCE
TALON	The assault on Akyab, early 1945
THURSDAY	The air-landing of Wingate's LRP Brigades, March 1944

TIGER FORCE	The Bomber Command force designated to join in the air assault on Japan, late 1945
U-GO	The Japanese offensive against Kohima and Imphal, March 1944
VACUUM	The second supply convoy for TIGER FORCE
ZIPPER	The invasion of Malaya, September 1945

3. United States Aircraft Designations

B-17	Flying Fortress
B-24	Liberator
B-25	Mitchell
B-29	Super Fortress
C-46	Commando
C-47	Dakota (DC3)
L-1	Vigilant
L-5	Sentinel
P-38	Lightning
P-40	Tomahawk
P-47	Thunderbolt
P-51	Mustang

Index